MILITARY ENTREPRENEURS AND THE SPANISH CONTRACTOR STATE IN THE EIGHTEENTH CENTURY

Military Entrepreneurs and the Spanish Contractor State in the Eighteenth Century

RAFAEL TORRES SÁNCHEZ

OXFORD
UNIVERSITY PRESS

OXFORD
UNIVERSITY PRESS

Great Clarendon Street, Oxford, OX2 6DP,
United Kingdom

Oxford University Press is a department of the University of Oxford.
It furthers the University's objective of excellence in research, scholarship,
and education by publishing worldwide. Oxford is a registered trade mark of
Oxford University Press in the UK and in certain other countries

First published 2016

Published in the United States of America by Oxford University Press
198 Madison Avenue, New York, NY 10016, United States of America

British Library Cataloguing in Publication Data
Data available

ISBN 978–0–19–878411–1

Acknowledgements

Behind each book lies a story, and it's almost always pleasant in the telling, spelling out the gestation of the book and how it became possible. Each book, after all, is a group story, of shared hopes and expectations, of countless and almost always unrepayable gestures of support from friends and colleagues. In my case, this story is particularly agreeable. The germ of this book was an invitation by Huw Bowen to give a lecture at Leicester University, United Kingdom, about Spanish eighteenth-century military entrepreneurs. The setting was an unforgettable 'brown-bag seminar', a format that certainly comes across as strange for a Spanish academic but that turned out be very fruitful. Professor Huw Bowen's unflagging initiative and vitality rubs off on one. With his collaboration we were able to bring more colleagues into the fold, the area of research as yet little explored that we all began to delve into together. With Stephen Conway, Agustín González Enciso, Richard Harding, and Patrick O'Brien we began to ferret out the role played by military entrepreneurs in the mobilization of warfare resources and state construction during the eighteenth century; at the same time the whole project became more international, attracting new colleagues and friends and creating new stimuli. Giving oneselves a name is always fun so we came to call ourselves the Contractor State Group (<www.unav.es/centro/contractorstate/> (accessed January 2016)). Without any doubt this book is the fruit of this thrilling collective academic adventure, which I was lucky enough to be part of. The research was funded by the Spanish government, ref. HAR 2015-64165-C2-1-P.

Many colleagues have chipped in over time with their critiques and comments in ongoing meetings and get-togethers to help flesh out the thesis of this book, but I owe a special debt of gratitude to the *savoir faire* and friendship of Paco Andujar, Alberto Angulo, María Baudot, Michael Beltran, Pepijn Brandon, Javier Cuenca-Esteban, Isidro Dubert, Anne Dubet, Joël Félix, Jeff Fynn-Paul, Farley Grubb, Marjolein 't Hart, Roger Knight, Cristina Moreira, Helen Julia Paul, Pierrick Pourchasse, Guy Rowlands, Margrit Schulte, Sergio Solbes, Christopher Storr, Toshiaki Tamaki, Iván Valdez-Bubnov, and Martin Wilcox. In recent years I have also run up a special debt with David Parrott, the firmest inspiration behind this book, who has offered me his friendship and shrewd advice since we first met in Brussels at that unforgettable seminar, 'War, Entrepreneurs, and the State in Europe and the Mediterranean 1300–1800'.

However, without doubt what make the whole journey more safe and agreeable are the emotional boosts offered day to day by one's nearest and dearest. Special thanks go to Ana, Jacin, Pedro, and Salva, for their unstinting efforts to improve the culinary level of the *enano de los Canales*. No less effective is the constant effort, with the collaboration of Badulaque's house, made by Diego, Javi, Laura, Natalia, and Waldo to offer unconditional emotional support. This was also the case with my brother Quico and Enca, and our balcony chats at La Manga, which proved a veritable hothouse of academic insights. But if this undertaking has borne fruit this is undoubtedly because I have been blessed by the support of the finest entrepreneur of all, my wife Jose, who has been able to mobilize the most valuable resources: my three children, Blanca, Laura, and Fernando, in what has been a real family project. To all of them my heartfelt thanks.

Contents

List of Figures

List of Maps

List of Tables

List of Abbreviations

AFB	Archivo Foral Biskaia, Bilbao
AGS	Archivo General de Simancas, Simancas, Valladolid
AHN	Archivo Histórico Nacional, Madrid
AHPM	Archivo Histórico Protocolos de Madrid, Madrid
AMN	Archivo Museo Naval, Madrid
BN	Biblioteca Nacional
DGT	Dirección General del Tesoro (AGS)
FCH	Fondo Contemporáneo de Hacienda (AHN)
Inv.	*Inventario*
leg.	*legajo* (dossier)
lib.	*libra* (book)
mrvs	*maravedis*
MS	manuscript
PRO	Public Record Office, Kew, London
RO	Real Orden (royal order)
rsv	*reales de vellón*
SSH	Secretaría y Superintendencia de Hacienda (AGS)

Glossary

administración Military supply system run directly by the state

apostaderos Smaller naval bases of the Spanish Royal Navy

Armada de Barlovento Windward Fleet

Armada del Mar del Sur The Southern Fleet

Armada Real Spanish Royal Navy

arroba Unit of weight equivalent to 11.502 kg

arsenal Royal dockyard and shipyard. Fully fledged state-run shipyard for naval warships and armaments

asentista Military entrepreneur or contractor. A businessperson running a military provision *asiento*

asiento Military supply contract signed between the state and an entrepreneur. It is also the generic name for the supply system carried out primarily by military entrepreneurs, in opposition to the *administración*

asignaciones Money that the navy or army lower ranks and officers ordered to be discounted from their wage for subsistence of their family for as long as their service lasted

astillero General shipyard and merchant yard

audiencia Court of justice

Banco de San Carlos A private bank, founded in 1782 under royal protection. It participated in state loans, the financing of public works, and control of the American silver trade

carta de pago Letter of payment given by treasurers to certify payments

Casa de Contratación Institution to regulate trade and navigation with the colonies. From 1717 in Cadiz

Cinco Gremios Mayores A major finance and trading company operating in the eighteenth century on a worldwide level. It was originally formed by the five main guilds of Madrid: silk, canvas, jewellery, broadcloth, and spices

contador general General comptroller

Contaduría General de la Provisión de Víveres de los Ejércitos General Army Victualling Accounting Office

Consejo de Hacienda Exchequer Council

Departamento Marítimo Maritime Department

Depositaría de Indias Indies Depository. The treasury in Cadiz that received American revenue, run by Tesorería General

ducados de plata Silver ducats

estancos State-monopoly wholesale and retail outlets for goods such as tobacco, spirits, chocolate, sugar, or stamped paper

excusado Tax; ecclesiastical tithe

factores Distribution agents of *asentistas*

fanega Unit of weight for cereals or flour, similar to a bushel

fondo vitalicio Life annuity and public debt

fuero militar Military jurisdiction

intendente Top government official in a given area to deal with military and financial affairs

intendente de marina navy intendant

Intendente General de la Armada Navy Intendant General

intendencia Territorial jurisdiction of an *intendente*

Intendencia de Marina Navy Intendancy

Junta de Estado State Cabinet

juntas departamentales Navy Department Boards

macuquina Hammered silver coinage of lower value used in America

maravedis (*mrvs*) Fictitious account unit

matrículas de mar Navy officials' registration of sailors

mayorazgo Primogeniture and entail

menestra Ration of dried, stewed, or cooked pulses given to troops and prisoners, consisting mainly of rice, chickpeas, and beans

mesadas Monthly or yearly advanced payments from the state to military entrepreneurs against the final cost of the military provision contracted with the state

pan de munición Bread made from wholewheat flour: an ordinary military bread ration, consisting of 24 ounces, Castilian weight, of baked bread

paja pelaza Barley fodder

patentes Open permits for the military entrepreneur to appoint employees and *factores* for the arrangement of provisions

peso de plata Equivalent to 20 *reales de vellón*

quintal A hundredweight, equivalent in Castilla to *c.*46 kg

quintas Draft of one out every five youngsters of military age

ración de dieta Food ration for sick soldiers and sailors

real cédula Royal Charter

real de vellón(rsv) Half-silver currency used as a yardstick for all other currencies in circulation during the eighteenth century

Real Giro Royal Remittance Office

Real Hacienda Royal Exchequer

Secretaría de Guerra, Hacienda, Marina War, Finance, Navy Ministry

Secretario de Guerra, Hacienda, Marina War, Finance, Navy Minister

situados Money transfers made by the Royal Exchequer from one part of the empire to another: A subsidy creamed off from the surplus of colonial income

Tesorería General Maximum institution of the Secretaría de Hacienda for controlling payments and bookkeeping information of the Real Hacienda

Tribunal Mayor de Cuentas The supreme accounting office

vales reales Interest-bearing state bonds

vara unit of length approximately equivalent to 83 centimetres

vía reservada Reserved affairs, i.e. a form of direct government management independent of council scrutiny

Map 0.1 Administrative and political geography of eighteenth-century Spain

Source: Author's own.

Map 0.2 Physical geography of eighteenth-century Spain (orography and rivers)

Source: Author's own.

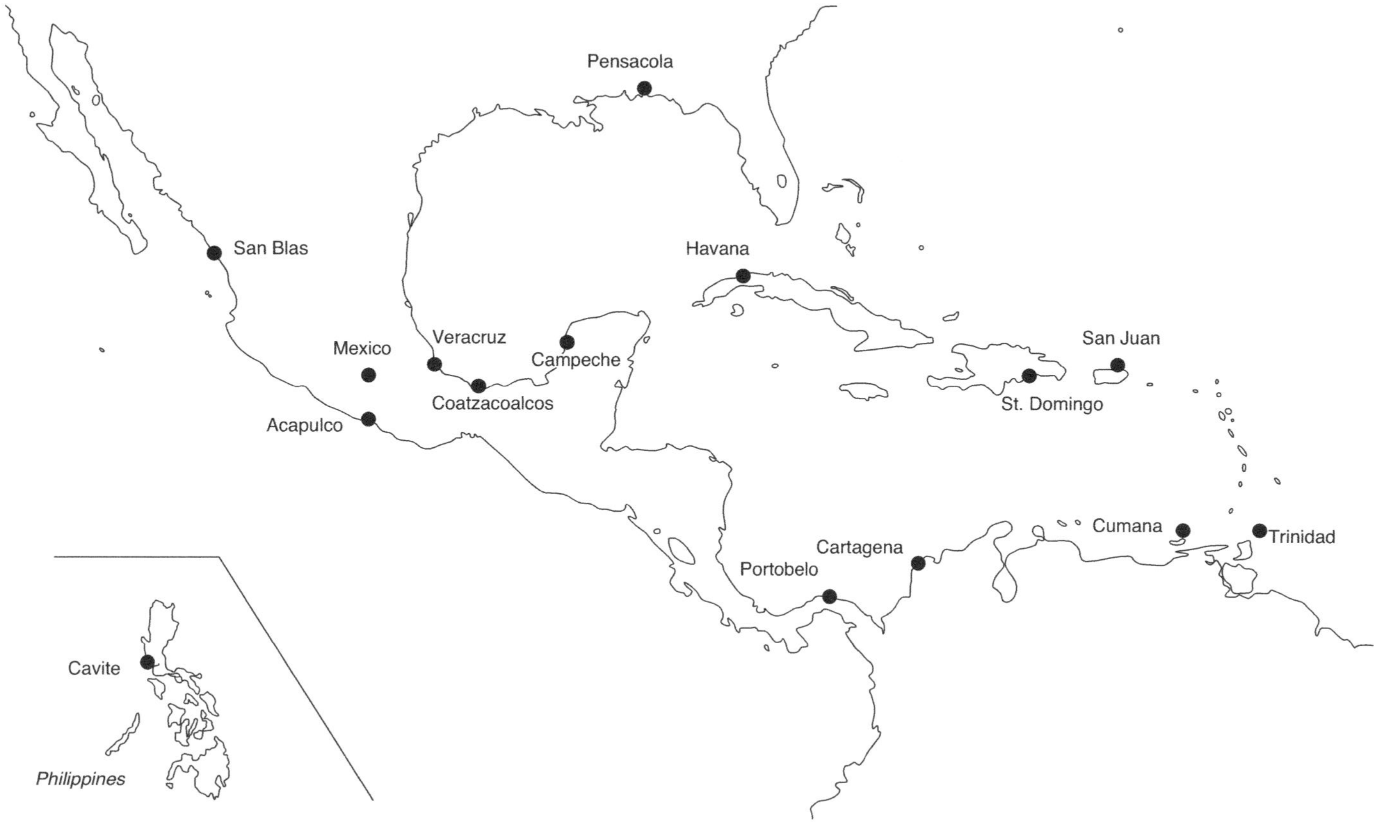

Map 0.3 The Spanish West Indies, Viceroyalty of New Spain, and Philippines

Source: Author's own.

Map 0.4 Spanish Atlantic Empire

Source: Author's own.

PART I

INTRODUCTION

1

From the Fiscal-Military State to the Contractor State

In February 1767 several members of the Spanish government exchanged reports and views on the best way of furnishing the state with the military supplies it needed. Asked for his opinion about whether or not they should turn to contractors (in Spanish, *asentistas*), a senior government official gave the forthright answer:

> this is a matter that, like all other commercial affairs, should be based upon a perfect economy if it is to be as successful as we wish. There is no doubt that a contractor tallies better with this overarching idea than any state commissary. The former, after all, looks after his own interest, on the strength of his own activity, efficiency and industriousness whereas the latter lacks this money-saving motive ... Furthermore the contractor looks beyond the short-term benefit of each individual contract and sets his eyes rather on the long-term business that might accrue therefrom ... which is the truest way of thinking in business houses.[1]

This official had no doubts about the superiority of these military contractors in terms of meeting the state's needs, satisfying as they did a series of prerequisites that were all particularly conducive to long-term managerial efficiency. This official of the Spanish state attributed them with a readiness to fulfil the state's commission in the best way possible, since they were driven above all by their own private interest. In his opinion they would therefore be sure to carry out their tasks efficiently, since their expertise was based on their superior commercial networking capacity. If the state turned to these businesspeople, he argued, the state itself would 'go further', that is, grow and develop. This example illustrates the theme of this book: how the Spanish state's pressing need for military supplies during the eighteenth century spurred, shaped, and constrained an emergent military-entrepreneur market and how state and contractors influenced each other's development and *ipso facto* the nation as a whole. This theme fits in with the thoroughgoing historiographical rethinking, in recent decades, of the traditional debate on the construction of the state; it aims ultimately to answer the question of why warfare, or rather the state's prime function of sustaining its armed forces, was a key factor in the growth and development of some nations and states and not in others. The key point, more specifically, is why for some states military enterprise became an authentic lever of wealth, helping to knit the whole society together, whereas for other states and nations it was a brake on development and a source of social friction.

Historians have long tended to link the emergence of modern states with the growth of military activity.[2] The driving force behind this relation was the constant rivalry between European states, and these states' desire to achieve security, stability, and sovereignty in the territories they governed.[3] An ever closer and stronger relationship between state and warfare was forged throughout the early modern era as the scale of warfare increased together with its cost and technological level. The state met this challenge by streamlining its administration and mobilizing economic and material resources. The response to these challenges apparently determined the differences in the states' various political models. Factors such as geography or the economy, and concepts like 'monopoly of violence', 'military revolution', and 'fiscal-military state' have helped to articulate and renew this historiographical discourse largely derived from the field of sociology.[4] Problems arose when these doctrinaire interpretations were set against the historical reality of the early modern era; then the ostensible differences in the political regimes of the belligerent states, parliamentarian or absolutist, turned out to be less crucial than previously thought as explanatory factors of historical developments. No automatic or universal relationship between state and warfare can in fact be postulated; neither did this relation even act in the same direction in all cases. What does seem to be clear is that the reason why the warfare–state interrelationship was more intense in Europe than in other parts of the world is that it was in Europe and its colonies where rivalry and competition were fiercest (dynastic, religious, economic, or national) and also it was in Europe where states proved themselves to be most imaginative and efficient in finding resource-mobilizing solutions, without causing any sort of rupture with the societies that sustain them. It is precisely in this bond between state and society where the study of warfare resource mobilization comes into its own. Thus Great Britain's success in the eighteenth century, the most highly taxed and indebted nation in the world, resided precisely, as Martin Daunton reminds us, in raising these taxes and running up this debt 'without serious political problems and with a remarkable level of compliance'.[5]

The traditional answer that states managed to raise their wherewithal by strong-arm tactics (in the words of Charles Tilly because 'coercion works'[6]) does not really hold up. It fails to explain European states' varying levels of effectiveness in the race to meet the growing demand for military activity in the early modern era. The fact that a state managed to raise enough money was no guarantee that this would be transformed into military wherewithal and much less that this would be done efficiently. Witness the naval confrontations of the Napoleonic Wars. The English lost 17 ships against the French toll of 229. Such a glaring difference cannot be accounted for solely on economic terms. In one way or another the English proved to be more efficient than the French at mustering seamen, fitting out and repairing their ships, training sailors, nursing the injured, providing pork fat or cannons and, as the author of a study on this subject, Douglas Allen, argues, doing so without stoking up social resistance or bringing down its economy or state structure.[7] The English were somehow more efficient than the French in recycling taxes as a perceived benefit to the society that had furnished them. Money without any doubt formed the sinews of war, but there was also a need for a consensus in those societies for it to be raised and then spent on military activity.[8] Once the underpinning society had learnt to see benefits for itself, it would be more likely to collaborate in the mutual endeavour. Everything would seem to suggest that collaboration did in fact override coercion in all European states' resource-mobilizing arrangements during the early modern era. In all probability, as argued by Peer Vries, this was precisely what differentiated European states from the rest of the world.[9]

Focusing on collaboration rather than coercion puts a different slant on the warfare resource-mobilizing process. The traditional view highlights the state's role as the main agent, unilaterally exerting all its coercive clout on its own society to obtain the military resources it needed. This view is now being ousted by a broader awareness of other types of collaboration and participation, in which the salient feature is beginning to be recognized as the resource-raising arrangements woven between state and society. As Stephen Conway claims, it is high time to start concentrating less on whether this relationship tended to strengthen or weaken the state and turn our attention instead to how the relationship came about and the consequences it might have for the prime end in view, which was none other than increasing military resource-raising efficiency.[10] One of the authors who have done most to bring out this new warfare-resource-raising relationship between state and society is David Parrott.[11] Parrott argues that there is not necessarily any incompatibility between the growth of state power and the development of significant participation of private agents and individuals in mobilizing resources for the military activity. He has even forthrightly shown that, without this participation, states would in fact have been unable to build up the resource-mobilization levels actually achieved. This new way of looking at things casts doubt on some long-held tenets. First, that there is no single and irreversible paradigm for growth driven by the state's ambition to increase its control over armed forces and to mobilize military resources. Moreover there is the possibility of change, of divergence in these developments, if the state's relationship with the surrounding society changes. Secondly, this new slant calls into question the traditional role assigned to private agents, whose performance ostensibly represented a weakening in state power. In other words it is no longer valid to continue assuming that if contractors and private agents collaborated they did so at the cost of the state's political capacity and authority. Rather would it seem to be quite the opposite, that the collaboration reinforced and enlarged the state's capacity for political action. Thirdly, if we admit that the mobilization of military resources is the result of the relationship built up between state and society, to the mutual benefit of both, the crux of the matter is then to ascertain why the private agents wished to collaborate and what were the consequences of this collaboration: for the contractors, for the state, and for the nation as a whole.

Centring the state-building debate on the relations between the state and military entrepreneurs is a promising way of dealing with the problems that have now cropped up in studies of the fiscal-military state. These studies have run into a serious initial limitation, deriving from the priority given to the study of only one side of the equation, namely the mobilization of economic resources. When John Brewer coined the term 'fiscal-military state' in 1989 it was intended to bring out the two main functions of the eighteenth-century English state: bringing in tax revenue and spending it on warfare.[12] Brewer's book paints the English state as a strong, centralized regime with a professional and highly skilled bureaucracy and administration, which pursued efficient fiscal policies and was capable of keeping up with the soaring needs of public credit and armed forces. The term 'fiscal-military state' spread like wildfire despite attracting some critical scrutiny.[13] As Peter Ertman pointed out, apart from questioning the Whig myth of a weak state, 'this is a book where one does not learn very much that one has not read elsewhere, except in respect of the excise where Brewer's own researches have established Britain's relative efficiency as a bureaucracy'.[14] Despite the criticism, the term 'fiscal-military' has been widely taken up, partly because it has come in handy for replacing the more hackneyed concept of 'absolutism'. As Chester Dunning proposed: 'there is a good chance that the model of the fiscal-military state will eventually replace the vague and hollow concept of absolutism as the preferred framework for the study of early modern Europe'.[15] But the very usefulness of the term, as anticipated by Dunning, has become counterproductive, ending up by blurring the concept itself. Max Edling refers here to two fiscal-military states with completely different political, economic, and social policies: 'If the American Revolution is regarded as a revolt against the extension of the British "fiscal-military state" to the colonies, it is of course ironic that the Revolution's very success should create the demand for an American "fiscal-military state".'[16]

The term 'fiscal-military' has gradually shed its original remit, that is, linking the state's two primordial functions in the early modern era, revenue collecting and military expenditure. Furthermore historians have tended to put too much weight on only one strand of this argument. Fairly logically, in the light of the very strength of economic history, historians have tended to concentrate on the economic strand in their studies of fiscal-military states: the capacity for mobilizing greater revenues. When a comparison is made between the various fiscal-military states, historians all too often refer only to how fiscal policies and administration enabled states to widen the tax trawl and increase available warfare resources. Efficiency, therefore, could be measured solely as the capacity to muster enough money to spend on military resources.[17] This focus upon the first function of the fiscal-military state has offered important clues to understanding the transition, already mooted by Schumpeter, from a 'domain state', with recourses taken from the king's property, to a 'tax state', where it is the kingdom and its subjects who come up with the resources, also currently dubbed as a 'fiscal state'.[18] In other words, stress was placed on explaining how fiscal-military states began piecing together public finance systems, doing so by curbing feudal or regional treasuries. Studies also looked at how financing resources were multiplied, using more secure, confidence-imbued public-debt financial markets, how accounting control instruments were enforced, and how public discourses turned to guaranteeing the legality of certain fiscal and financial policies.[19] The significant interpretative headway made in this emphasis on the fiscal and financial aspects has absolutely no parallel in the fiscal-military state's other function, military expenditure. This has created a certain narrow sense of the term 'fiscal-military state' and hence biased the direction of research. A paradigm has been established, in which the most developed and efficient fiscal-military state is precisely the one that can bring in most revenue and better feed military demand; the other states, if they fail in this remit, could even forfeit the right to call themselves fiscal-military states. For Jan Glete, for example, Spain declined and had ceased to be a fiscal-military state by 1700 because it failed in the protracted attempt to sustain its imperial military expenditure.[20] As Guy Rowland has masterfully shown, a fiscal and financial crisis is part and parcel of the political system itself and by no means spells the end of the state, because power relations are continually being readjusted, including the relations between the political, economic, and financial elites and hence the relations between state and nation.[21]

The methodological overlooking of the fiscal-military state's second function, military expenditure, is especially grave, since it is precisely here where the revenue raised reverted to the society and economy that generated it, or, what comes to the same thing, where the relation between the state and entrepreneurs becomes most visible. Some studies have helped enormously to flesh out this relationship.[22] The growing interest in how states actually went about undertaking military expenditure has been fuelled by a new concept or term that could be an extraordinary research catalyst.[23] The term in question is 'contractor state', coined in 2010 by Roger Knight and Martin Willcox to express the historical character of the eighteenth-century British state, which turned to contractors for most of the military supplies it needed.[24] An analysis of thousands of the navy-provisioning contracts signed between the English state and contractors, and also of the different supply methods used and of administrative control, has allowed these authors to demonstrate how the state mobilized the resources of the private sector to achieve its military and strategic targets. The conclusion they draw is that 'success in war was not only dependent upon a plentiful supply of money, but also the ability to spend it to best effect'.[25] Success and efficacy here are gauged in terms of how the state managed to muster necessary naval victuals with the necessary quantity and quality, despite the multiplication and dispersion of delivery sites, doing so within deadlines and with the necessary flexibility. The English state 'went further', in the words of the abovementioned Spanish official, because it was capable of transforming tax revenue into navy victuals extremely effectively. In this case, by sole means of massive recourse to military contractors, the English state managed to solve the problem of growing military demand and, above all, to cope with the wild swings in this demand, because it was only the English state that had enough information, creditworthiness, and business contacts to tap into national and international markets and commercial networks. In other words he came to exactly the same conclusion as David Parrott to explain the recourse of the belligerent states of the Thirty Years War to military contractors and their financial and commercial networks and national and international production outlets. In the English case, moreover, the triumph of the contractors was more evident, as were its knock-on effects for the rest of society, because the English state offered the contractors reliable and secure trading arrangements, with contracts that the state always honoured and with a diligent administration capable of introducing continual improvements to boost control over supplies and contractors. The upshot was a climate of business confidence, within which the powers and responsibilities of each participant were neatly ring-fenced and abuse was largely forestalled, whether of the state over contractors or the contractors themselves over the Victualling Board. In this case the established relationships between state and contractors managed to turn war and British navy victualling arrangements into a source of opportunities and economic growth, into a lever of wealth and development, of the state and the nation.

The concept of 'contractor state', moreover, feeds into the specific historical studies of military entrepreneurs, deeply rooted in the seminal study of Fritz Redlich and also fuelled by the long debate on Military Revolution.[26] These studies show a marked upward development in historians' appreciation of the military entrepreneurs. Simplifying matters, this development can be boiled down to two clearly differentiated stages. In the first stage this view was overwhelmingly negative. The military contractor was presented as the corollary of the weakness of a bureaucratized state, flourishing only because the Weberian states in which they operated were still callow and poorly developed. In contrast to the even-handedness, uprightness, and rationality of public service, the military contractor was considered to be a synonym for private corruption, looked down upon because this profit was earned with no apparent concern at all for state interests or national wellbeing. And they might come in for even worse handling when this profit was gleaned on the strength of their political clout and influence. The military contactor was written off as a selfish and corrupt agent opposed to state development and growth, and national prosperity. These military contractors, who furnished military supplies and financing, were seen, in short, as exploiting the state's weakness and inability to run its business in its own right.

Studies like those of Bernard Pool, Norman Baker, David Syrett, and Christian Buchet,[27] among others, began to suggest that, as well as all the above, military contractors could sometimes be efficient. In these studies, which we could qualify as the transition to a new appreciation, the 'Old Corruption' ideas of Sir Lewis Namier continued to linger on. A somewhat more positive interpretation, however, did begin to filter in, whereby the state might also benefit from the efficacy shown by these entrepreneurs. This change of mind ushered in the second stage of interpretation, clearly differentiated from the former in the work of Gordon Bannerman, who masterfully showed how the state could 'go further' if it was backed up by military contractors, prolonging and connecting the state's administrative structures in the production and distribution markets.[28] They could tap into their relational capital (kith and kin, friends, colleagues) to access information, production, and creditworthiness within wider-ranging supply networks, doing so with extraordinary flexibility. Neither were they necessarily so corrupt.[29] The efficacy and flexibility that military entrepreneurs offered the state could be interpreted as essential in understanding England's success. Within this trend the work of David Parrott confirmed the vitality of this interpretation and did so, moreover, by returning to the original material and concepts of Redlich. His thesis laid down the bases of this second stage, which we could characterize as an effort to understand military contractors in their historical context, eschewing former doctrinaire interpretations and paradigms and accepting the contractors as an essential part of state action. In recent years this interpretation has been strengthened and enriched by inputs dealing with other European states: Jeff Fynn-Paul, Marjoelin 't Hart, Thomas Goossens, Andrea Thiele, Pepijn Brandon, Agustín González Enciso, Joël Felix, Sergio Solbes, Carlos Álvarez, Rhoads Murphey, and Kahraman Sakul, plus interesting British contributions from Richard Harding, Aaron Graham, Stephen Conway, Huw Bowen, and Helen Julia Paul.[30] This second contractor-state interpretation has produced a flood of studies on military contractors, with a very appreciable proportion of joint inquiries. There was also a perceived need for more national studies to fuel a comparative investigation of this phenomenon widely shared by all states.

The present work aims to offer a first book on what it chooses to call 'the Spanish contractor state'. In view of all these recent historiographic trends, the intention is to offer a revision of all the existing studies and research undertaken on Spanish military organization. This study addresses the relationship between state and military contractors in the eighteenth-century Spanish monarchy. The decisive moment for the historiography of early modern Spanish military organization was the seminal and influential work by Irving A. Thompson, *War and Government in Habsburg Spain, 1560–1620* (published in English in 1976, and translated into Spanish as *Guerra y decadencia, gobierno y administración en la España de los Austrias, 1560–1620*).[31] According to this well-known work, the seventeenth-century Spanish state's inability to mobilize the military resources needed to keep pace with its rivals forced the state to turn over these tasks to *asentistas*, private middlemen, regional elites, and nobility, as a result of which the state forfeited its own authority and entered into a period of decline. In the interpretation of Jan Glete, who stuck very closely to this thesis, this led to its decadence as a fiscal-military state. In Thompson's eyes this decline ended only when the state again took over direct control of the mobilization of military resources, a moment that Thompson locates in the eighteenth century. The problem is that Thompson considered the essence of the problem in the relation between state and military contractors to reside in the strength of the state itself. He therefore argued that the state's weakness, evident in its dependence upon contractors, had ended in the eighteenth century when a more absolutist, centralized state arose, capable of enforcing its own authority and better run on French lines. This strength, he concludes, enabled it to take back control over its military supplies, producing them directly and watching out for their quality and distribution without needing to fall back on military contractors. The state, in other words, recovered its lost power. On this argument, it was the sharing-out of power and authority that was at stake in the state's military supply needs. With the increasing participation of private middlemen, it was argued, the state forfeited its own capacity for political action, and recovered it only when it reasserted control. In Thompson's thesis the state–contractor relation was not one of collaboration but confrontation, of imposition and loss of control. What was at stake, therefore, in the mobilization of military resources was the supposed strength of the state, without which no other type of growth was possible.

The aim of this book is to test whether such a thesis really holds good in the eighteenth century and address the problem in terms of the abovementioned historiographical evolution of the contractor state. It argues that understanding the enduring relationship between the Spanish contractor state and military entrepreneurs gives a better appreciation of the true nature of Spain's fiscal-military state.

The book tackles the problem from four complementary viewpoints. First of all the Spanish government's eighteenth-century military supply policy is analysed. The relationship between the state and entrepreneurs was by no means written in stone; quite the contrary, it depended on a host of ever-changing factors. Variables such as military exigencies, the change of a minister, diplomatic shifts, or commercial or production difficulties in ensuring the maintenance of supplies, all exerted their influence. History shows us that all these shifting circumstances in turn could change the prevailing military policy. The crucial point here is how the Spanish state's supply policy reacted to these changing circumstances. To find out, the Spanish state's military provisioning models are analysed by focusing on various types of product supplied, aiming to shift many of the assumptions that have prevailed about eighteenth-century military supply. One critical aspect of this will be to examine the assumed dichotomy in supply: either production and management by the state itself, or resorting to the market and military entrepreneurs. The distinction, as will be argued, is misleading, since one of the most notable features of the period is that public and private spheres were not delimited as previously thought. The real problem, in fact, lies not in determining which sphere was uppermost but rather in understanding the interactions between them. This point is crucial because it turns out, notably, that both of them, state and entrepreneurs, might sometimes share the same objectives, not only economic but also ideological.

A second section looks at research into army victualling. All military supplies are strategically important but food supply overrides all the rest; first, because of the sheer cost—it is always the largest item of expenditure for the state, and secondly, because of the political and strategic character of victualling. The sensitivity of politicians and military personnel to food supply made it the factor of most concern to the Spanish government; it is therefore the best litmus test of the practical application of the policy and relations with entrepreneurs. Unfortunately, there are no private files of military entrepreneurs to work from, so there is inevitably a risk of viewing this problem only from the state's perspective. An attempt to reduce this risk has been made, by including varied sources; looking, for example, at the negotiation processes in between signed contracts, which include correspondence with entrepreneurs and other members of the state's administrative apparatus. Secondly, I have examined the evidence provided by the private documentation of professional notaries, which reveals entrepreneurs making agreements with their own factors and with other national and foreign businesspeople. The study shows that the strategic importance of victuals meant that the policy concerning them might come to dominate military supply as a whole. Victualling was also a powerful source of upward mobility for the contractors involved. The geographical extension and scope of this supply arrangement, with a host of delivery points and intervening agents, public and private, also give insights into military supply arrangements as a whole throughout the whole nation.

The third section focuses on the navy. In this case the aim is to ascertain whether or not a 'fiscal-naval' state existed, in terms of how much revenue was spent on the navy, while looking at the distinctiveness of the naval supply system,[32] taking into account too the particular characteristics of naval finances in Spain. The chosen touchstone is shipbuilding, the most important and costly of all naval supply operations. The objective is to find out how the Spanish state met its demand for ships and how far military entrepreneurs participated in this shipbuilding process. This question is important because, as in the English case, the navy's growth was achieved through an increasing contribution from private shipyards.[33] The transatlantic imperial dimension looms large in all the documentation, and has therefore been brought into the discussion. The transfer of the bulk of the shipbuilding to Havana and the need to supply Havana with crucial raw materials and equipment from Spain after the Seven Years War spurred a major mobilization of military resources and fuelled the activity of military entrepreneurs who were actively trading in the Atlantic and throughout the whole empire. The sheer quantity and variety of products involved in shipbuilding multiplied supply methods and encouraged all types of military entrepreneurs to offer their services. The final stage of actual shipbuilding is only the tip of the iceberg in a world of business and contractors that needs to be explored.

Finally, in the fourth section, we analyse what this book calls 'the contractor state in action': that is, how the state reacted to a particular problem. The aim is to weigh up the true nature of the Spanish contractor state and ascertain, first, if it acted consistently with its political shibboleths and, secondly, if it was capable of reacting fleet-footedly to any urgent changes in the demand for military supplies. The first thing we find is that the much-vaunted mercantilist tenets were often reduced to mere lip service as the state had to look well beyond national production capacity to meet the demand for its military supplies. Our test case here is the supply of hemp and the ongoing dilemma of encouraging national production or buying hemp in from abroad, assuming therewith an outflow of funds and a forfeiture of the chances to boost Spanish entrepreneurs and the national economy. This particular product shows us that the mercantilist policies ostensibly pursued by all states alike, England included, which was, according to Patrick O'Brien, the biggest of all mercantilist states, sometimes had to bow to inevitability at times of pressing need and surging demand, and to look abroad as the only way of solving the problem of supply.[34] In the final chapter the Spanish contractor state's efficiency will be assessed in terms of one particular military action. The yardstick chosen is an amphibious expedition. As Richard Harding has shown, operations of this type called for high levels of administrative coordination and a massive and almost instant mobilization of all military resources, both by the state itself and by military entrepreneurs. The aim is to show how Spain managed to organize a great amphibious expedition and what the relations were like with the military entrepreneurs who participated in it. The short timescale and the specific conflict gives a challenging and focused perspective on how the Spanish contractor state operated and what the possibilities and limitations were of drawing military entrepreneurs into such operations. More generally, and pulling the threads of these focused investigations together, the book will ask whether the Spanish mobilization of military resources boosted its economy or hampered it. The relations developed between the Spanish state and military entrepreneurs were important because they stood at the centre of what was the nation's largest public and private business.

2

Economic Policy and Military Supplies

THE RESOURCE-MOBILIZATION POLICY OR THE NATURE OF THE STATE

The mobilization of military resources was essentially a political matter: it was in the political arena that decisions were taken on what to mobilize, when, and how. This fact needs to be stressed from the start since historians have traditionally accounted for national military resource-raising differences on the basis of more structural factors, which factors then ostensibly drove those states along their historical course into the future. Factors such as ideology, financial systems, or geography have all been put forward as the grounds for these national differences. Although it is indisputable that all factors were in some way and to some extent relevant, it nonetheless needs to be pointed out here that these allegedly structural factors were just one more variable to be brought into the whole picture, and not always the most decisive in terms of understanding the mobilization of resources for war. As we shall see later, there was even a certain sequential order, initial political action coming first before the restraining conditions were then brought into play. States almost always worked with a short-term outlook; what came first, therefore, was the political decision and then everything else had to fit in; only if the fit proved impossible was the original decision tweaked. The mobilization of military resources was hence born from a political decision, from the political action of a government that could then modify a given policy with remarkable fleet-footedness if need be, without the state's enveloping ideological, financial, or geographical coordinates changing at the same rate.

It is precisely this political aspect that must be examined first. It will be argued that there was indeed an overarching resource-mobilizing policy. As will be shown later, the same government, the same state, or the same dynasty was capable of imposing it, modifying it, or rejecting it and, in so doing, changing the ground rules with entrepreneurs and the financing conditions and supply-market access entitlements. It will be argued particularly that this policy was not necessarily hemmed in by ideology, finances, or geography. Factors such as urgency (short-term outlook, in sum), the ups and downs of war and threatening war, political infighting, or the across-the-board consequences of former policies could all trim the course of the policy finally imposed by the government.

In the Spanish case the problem is even more complex, since we have to work against a firmly entrenched interpretation of what the military supply policy was like and how it edged the state irrevocably towards decadence and absolutism. Thompson's *War and Government in Habsburg Spain, 1560–1620*, is still the starting point for most discussion of military resource mobilization.[1] Thompson showed that the state's chosen military supply system had a profound effect on the constitution of the state itself. In Thompson's view the state's decadence on the threshold of the seventeenth century can be put down to the administrative decisions that grew out of the military supply system based on private military entrepreneurs and the role of regional and local oligarchies. His conclusion is forthright: 'Choosing between direct *administración* and *asiento* therefore involved taking a parallel decision about the nature of the state itself. This was clearly acknowledged in the eighteenth century.'[2] With this seminal idea Thompson not only established the political dimension involved in the study of military supply but also identified a trend whereby state decadence was finally ended when the eighteenth-century governments cottoned on to the importance of recovering state control over military supplies, returning to a situation supposedly attained under Philip II. Thompson argues that the important point of Spain's case was that reliance on contractors implied a backward step in the state-intervention and -centralizing trend prevailing elsewhere in Europe, and which had been largely achieved under Philip II: 'in many senses Philip II, by directly controlling the war machine, had marched at the head of his European peers'.[3] Thompson's conclusion is therefore that the recovery of this state control during the eighteenth century was the result of the revived strength of the Bourbon state, and the seventeenth-century crisis is interpreted as an interregnum in an apparently inescapable trend of growing state control over military supplies.

Thompson's thought-provoking thesis offers a rich vein of insights into the relation between the nature of the state and military supplies, or, amounting to the same thing, state-building and the mobilization of military resources. But it also seemingly closes down the range of possible interpretations of the role played by military supply in Spanish development. A good example of the perils of a one-size-fits-all approach can be found in the picture of the Spanish case painted by Jan Glete. Although Glete was writing in an era when historians had begun to shrug off a coercion-based interpretation of the relationship between state and warfare, working towards a more fruitful idea of cooperation and coordination, his interpretation of the military supply policy and the construction of the Spanish state was negative, precisely because he considered that Spain strayed away from the supposed path of greater state control. Thompson's conclusion that an alleged loss of state control over military supplies was bound up with its decadence became an *idée fixe* for Glete; this led him to present the Spanish case as 'different' from the overall European context. In his words 'the Spanish decline was a unique case among the European states that at some time developed a fiscal-military state.'[4] In other words, and taking up Thompson's thesis, Glete considered Spain to be a fiscal-military state in the times of Philip II because it was supposedly capable of directly handling the mobilization of its military resources, but ceased to be so upon losing this control and falling back on the role of private military entrepreneurs.

This interpretation chimes well with social scientists' methodological explanations of the relation between state-building and the role of war, but raised more doubts when historians checked it more closely against historical reality.[5] David Parrott has questioned this, in his judgement, paradigm, concluding that the increase in warfare, in terms of scale and technology, did not imply in the Early Modern Age an irreversible state monopoly upon the recruitment and maintenance of armed force. He therefore shuns overly theoretical interpretations and argues that there is no incompatibility between the growth of state power and the development of private participation in military affairs. In his judgement the wider experience of early modern European warfare shows that coexistence was the norm and could even be conducive to an increase in the state's authority and capacity. Parrott argues that the public and private spheres are not a seesaw where the gain for one is loss for the other. The important point is how both sectors interrelated in particular historical contexts, with results that were frequently distinctive and diverse rather than following a common trend.[6]

Sticking rigidly to the argument that the crux of military-supply studies lies in the dichotomy between state *administración* or *asiento*, as an aid to understanding the nature of the state, would be to limit the discussion from the start and divert attention from the truly important aspect for the early modern state itself, that is, ensuring military supplies. Without leaving the Habsburg stage, the excellent studies by, among others, Antonio Jiménez Estrella and Alicia Esteban Estríngana have clearly shown that, in the case of gunpowder supplies, the 'nature of the state' was not at stake in the switch from *administración* to *asiento* but rather the economic development underpinning the strength of that state.[7] Similarly, Carla Rahn Phillips, who analyses in detail the start of the Spanish navy's practice of contracting private entrepreneurs for shipbuilding, argues that the evidence may point in the exact opposite direction from Thompson's thesis, suggesting that only when the state considered itself to be strong, that is, capable of enforcing its own laws and ordinances, did it cease to hire or buy ships and begin instead to impose private shipbuilding contracts with precise terms and conditions to suit the state's geostrategic needs. Phillips concludes that only when a state is itself developed can it begin to regulate the productive capacity of non-state agents.[8] There is room for more interpretations and approaches than those established by Thompson. It would seem a propitious moment to address the apparent dichotomy between *administración* and *asiento*, but without linking this discussion to debates about the nature of the state or in relation to any particular paradigm about state-building.

The value of this approach is evident in an examination of eighteenth-century Spanish military mobilization. Thompson's thesis was that Spain, emerging from the decadence of the seventeenth-century 'crisis', was now fighting successfully to recover the 'lost' direct *administración* of military resources. The evidence of a military reconstruction of the Bourbon state and the notable state effort to reform the armed forces inherited from the Habsburg monarchs, have been deployed as evidence pointing to the traditional arguments that a strong state would lead to a redefined relationship between the state and the system of military provisioning. Witness Teijeiro, who seconds the deeply rooted theory 'that enlightened statesmen must have been disgusted by the system (of *asientos*)'.[9] The real situation, however, is much more complex. After examining the evidence of so many ordinances, administrative initiatives, shipyards, and factories, it is now becoming obvious that there was in fact a hidden and bustling world of military supply-contracts, much more deep-rooted and widespread than has habitually been admitted and not at all at loggerheads with the state's own interests and policies. The evidence now coming to light, showing a concurrence of private and public arrangements in the eighteenth-century mobilization of warfare resources, exactly as also occurred in the previous century, proves that the response to military resource mobilization and organization was not simply a question of the nature of the state.

THE MILITARY RESOURCE-MOBILIZATION METHOD: URGENCY AND ROYAL AUTHORITY

Set apart from historians' much-discussed theories about the significance of the mobilization of military resources for the constitution of the state, is overwhelming empirical evidence derived from the actual processes of resource-raising and management undertaken by the governments of the time. It is these practical concerns considered in the political forum that best indicate the true nature of the problem. The decisions finally taken and the considerations given about the methods to be employed give us key insights into the real significance and meaning of the resource-mobilization policy. The first point to make is that there was not a single approach to resource-mobilization in eighteenth-century Spain or even the conviction that one method was better than any other. Military resource mobilization as actually pursued tells us on the contrary that public and private methods overlapped. On the public side there was direct state administration; private arrangements were in the form of state contracts with private agents (entrepreneurs, merchants, or financiers) called *asientos*. The great interest here is seeing how practical reality shaped the choice of methods actually chosen, which occurred without any preconceived ideas about one dominant method or even one single administrative trend throughout the eighteenth century. As we are told by a shrewd judge of Spain's late eighteenth-century administrative and military apparatus, Luis María Salazar, who held the top posts within the navy and finance ministries, the picture throughout the whole century was of the concurrence of both methods. In 1814 Salazar, as Navy Minister, wrote a book in the form of 'letters to a friend' reflecting on the history, characteristics, and problems of the Spanish navy.[10] Among the aspects addressed in Salazar's 'critical judgement' he was particularly concerned about the existing relationship between naval suppliers and the development of the economy and society of the Spanish monarchy, or what he called the 'State'.[11] This led him to deal at some length with the problem of which military supply policy had been followed during the eighteenth century and which one he believed to be best for the state: *administración* or *asiento*. His conclusion in reference to the Spanish navy were clear: 'speaking of the stockpiles that have been created and the responses of the navy we have found that as a general rule the *asiento* system is preferable to *administración*'.[12] For Navy Minister Salazar this stood to reason: 'any minimally educated man must surely agree with the self-evident maxim that the king should never meddle as farmer, manufacturer or merchant'.[13]

Without delving too far into Salazar's thinking processes here, what his ideas clearly show us is that, even at the end of the eighteenth century, the 'debate' had by no means been settled one way or the other. That a member of government, boasting a wealth of experience in the political management of military provisions, should question one of the Bourbon state's apparently key political principles is telling. If the debate still lingered on, this was precisely because both systems actually coexisted in eighteenth-century Spain, regardless of the 'nature' of the state.

It is a risky business to draw conclusions here, particularly when they clash with a powerful line in historical argument that has upheld the exact opposite, but it seems that the Bourbon state, like the Habsburg, based its military provisioning system largely on contractors and private intermediaries. A very high proportion of military resources were obtained by means of contractors. The list of private contracts is still incomplete, the circumstances vary with each one, and they also developed differently over the century, but the common thread we tend to see running through all of them is a continual switchback of management methods, contractors winning out over administration. It seems likely that what lurked behind this apparent fluidity is a particular historical situation in which the division between *administración* and *asientos* was much more blurred than has commonly been supposed. For the historical actors the crux of the matter was not the ostensible dilemma between 'public' or 'private' but rather the question of whether the product demanded was actually obtained and whether the king's authority was strengthened or not by the possession of these military resources. So the mobilization of military resources actually carried out was governed by the political priorities of the time, which in the eighteenth century came to mean urgency and authority (see Figure 2.1).

A quick review of the main military supplies confirms that both methods coexisted throughout the eighteenth century, with a higher proportion of military supply-contracts. In the state's main military supply expenditure, victuals for armed forces, the Bourbon's preferred provisioning method was *asientos*. As we will see in detail in the next chapter, the state tried on several occasions to bring victualling under direct *administración*. The most important attempt was made in the 1730s, when *intendentes* took on the duty of provisions managers, with the remit of procuring the purchases from producers, preparing them and distributing them to the troops, and army treasurers took on the preparation of managerial accounts. The new system was in operation for barely a decade and

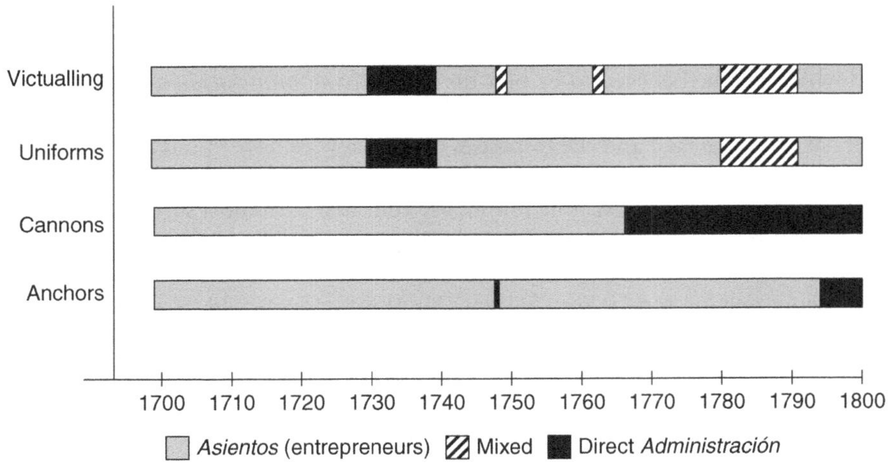

Figure 2.1 Concurrence and variation in some military supply methods: *administración* or *asiento*

Source: Author's own. Adapted from Rafael Torres Sánchez, 'Cuando las reglas del juego cambian. Mercados y privilegio en el abastecimiento del ejército español en el siglo XVIII', *Revista de Historia Moderna* 20 (2002), 487–511; Sergio Solbes Ferri, 'Campillo y Ensenada: el suministro de vestuarios para el ejército durante las campañas de Italia (1741-1748)', *Studia historica. Historia moderna* 35 (2013), 201–34; Agustín González Enciso, 'Del *contractor state* al Estado fabricante. El cambio de propiedad en la fábrica de municiones de Eugui en 1766', *Revista de Historia de la Economía y de la Empresa*, BBVA 7, 2014, 455–84.

with notable limitations; finally, in 1739 the government had to resort anew to private entrepreneurs.[14] This system was kept in place until the end of the century, when in 1799 an Army Victualling Accounting Office was again created, dependent on the Finance Ministry; but this again was to last only a few years because, as Salazar points out, 'this marked the start of shortfalls, haste, poor quality of the goods, clamours, complaints and, in sum, complete and general disorder in these supplies'.[15] In the case of military uniforms too, we find an overwhelming predominance of private supply during the whole century. Once again it was in the 1730s, with the War Minister, that there was an attempt to bring in direct *administración* for this supply operation, with a similar result to the aforementioned one for victuals.[16] As well as this project the state also tried to bring the supply of uniforms for navy battalions under state control.[17] When the government finally opted for direct *administración*, in 1786, it was still not a clean-cut decision; the ensuing method was mixed, with continuing participation by private entrepreneurs. The state nominally brought the provision of uniforms under direct *administración* but it was run by Banco de San Carlos, a bank managed by private merchants and financiers, which tapped into its own private credit and commercial networks to provide the uniforms on a 10 per cent commission basis. In 1789 the bank was replaced by a group of entrepreneurs of the Cinco Gremios Mayores, with the same private, commission-based method. Even this mixed method failed to prosper, however, and direct dealings with merchants were restored in 1797. For Sergio Solbes 'army provisioning engendered a permanent schizophrenia in the crown's ministers, for the aforementioned recourse to provisioning *asientos* really worked and became the predominant arrangement throughout the whole century'.[18]

The military wherewithal supplied with a clear prevalence of military supply-contracts also included the recruitment of soldiers, since levying troops entailed the same supply-method choices. As Francisco Andújar has clearly shown, private levies were not exclusively a seventeenth-century resource; they were often turned to in the eighteenth century too. The option of a state-managed recruitment system, under various arrangements known as *quintas* (draft of one out every five youngsters of military age) and *reclutas* (conscripts), was, in Andújar's opinion, inefficient and insufficient, and the Bourbon state had to resort to the system of private military supply-contracts to muster the military corps it required.[19] For his part Thomas Glesener has recently concluded that 'the concern about the "public" character of recruitment has cloaked an important facet of the system that was largely assumed by private entrepreneurs'. In his view historians have tended to overlook this aspect, preferring 'to dwell on the opposition between military supply-contracts on one side and *quintas* on the other, considered as two successive stages along a straight-line trend'. He concludes that 'it is now necessary to revisit the specific experiences of the eighteenth century modus operandi, which sought new forms of collaboration among entrepreneurs, the military and the royal administration'.[20]

As regards other supply needs there is less certainty about the procedures used, largely because they have not yet been studied, but we do know that even when part of the supply went over to direct *administración*, private contractors continued to play their part. In the supply of gunpowder, for example, we know that 103,480 *arrobas* of saltpetre were produced in Spain in 1760, of which 23 per cent was produced in 'king's factories' and the remaining 77 per cent in 'private factories'.[21] In the Americas private contractors were even more widely used. In the main production centre, Mexico, the *asiento* system was the only one used until 1767, but the switch to direct *administración* went hand in hand with continual state business with the main contractors, as in 1781, when state production fell short of its needs and a massive gunpowder purchase had to be made.[22] This coexistence also obtained in Spain, as shown by the huge gunpowder contracts with the merchants Francisco Cabarrús and Juan Gil Meester.[23]

The area where the state showed the firmest determination to intervene directly was naval supplies, but behind the big effort made in state shipyards and shipbuilding lurked a thriving military entrepreneur business. Throughout the whole of the eighteenth century the state procured most of its anchors by private contracts, albeit with several attempts to switch to direct *administración* in the mid eighteenth century.[24] Anchors, for example, were provided by military entrepreneurs until the end of the century, when the state factory was set up in Marrón, Santander, above all for strategic reasons and to avoid the perils of proximity to the French border. Even so, direct *administración* did not last a decade and, in 1804 the supply was once more contracted by *asiento*.[25] Provision of the navy's bitumen and tar was also exclusively by contractors. Although there were for several years up to three bitumen factories up and running for naval supply, the state still depended on private contracts to fill out supplies.[26] Even clearer was the military supply-contracts option in the provision of iron fittings and nails. The existence of forges in the shipyards did not limit the state's complete dependence on private merchants and producers. In other products, such as hemp and wood, the state was much more interventionist, but there was an ongoing need of private contracts, which in fact became the main supply method in the second half of the eighteenth century.[27] The predominance of *asiento*-based naval supplies was reflected in financing arrangements, which were withdrawn from the management of department councils in favour of the Treasurer General, who finally paid the naval entrepreneurs.[28] Furthermore, all these contracts fuelled a constant traffic of supply transport around the whole country, in carts and boats, almost always contracted by military supply-contract. As Ministro Arriaga acknowledged in the transport of bitumen for the navy, 'special care has been taken to carry out this transport by contract since to do so by *administración* would lose out in terms of punctuality, conveyance capacity and price'.[29] Transport in fact launched a whole world of small military supply-contracts, dubbed by Francisco Andújar '*microasientos*' with the state or between private parties, multiplying the importance of these military supply-contracts.[30] The importance built up by transport military supply-contracts was enhanced by the complicated geography of military supplies in Spain. As Map 2.1 shows, military entrepreneurs had to cope with a serious structural problem, namely, the concentration of military supply production in the north of Spain, while they were consumed mainly in the south. The best option of sea transport could turn out to be very risky in wartime, precisely when needs were most pressing. Overland transport, however, had to tackle the problem of very hilly country and few navigable rivers, with no rivers actually running from the north to the south of the country. Additional transport costs were no doubt a complicating factor of military supplies in Spain.

These military supply-contracts also loomed large even in the area most zealously controlled by the state, namely weapons and shipbuilding. Taking weapons first, González Enciso argues that up to 1760 the system of contracts was the only arrangement, and only from then on did direct *administración* win out.[31] Nonetheless, in the programme that he himself calls *estatalizador* (nationalization) of armaments production, private contracts still played some part and, once more, the process was not irreversible. With cannon supply, for example, state factories continually fell short of needs and huge purchases had to be made abroad; the provision of materials was always by contract and at the end of the century the system of contracts with private parties was even introduced.[32] Even more important was the presence of *asientos* in the supply of hand weapons such as rifles, pistols, and swords, where the state resorted overwhelmingly to private entrepreneurs throughout the whole century.[33] Much the same goes for shipbuilding. When Professor Merino commented on the graph of ships built in the eighteenth century he made a very telling remark: 'I confess my surprise at the result of the "ships of the line" graph in the first half of the eighteenth century.'[34] His surprise stemmed from the fact that the bulk of shipbuilding in the first half of the century

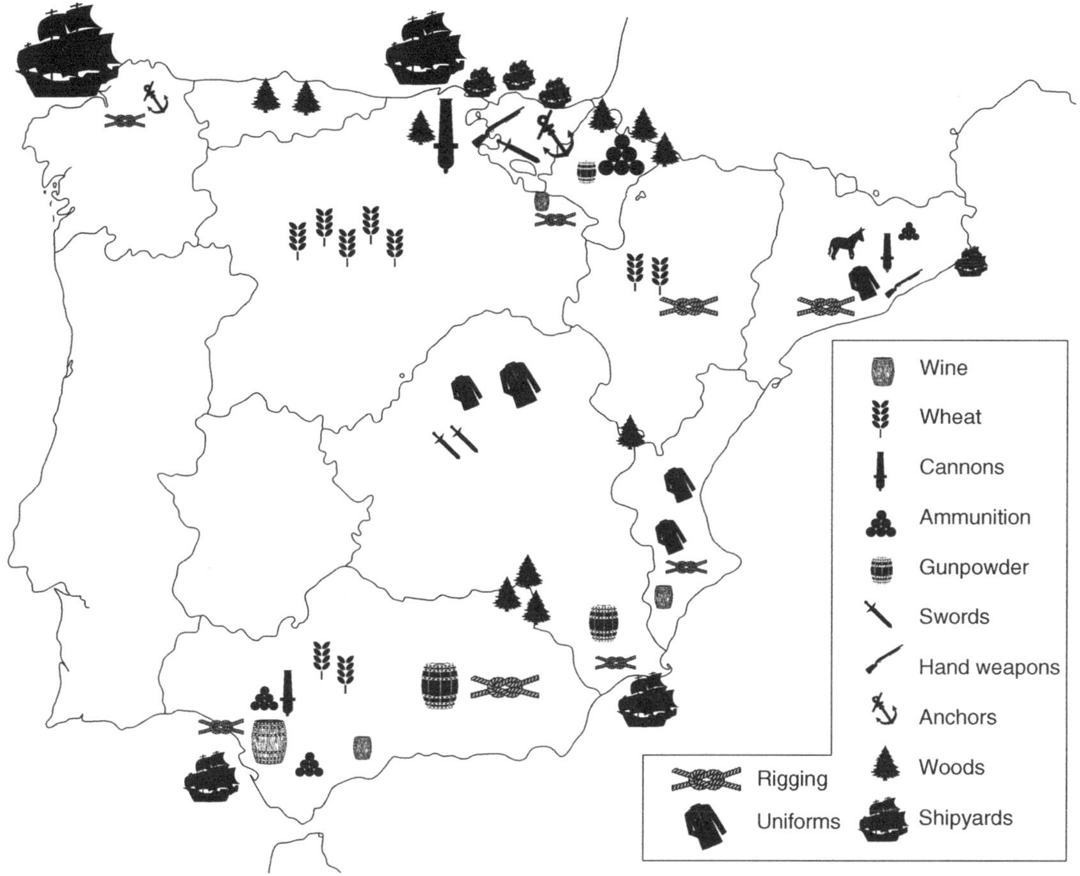

Map 2.1 The geography of eighteenth-century military supplies

Source: Author's own. NB the pictogram size reflects the output.

came not from the state's newly constructed shipyards in Spain but rather from Havana and Guarnizo, made, to boot, under private entrepreneurs.[35] This idea has since been ratified and fleshed out by the study by Iván Valdez-Bubnov, who has shown convincingly that shipbuilding by military supply-contract featured much more prominently in the Bourbon's shipbuilding programme than had traditionally been thought; furthermore, here as elsewhere, there was no irremediable and irreversible trend of growing state administration. As the author himself reminds us, towards the end of the 1780s 'contracts and military supply-contracts were systematically brought back into the naval system as a strategic priority, showing that the ideal of direct *administración* came across as the less feasible alternative among government high-ups. The documentation kept by the navy departments of Spain, moreover, completely bear out his view.'[36] Private suppliers might also be readily turned to whenever quick action was called for due to technological developments in warship performance. Witness the demand for copper needed for copper sheathing ships of the line during the American War of Independence. The government then had to decide between obtaining the copper in the Americas or turning to European entrepreneurs who could obtain it from Hungary. In the end, under pressure from the Spanish navy itself, which feared delays, the state opted to enter into a contract with the Greppi company, which duly informed its shareholders 'that the Spanish government had decided on supply by private merchants rather than direct state control'.[37]

It would seem reasonable to conclude that, in the eighteenth century as a whole, the Bourbons, just like the Habsburgs, used military supply-contracts with private parties as the main means of obtaining military supplies, even though the 'nature' of the state had moved on. The moot point now is to explain the reasons behind the Bourbon's supply policy and why there was no clearer party line on the path to follow, whether direct *administración* or by *asiento*. In sum, we believe that Bourbon governors took a pragmatic stance in their military supply policy. Any method was good as long as it served the immediate goal of ensuring the provision without forfeiting royal authority.

The essential thing for the Bourbon state was to make sure it had soldiers when it needed them and that these soldiers in turn had uniforms and swords; how this was done was of secondary importance. Any breach of a supply arrangement or fear of a shortfall could therefore be the spur to changing the method. Many examples bear out this order of priorities throughout the entire eighteenth century. Thus, the new administration-based uniform-supply method ordered by the state in 1763 for navy battalions had to be scrapped in 1776 at the behest of the Navy Minister on the grounds of 'the damage done to the navy's battalion troops by the current practice of supplying uniforms by the *Royal Exchequer*, due to the losses or breakdowns of the transport at sea and the delays they suffer'.[38] The fact that interventionist methods were then in full swing counted for little, overridden by the importance of this unit receiving its clothing properly. Likewise the failure of anchor production by the Royal Factory in Rentería in 1749 led the state to cut its losses and fall back on *asiento*-based supply.[39] The regularity from then on in the state's anchor supplies dissuaded any attempt to return to *administración*, and the supply henceforth was assured by those whom the state itself called *Ympresarios de anclas* (anchor entrepreneurs).[40] Germán Luis Andrade's findings are similar when analysing naval supplies in Mexico, coming to the conclusion that 'the failures and cost overruns experienced in the shipyards of Havana and Coatzacoalcos ... caused the navy to return to the military supply-contract-based system'.[41] He came to the selfsame conclusion when analysing the revival of *asiento*-based shipbuilding in Cantabria and Havana in the first half of the eighteenth century, a move that cannot be understood without factoring in the slowness and failure of Patiño and Ensenada's shipbuilding plans in state shipyards. Julián Arriaga, the Intendente General de la Armada (Navy Intendant General), argued as follows after suffering slowness and snags in La Carraca shipyard and the impossibility of meeting the scheduled shipbuilding programme, 'it is true that military supply-contracts are not good but the shortfalls of *administración* make them a necessary evil'.[42]

Supply failures or shortfalls could thus spur a change of method but this was not all one-way traffic: the failure of a military entrepreneur could also be the main reason for returning to direct *administración*. In 1753 the Marqués de Ensenada ordered that victualling of troops be done by direct *administración* to bypass the difficulties and failings of provision by military supply-contract; after two years of *administración* the system returned to contracts.[43] The same happened again ten years later when, in a period of soaring farm prices, the Cinco Gremios Mayores wanted to opt out of the provision. The reaction was the same and the state ordered that the supply be effected entirely 'by the *Royal Exchequer* itself', with the Cinco Gremios Mayores now acting as king's employees. Once the farming crisis had subsided the state went back to the former *asiento* system.[44] Once more, in the next decade, when the Banco de San Carlos ran into problems in performing its military supply-contract-based victualling contract, the Finance Minister Pedro López de Lerena ordered the method to be changed 'otherwise the shareholders (of the bank) will be ruined', and arrangements were made with the Cinco Gremios Mayores to supply this provision, explicitly 'by *administración*'.[45] The state's priority seemed to have been ensuring that the troops were duly provisioned and therefore operational; the method used was of secondary importance. In fact this modus operandi was not too different from Great Britain's, where the failure of suppliers was the main reason for changing the supply system, as occurred in the War of Jenkin's Ear.[46]

ECONOMIC PRICE OR POLITICAL PRICE?

The *administración* versus *asiento* dichotomy has traditionally been interpreted from an economic stance, that is, on the assumption that the choice of one option or another was based on cutting costs. Here too the picture is somewhat blurred and we find nothing as well defined as the declaration of principles made by the British Victualling Board when asked expressly about the cheapest means of victualling the British armed forces: 'It is scarcely necessary for us to remark that upon a *general principle* Governments obtain their supplies by contract at a cheaper rate than if they were procured by their own immediate servants.'[47] Once more the question begged is why there were no clear, sustained arguments in favour of any particular option. One of the reasons for this ongoing vagueness was precisely the price of supplies, or more strictly speaking the lack of an economic price. Failing any precise economic information to work from, both the state and military entrepreneurs placed much more emphasis on political aspects that had little to do with market rules.

An analysis of the negotiation processes used in some contracts seems to show that the price of supplies was an essentially political construct, not an economic one, as might have been thought a priori. The state was always hard put to establish a precise supply price, a *sine qua non* for deciding which system would work best economically. When the *contador general* of the Consejo de Indias, Tomás Ortíz de Landázuri, asked in 1772 for a calculation to be made of the real cost to the state of the production of Mexican gunpowder in the king's factories, the response he received was surprising: that it was calculated on the basis of 3 *reales* per pound. This was 'the price at which the last gunpowder military entrepreneur had sold his wares to the crown' and was in turn the same price that the state had fixed in 1642 as part of a negotiation that included revenue management. In this example the price is not determined in terms of anything comparable to a supply/cost analysis but rather institutional inertia. The final recommendations of the comptroller were 'not to include some imaginary revenue and expenditure by virtue of the ideal price of three *reales*', but not even this was actually taken up as a policy and the price of gunpowder produced by the state at the end of the eighteenth century was still determined by the mid-seventeenth-century price.[48]

Many other examples support the argument that the state worked with only a very vague idea of supply costs, even after all the ostensible progress made in the budget control measures, such as the Tesorería General. A detailed list of the cost to the state of victualling the army from 1744 to 1757 apparently managed to establish with some precision the cost of each *asiento*-supplied ration of bread and barley in each year, though this excluded the two years 1753 and 1754 in which 'there was no military supply-contract and supplies were provided by the Royal Exchequer and Tesorería General and there are no records of the cost'.[49] The reason is that the Royal Exchequer knew perfectly well how much it paid the military entrepreneur but acknowledged it was unable to pinpoint the administration costs because many expenses were not calculated. The traditional argument in favour of state-managed supplies, namely that direct *administración* did not need to keep up a network of correspondents since it could tap into the state administration itself, was in fact the main stumbling block to keeping a tag on the supply price.[50] Even in the most closely vetted supplies, such as, in general, those of the navy and especially in shipbuilding, the state never really managed to find out the final supply price, particularly of a constructed and fully rigged-out ship, and how this varied according to whether it was supplied by direct *administración* or *asiento*, despite countless attempts to do so throughout the eighteenth century. Even as late as 1790 the Navy Ministry carried out a last study of construction costs to decide 'the method that should be used in the construction of new ships' without any clear conclusion being drawn even in this case, because the final decision was spurred mainly by lobbying from the navy officials themselves.[51]

If the Bourbon state had serious difficulties in finding out the price of supplies, there do not seem to be any well-founded grounds for the accusations of overpricing often levelled at the contractors. For example, when Gabriel Arrieta wrote his popular *Alphabeto y Cartilla Militar* he openly criticized the military entrepreneurs' supply methods for the 'gains and profit creamed off' by them, but he offered no precise figures on what gain or profit might accrue from administration. The most surprising thing is his acknowledgement that to make his speculative calculations 'it has been necessary, to ascertain the quantity thereof with any precision, to fall back on the military supply-contracts'.[52] In all likelihood many criticisms of the contractors, most coming from state administrators, were not based on hard figures of any type, and they argued only on the general conviction that the money paid by the state was a waste for the Royal Exchequer. In the pithy words of the Marqués de Castejón, Navy Minister, echoing the complaints and criticisms made by several Navy Ministry employees, 'everything is a loss for the king's *hacienda* and gain for the military entrepreneurs' (see Figure 2.2).[53]

What does seem to be clear is that the state's difficulties in keeping a tag on supply prices, especially with direct *administración* arrangements, tended to load military supply-contract prices with political content. The state could check prices only against a vague institutional memory of historical prices and the final decision was negotiated largely on political grounds. Analysis of *asiento*-awarding processes shows that the final price was hardly ever established by market rules, and the legal public auction process was in fact compatible with legal negotiation. In a modest military supply-contract for oak planking in Navarre the entrepreneurs imposed the condition that the contract prices should not be published because 'there is a danger that if this [*asiento*] is published as wished the owners [of the trees] might hike up their prices'.[54] The state ordered their representatives on the auction site to negotiate directly with bidders, even before the auction was held, to agree a price beforehand. As the Marqués de Ensenada asked the Navy Minister of Bilbao, while in the process of awarding a nails and iron-fittings provision contract in 1750 for the whole navy, 'it behoves your excellency to draw on all your guile as well as intelligence to ensure this contract is conducive to the Royal Exchequer's interests in terms of the gross sum advanced to the military entrepreneur and the sure and punctual payment of all that might be provided'.[55] The price did not reflect exactly what the supplied goods were worth, rather what had been negotiated, and in a contract practically anything was open to negotiation: the contract term, the *asentista*'s performance bonds, the mode of payment, the advanced payments made by the Royal Exchequer, numbers of supplies, delivery sites, taxes, privileges, and many more factors. A change in any of these items could alter the final price without any modification in market conditions, and the state learned the advantages of buttonholing the military entrepreneurs in a parallel negotiation to the public auction procedure: 'the king orders that Aragorri be confidentially told that the guilds have dropped prices … in case he is disposed to improve his offer'.[56]

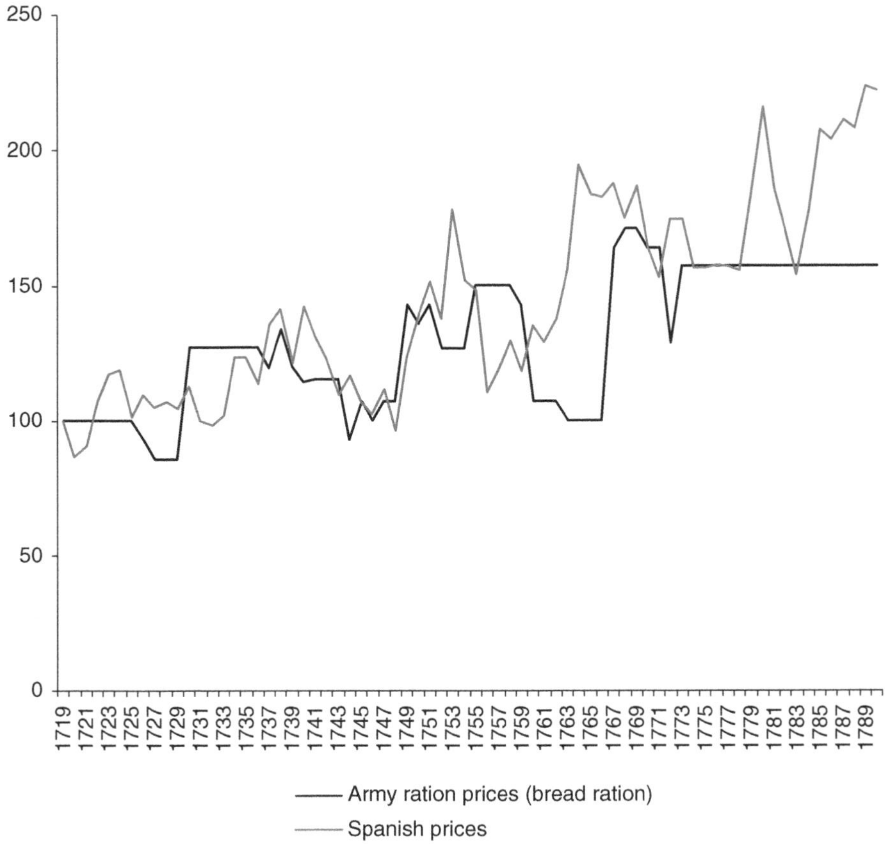

Figure 2.2 The political price of military supplies (1719 = 100): comparison between the final state-entrepreneur price and the general price trend in Spain

Source: David Sven Reher, 'Precios y salarios en Castilla la Nueva: la construcción de un índice de salarios reales, 1501–1991, *Revista de Historia Económica—Journal of Iberian and Latin American Economic History* 11 (1993), 101–51; and Enrique Llopis Agelán, 'Índices de precios de tres ciudades españolas, 1680–1800: Palencia, Madrid y Sevilla', *América Latina en la Historia Económica* 16 (2009), 29–80.

In these parallel negotiations between state and military entrepreneurs there was a surprising limit: public opinion. For the whole eighteenth century, but especially in the second half, the state strived to ensure that military supply-contract prices did not increase on previous contracts. Institutional memory acted as the main price regulator, and whenever any new negotiation started, reports were requested on the previous prices. The aim of these backward looks was to justify the maintenance, reduction, or, in the worst of cases, slight rise in the new price, mindful as they were that the price would finally become public knowledge. Strange as it may seem, the Spanish state was very concerned about what 'the public' might think, and it bent over backwards to ensure that the published price should be what they called 'economical'. We have even found cases of supply prices being concealed from the public, presumably due to a fear of public opinion. This was expressly recognized in an army victualling contract of 1756, with the admission that, to ensure that the final price agreed between the Finance Ministry and *asentista* was the same as the previous one, the prices could be offset among the various goods supplied in the contract: 'to forestall any untoward surprise in the inexperienced, this latter price could be increased for the bread ration and lowered accordingly for the barley'.[57] In any case the negotiation involved concealment of the real price agreed between state and military entrepreneurs, even with the express authorization of the Finance Minister himself: 'I give you my word that the prices will not be published.' (See Figure 2.3.)[58]

Another salient factor in price negotiations between state and military entrepreneurs was the form of payment. The thorniest point was whether the Royal Exchequer should pay the contractor the total cost beforehand in monthly or annual payments called '*anticipos*' or '*mesadas*'. The cost was estimated from the state consumption figures in each supply arrangement of previous years. These *mesadas* forestalled an important accounting problem. Before going ahead with payment of the goods supplied, the state had to check the certificates issued by

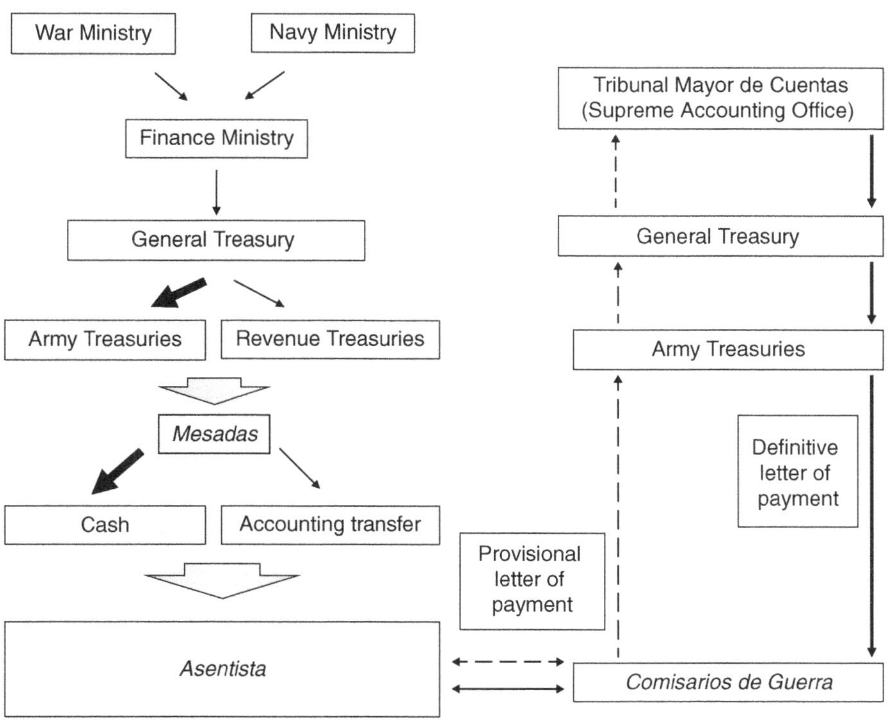

Figure 2.3 Form of payment and accounting control of *asientos*

Source: Author's own. Adapted from Rafael Torres Sánchez, *La llave de todos los tesoros: la Tesorería General de Carlos III* (Madrid: Sílex, 2012).

the *comisarios de guerra* and *ordenadores*, pooled by the army treasuries, sent up to Treasurer General and finally vetted by the Tribunal Mayor de Cuentas. This was a long-winded accounting process that could take several years, provoking unconscionable delays for military entrepreneurs. For the suppliers these consignments represented a way of receiving payments without building up intolerable delays, whilst also comprising an efficient financing arrangement to shore up their creditworthiness. The contractors running the bronze cannon factories of Seville, for example, needed these consignments precisely to service the loans they took out to buy raw materials on the world markets,[59] and we know that some entrepreneurs even negotiated using these advanced payments.[60] For the military entrepreneurs therefore these *mesadas* became an essential feature. In some cases, as in the military supply-contract for building six ships of the line in 1766, they were written into the contract: 'Upon the cessation of any monthly payment the work shall cease forthwith and compensation will be paid for the suspension.'[61] This method of advanced payments cannot be construed as a condition imposed on the Spanish state by military entrepreneurs; rather was it the habitual state of affairs throughout Europe. Even the British state used this system with its contractors, and it was also considered as 'a system that encouraged the rapid performance of contracts'.[62] Nonetheless, the method of advanced payments was a leitmotif in the administrators' arguments to demonstrate precisely the opposite, that is, the 'profligacy' of the Royal Exchequer, and a conclusive proof of military entrepreneurs' excesses. In the words of Fermín Buenaventura, 'it must be admitted that if the Administration is given the advanced payment and consignment asked for by Manuel Santos, it would not seem to me to represent more expense than this supply is worth, because the three million *reales de vellón* up front would ensure the supply of wheat within and without the kingdom with some ease'.[63]

What brought this feature into the very centre of negotiations was the fact that it forced the Royal Exchequer to face up to the problem of needing more liquidity in its royal coffers. It was precisely its chronic lack of liquidity throughout the whole century that made the *mesadas* such a key element in the supply-contract negotiation procedures. The military entrepreneurs claimed the monthly payment punctually and as agreed in the contract, while the Royal Exchequer tried to reduce and delay these payments as much as possible. The Royal Exchequer's room for manoeuvre grew increasingly cramped. In the first half of the eighteenth century it was able to solve the payment of the *mesadas* by tying them into the income received from specific revenues, but in the second half of the century, when some royal revenue had been taken into direct *administración*, the state was forced to toughen its negotiations for advanced payments with the military entrepreneurs.[64] The negotiation of each military supply-contract renewal thus became more complex, especially for the most important military supply-contracts. The state's attempts to bargain down advanced payments were accepted by the military entrepreneurs only in exchange for an increase in the number of contract years or for some other privilege, including monopoly rights. This was a dangerous game. The more significant were the advanced payments, the more complex were the negotiations and hefty the trade-offs. In fact some administrators, mindful of the danger, preferred to exclude advanced payments from the negotiations, as admitted by the Junta del Departamento Marítimo of Ferrol, which concluded in a military supply-contract negotiation, 'for which reason nothing should ideally be advanced to the military entrepreneurs; advanced payments also have the drawback that they call for non-contractual arrangements'.[65] Needs must, however, and in practice advanced payments were in the end almost always included in the negotiation package. Juggling with all these factors led to very different solutions in each case, but the bottom line was always that the final published price should not be 'scandalous'. Military supply-contract prices, therefore, almost always held steady or fell, sometimes even by covering up an actual increase in the sums advanced by the state. Things might also work the other way and waiving of the advance payment could be the best way to win an *asiento* over another bidder offering the same price.[66]

If the government was often hard put to ascertain the real price of state-supplied goods, therefore, and military supply-contract prices were established more in terms of multi-factor trade-offs and negotiations, the upshot was that the state did not work towards finding out and imposing the most efficient method, at least from the economic point of view. If the real economic calculations were less important, a pragmatic interpretation once more won out: the crucial factor was to obtain the product; how much it cost was secondary. In the middle of a complex negotiation of a victualling military supply-contract between the Cinco Gremios Mayores and the Finance Ministry in 1772, Miguel Múzquiz went for broke in an attempt to beat down the military entrepreneurs' claims: he threatened them

> with changing the two activities [provision of victuals and management of the *Excusado* tax] across to administration ... and if they still do not knuckle under, order that the administration arrangement be enforced by such offices as you may deem most fitting but that it be none of the Guilds so that it may turn out cheaper for the king and their demands more moderate.[67]

The priority for the minister was clear; the rest was all negotiable, including the supply method, the privileges granted, the price, and or advanced payments. And in this negotiation the king always had the last word because it was he who gave the exact value to the contract granted, reinforcing his authority with each renewal.

This growing politicization of the supply price was bound up, as we will see later, with the political room for manoeuvre in fact offered to the state by a supply-contract, thus blurring the distinction between *asiento* and *administración*.

POLITICAL ACTION: SHARED MERCANTILISM

According to Thompson's thesis, by resorting to *asientos* the state forfeited part of its capacity for direct political action. Yet this was not so clear-cut for the Bourbon state. In fact it can be argued that one of the reasons why no one provisioning system won out definitively over the other was precisely because the Bourbon state was able to pursue political action without any major constraints. The state was able to enforce its full authority without limits, regardless of whether the goods it needed were supplied by direct *administración* or by *asiento.*

Perhaps the clearest defining trait in the state's military supply policy was the pursuit of mercantilist principles. Although it might seem almost a commonplace to affirm that the state's political action was largely ruled by mercantilist tenets, the fact is that this characteristic went even deeper than is generally believed. As historians have been insisting for some time now, mercantilism was not only a current of thought but also one of the main driving forces behind political action throughout the whole eighteenth century, particularly, it could even be said, in Great Britain. According to Kenneth Morgan, its 'mercantilist policies, underpinned by a fiscal-military state and successful prosecution of war, enabled Great Britain to forge a world empire'.[68] Patrick O'Brien even goes so far as to argue that a historical view guided by what he calls 'liberal myths and mercantilist realities' shows that English success during the eighteenth century was fundamentally the success of Europe's most mercantilist state, because it was the state that most successfully built up 'security, stability and sovereignty' throughout the kingdom, ultimate objectives of the state and the essential base for sustained growth.[69] In eighteenth-century Spain there was also an almost entire unanimity about pursuing these goals, and Uztáriz's mercantilist ideas were a permanent lodestar through the whole century. The main objective of political action was national security and the profitability and stimulation of the kingdom's economy. Both elements could be merged by means of a military provisioning policy fuelled by express national production, thereby preventing the engendered wealth from ending up in the hands of foreigners, either because the suppliers were not national subjects or because the supplies had to be paid for abroad. When, for example, the Navy Minister, Marqués de Castejón, declared in 1781 that the best and only way of supplying hemp was to foster its production in Spain, he based his arguments on the idea that this supply arrangement would become a useful political action 'to sustain our Navy, that of national trade, and avoid hereafter the drain of so many millions abroad'.[70] In other words, his arguments were limited to the reiteration of Uztáriz's mercantilist ideas. For most of Spain's public administrators it was an unchallengeable tenet that the provision of the armed forces by national production would produce huge economic and political benefits; the role model was Great Britain. As late as 1792 the Finance Minister, Diego Gardoqui, was still arguing that the economic policy to follow was 'the English model', which, in the minister's words, could be summed up as the intelligent use and protection of national demand: 'three kinds of measures as well as prohibitions have been followed by the English, which are without doubt those that have been most zealously, watchfully and fruitfully nurtured to boost national wealth'.[71] As Guillaume Garner argues, the presence and influence of mercantilist ideas in the political discourse of the eighteenth century is explained by the state's need to enforce its authority and sovereignty, something he calls 'territorial economy'.[72]

The ongoing validity of these ideas among Spanish governors during the whole century was reflected in the best supply-policy recommendations made by the Navy Minister and Finance Minister, Salazar. He advocated a clear mercantilist programme:

> as Mr Ustariz and all economists quite rightly claim … on the grounds that supplies of all types should whenever possible be made in national goods, even if they be of lower quality and higher price than foreign goods, because the wealth of the state is the same as the wealth of the members who make it up, the funds that pass from government coffers into the hands of private merchants, insofar as this remains Spanish property, do not impoverish said state in any way whatsoever but rather through myriad twists and turns return to swell its funds; and this perpetual circulation gives life to governments just as the circulation of blood gives life to animals.[73]

Once more the priority was not the price of supplies; for Salazar the most important factor was the possibility of politically motivated economic action.

The mercantilist ideas expounded in 1814 tell us we are not talking here merely about theoretical ideas or tenets applicable only to the early decades of the eighteenth century; on the contrary, they profoundly marked state military supply policies during the whole century. That said, the crux of the matter for our purposes here is whether this mercantilist 'programme' could be carried out only by means of direct *administración*, a factor that would have justified the choice of this system as an instrument of political action. What we are told by the relationships between the state and military entrepreneurs is that these mercantilist ideas were largely shared by military entrepreneurs too, who echoed the government's shibboleths, and that the military supply-contracts also helped the Bourbon state to implement its markedly mercantilist policies. When the textile military entrepreneur Marcos Antonio de Andueza proposed in 1780 a new 12-year contract for military uniforms for the troops of the Americas, Andalusia, and Ceuta, he justified it on mercantilist grounds, chiming in completely with the state's desires:

> to the end of fostering factories and manufacturing activity, extending the profit from this business that up to now has been engendered only in the Principality of Catalonia further afield to (a) the other provinces of the realm … thereby banishing the greater part of the mendicity … That it being Your Majesty's will to promote and foment as far as possible the factories in those four kingdoms of Andalusia, I hereby undertake to make the said uniforms from broadcloth and serge from the factories of those provinces of Andalusia …[74]

Equally mercantilist are the ideas expressed by the directors of the Banco de San Carlos to justify their interest in managing the victualling military supply-contract: 'preferring, however, the production of these realms insofar as they may be compatible with the purpose in view, in keeping with the provisions laid down in the Real Cédula de Erección del Banco (bank's foundational charter) for promotion of the agriculture and industry thereof'.[75] Examples are rife but the conclusion is always the same: the state could carry out a mercantilist policy on the back of military supply-contracts too, because the military entrepreneurs, from convenience or conviction, fully shared the prevailing ideas. This synchrony further reduced the political importance of choosing between direct *administración* and *asientos* and fuelled the ongoing validity of both systems.

Nonetheless, the fact that both supply methods could be applied to the pursuit of the same mercantilist objectives does not in itself ensure that these objectives are fulfilled; neither does it mean that one or other method might guarantee a higher level of success in pursuing the mercantilist ideal. In the practical results of mercantilist politics we do find a notable difference when breaking down the overall picture by military entrepreneurs or supplies. As regards businessmen the success was complete, with a concomitant triumph of the Bourbon state's mercantilist principles. Throughout the eighteenth century the dominance of Spanish suppliers in military provisions was total and constant. The nationalization of military entrepreneurs has been little studied and understood as yet. Nonetheless, there are some studies stressing that the strong inroads into this business made by foreigners since the end of the sixteenth century, as pointed out by Thompson, were compatible with the continued operations of Spanish suppliers in the seventeenth century, and with a pre-1700 process of substitution and expansion. Constant outbreaks of war in Spain itself and the local mobilization of military resources nonetheless fostered the development of Spanish military entrepreneurs, some of whom managed to set up trading houses of great capacity, to the point of extending their business to other territories of the monarchy.[76] There was no brake on this expansionist dynamic of Spanish military entrepreneurs with the change of dynasty and the advent of French policies, military entrepreneurs, and supplies. Not even Jean Orry's political clout and his past connections with French military entrepreneurs,[77] nor the need of massive imports of supplies from France during the War of Succession,[78] managed to create the effective conditions for the permanent infiltration of French suppliers. As Jean Pierre Dedieu argues, it was Philip V's financial needs that finally swung royal favour to the Spanish, thereby ensuring survival of Spanish military entrepreneurs, in a confrontation defined by Dedieu as between 'the group' of Jean Baptiste Orry and the Goyeneche 'conglomerate'.[79] This clash should probably be understood in the wider context of a simmering but fierce struggle by various European countries for the Spanish market. In this ongoing struggle, as Pérez Sarrión has shown, there was no going back, and Spanish interests flourished.[80] This whole process came to a head after the War of Succession, when military supply-contracts at all levels, from contract holders to *factores* and guarantors, were controlled by Spaniards. We do not yet know the key features of the triumph of Spanish businessmen and women but the firm support of royal authority must have played a leading role, without doubt due to the state's own financial weakness, the need of a stable of solvent capitalists, and the entrance of some of them into the machinery of the state itself. However it may have come about, the dominance of Spanish businesspeople in military supplies was absolute and unquestionable for the rest of the century, without doubt an outstanding mercantilist success story.

The continuance of Spanish dominance cannot be explained simply by inertia; it was a struggle to sustain this dominance over time, and Spanish military entrepreneurs collaborated in this struggle. In some cases they are known to have contributed actively to the maintenance of national dominance, fending off foreign encroachment. It was not the state but the Spanish military entrepreneurs themselves who defended the 'territorial economy' and thereby managed to fortify the state's mercantilist principles. The success of the French entrepreneurs and their advent in the provisioning business should be construed along the same lines. When Francisco Cabarrús, as head of the Banco de San Carlos, won the lion's share of this business, it was interpreted as another French triumph.[81] Cabarrús was not interested in military supplies. His main goal was a monopoly on silver exports, which the state granted as a trade-off for the *vales reales* solution to the problem of public debt. But his appearance in the military supplies business brought him into conflict with the previous military entrepreneurs, who, with the Cinco Gremios Mayores to the fore, the support of the treasurer general Francisco Montes, and the approval of the Finance Ministry, Pedro Lerena, managed to discredit him within a few years and oust him from their business.[82] Once driven out, and with the Marqués de Hormazas (former navy victualling military entrepreneur)[83] at the head of the bank, all the military supply-contracts were once more granted to Spanish military entrepreneurs. Cabarrús's triumph in military supplies lasted barely five years and the cause of his failure was the opposition of the Spanish. The rapid and decisive fall of Cabarrús speaks less of French influence and more of the strength built up by Spanish businesspeople to fend off foreign inroads. Without doubt another mercantilist triumph.

The Bourbon state, with the participation of Spanish military entrepreneurs, managed to keep military supply-contracts in Spanish hands, but was not so successful at limiting supplies to Spanish goods, produced either at home or in its colonies. In truth the mercantilist idea of self-sufficiency was not achieved.[84] Almost all supply arrangements had to be topped up by imports of foreign goods: gunpowder, cannons, ships, tar, nails, iron fittings, victuals ... even soldiers. Of the 82 infantry battalions existing in the mid eighteenth century, 21 per cent were made up of foreigners,[85] and there was a growing need for foreign mercenaries during the rest of the century.[86] Yet the inability to meet the ideal of mercantilist self-sufficiency should not be overstated. In practice this ideal was not achieved by any European country, not even Great Britain, where, for all its extraordinary productive capacity, it could keep up its naval expansion only by means of huge imports of military supplies.[87] Foreign markets of raw materials, finished products or technical products were tapped into fairly fluidly in the eighteenth century, largely because it was precisely in Europe where most states interested in spending all their resources on warfare were concentrated, and this gave rise to European markets of military supplies, little studied as yet.[88]

The important question for our purposes here is whether or not the Bourbon state's military supply policy managed to reduce this irremediable dependence on foreign markets, which was at the end of the day the ultimate objective of a mercantilist approach. Here it can be argued that the constant switching from direct *administración* to military supply-contracts may have boosted the state's authority, but it also curbed national production capabilities and therefore strayed from its mercantilist principles. To understand this apparent paradox—more authority and less mercantilism—we need to factor in another key feature, namely the exclusivity principal underpinning the Bourbon dynasty's military supply policy.

EXCLUSIVITY, PRIVILEGE, AND COLLABORATION

The Bourbon state's political actions were also driven by another guiding idea that has been little studied as yet, namely exclusivity. The state developed a supply policy in which all the public and private stakeholders shared the same aim of achieving exclusivity, privilege, and even monopoly in some cases. Both sides came out winning. The state secured a given supply of goods without hiccups; the private merchants were brought closer to the centres of power and authority within that society and hence found it easier to forge their own careers and promotion. Thompson insists that this condition was always imposed by one party on the other, either the state on the military entrepreneurs or the *asentistas* on the state. In fact the picture that seems to emerge quite clearly from a study of the eighteenth century is a constant quest by both parties for the same exclusivity or, to put it another way, a collaboration between state and military entrepreneurs to serve their mutual interests, thereby helping to blur even more the limits between direct *administración* and *asientos*.

We cannot actually work out who was most interested of the two, whether the state or the military entrepreneurs, but we do know that it was mutually beneficial. As Rafael Guerrero has cogently shown, competition between the Gipuzkoa and Biscay ironworks was sharpened not by production or market forces but rather proximity to the king, either by way of an military supply-contract or by holding the post of an administrator in a royal factory. Obtaining an *asiento* or royal appointment could greatly alter the beneficiary's production capacity but it also had a knock-on effect on the other local producers and so reshaped social and political relations for an entire area. Witness the comments made by a friend of the weapons entrepreneur Pedro Bernardo de Villarreal as part of the flood of news unleashed by his recent military supply-contract, leaving no doubt at all that much more was at stake than just a piece of business: 'you must know that the military supply-contract and offices in Bengolea have ruffled the feathers of not a few dukes and counts, armed and unarmed of this whole land'.[89] Becoming a 'right-hand man of the king' represented a seismic shift in the power alliances and relations and authority of a given area and raised the beneficiary to the status of an inner and national elite. If the king was the only source of authority, then a military supply-contract or royal appointment offered a crucial promotion and badge of social eminence. This dynamic of social promotion under the wing of royal authority worked in a bottom-up direction, that is, levering up the individual towards the local elite and oligarchy and, at the very top level, towards the national groups and elites. This achieved several things. First and foremost the local elites became more interested in participating in the state's supply needs. This was not an imposition of the state and much less an assignment of power; quite the opposite in fact. It was the military entrepreneurs and local elites themselves that sought to participate in and satisfy state needs and so helped to reinforce the source of power, that is, royal authority. Secondly, it could help to pull out the carpet from under the old elites, as in this example, and replace them by others closer and more loyal to the king; this was an essential factor in the reign of Philip V. One way or another, the king's authority was enhanced.

The cost to the state of this exclusivity was apparently cheap, since the number of privileges granted was to be kept to a set minimum. But the privileges conceded to royal factories and trading companies were merely the tip of the iceberg of a much deeper traffic of privileges with military entrepreneurs, little studied as yet but without doubt affecting many individuals and groups.[90] The important factor to stress here is that these privileges could be essential for management of the business; this guaranteed two essential aspects, the interest of the military entrepreneur and the strength of the state's position and royal authority. Prima facie the *asiento* involved a series of privileges with an economic value and business possibilities that transcended a mere supply-contract. One of the most important associated business boons was the relaxation of traffic controls on merchandise and money. For instance, the granting of permission to export silver abroad, on the pretext that it was necessary for making certain purchases, could well become even more important than the military supply-contract itself. Likewise, the permission, with the support of local authorities, to requisition means of transport such as carts, oxen, or boats could also be an important advantage. The Board of the Banco de San Carlos, for example, obtained for its navy victualling military supply-contract the right of demanding 'provision of sailors from Navy Ministers'.[91] As acknowledged by the military entrepreneur, the Marqués de Valdeolmos, without any state instrument to vouch for their authority to seize carts or buy at fixed prices, this business should be governed by market rules, and this was not to the liking of these military entrepreneurs: 'an *Asentista* lacks the power to strike a hard bargain when sellers of grain, carters or boat captains hold out for high prices and there is no other remedy, to avoid greater damage, than paying each one his asking price'.[92]

The advantage obtained by any privileged military entrepreneur over other producers and sellers meant that the number and quality of privileges obtained marked the crucial difference. Here, as elsewhere, the state distinguished cases according to the risk of supply shortfalls. Thus, while it authorized the Cinco Gremios Mayores to seize conveyances for the transport of victuals, it withheld the same right from a small military entrepreneur transporting bitumen to the port of Almería: 'the *asentista* is not granted the privilege it seeks for stockpiling carts, since this should be its own business without detriment to private parties, nor the grace it seeks of the privileges of the Cabaña Real de Carreteros [Royal Carters' Association]'.[93] Among the privileges that featured as bargaining tokens there was one of extraordinary value: the number of *patentes*, open permits for the military entrepreneur to appoint employees and *factores* of the provision congrats.

The system faithfully reproduced the scheme employed in the private recruitment of soldiers, where the number of appointments was also negotiated, in this case jobs that could then be sold.[94] In military supplies the negotiated *patentes* conferred valuable advantages on their holders, such as entitlement to the *fuero militar*, exemption from militia drafts, the right to carry weapons, exemption from some taxes, and an evident boost in local status. These were without doubt sufficient lures for the military entrepreneur to attract employees and sustain its network of *factores*, distribution agents whose collaboration was crucial to make the military supply-contract feasible. Under these conditions it was the military entrepreneurs themselves who were the first to ask for and sustain exclusivity as a means of political leverage.

The state, for its part, was keen to demand this exclusivity arrangement in its dealings with private contractors, in order to guarantee the supply. To understand this way of thinking (that an exclusive supplier is the best guarantee of military supply) it should be borne in mind that this was precisely what the state itself sought: absolute control over military supplies. Whether this control was achieved with a single private contractor or public administrator was secondary; the important point was to guarantee unbroken supply. The alternative to this modus operandi would have been to trust in free market competition, albeit exclusively national, but this option apparently posed so many risks and so much uncertainty that the Bourbon state was never ready to take it. Thus the real problem for the state was not choosing public or private administration, but rather the degree of control it achieved either way, and ultimately the authority that the state managed to wield in the supply of military provisions. Viewed through this prism, free market forces would appear as uncontrollable; the option was therefore ruled out from the start. A military entrepreneur who claimed privileges and an authority that granted them and assigned a precise value to each privilege was just as useful as direct *administración* would have been in terms of fulfilling the main supply-control goal. The demand and concession of exclusivity, of privileges, became the true essence of the Bourbons' military supply policy and system.

The principle of exclusivity brought into play an increasing identification of objectives and of the modus operandi between state and military entrepreneur, and fulfilled a relationship of mutual dependence. Experience had taught the state the perils and insecurity of opening up military supplies to the uncertain competition of military entrepreneurs. There was a real risk of not enough entrepreneurs coming forward, or doing so with insufficient guarantees and solvency or even, in the worst case, falling down on a contract. The chosen way of reducing these risks was precisely to increase exclusivity and thereby privileges. Indeed, an aspect of Bourbon politics that has been undervalued hitherto is precisely the growing trend over the century of using privilege as a means of political action. In its relation with military entrepreneurs this translated into increasingly privileged and state-supported contractors, a clutch of military entrepreneurs that, on the principle of exclusivity, were also pared down in number. This development explains an evident and apparently contradictory feature of eighteenth-century Spain: namely, that just at the moment of increasing state intervention and direct *administración*, in the reign of Charles III, there was also a greater concentration of military supply-contracts in the hands of fewer military entrepreneurs. The success of the Cinco Gremios Mayores was possible thanks to this situation, with a brief continuation in the hands of another military entrepreneur, the Banco de San Carlos, who negotiated with the state using words that made no bones about the game rules, such as: 'with preference over any other privileged firm'.[95] By late in the century the ante between state and military entrepreneurs had been upped to such an extent that it ushered in the last stage in the process of growing exclusivity: de facto monopoly. This trend had been growing throughout the whole century. Orry had already spoken of the wisdom of bringing the army's whole supply under the exclusive control of one single military entrepreneur.[96] The pace of change then picked up from mid-century onwards, since the state could no longer fob off military entrepreneurs with revenue farming arrangements and also wished to make the supply more secure. The result was a growing interdependence between state and military entrepreneurs and the need for the state directly to support and shore up the military entrepreneurs. As the Marqués de Esquilache reminded the *intendente* of Extremadura in 1767, faced with the possible bankruptcy of some *factores* of military entrepreneurs in that region, 'it behoves us to treat them with even-handedness for neither these nor others can now fulfil the defaulted supply-agreements'.[97] A group of military entrepreneurs trading under state authority, who claimed and obtained business privileges as a trade-off for guaranteed supplies, who identified with the state's mercantilist goals, and, in case of difficulties, would be directly shored up by the state itself for fear of supply shortages, represented in essence a mere extension of the state itself. So in practice, the dividing line between *administración* and *asiento* grew very vague or even non-existent. This is borne out too by the switchback management model and the tolerated role of the same businessmen as military entrepreneurs and administrators alike.

The principle of exclusivity was equally applicable when the state managed a supply arrangement directly itself. The fact that a certain good was produced and supplied by the state did not necessarily rule out other sources of national supply, which might turn out to be perfectly compatible or even advantageous, as is shown by the English example. But the picture revealed by studies and documentation is that the Bourbon state, whenever it could, tried to impose an exclusivity condition on the production arrangement. Historians traditionally account for this on the basis of the state's desire to boost national technology and unify and control quality, but these arguments are questionable at best. The technology component was indeed important in some of the products supplied to the armed forces. More direct state control could favour implementation of a new technology because it wielded direct control over the mode of production and any obstacles that might crop up in its application could be eliminated more directly too. The state's engagement in technological renewal has traditionally fascinated historians, who tend to interpret it as a calculated bid for modernization.[98] The problem is that it has not always proved possible to ascertain or cross-check the real costs of its introduction, whether in terms of creating the necessary infrastructure and wherewithal (buildings, experts, and tools) or because of the destruction of existing activities and firms. Neither has due consideration been given to its effects on the overriding goal: to ensure the best supplies for the state. Rather more attention has been paid to technological breakthroughs than to these real effects.

There are many examples of this, particularly in the metal industry. In the case of the production of bronze cannons the state decided after the Seven Years War to introduce a new cannon production procedure, casting the cannons solid and then drilling out the bore instead of casting them hollow in moulds. This decision was taken even though tests conducted with this new technique in Seville in 1757 had failed and despite the higher copper input required, just when Spain's metal market was being squeezed. Application of this technique involved luring in technical experts with high salaries and disproportionate additional benefits, constructing a new factory at a cost of over six million *reales* (until the 1760s the factory's monthly allocation from the Royal Exchequer was 720,000 *reales de vellón*),[99] and shutting down production, which between 1767 and 1774 dwindled right down to 84 pieces as against the 300 chalked up in the 1750s. The end result of all this effort was technically poor and extremely costly,[100] as the English ambassador told his government after attending the tests, opining that these cannons had turned out 'too costly to render any service other than adorning the entrance to a shipyard'.[101] Even graver were the consequences of technological renewal in the production of iron cannons in Liérganes and La Cavada, provoking administrative chaos, lowering production, and resulting in the century's biggest importation of cannons: 4,498 bought from Great Britain.[102] This comes as quite a surprise when the state seemed to have no problem in imposing on cannon-producing military entrepreneurs the new official artillery calibre regulations without bringing them under direct *administración*.[103] Likewise, the mid-century introduction and enforcement of the new English-style shipbuilding system sparked off grave problems and delays in Spain's shipyards and could be finally carried out only when the state turned back to the Cantabrian and Havana military entrepreneurs and imposed this as a condition in the military supply-contracts.[104] In other words, technology, like authority, could not be applied exclusively behind the walls of a shipyard belonging directly to the king.

The state had no real problem in imposing a given standard of quality on the supplies it needed. In fact the supposed quality problem was no such thing. It sufficed for the terms and conditions in military supply-contracts to be clear and for the person in charge of receiving the goods to certify that they complied with the state's contracted terms. As agreed in a clothing contract, the military entrepreneur undertook to 'provide wherever I am asked a complete uniform with all clothing items as a sample to be checked beforehand, sealed and deposited, so that the rest produced thereafter abide thereby'.[105] The state therefore needed only a regulation and a sample to unify the quality of all supplies, as occurred in the English case, where it was specified that any contractor who supplied products lower than the stipulated quality would be excluded from all future contracting procedures.[106] The problem of quality as such did not seem to exist. What actually occurred was that, as part of this growing spiral of identification and interdependence between state and military entrepreneurs, the state was often prepared to accept lower quality levels than those stipulated in the contracts. Administrators were also quick to use quality as an argument to justify keeping a particular supply arrangement under their control. When a debate was underway about whether an *asiento* system should be restored due to a gunpowder production shortfall in state factories, the factory administrators argued that this would involve an inevitable reduction in quality. The inspector of the Royal Exchequer had to counter the administrators' arguments by pointing out that when the state entered into a contract it paid nothing until 'the testing and examination of the gunpowder delivered, pursuant to ordinances ... thus circumventing the supposed objection to accepting the contract without knowing the goodness, virtue and consistency of the goods to be manufactured'.[107] In the inspector's opinion there should be no debate about any supposed variation in quality; the only meaningful requisite was to ensure that the state paid only for what it wished to buy with the quality stipulated in the contract.

If the state had the real possibility of controlling the quality of supplies and it was not essential for the state itself to produce the good in question, why was it so interested in applying the principle of exclusivity? Curiously enough, this very point greatly preoccupied Navy Minister Salazar in 1814. In the opinion of this minister the problem resided in the state's political tendency throughout the whole eighteenth century, in his case seen in the navy, towards what he called the question of *cosechas propias* (home harvests). With this expression the minister wished to illustrate what, in his judgement, was the principle of exclusivity that had dominated the supply policy during the whole eighteenth century. Salazar reasoned that, with the objective of ensuring the supply of certain naval goods, the navy had directly controlled production. The examples of hemp and wood influenced him. All navy officials agreed that home production and consumption of hemp, for example, should be encouraged, but the navy's attempt to soak up all production exclusively tended to 'diminish hemp harvests ... and the navy had to turn back to foreign hemp supplies'.[108] The minister's interpretation here must have been based on knowledge of the actual situation, because we have found sufficient evidence showing that navy commissioners in charge of procurement tried to reserve all production exclusively for the navy. Words such as 'seizure', 'rate', and 'fixed price' illustrate the increasingly complex tenor of relations between commissioners and the products they tried to procure.[109] The navy's attempt to impose itself as the sole purchaser must have dampened the ardour of producers, who then dropped out en masse when the navy treasuries even began to fall down on payments.

Something very similar must have happened with the policy of exclusivity applied to the supply of wood for shipbuilding. Although a major shipbuilding effort was made in the first half of the eighteenth century, there was no serious dearth of wood at this time; neither did the state need to organize any massive imports of wood. The situation changed radically after the Forestry Regulation of 1748, which aimed to encourage the planting of trees for the navy. It turned out to have quite the opposite effect: restricted use of forestry resources brought the state into confrontation with private owners and towns, which also had to foot the reforestation bill. A spiral of suits and fines served only to discourage any planning of production or marketing, as well as eating into the communal profits of these resources.[110] The supply of wood dried up from that point and the state was forced to address as a political question the mass importation of wood from the Mediterranean or Baltic. The Navy Minister, Salazar, commented in some detail on this rapid decline in the availability of national wood for shipbuilding, which he attributed to the political decision to ensure 'a home harvest', an exclusive harvest that hindered production and marketing and to top it all had to be supplied by private owners. The solution to this problem, in his opinion, was to return to the situation of the first half of the eighteenth century, to allow and even favour the free market in shipbuilding wood, thereby fomenting the tree-planting interest of landowners and towns. Salazar argued that the problem stemmed not from any lack of resources but from the wrong supply policy. With tongue in cheek he summed up the situation thus: 'to speak truthfully I hold no doubt that if similar legislation had been introduced to regulate and promote the production of grain, then such wise lucubration would soon have produced a general famine'.[111]

It thus turns out that Thompson's thesis about the crucial importance of the decision between *administración* or *asiento* in understanding the nature of the state can be insightful and certainly offers food for thought. It cannot be applied in doctrinaire fashion, however, for it sits ill with the actual eighteenth-century military supply policy. This chapter has tried to show that the Bourbons' overriding priority was never to develop one or other of the two supply methods. This was so not for ideological reasons or in the interests of consistency with the state model that the Bourbons were trying to build up. The chosen supply policy pursued was more of a pragmatic decision about the best way of guaranteeing supply of the goods in each case. No other consideration was more important for the state than the essential wherewithal for its own constitution: its armed forces, its conservation, and supplies. In pursuit of this end the state applied throughout the eighteenth century all available means and methods, public or private. The differences and ostensible limits between both methods do not seem to have been as clear-cut as has traditionally been thought because the state could depend on the collaboration and cooperation of private military entrepreneurs who in general identified closely with state interests. The Bourbon state never really seemed to have to confront or oppose military entrepreneurs to obtain its supplies and much less hand over to them any of its power or authority. In fact, quite the opposite occurred: the Bourbon state's military supply policy helped to strengthen its authority. As the main source of power and authority the state offered private agents means of social status and promotion. In exchange the military entrepreneurs understood the advantage of identifying with the state's mercantilist goals, as national subjects and agents of state political action. They also harnessed all the advantages of the principle of exclusivity with which the state tried to ensure its supplies, by public or private means. The military supply policy, in short, fortified the state and expedited the exercise of its authority, thereby strengthening at the same time the Bourbon's model of political effectiveness.

PART II

VICTUALLING THE SPANISH ARMED FORCES

3

Public and Private Business

Soldiers' Bread Ration

The contractor state's first and foremost objective was to keep its armed forces operational in the field. This obliged the state not only to pay the soldiers' salaries but also to maintain a constant, wide variety of supplies, ranging from arms to food and taking in many other things, such as accommodation and healthcare, along the way. In all the armed forces of the early modern period, and no less in the eighteenth century, the second most costly supply after salaries was food, always way above the cost of arms or any other military resource. Witness the words of Marshal Villar of Louis XIV: 'we can go some time without money, but without bread nothing can be done'.[1]

Feeding the troops was the most important military supply operation in every army and often the most complex to manage. The main problem was money, due to the high cost of bulk provisioning, but availability of foodstuffs was a constant headache too. Agriculture in early modern Europe faced immense problems in seeking to increase its yield; surpluses were therefore few, at least in the quantity and quality needed to meet military demand, even in times of peace. The interventionist policies of the state and local authorities, fixing prices and regulating the victualling market, did not help to solve the low-productivity problem; it probably worsened matters by making distribution more complicated still.[2] If the military victualling management process was complex, this was largely due to the limited output of early modern farming.

Since the mid seventeenth century, European armies had found they could not rely on the requisitioning and confiscation of foodstuffs. Risks run in any confiscation process were so vast they might even bounce back against the army itself and jeopardize the successful prosecution of the conflict in question.[3] But solutions were also found in this century. The most effective was to fall back on private provisioning arrangements, tapping into an ever wider and more extensive trawl of commercial networks and production markets. As David Parrott has shown, during the Thirty Years War, for example, it was private suppliers who managed to connect distant production markets with the target arsenals and stores near the battlefields. Close relationships were often built up between these private suppliers and military commanders, who found thereby a means to ensure regular supply.

This system also proved sufficiently fleet-footed to adapt to the ever-changing geographical, quantitative, and strategic needs of armed-forces deployments.[4] The problem of this private contractor option came to a head whenever the state was unable to pay them. Any return to a direct purchasing or local requisitioning system was no longer feasible or even advisable, in view of the sheer size of armies and navies by that time. The state, henceforth, had to decide at each moment between returning to private suppliers or resorting to direct supply by government agents. A study of Louis XIV's army victualling policies shows that no single solution was possible.[5] Moreover, one thing was clear: if it was not the state that managed this military supply, either through private suppliers or direct *administración*, then the alternatives, at best, were continual problems or, at worst, utter chaos.[6]

Feeding the armed forces became an even bigger problem in the eighteenth century. The burgeoning increase in the number of mobilized armed forces could never be catered for by the modest increases in European farming output. But the biggest victualling problem of all was the soaring food demand of Europe's navies. Not only was there a quantitative increase in the scale of armed forces, therefore, but also a qualitatively new demand for naval victuals. Regularly feeding a navy like the English one, which had 140,000 men on board by 1810, was a titanic task.[7] As Roger Knight and Martin Wilcox have shown, the British contractor state had to deploy extraordinary administrative, commercial, and financial capacity to sustain its fleet.[8] As well as the growth in the navies' food demands, what made this all the more complex was the specific conditions imposed by this type of naval supply. Stocks of food had to be laid on beforehand at boarding points in sufficient quantities to ensure crews had enough for two or three months. The range of products to be supplied was much more varied than for army victualling and the quality had to be higher, including as it did diets for the sick to mitigate the high illness rates among sailors. These additional demands of foresight, quantity, and quality made navy victualling much more complex than the general problem of food supplies for land forces.[9]

The demands related to supplying food to eighteenth-century land armies also underwent significant changes. As well as the conditions imposed by their swelling size, the armies also had to be supplied for longer periods as lengthier wars proliferated and a greater proportion of armies were made up of professional and permanent troops. The construction of fixed barracks fuelled more permanent demand and also helped to make geographical supply needs clearer and more foreseeable for the states involved.

As well as the regular factors of more numerous, more permanent, and better-located troops, the eighteenth century also threw up extraordinary supply needs, such as the despatch of amphibious expeditions outside Europe. As colonial conflicts became greater and more frequent throughout the eighteenth century, states needed to strengthen their armed forces in extra-European zones of conflict; this implied mustering and sending huge, often thousands-strong, contingents of troops.[10] These major amphibious expeditions forced European states to deal with a sudden and spectacular increase in the volume of military supplies.

These quantitative and qualitative changes in eighteenth-century military supply demands obliged the state to set up special arrangements to ensure these new needs were met with the necessary rapidity and completeness. This posed a sterling challenge for the fiscal-military state, with the efficacy of its armed forces at stake. This challenge could not be shirked, not only because the operational capacity of its armies and navies rested on it but also because it represented a gilt-edged chance of improving the state's governing capacity. As we have already seen in the previous chapter, the state's military supply requirements continually and clearly moulded the economy's ground rules. Its provisioning demands generated business opportunities or modified the conditions under which the economic stakeholders exploited these opportunities. This two-way play between state and economy is without any doubt the main nexus between the fiscal-military state and the particular circumstances of the society that underpinned it. Such interaction might even take in the military personnel itself. Control of supply policy, for example, offered the state the chance of tweaking its relations with senior military figures, by bringing them into this activity or ousting them.[11] It might even impinge on soldier loyalty: effective control of supplies could be a way of limiting desertions.[12]

This constant interaction between the state and the underpinning economy and society obliged the state to apply a victualling policy that fluctuated with changing circumstances and could have important and different consequences both for the economy as a whole and the state itself. There was a host of options; the bookend cases were, on the one hand, the military making their own arrangements for the supplies they needed and, on the other, state development of administrative instruments and institutions capable of controlling private victualling arrangements. In between came other options like direct state *administración* of supplies by means of public officials and other intermediate options in which private or military agents acted as stand-in functionaries. This wide range of victualling solutions, all born from political options, could affect victualling efficacy. Although this aspect has been little studied as yet, the argument here will suggest that in the Spanish case efficacy was not a strictly economic question; rather was it bound up with the chosen supply policy, the relations between state and society, and the economic stakeholders. Indeed, it is in this terrain of military supplies, of public and private business, where the fiscal-military state most clearly revealed its capacity to turn tax revenue into public goods (in this case military supplies). How the state obtained these supplies, at what price, quality, and political cost, could be a telltale sign of the state's particular nature.

VICTUALLING THE SPANISH ARMED FORCES

The supply of the armed forces was a huge and complex logistical problem, quite possibly the biggest challenge any contractor state had to tackle. This was mainly because of the complex arrangements needed to make sure supplies kept up with soldiers and sailors on the move. To this extent it made little difference whether the wherewithal was supplied directly by the state, using its own officials and public agents, or by *asentistas* using their own factors. They both faced the same problem of knitting together sectors and activities and connecting up scattered geographical areas. This meant bringing together and collaborating with a whole host of stakeholders: crop and animal farmers, transporters, millers, bakers, etc. The main product to be mobilized was grain (wheat or rye), the price of which always served as the main touchstone for fixing the supply-contract price. But many other types of products were also involved (wood, flour, pork fat, peas, fruit, wine, etc.), and these also had to be detailed in the contracts.

The supply tasks to be tackled were many. First of all it was essential to deal directly with the producers. This called for a wide-ranging network of government officials or *asentistas*' factors capable of procuring the necessary products making up the government's established diet for soldiers and sailors. The fact that the purchases were made directly from producers meant that the necessary network of public or private agents had to be supplied with efficient means of payments, preferably cash. Any other means of payment implied a credit arrangement, with a concomitant payment delay for the producer and distancing from the payment site. All this worked against the public agents, with fewer credit outlets, and also against the small *asentistas*, incapable of extending their factor network and sustaining their creditworthiness. The differences between public and private agents were even greater when international markets were involved, because credit then became essential.

Once the necessary products had been bought for the soldiers' and sailors' diet, the distribution problem then raised its head; this involved the problem of packaging and, above all, transport to the processing sites or direct pick-up sites. Although historians' attention has traditionally tended to focus on the production side, the bigger problem was in fact distribution. This meant that the degree of market integration and the availability of means of transport, as we will see, could spell the difference between success or failure. Lastly, the public agents or factors of the contractors had to deal with the no less prickly problem of running facilities for preparing the products for consumption, such as mills and ovens. Such facilities became a continuous bargaining point between the state and entrepreneurs, partly because the state wished to retain its ownership of them and then rent them out to the entrepreneurs ad hoc, but also because the *asentistas* exploited this desire of the state to lever down their costs. In fact the various supply stages (production, distribution, and preparation) were all bargaining tools because all of them had their price.

Spanish army victualling was not controlled by a single and specific administration and institution throughout the eighteenth century. The eighteenth-century Spanish state preferred to keep its army and navy victualling arrangements separate according to the geographical region or armed force involved. The first major division can be made between the victualling of Spanish armed forces operating at home and overseas. This difference yawned wider as the eighteenth century developed and brought out the growing strategic importance of the Americas.

In the American and Philippine territories the Spanish state turned to local economic agents and powers to meet its armed-forces victualling needs. Local colonial merchants, trading corporations, guilds, or local councils provided the necessary military supplies. These local victualling arrangements often implied loans to the state from these same local suppliers (private or institutions), who then furnished provisions on credit, called *situados*.[13] Payment for these military supplies might have been tardy but it was at least assured, and in strong silver currency; this was reason enough to keep private agents interested in the victualling business. This business never stopped growing throughout the whole century, in line with the increasing scale of armed forces in the Americas and Philippines; there was also the business of moving troops about the Spanish mainland and a notable increase of local militias. Largely on the strength of rising silver production and the monarchy's tax revenue capacity, there was also a parallel increase in the money available to the Spanish state in the Americas and Philippines to defray these provisions and pay off the credit granted by local suppliers.[14] This *situados* system, continually swelling in size and improving in distribution efficiency, kept the wheels oiled and was even capable of coping with the heavy military deployment in the colonies in the second half of the eighteenth century. It was precisely while the *situados* private credit system was up and running (a model similar to the British one), that the state could most confidently rely on the interest of local suppliers. The problems and the weak points of the system became evident at the start of the nineteenth century, when state demands outgrew local supply capacity working on credit, and when the state had to divert resources to mainland Spain to nurse the growing national debt, whereupon the whole victualling system in the Americas quickly crumbled. Under these circumstances of mainly local financing and autonomy of military supplies in Spain's empire, it is understandable that the state was loath to tamper with the supply policy for its armed forces, until the system finally collapsed under its own weight. The Spanish monarchy preferred to fall back on American resources, its coffers and economic agents (public, institutional, and, above all, private), for managing military supplies. To some extent there was a de facto chasm between supplies at home and supplies abroad in the colonies.

Such geographical separation was further widened by the difficulty of maintaining in the Americas the same terms and conditions that had been agreed for Spain. The price of victuals in the Americas was always higher than at home, partly due to the different value of American currencies and partly because of the less sophisticated food markets in colonial territories and the greater distance from the more efficient European markets. The quality of the procured products also differed. Wheat flour, in particular, was harder to come by in Spanish America, so replacement products had to be sought; these were not warmly welcomed by the soldiers and sailors who had to eat them. The use of corn to replace wheat, for example, was rejected by the soldiers themselves on the grounds that it affected their health, even going so far as to claim graphically that it was responsible for 'an infinite number of Spaniards buried below the earth'.[15] This problem was gradually ironed out during the century as Mexican flour production was stepped up, as was production across the rest of Spanish America, especially in the Caribbean.[16]

Under this main dichotomy came several subdivisions between the various types of homeland victualling. The Spanish state's main problem was provisioning the armed forces in Spain. Throughout the entire eighteenth century the Spanish state maintained a fourfold distinction between the army, the navy, the household guard, and the African garrisons. The state always managed the victualling of these four areas separately. There was no common policy or centralized management by a single institution; the state always preferred to distinguish the supply arrangements by the armed body they were meant for. If any of these supply arrangements were managed jointly this was only a temporary arrangement and always because they remained under the control of the same *asentista* or group of businesspeople, not because the state thought it best to merge them. This distinction and separation between different types of victualling in Spain was largely kept up because each one of these provisions had different characteristics and even different meanings for the state itself. We will now look at each one of these four victualling groups in Spain.

The most important of the four groups was the army. The victuals that the state was bound to supply to the army were bread rations and barley. The bread ration, sometimes called in Spanish *pan de munición*, consisted of 24 ounces, Castilian weight, of baked bread. This meant that each *fanega* (*c.*bushel) of wheat produced 66 bread rations, or, what came to the same thing, 100 rations for each *fanega* of flour. These ratios were important because they regulated the amounts to be supplied to the military units if the victualling was done directly in wheat or flour and the bread then made by the army itself. The *fanega* ration comprised one *fanega* of barley, measured according to the *marco de Ávila* (Ávila standard), from which eight barley rations were extracted. The ordinary ration of bread and barley was topped up with a ration of *paja pelaza* (barley fodder) for cavalry corps, measured as one *arroba* of 19 *cuartos*. Such other victuals as the Spanish soldier might need were his own responsibility. Nonetheless the state did top up these victuals with other products necessary for accommodation and food preparation, such as firewood, oil, vinegar, salt, and pepper, the cost of which was also defrayed by the Royal Exchequer. The usual procedure in this case was for these products to be provided by the towns and villages where the soldiers lodged or passed through. These products formed part of the towns' obligation to contribute towards the accommodation of military units. The state then cancelled out this cost against the town's tax liability, a practice that gave rise to many jurisdictional problems and much uncertainty for the troops.[17]

The state therefore undertook to furnish the military unit with its bread rations and barley, either by a contract with *asentistas*, by public officials, or, in the last instance, directly paying military officials for market purchases or requisitions at the cost to the Royal Exchequer of procuring it by other means. As in all armies of the world, this undertaking did not stretch to the quality of the goods supplied; complaints from the military about scarcity and quality were constant. As the infantry inspector O'Reilly recognized in 1770, '[w]ith 24 ounces of bread, which still falls two short under the best husbanding, how is the soldier expected to keep up his strength?'[18]

Overall, though, the victualling of the army did not seem to run into other complications than the sheer size of state demand and the political options about the best way of meeting it. This fairly straightforward situation contrasts sharply with the extraordinary complexity of navy victualling. Most probably the reason why the state kept up a watertight distinction between army and navy victualling arrangements throughout the whole eighteenth century was precisely because of the huge difference in character between the two, vastly more problematic for the navy. Its complexity arose from the technical constraint of working with perishable goods, the difficulty of planning their consumption over the period of a voyage and the higher cost of navy victuals. As we are reminded by David Goodman, 'victualling was the most time-consuming naval preparation'.[19] After weighing anchor, sailors had no more chance of adding to the supplies originally taken on board, so the state was duty bound to provide a much more varied range of victuals to keep them going at sea. These provisions also had to cater for the crew and boarded troops when the ship was in port (see Table 3.1).

For navy victualling purposes a distinction was made between *ración ordinaria* (ordinary ration), eaten by the crew as a whole, and the *ración de dieta* (diet ration) provided for the ill, both in hospitals and at sea. A mere glance at the make-up of both these rations shows the vast difference from army victuals, where the state procured only bread and barley, and the products actually supplied were limited to wheat, barley, and straw. The supplier of the navy's *ración ordinaria*, in contrast, undertook to supply the sailors with hardtack, wine, pork fat, salted meat, *menestra* (rice, chickpeas, or beans), cheese, oil, cod, vinegar, garlic, firewood, salt, and water, in all about 23 products.[20] The variety of products and quality was even higher in the *ración de dieta*, with an increased amount of 'white' hardtack, semolina, egg, almonds, raisins, sugar, firewood, coal, and, the most important and dearest, chicken or mutton. All this also called for a much more varied range of shipping containers: pipes, casks, sacks, tuns, puncheons, or barrels, none of which were necessary for army supplies (see Table 3.2).

The greater variety of products needed for navy victuals and the more time-consuming preparation were therefore additional management burdens both for the private procurement agents and the public officials controlling and monitoring them. Furthermore this effort might even be racked up to higher levels for an amphibious expedition when the troops carried on board also had to be provisioned, with a preparation time of only a few months or even a few weeks. The preparation of victuals for an 8,000-strong fleet, to last for three months (the time laid down by law), involved organizing a complex logistical operation, bringing together between 5 and 6 million victual rations at the boarding point in less than two months.[21] The upshot was that the management of navy victuals was a different proposition. A telltale sign is that the public state auctions for *asiento*-based provision of army victuals always attracted more bids from businesspeople than did navy victuals. Many businesspeople saw themselves capable of managing

Table 3.1 Make-up of the navy's victuals ration, 1776

	Products	Quantity									Price (*mrvs*)
Navy ordinary ration											
Common	hardtack	18 ounces									33.4
	wine	1.5 *cuartillo* (½ kilo)									26.7
	oil	1 ounces									3.15
	vinegar	1 *cuartillo*									1.9
	firewood	1½ pounds									2.5
	salt	1/1000 *celemín* (*c.*5 litres)									0.8
	water	1 *azumbre* (*c.*2 litres)									2.1
Options	pork fat	4 ounces	*menestra*	5							26.8
	salted meat	3 ounces	pork fat	2	*menestra*	5					26.8
	cheese	5 ounces	*menestra*	3	oil	1					26.8
	fresh meat	8 ounces	pork fat	2	*menestra*	2					26.8
	cod	4 ounces	*menestra*	5	oil	1	vinegar	1 *cuartillo*			26.8
	menestra	9 ounces	oil	2.5							26.8
	hardtack	3 ounces	oil	1.5	garlic	0.5	pork fat	2	*menestra*	2	26.8
Total ration											96
Navy diet ration											
	'white' hardtack	12 ounces									32.7
	chicken	8 ounces	Mutton	8							83.8
	coal	8 ounces									2.1
Final ration price											118

Note: All amounts are in ounces unless otherwise stated.
Source: AGS, DGT, Inv. 25, leg. 15.

Table 3.2 Products and amounts necessary for making 16 million rations for the fleet in Cadiz, 1781

Products	Amounts	
Hardtack	184,830	*quintales*
Wine	764,062	*arrobas*
Meat	4,368	*quintales*
Pork fat	30,562	*quintales*
Cheese	7,144	*quintales*
Menestra	43,660	*quintales*
Oil	14,767	*arrobas*
Firewood	244,500	*quintales*

Note: This was to cater for daily consumption of 23,500 sailors. The listed ingredients produced 16,325,500 rations at an average price of 96 *maravedis*; the total cost would be 46,101,176 *reales de vellón*. As a detail, making 20,340 *quintales* of hardtack called for 23,010 *fanegas* of wheat. These supplies were to last from 22 Sept. to 31 Dec. 1781.

Source: AGS, SSH, leg. 51.

provisions made up by wheat and barley, but this number plummeted when dealing with over 20 different products. The nature of navy victualling could no doubt affect the levels of competition between traders and reinforced the state's policy of managing them separately (see Figure 3.1).

One of the consequences of the *sui generis* navy victualling procedure was a higher price than that paid by the state for land-based troops. This was undoubtedly another factor that contributed towards the idiosyncrasy of navy victuals and kept them separate from the rest. On average the Spanish navy's eighteenth-century ordinary ration was five times dearer than the army ration. In hard figures the average eighteenth-century cost to the state of the army 'bread ration' was about 18.1 *mrvs*, whereas the ordinary navy rations cost 89.6 *mrvs*.[22] The gap is even greater when the navy's diet rations for the sick are factored in. The better quality of these special rations meant that the price was even higher, about 117 *mrvs*, or six times the cost of the land troops' 'bread ration'.

It is also revealing to track the trend of the price paid by the state for these victuals. The price of the troop's rations increased by 57 per cent throughout the eighteenth century, peaking at 71 per cent in 1768 in relation to the start-of-the-century price. The price of the ordinary navy ration, on the contrary, fell by 2 per cent during the eighteenth century, with peak falls on the start-of-century price of up to 23 per cent. This contrary price trend suggests also a different aetiology of the factors making up the final cost paid by the state. The price of army victuals tended to change in line with agricultural prices, especially for cereals, i.e. a sharp price increase from the 1760s onwards and maintained during the last third of the century.[23] The cost of navy victuals, on the other hand, strayed further and further from the general trend, even though most of the products making up the navy ration also followed the cereal price trend closely. This growing gap

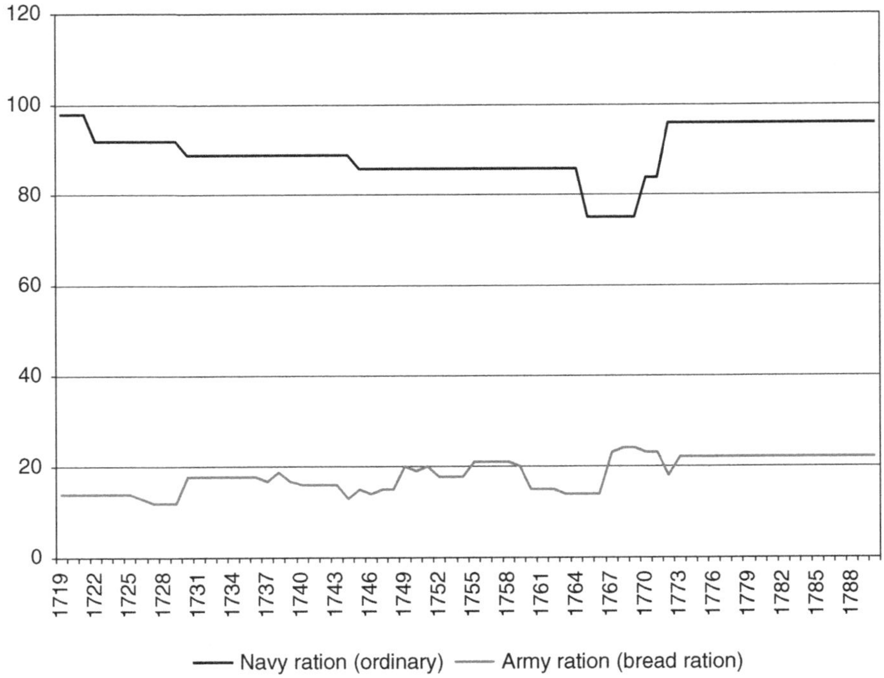

Figure 3.1 The price of state-procured victuals (in *mrvs*)
Source: AGS, SSH, leg. 640–9.

between navy victual prices and market price indicators suggest that other factors must have been in play when determining the cost of the victuals for the state. As we will see, the production and distribution markets were not the only price-determining elements to be factored into the equation here. Political variables, involving the relations between the suppliers and the state, might provide a better explanation of price trends. In the specific case of naval victuals the suppliers continually dropped their asking price in exchange for the state's assurance that the business would remain in the hands of a particular family group. This circumstance might have been yet another factor persuading the state to keep army and navy victualling arrangements separate.

The third victualling group kept separate by the state involved the troops garrisoned at the court. The main remit of these troops was to protect the royal family in court and on its continuous journeys to the other royal residences (leisure palaces and hunting grounds of Aranjuez, San Ildefonso, and Escorial, close to Madrid), although also on longer journeys as when the whole court was moved to Seville.[24] The contracts signed for the victualling of these armed forces show that the military units posted to this service fluctuated according to circumstances, but the main ones were: Reales Guardias de Corps, Infantería Española, Infantería Walona, Destacamento de Inválidos, and Compañía Suelta, both in El

Pardo and in the royal estates, plus a varied selection of troops passing through Madrid. The victualling arrangements for these troops also included the supply of bread rations, straw, and barley for the servants of the royal household and draught animals and horses (*Reales Caballeriza*) used in the court and on trips to other royal palaces and estates. There were also other one-off remits, according to the whim of each king, such as supplying bread for the poor of San Fernando Hospice in Madrid.[25]

Although the products involved were similar to those supplied for the rest of the army (bread, wheat, barley, and straw fodder for the infantry and cavalry), the state kept this victualling arrangement separate through the whole century. Something must have lain behind this different treatment. During that period, and quite clearly during the first half of the century, the government dealt with the victualling of the household guard in a completely separate way. The reasons for this distinctive treatment are not clear but we do know that it was habitual. A factor that probably weighed heavily in this policy was this troop's continual exposure to observation by foreign ambassadors, who also accompanied the royal family on its journeys. The victualling of this troop was therefore probably considered to be top priority because it affected the king's image as projected abroad. Indeed, the government always tried to cream off the best troops for protection of the court and royal family.[26] In short, these victuals had an upfront diplomatic facet to them.

Whatever the reason behind it, the truth is that the state always dealt with this victualling arrangement separately, even when efforts were being made otherwise to unify victualling procedures.[27] In 1727, for example, the supplier Urban Ruiz Velarde, who had already carried out several victualling *asientos* for the armed forces of Aragon, Valencia, and Catalonia, won another *asiento* called in the bidding documents, 'General Provision of Victuals for the Troops in Mainland Spain', but expressly excluding 'the guards and infantry of the Court and twenty leagues thereabout'.[28] Likewise, when a provisions-accounting office was set up in the decade of 1730–40 for the whole army other than the court troops, this victualling arrangement was kept separate for both administrative and accounting purposes. From 1732 to 1743 or even earlier a 'factor's office' was up and running for victualling the royal guards and royal stables 'and others receiving a ration at court'. This 'factor's office of the court and royal estates' was kept apart from the General Army Victualling Accounting Office, set up by Patiño in an attempt to rectify the general disorder apparently produced by private victualling managements and also to keep a track of 'the price at which each bread ration and *fanega* of barley went out to the troops'.[29] Even when these calculations were made, the public officials conducting them were always careful to specify the cost of the bread ration or *fanega* of barley supplied 'including or not the court and royal estates'.[30]

As well as the personal interest of the monarchs and the diplomatic dimension, another factor that must have contributed to the separate treatment of household-guard victualling was its fixed and sizeable budget. Prima facie this might be thought to be only a tiny part of total armed-forces supplies but it still represented a significant state disbursement. In 1738, for example, over 10 per cent of the total cost of bread rations and *fanegas* of barley supplied to the Spanish army was accounted for by victualling of the troops of the court and royal estates.[31] The higher proportion of cavalry among the royal guard brought about a clear difference in the proportions between the various products. Bread rations to the court troops represented barely 2 per cent of the army total, whereas barley accounted for nearly 20 per cent of the total cost of this provision for the armed forces as a whole.[32] In any case these victuals were considered apart from the rest of the army and managed under different procedures, consequently giving rise to different public and private businesses.

The last group for which separate victualling arrangements were made was the African garrisons. The garrison cities and military enclaves in North Africa were permanently manned by armed forces who needed to be provisioned regularly from Spain. These included Ceuta, the minor garrisons of Melilla, Peñón, and Alhucemas, plus Orán and Mazarquivir. Here the state made a distinction from one stronghold to another, laying down different terms and conditions relating to price and quality for each one, all differing from the victualling conditions for the rest of the Spanish army. Ceuta, for example, was furnished with flour for the necessary bread rations to be made up there, plus wheat for the '*moros de paz*', that is, Spain's Moroccan allies. In the other enclaves there was a *presidios*, or garrison ration, which was similar to the navy ration. The hostility of the surrounding terrain and the difficulty of tapping into any alternative provisioning sources prompted the government to treat these enclaves as a sort of ship on land. Melilla's *presidio* ration, for example, included 'flour, fresh beef, mutton, chicken, pork fat, cod, *menestras*, wine, vinegar, oil, raisins, sugar, and firewood', rations that might also be offered to hospitals and civilian neighbours.[33] For a good part of the century these garrison provisions also extended to the fleet of galleys set up to combat Berber corsairs and keep communications open between Spain and North Africa, which often put into the garrison cities. A good idea of the complexity and variety of the garrison victualling supplies is given by the prices contracted by the state with the *asentista* Marqués de Murillo in 1745 (see Table 3.3).[34]

Table 3.3 Victualling variety, destination and price, 1745

Destination	Type of victuals	Price	
Orán	Bread ration	15	*maravedis*
	Fanega of barley	15	*reales de vellón*
	Arroba of straw	3	*reales de vellón*
Ceuta	Bread ration	16	*maravedis*
Melilla	Ordinary ration	55	*maravedis*
	Special diet for the sick	72	*maravedis*
Galley fleet	Navy ration	58	*maravedis*
	Galley rowers' ration	30	*maravedis*
	Bread ration	14	*maravedis*

Source: AGS, SSH, leg. 113.

Finally, each one of these four categories had a different budget. Figures from the reign of Charles III (1759–88) show that the Royal Exchequer spent on average 48.5 million *reales de vellón* a year in this period.[35] Nearly half this sum was spent on the army while the navy received just over one-third of the total victualling expenditure. The other two groups lagged well behind. Garrison victuals topped 11 per cent, while the household guard accounted for only 7 per cent (see Figure 3.2).

For the Spanish fiscal-military state, therefore, armed-forces victualling was not a single, one-size-fits-all but rather a horses-for-courses process. On grounds of past tradition, technical idiosyncrasies, and diplomatic or political considerations, the state saw fit to deal with each of these categories using separate contracting and management procedures. Against this inherited backdrop, maintained in essence, the Bourbon state applied certain more specific supply policies. It was precisely via the way the state chose to solve its military victualling needs that the fiscal-military state really came to the fore as an operating system. It was, in other words, the supply policy that brought the state most directly into contact with the economy and society in an attempt to muster its tax revenue and convert it into military supplies. Homing in now on the question of how the state procured these victuals will show us the contractor state in action and permit an analysis of the consequences of its policies.

THE VICTUALLING POLICY

During the first half of the eighteenth century there was a series of significant changes in the victualling policy. First of all French military entrepreneurs,

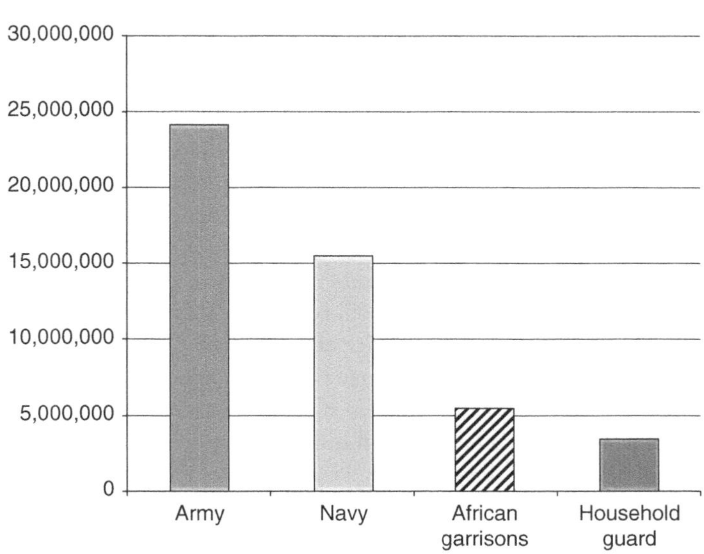

Figure 3.2 Armed-forces victualling groups, 1759–88. (Supply per annum in *rsv.*)

Source: AGS, DGT, Inv. 16, Guión 24, leg. 49.

dominant hitherto, were systematically ousted from the business; this was followed by a few decades' experimentation with direct *administración* and, finally, the policy of nurturing a greater involvement by Spanish military entrepreneurs in the victualling process. The growing role of Spanish contractors broke the seventeenth-century stranglehold held by foreign entrepreneurs over the Spanish military supply business. The transformation was fuelled by two main factors: mercantilist ideas and the post-Utrecht shrinkage of Spain's European empire.

During the Habsburg era foreign entrepreneurs had made steady inroads into military supply-contracts as the best way of securing other loan and credit services for the Spanish monarchy.[36] The Habsburgs linked their need for credit with the opening up of the military supply business to European financial and entrepreneurial groups, mainly Flemish. This led to a dangerous dependence, which has been traditionally seen as a backward step in terms of state authority[37] and, in general, as a poor economic policy, though this view has come in for reassessment lately.[38] Be that as it may, the Spanish state's military-supply dependence on foreigners had become a stark fact during the reign of the last Habsburg king.[39] This proven dependence brought out the attraction of the mercantilist ideas then being embraced and circulated by political thinkers and government authorities, a development that picked up pace as from the 1680s.[40] The writings of Spanish mercantilists laid down a platform for political action; these principles then underpinned the political agenda for a good part of the eighteenth century. The most comprehensive expression of these principles came from Jerónimo de Uztáriz in 1724. Although he picked up on ideas that had been widely debated by Spanish thinkers and politicians of previous years, Uztáriz managed to systematize them into a real programme of political action, which then turned out to be crucial for understanding the development of relations between the state and military entrepreneurs. Uztáriz argued that Spain was capable of procuring all its military supplies from within its European or American territory. There was no longer any need to resort to foreign supply markets and even less to do business with foreign entrepreneurs. Uztáriz analysed each one of the supplies needed by the armed forces in support of his arguments. He considered that it was essential for the state to take the initiative in organizing military supplies. The reason why Uztáriz stressed the importance of state intervention was the beneficial effects this would have on the monarchy itself. If the state managed to nationalize supply this would sidestep import payments. Uztaríz argued that it was essential for the supply expenditure to be kept within the national economy. This would be the only way, he argued, of tapping into the multiplier effects of the 'war business'. State and national entrepreneurs could both impinge positively on economic development.[41]

The moot point was how to apply these mercantilist ideas. Philip V inherited a negligible and poorly controlled national military supply business with little tradition of state intervention. Most supplies were still procured via contracts with foreign entrepreneurs. To make matters worse, foreign entrepreneurs were also called upon to broker any attempts to reform the Spanish armed forces. These attempts affected the whole institutional organization but also the supplies used, including any renewal of regulation armaments. Philip V's chances of breaking this dependence on external supply sources, already bleak, became zero when the War of Succession broke out. During this conflict the monarch had to turn increasingly to French military entrepreneurs as Dutch and Flemish dealers progressively lost interest in trading with the Bourbon king of Spain. The overwhelming presence of French counsellors and ministers in Philip V's first administrations suggested that the likeliest scenario would be a reshuffling of foreign military entrepreneurs, to the clear benefit of the French. At this time Louis XIV facilitated Philip V's access to French military entrepreneurs, from which he obtained much of the material wherewithal for this war, ranging from cannons to shoes and tents.[42] This recourse to French entrepreneurs was not only a sign of the Spanish state's weakness in terms of implementing mercantilist ideas; it was no less the result of Louis XIV's bid to increase the French court's influence over the new Spanish monarch.[43]

The problem came to a head in the victualling procedures. The emergence of the French financier Juan Orry, sent by Louis XIV to Philip V in January 1703, posed the risk of the victualling business being snapped up wholesale by French military entrepreneurs and merchants. A French supplier, Onfroy de Servigny, was in negotiation with the Spanish government from the outset. Orry, as Secretary of War, even went so far as to propose that the victualling of Spanish armed forces should be handled directly from France. Orry's pro-French bias in handing out contracts seems to have been spread across all military supplies.[44] In Juan de Orry's eyes the best-case scenario was concentration of all supply *asientos* in a single provider, reimbursed by concession of a Royal Exchequer revenue-farming contract.[45] Despite the shift of foreign suppliers from Flemish to French during the War of Succession, there was still leeway for further change, which ended up with the definitive ousting of foreign military entrepreneurs. French suppliers did not always turn out to be efficient in terms of meeting the needs of the allied armies operating in Spain. The difficulty of finding French suppliers capable of supplying victuals on the scale required prompted the state to turn in addition to local Spanish suppliers, who would see to provisioning regional armies, such as López de Castro for Galicia, Extremadura, and Andalusia or the Marqués de Valdeolmos for Catalonia. On a surprising number of occasions the state had to fall back ad hoc on local Spanish producers and traders, especially for the supply of victuals to armies on the march. Small local or regional financiers managed to gain a foothold in the supply business for Spanish and even French troops. Witness the case of the Navarre merchants who offered their services to the new Spanish king on the strength of their proximity to the Aragon front and the passage through their area of troops from France.[46] This business turned out to be crucial for a swelling group of military contractors. In no time at all these entrepreneurs managed to tie in the Spanish and French troop victualling business with the supply of other military products such as swords, pistols, munitions, and even cannons. But the important thing about this rapid development is that it occurred during the war itself. At the end of the conflict, therefore, Philip V could call on the services of a group of military entrepreneurs, still small as yet, for drawing up the new supply-contracts. First working alongside the French merchants and then progressively ousting them, they paved the way for Spanish domination of this business. Tellingly, some years later, an important Spanish politician and writer, Campomanes, referring to the way that the War of Succession had offered chances for the development of Spanish entrepreneurs, opined: 'Spanish business houses were then built up and our Spanish learnt how to handle military supply-contracts, which remained exclusively within the nation.'[47]

After the war the French court, with its sights firmly set on the American trade, remained keen to increase its influence over Spain's economy and policy. Any temptation by the triumphant Spanish monarch to continue nurturing this French ambition was nipped in the bud by the Spanish ministers making up his first governments and their eagerness to begin at last applying the mercantilist ideas that had for so long been uppermost in their minds. The ministers of the Spanish governments, notably Alberoni and Patiño, facilitated the entrance of the Spanish entrepreneurs who had been doing business with the state during the War of Succession.[48]

In this context of political favour and revamped relations between the state and military entrepreneurs, another important factor also loomed large: the contraction in Spain's European empire. Thus, the War of Succession boosted military entrepreneurs' state supply business in another equally important way. The territorial losses in the Treaty of Utrecht reshuffled the Spanish state's military supply needs. Spain was no longer burdened with the tricky problem of supplying the army deployed in the Low Countries. The removal of this obligation had a two-fold effect. First the territorial losses cut down the scope of supply needs so that these focused upon the forces deployed on the Spanish mainland. As yet the needs in the Americas were few and could be fielded with one-off shipments from Spain or purchases in American ports. Secondly, the ousting of the Spanish troops from the Low Countries made Flemish financiers and entrepreneurs even less keen to continue working with the king of Spain. The advantage of the Flemish military entrepreneurs lay precisely in the proximity of the Spanish troops and their commercial shrewdness in linking local production for military purposes to the credit needs of the Spanish monarchy. The Treaty of Utrecht spelt the end of these Flemish entrepreneurs' business sway. These two factors—a concentration of military expenditure on the mainland and the removal of foreign military entrepreneurs—a voluntary withdrawal in the Flemish case and obligatory exit in the French—all boosted the opportunities of the Spanish set of military entrepreneurs.

In other words the War of Succession at last facilitated the implementation of mercantilist ideas that prioritized the relation of the state with national entrepreneurs. The conflict offered the state and Spanish entrepreneurs the chance to continue moulding and redesigning the relations between them. At the end of the conflict, the war-induced territorial losses further enhanced these business opportunities and the chance for the switch to national entrepreneurs, bringing political will into line with state needs. From then on and throughout the whole eighteenth century, the state's military supplies were largely the business of Spanish entrepreneurs, although, as we shall see later, there was no lack of attempts to change this situation. This meant that the whole effort of increasing the armed forces and expanding them towards the Italian and, above all, American fronts played into the hands of Spanish military entrepreneurs and boosted their business opportunities.

These beneficiaries of the military supply system included some major *asentistas* who amassed huge fortunes and, even more importantly, established a track record of serving the crown. Examples such as the house of the Marqués de Valdeolmos illustrate the rise and consolidation of Spanish military entrepreneurs, who harnessed the war to boost their fortunes and publicize their role as servants of the new dynasty. In the mid seventeenth century the brothers Pedro and José de Aguerri, originally from French Navarre, built up a long record of business with the Spanish Habsburgs, José kicking things off by taking on responsibility for victualling diverse military units in Spain, mainly the troops in Catalonia, Pamplona, and Extremadura.[49] Their services won them rapid naturalization, and despite a rather up-and-down relationship with the crown thereafter, José de Aguerri was finally rewarded in 1697 with the title of Marqués de Valdeolmos.[50] With this history of crown service behind him, Valdeolmos identified with the new reigning dynasty from the outset and managed to tap into many of the business opportunities thrown up by the war. His biggest success was to tie in state victualling-*asiento* debts and payments with revenue farming. This was by no means a new strategy but it enabled him to assure payment of the heavy debts that the crown had built up with this trading house during the war.[51] For the trading house of the Marqués de Valdeolmos the doors remained open for future collaboration with the new dynasty. It continued to tender for army victualling during the 1720s, and its proprietor managed to work his way onto the state's financial machinery when he was appointed treasurer general of Santa Cruzada de Aragón.[52] His relation with the new dynasty facilitated access to information about the state's victualling requirements and the crown's service-contracting preferences, as demonstrated in 1740 when, in the words of a senior figure within the Contaduría General, he was 'urged' by the War Ministry to participate in a general provision arrangement for all the armies of Spain, Mallorca, and Garrisons, a business worth over 25 million *reales* a year (see Figure 3.3).[53]

A similar success story was achieved by the Spanish victuals supplier Urbán Ruiz Velarde, who, after the War of Succession, got his foot in the door by building up a victualling portfolio for several regions. In 1726–7 Ruíz Velarde managed to persuade the state to unify the regional victualling contracts, which had been the old ambition of Juan Orry. Ruiz Velarde had been a known victualling *asentista* for the armies of the Crown of Aragon since the War of Succession, and was shrewd enough to link payment for these military supply-contracts with revenue farming rights in the provinces of León, Murcia, Extremadura, Córdoba, and Granada. It was in fact his outstanding position within Philip V's financial establishment that won him this important business. The terms agreed by Ruiz Velarde and the crown were far-reaching because they then served as the base for subsequent army victualling contracts until the end of the eighteenth century. But they also mooted the possibility of unifying the whole national territory under a

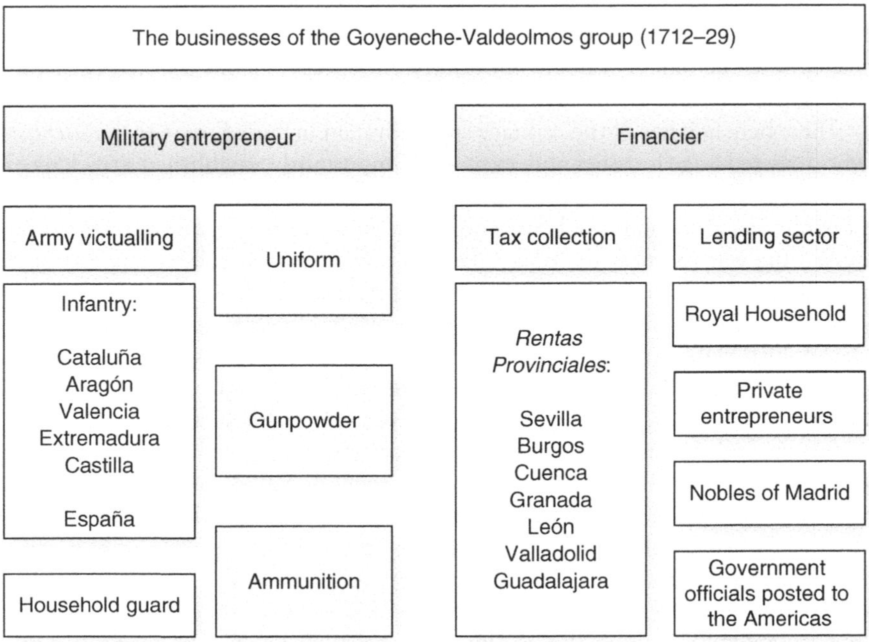

Figure 3.3 The links between public finances and military provisioning. The businesses of the Goyeneche-Valdeolmos group, 1712–29

Source: Author's own. Adapted from Santiago Aquerreta, *Negocios y familias en el siglo XVIII: la familia Goyeneche* (Pamplona: Eunsa, 2001).

single contract.[54] This was hugely important, spelling a change in the victualling business from a local to a national affair. A single *asiento* for each type of victualling supply meant that from then on only the grandest entrepreneurs could afford to assume the contracts. There was hence a hugely significant shift in the victualling business from the local sphere to the economic and political circles surrounding the Madrid court.

Although this was the path that finally triumphed, Ruíz Velarde's experience lasted only a few years, partly because he died in 1730,[55] but also because the state decided to change its victualling policy. During the 1730s it began to consider a serious overhaul of the crown's relation with the military entrepreneurs. In an intellectual climate shaped by outrage at the excesses attributed to revenue farmers and military entrepreneurs, and with the government's ministers such as Patiño becoming increasingly reform-minded, an attempt was made to increase the crown's control over the military supply-contracts.[56] Patiño aimed at direct crown control of *asientos*, basing his attempt on the military administration itself. In 1730 he ordered that army victualling procedures should be managed directly by army *intendentes*.[57] The previous victualling contract, in the hands of Pedro López de Ortega, came to the end of its term at the end of November 1729, and he seized this chance to bring in a new system. From here on these *intendentes* would act in their own provinces as victualling directors; their remit would be to procure the necessary supplies, coordinate the local authorities involved, and ensure proper distribution. Each treasurer of each army would keep an account of supplies received and pass it on to provincial *contadurías* (accounting offices) who would be finally supervised by the *intendentes*. Patiño ordered special funds to be released for army treasurers, who would then be charged with all victualling costs. The new system was completed in March 1732 with the setting up of a new Contaduría General de Provisiones (General Victualling Accounting Office) for control of the accounts (see Figure 3.4).[58]

The system aimed at would be similar to the one under construction in Great Britain, where a Victualling Board took on responsibility for organizing the necessary purchases through commission agents, paying producers or merchants with bills drafted against the Board. From 1684 to the second decade of the eighteenth century the Victualling Board was disorganized and inefficient. Above all in the reign of William III there were various attempts to return to the previous system of state contracts, and one of the measures taken to shore up the new system of direct administration was the inclusion, at the head of this body, of one of the greatest merchants of the victualling syndicate of the reign of Charles I, Thomas Papillon.[59] This is also paralleled in the Spanish case, where we find the Dirección General de Provisiones headed by Pedro Astrearena, Marqués de Murillo, military entrepreneur, partner, and direct family relative of the group of Navarre financiers at the Madrid court.[60] The development of the English provisioning system paralleled the development of the financial system; the slowness of establishing it in the eighteenth century during the readjustment phase of English public finances can be contrasted with its development in an era of expansion of

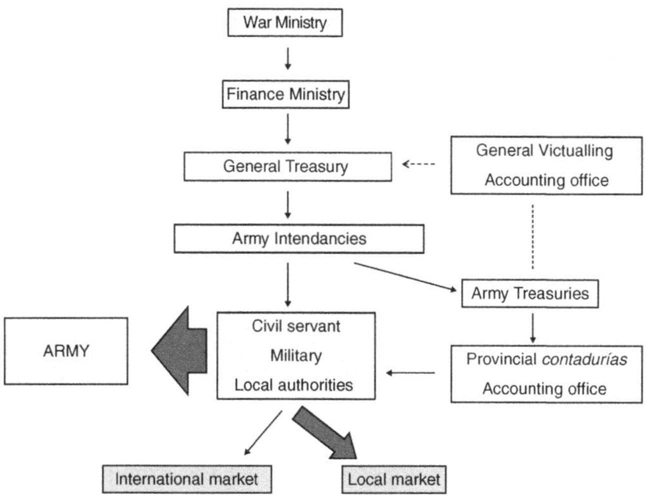

Figure 3.4 Victualling by direct *administración*, 1730–9

Source: Author's own. Adapted from AGS, DGT, Inv. 25, leg. 14, and AGS, SSH, leg. 640.

the state's financial resources.[61] The slowness of Spanish direct *administración* can be compared with the Victualling Board's severe difficulties and limitations in assuring military provisions at the end of the 1730s, forcing the state temporarily to switch back to private contractors.[62] The new English system proved very slow and unwieldy to introduce, showing the enormous difficulties of making these changes. If success was finally achieved this was because Great Britain's financial system was sounder, making the system completely trustworthy to the merchants (the Victualling Board accepted on principle any bill of exchange drawn against them from anywhere in the world), and because it was able to combine continual improvement in service control and management with a progressive increase in the supply of products on the strength of national economic development and Great Britain's expansion overseas.[63]

But the situation of Spain's public finances was not exactly conducive to management improvement initiatives. In fact the outbreaks of war and the revenue collection system limited the scope of any reforms of the victualling system and once more forced the state to turn to private vcontractors. Although the measures proposed by Patiño turned out to be fairly effective in solving the crown's victualling needs in one-off crises, especially in terms of enforcement measures and the indiscriminate use of the *vía reservada* to mobilize affected authorities, it was less expedient in normal times, when the crown had to fall back on the producers' offers of supply and the merchants' capacity to coordinate distribution of products they had procured.

A further, even bigger opportunity arose for the crown to reform its relations with entrepreneurs. This came after the crown's suspension of payments in 1739, when measures were taken to bring in more centralized and interventionist government, enabling revenue collection to be set up under a direct-*administración* arrangement during the following decade. But the crown did not show the same determination to put an end to the system of military *asientos* and their beneficiaries. The reason for this probably lay in the urgent demand for war materials generated by war with England and the concomitant need to ensure the continuity of military supplies above all else. Even if there was a political will to make the switch, now was not the moment to introduce wholesale changes that might disrupt the entire supply system for the king's army. Some entrepreneurs, moreover, found in the military supply-contracts a means of recouping their losses from the crown's 1739 suspension of payments. The *asiento* became an efficient instrument for linking a lower asking price, always to the crown's liking, with payment by the Royal Exchequer of suspended debts and credits. The weakness of Spain's finances finally stymied the implementation of a genuinely new military supply system and condemned the fiscal-military state to return to the system of *asientos* with private entrepreneurs. That said, despite this apparent backsliding, the state did slip in a new policy: the strengthening of the supplier.

The poor outcome of even the state's most determined attempt to set up direct *administración* of military *asientos* prompted the dropping of this policy in the early 1740s and the return to private suppliers. This meant that the state passed on to entrepreneurs the responsibility for coordinating the production and distribution of the victuals it needed. In so doing the state constrained the potential knock-on and multiplier effect of military demand to its relations with suppliers. Henceforth the market response to this potentially economy-stimulating demand would depend not so much on the size and variety of this demand but rather upon the military entrepreneurs' business strategies, and the latter, as we will see later, were influenced by their relation with the crown. The state-supported system was then deadlocked until the end of the century by maintenance of army supplies as top priority over and above the economy as a whole or any other kind of private businesses.

The Spanish state was caught in a cleft stick here. Its priorities were clear but it lacked the managerial capacity to control suppliers directly and its long-standing experience in this terrain had taught it not to depend on strict military entrepreneur compliance with assumed obligations or even the producers' capacity to generate enough goods to meet demand. To escape this dilemma it chose not only to continue relying on contractors but, even more importantly, to shore up the military entrepreneur as the simplest and most efficient means of ensuring the supply of victuals and *ipso facto* its strategic interests. The state found it more useful to liaise with a known quantity, who could be held to account for any contact breach, than to negotiate with a host of free-trading businesspeople.

But this strategic decision to strengthen the military entrepreneur had huge repercussions. To start with, it undermined any positive effect on the *asiento* system that might otherwise have stemmed from the success of the reforms of the financial system initiated at that time. When the state took over direct *administración* of the Royal Exchequer's main plus provincial revenue (from 1742 to 1750, barring the revenue of Madrid), this wiped out much of the private business tied in with the management of state finances; this must have kindled entrepreneurs' interest in the military supply-contracts. In other words, the reform of the Royal Exchequer, its direct control by the state, broke the traditional bonds established between public finance and military supplies. A good example of this complex relationship is the web of business activities established by the Navarre businessman Miguel Arizcun during the 1720s and 1730s (see Figure 3.5). It was therefore the state itself that was encouraging businesspeople to participate in the military supply business. At first glance this would seem likely to encourage more private contractors to become involved and boost the state's bargaining power in negotiating military *asientos*. It did not in fact turn out like that because of the way negotiations were finally conducted with victual suppliers. If the state decided to strengthen a single entrepreneur then the government was also duty bound to offer him or her general protection at all times plus surplus profits: in short, incentives to encourage the military entrepreneur to enter a business of vast scope and therefore higher risks. The chosen way was to grant monopoly-based privileges to a single military entrepreneur.

The path ahead was now strewn with uncertainties for both state and military entrepreneurs. For the state because the channelling of all military demand towards a handful of privileged entrepreneurs limited the size of the market and cut down competition. The crown also increased its dependence on the military

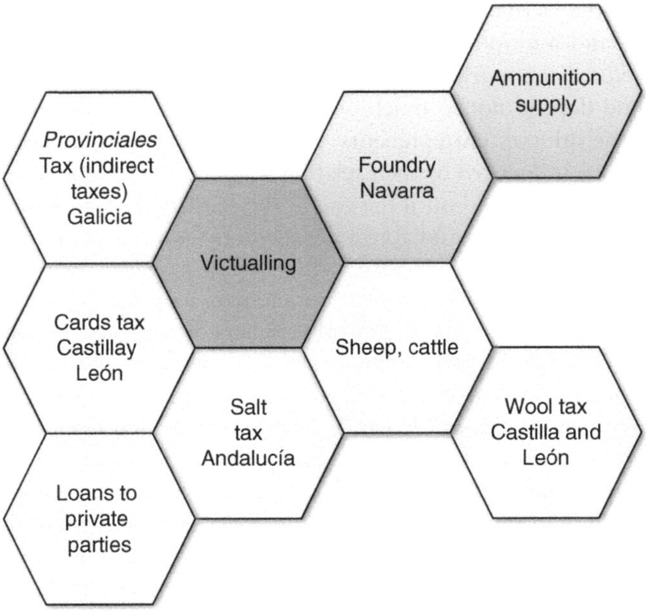

Figure 3.5 The business web of the entrepreneur Miguel Arizcun, 1725–41

Source: Author's own. Adapted from Santiago Aquerreta, 'La casa de Arizcun 1725–42: las estrategias financieras de un hombre de negocios en el Madrid de la Ilustración', in José A. Ferrer Benimeli, ed., *El Conde de Aranda y su tiempo* (Zaragoza, Institución Fernando el Católico, 2000), 659–78.

entrepreneur, because limiting the size of the market also cut down the chances of pressurizing or replacing any who were inefficient. Opting for an ever-dwindling, albeit more controlled market exacerbated the military entrepreneur replacement problem because there would be fewer and fewer contractors or economic groups with the necessary knowledge and economic capacity to match or replace the current incumbents. For the privileged, bolstered military entrepreneurs themselves it was a path plagued with uncertainty because the organization of their business was based on safeguards promised and contracted with the crown. The viability of their business no longer depended on a greater or lesser managerial capacity but rather the winning of a safeguarded contract. On this premise any government tweak of this general framework, any modification to the tenor of the privileges at any one time, could have disastrous consequences for the businesses concerned.

Against this backdrop the 1740s proved a very favourable decade politically for those seeking a victualling *asiento*. Significantly, the first step was taken by the crown itself by offering a general victualling contract for the entire military establishment of 'Spain, Mallorca, and Oran' to the trading house of the Marqués de Valdeolmos. The house itself estimated this victualling contract to add up to 30 million bread rations and 650,000 *fanegas* of barley.[64] This trading house, which by now had built up a long track record of services rendered to Philip V and an encyclopaedic knowledge of the victualling business, pressed home its advantage after the state's change of mind and upped its asking price—excessively, in the crown's judgment. Negotiations were tough and the arguments broached by Marqués de Valdeolmos, through his spokesman Inocencio García, are a veritable compendium of the complexity of this business. Ostensibly, the state had switched back to *asentistas* to remedy its governmental limitations, but times had changed and with them the modus operandi. The order went out for a detailed study of the victualling costs during the previous decade. Reports were requested concerning the rations provided for each army unit and the locality; seeking, in other words, a definitive idea of the real past cost to serve as a clear benchmark for negotiations henceforth. No longer was it a question merely of who would provide the service, but how and, above all, for how much. In the end this calculation was decisive in the decision to turn down Valdeolmos's bid; but the door to establishment of a general *asiento* had been shoved open, and it was now only a question of time before the parties came to terms, and a military entrepreneur with knowledge, networks, and public credit should clinch the deal. This was when another victualler appeared on the scene: Francisco Mendinueta, who would be capable of enforcing the state's new policy.

4

National and State Capitalism

REINFORCEMENT OF ENTREPRENEURS, MONOPOLY, AND TERRITORIAL UNIFICATION

During the first half of the eighteenth century it became evident that armed-forces victualling was a private matter within a framework of national capitalism. Foreign businesspeople, hitherto so dominant, gradually faded out of the picture completely. By the time the War of Succession had ended, victualling was being almost exclusively dealt with by Spanish entrepreneurs and financiers. How this came about can best be shown by focusing on one of these entrepreneurs, Francisco Mendinueta, who, from the 1720s onwards, became the leading figure in what might be called the triumph of national capitalism.

The Spanish army's victualling business represented the peak of Francisco Mendinueta's career as entrepreneur and financier. This peak lasted for nearly two decades, from 1744 to 1763, when Mendinueta was continually at the head of a business that was arguably the most important that any private businessman might undertake at that time. Reaching the top of the pile was the aspiration of all entrepreneurs, not only because it allowed them to manage gigantic businesses but also because it meant being very close to the crown, even serving it directly, face to face. These direct dealings with the Royal Household could in the end become much more important than any business profit. We should not forget here that the crown held the power of creating privileges and honours. Once bestowed on any individual, these then attracted universal recognition and respect. If upward social mobility had any ceiling in the eighteenth century, it was arriving at the summit through the support of royal power, recognition, and favour. Francisco Mendinueta could stand here as a fine example of many other Spanish contractors who sought social and economic promotion in the king's service. This, logically enough, was nothing new; many had attempted it beforehand. The new feature here was the resounding success with which these eighteenth-century entrepreneurs managed to participate in the economy of the Royal Exchequer and the way they ousted the foreign financiers and merchants who had dominated royal finances since the reign of Charles I. Historians have tended to overlook the importance of this development, which we could quite safely dub a 'nationalization' of mercantile capitalism. No eyebrows seem to have been raised by the fact that, during the second half of the eighteenth century, practically all the major merchants and financiers associated with the state's big economic projects were Spanish. This had clearly become the case by the middle of the century and the situation was built up during the first third, if not earlier. In fact this should be understood as part of a general trend towards more nationalist conceptions of economic policy.[1]

Francisco Mendinueta, therefore, was one of the prime exemplars of a Zeitgeist change and, at the same time, was helped in turn by the way this Zeitgeist favoured the initiatives of Spanish entrepreneurs. But Mendinueta's career was also spurred on by his membership of one of the most active groups of business-people at that time: the Navarre clique. This membership was by no means merely circumstantial; it was fuelled by a strong economic factor. In a mercantile world in which entrepreneurs, more than their counterparts nowadays, stood in need of safeguards and trust, membership of a group closely knitted together by family bonds and kinship was a much more efficient way of doing business and offering services.[2]

The family group provided the economic bases and essential business connections for one to become a highly successful businessperson working within the structures of the state. First and foremost in this particular case was the legacy of Francisco's father, Juan de Mendinueta y Arizcun.[3] This represented a direct family link with one of the most active families of the Navarre clique: the Arizcun family. Arizcun's household and company managed to keep in its power the navy victualling contract from 1722 to 1783, the longest known possession of an important *asiento.*[4] This continuity, and the sheer importance of this navy supply-contract, served as inexhaustible sources of relations via the Navarre group with other Madrid merchants and financiers, with other state business—in short, of a *cursus honorum* of crown services, all of them essential for keeping up the current position and bringing in new family members.

From his father Mendinueta had also inherited his business, his public credit, and relations; but compared to him Juan Mendinueta never became a great merchant or financier. However, he knew how to exploit the crown's border-zone needs in connection with the demand for services from the Navarre financiers in Madrid for doing business in the kingdom of Navarre; this arrangement represented a veritable business and service triangle. During the following years and, above all, during the War of Succession, Juan de Mendinueta worked this business and service triangle for all it was worth. Supplying the king's troops in Navarre and Aragon was a key business underpinning the rest of his business activities. From 1714 a whole string of military *asientos* came one after the other: gunpowder, victuals, and munitions. The family relatives in Madrid served as a privileged information channel to plumb the crown's needs and offered Juan de Mendinueta the possibility of networking or acting as factor or commissioner. The tangled web of relations woven by this business, where it was hard at any one moment to work out who was serving whom, considerably boosted his chance of building up service capacity and, above all, reinforced his public credit. Juan de Mendinueta called on this credit to attract friends and capital towards local business: revenue farming in Navarre, *estanco del tabaco* (fiscal monopoly on tobacco), *tablas de Navarra* (dry port customs), or *rentas episcopales* (episcopal revenue).[5] Juan de Mendinueta contributed as his life's work to cram that triangle of crown business and services with content. For that very reason he was mindful of the importance of getting his heir, Francisco de Mendinueta, to Madrid as soon as possible to join the Navarre group of courtiers. By the age of 24 it would seem that Mendinueta was already definitively settled in Madrid and by the time he was 28 he was a member of the clique of Navarros set up around the Congregación de San Fermín de los Navarros. The legacy of his father, therefore, was a crucial factor in the ascent of Francisco Mendinueta.

Francisco Mendinueta's presence in Madrid might have been expected to spell the end of that triangle of business and services. Nothing of the sort, and this proved indirectly just how robust it was. Mendinueta in fact continued to nurture the business in Navarre and the king's service in that region. During the 1720s and 1730s there was another stream of military *asientos* for supplying the troops in Navarre or making military artefacts in the Navarre mountains. In these *asientos* Mendinueta features in association with direct relatives: in Madrid with Miguel Arizcun, first cousin, and in Navarre with Pedro Fermín Goyeneche, brother-in-law, who themselves held leading positions in the military supply business. Arizcun, in other words, controlled the navy victualling business while Goyeneche took charge of gunpowder provision throughout the whole of Spain and victualling the troops of Navarre.[6] Without doubt these were peerless family connections.

The business experience built up by Mendinueta while working with these relatives in the military supply business was decisive in his training and rise through the ranks. With Miguel de Arizcun he was able to learn the strategic importance of amassing *asientos* and leases to fend off Royal Exchequer payment arrears and increase managerial efficiency. The state's financial shakiness and frequent payment defaults set up a spiral of state debts reinforcing the political and economic clout of the *asentistas*, providing they remained prepared to take on further business with the king. Arizcun, like many other Spanish businessmen, took up the cudgel, agreeing to continue participating in this profitable but also increasingly risky spiral of crown indebtedness. Thus navy victualling debts were set off against revenue from Galicia or wool revenue, and then this new link with the Royal Exchequer in turn spawned a new munitions-manufacturing military supply-contract, the payment default on the latter then forcing the crown to fob off its creditors with yet more services, specifically in this case the distribution of war materiel throughout the whole of Spain.

From Pedro Fermín de Goyeneche, Mendinueta learned another essential trick: the importance of wheedling your way into the state's administrative machinery and then doing business under this cover. Goyeneche got himself appointed victualling director of the Kingdom of Navarre; from Pamplona he served the troops of Navarre and neighbouring regions. His salary was a percentage of purchases. This post won him considerable kudos with the Secretaries of War and Finance and it was by no means incompatible in his opinion with other major business interests on the side. In fact this combination of public official and trusted merchant won him enormous earnings. In the victualling business urgency was the order of the day and trusted merchants often had to be called on to meet this demand. The biggest problem was not dominating the international grain market but rather juggling the urgency of a supply operation against the amount needed and necessary credit. Goyeneche was a past master of the wheat market of Bayonne, where he could easily contact French and Navarre merchants, who in turn were well connected with Dutch and English trading houses that dominated grain markets stretching right up to the Baltic ports. Witness the crown's urgent need in 1733 to increase victuals by 40,000 *fanegas* of wheat and 20,000 *fanegas* of barley. The crown turned to Goyeneche, who in turn made the purchase from the Bayonne house of Olagara y Hermanos. Goyeneche made all the necessary logistical arrangements for delivering 20,000 *fanegas* of wheat in Seville, 8,000 in Coruña, and 12,000 in San Sebastián, plus another 20,000 *fanegas* of barley in Seville. All this was achieved in record time and with a notable surcharge: 25 *reales de vellón* per *fanega* of wheat and 17 *reales de vellón* per *fanega* of barley, 'Pedro Fermín Goyeneche himself being responsible along with the aforementioned businessmen for paying the cost of this grain and receiving same from the Real Hacienda'.[7] To carry out these transactions Goyeneche forwarded payment to these European traders and later received reimbursement from the Royal Exchequer. Goyeneche's credit after paying the traders was then set off against a whole host of private business, including contraband of all types of products, such as wool, silver, or tobacco.[8] Goyeneche's experience and position were so crucial to Francisco Mendinueta's plans that when he won the general victualling *asiento* for the whole of Spain in 1744, he immediately appointed him director-general for Navarre and Guipuzkoa. All these influences and experience helped to train up the young Francisco Mendinueta in state business. When Mendinueta won this victualling contract covering the whole of Spain in 1744 he was 48 and had by now built up all the necessary knowledge, public credit, and family connections to carry it off.

This military supply-contract that Francisco Mendinueta then embarked on was no different from the previous ones in essence but had one idiosyncrasy that set it apart from the rest: this was its sheer volume, which in turn swelled and magnified everything else to do with the business: the logistics, the credit, the factors, employees, and many other variables. A good idea of the scope of this business can be gleaned by comparing its worth with the other main *asientos* of the time. By the mid eighteenth century the army victualling contract was by far the biggest possible military supply-contract in Spain. It was more than double the state's expenditure on artillery and fortifications, and more than triple the navy victualling expense, overwhelming the expenditure on army uniforms and weapons or victualling for the household guard or garrison troops (see Table 4.1).

These figures are probably an understatement. There are frequent cases of victualling costs being shifted to other budget items of the Royal Exchequer to be found in the archives. Sometimes these concerned emergency purchases; in other cases they were freightage and insurance costs, paid against very different income. These shunted costs might have added up to a considerable sum, even exceeding the amount of the most important *asientos*. In this same year of 1756, for

Table 4.1 Cost of the monarchy's main *asientos*, 1756 (*reales de vellón*)

Army victuals	26,337,202
Artillery and fortifications	10,666,970
Navy victuals	7,553,971
Uniforms	2,560,126
Household guard victuals	1,714,520
Garrison troop victuals	1,200,000

Source: Figures taken from AGS, SSH, leg. 293. *Cuentas de la provisión de víveres de la Corte y Reales sitios a cargo de José Florenza, vecino de Madrid, desde el 1-7-1756 hasta el 30-1-757*, AGS, DGT, inv. 25, leg. 14. For garrison victualling figures see *Asiento de Francisco Bartolomé de Huarte, con abono de Pedro de Astrearena, Marqués de Murillo*, AGS, SSH, leg. 641.

example the Royal Exchequer took on responsibility for diverse army-victualling grain contracts worth 3.2 million *reales*, recording the expense as 'Extraordinary of the Royal Exchequer'; the purchases made in 1757 were even greater: 6 million *reales*.[9] Furthermore, when the army fought a campaign abroad the supplier was not bound to meet this extraordinary expense: the crown either had to haggle with the supplier, to be paid outside the military supply-contract, or enter into an agreement with another financier, as occurred during the 1740s for the many Spanish troops sent to the Italian wars. In any case these extraordinary expenses were normally not recorded under the ordinary victualling costs so the real cost to the crown was even higher than the vast figure recorded in national accounts; the gap between this supply and the rest was therefore even wider. If we look at the trend, the Spanish state continually stepped up its army victualling expenditure, although this expenditure's percentage share of total public spending fell, mainly due to the increasing share of naval expenditure (see Figure 4.1).

In any case the king's ordinary victualling expenditure underwent no great changes during Mendinueta's spell at the head of the business. From the beginning of the 1730s to the end of the 1760s, the crown spent between 20 and 25 million *reales* a year on this business, representing about 5 per cent of total state spending. The expenditure therefore gives a ballpark idea of the importance of this business, but the contract also possessed a series of idiosyncratic traits that made it extraordinarily complex and hence difficult to manage.

This complexity arose mainly from the impossibility of clearly determining either the supply or demand. The supply was the wheat, barley, and rations needed to keep both soldiers and their various beasts of burden regularly fed. In Spain this supply depended mainly on each year's harvest. In the middle of the eighteenth century cereal production was based almost exclusively on an extensive farming system. Yield was low and fickle, depending on the weather each year. The possibilities of increasing the yield and breaking this weather dependence were slight and restricted to a few regions in the north of Spain. The resulting picture was very patchy from region to region and, even worse,

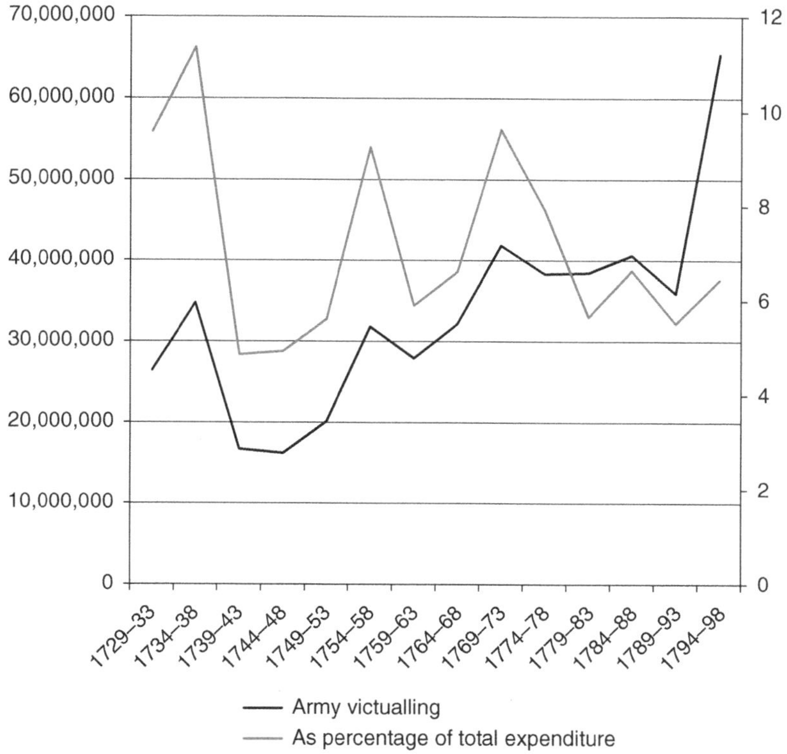

Figure 4.1 The ordinary Spanish army victualling costs (in *rsv*)

Source: Rafael Torres Sánchez, *Constructing a Fiscal-Military State in Eighteenth-Century Spain* (Basingstoke: Palgrave Macmillan, 2015).

displayed wild and unforeseeable swings over time. The problem was exacerbated by the eighteenth-century tendency to cluster armies in the southern half of Spain. Bucking the general trend, the exceptionally high yield of the Lower Guadalquivir in Andalusia turned out to be a goldmine when most of the armed forces ended up concentrated in that region in the second half of the eighteenth century (see Map 4.1).

Things were not much better on the demand side, that is, the state's calculations of the future supply needs of its soldiers and their beasts of burden. Until the second half of the eighteenth century most of the army had no fixed locations or barracks and was constantly moving from one site to another; there was also constant fluctuation in the number of units to be victualled.[10] All this made it very difficult to calculate needs beforehand. The director of the Contaduría General de Provisiones himself warned about the complexity of this business in 1740: 'All the businesses,' wrote Fermín Folch,

> whether revenue leases or other forms of *Asientos*, have rules for calculating their worth, and so some idea can be given a priori of the total sum or benefits. The general

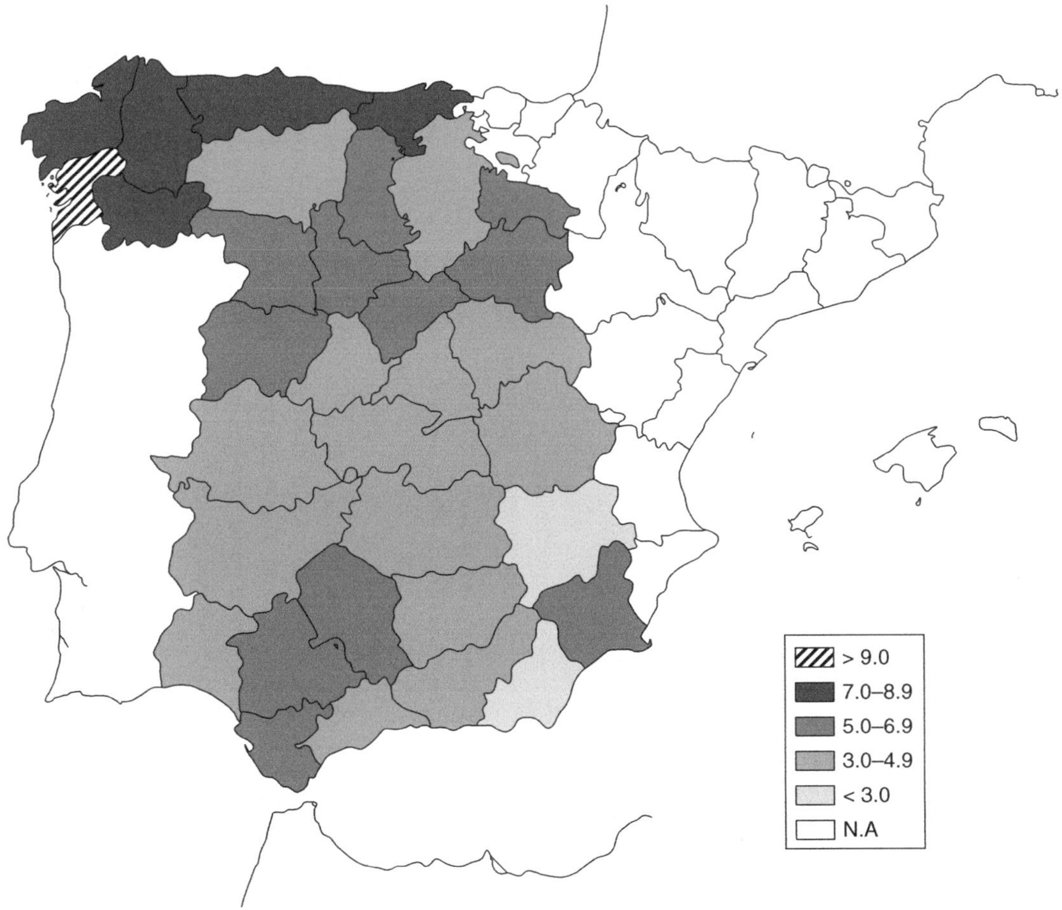

Map 4.1 Wheat yields, 1750s (*Quintals* per hectare)

Source: Adapted from Carlos Santiago-Caballero, 'Trapped by Nature: Provincial Grain Yields in Spain in the Mid 18th Century', *Revista de Historia Económica/Journal of Iberian and Latin American Economic History* 31 (2013), 1–28.

> victualling military supply-contract is an exception, however, for there is no rule and neither can any examples be given ... either of the price of grain or the number of troops to be catered for.[11]

The general terms and conditions of production complicated military supply-contract management; the contractor's main problem became to bridge the gaps in time and place between supply and demand. This overriding concern is clearly brought out by a simple comparison between the regions where the victuals were bought during the year and the sites where the bread rations were effectively delivered to the soldiers and the *fanegas* of barley to their livestock (see Table 4.2).

According to the figures in Table 4.2 there was a marked regional lopsidedness. Before the 1740s the army's most important victual producing regions were Andalusia and Aragon, while other regions such as Catalonia were net consumers. Andalusia furnished nearly half the army's total grain while its own armies consumed only one-quarter. Even greater was the supply–demand lopsidedness in Aragon, which acted as a vital granary. Catalonia, on the contrary, accounted for 15 per cent of all purchases while its own bread consumption added up to nearly 40 per cent. This meant that, at the beginning of Mendinueta's victualling provision, victuals from the south and north had to be sent to the eastern part of Spain. This was due to the eastern region's heavy militarization in the aftermath of the War of Succession, while it also served as the main base of armies being shipped off to Italy.[12] In this case geopolitical strategy called for a distribution of armed forces that married badly with the country's production capacity. In fact a true understanding of how this business worked called for a close eye to be kept not only on changes in farming yield in the various regions but also the shifting map of military needs. As we have already pointed out, as the century wore on the main destination of most of the victuals shifted to Andalusia, partly correcting this problem. This change in the military geography of the eighteenth century can be seen by comparing Maps 4.2 and 4.3.

The supply–demand mismatch was repeated in all products, because each one had its own particular geographical characteristics. Take the case of barley, the other major victualling ingredient. Although other products such as rye, flour, straw, and chaff might also be bought, their cost was only a tiny percentage of that of barley. Table 4.2 shows that the barley supply was spread much more widely around Spain than wheat, albeit with a peak in central Castile. This distribution is bound up with the greater presence of cavalry around Madrid and the court. This concentration of demand at one point was a boon from the business point of view and probably accounted for a growing interest of other financiers in supplying the court, as we will see later with the business group called the Cinco Gremios Mayores de Madrid.

The supply–demand mismatch was increased by the frequency with which *asentistas* purchased their grain abroad. The main attractions of overseas markets were price, which was often low enough to cancel out freightage and insurance costs, but above all the quantities that could be procured. This factor is crucial

Table 4.2 Sites where Spanish army victuals were bought and consumed, 1734

Site of Purchase			Site of distribution		
	Wheat	Barley		Bread rations	Barley (*fanegas*)
Andalusia	49.4	23.4	Catalonia	38.4	27.8
Catalonia	15.3	4.2	Andalusia	24.3	21.4
Aragon	13.5	7.4	Valencia	8.1	2.4
Valencia	6.2	6.8	Navarre	6	0.1
London	5	0	Madrid	5.6	29.6
Navarre	3.9	0.1	Galicia	4	1.1
Castile	3.3	17.3	Castile	3.9	8.8
Extremadura	1.9	6.4	Mallorca	3.8	3.6
Madrid	1	18.2	Aragon	3	1
Galicia	0.6	1.5	Extremadura	2.9	4.1
Murcia	0	14.8			
	100	100		100	100
	8,326,023 Rsv	4,576,006 Rsv		13,111,972 Rsv	350,359 Rsv

Source: AGS, SSH, leg. 640.

because urgent military demand usually coincided with poor harvests at home. However, this international supply also had its own particular system. The problem was not in finding the market—Amsterdam or Genoa, for example, would be perfect choices for any Spanish *asentista*—but rather in bringing to this market enough credit to persuade these local merchants to accept the deal. It is worth bearing in mind here that the privileges and security with which the Spanish king ended up surrounding the contractor counted for very little in international markets, so their bargaining power was much less abroad. This promissory aspect was essential in Spanish public credit but very tricky to manage for private agents. In the world of private business, even when backed up by the implicit endorsement of being an established state supplier, a certain liquidity was still needed, and this was by no means habitual for financiers of this type. In the Spanish case this liquidity could be offset by the proven capacity to export silver to these markets, which was one of the eighteenth century Spanish merchants' most habitual ploys: silver was highly valued by European financiers and merchants. For military entrepreneurs, therefore, it was de rigeur to work also in silver exportation directly or to collaborate with merchants who did so. Possession of a Royal Exchequer silver export permit could be a vital calling card for breaking into European victual markets. All this gave rise to alliances of suppliers with Spanish and foreign merchants who had a handle on wheat markets and were also capable of catalyzing interest around the silver trade. The upshot of all the above is that actual recourse to victual markets abroad did not depend so much on their level of development and efficiency but rather on the suppliers' real possibilities of trading in broader exchange networks; in Spain's case this largely boiled down to silver and, secondarily, wool. In the case of the Navarre merchant Mendinueta, the connection with the Navarre group and the exportation of silver and wool to the French market of

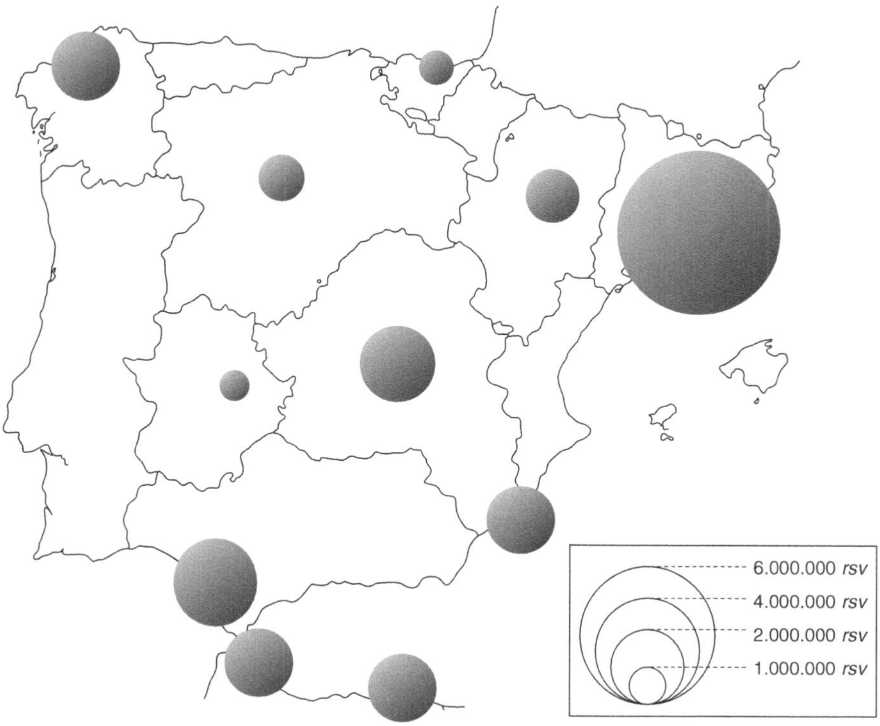

Map 4.2 Geographical breakdown of army victualling, 1730–9
Source: Author's own. Adapted from AGS, SSH, leg. 640–2.

Bayonne, legally or illegally, offered a fine chance of breaking into Europe's wheat marketing networks.[13]

Whether trading at home or abroad, the management of businesses of this type was highly complex. In the words of a functionary of the Finance Ministry in 1740, everything in this military supply-contract was highly priced and varied and a whole host of separate arrangements had to be made: 'carriage, freightage, salaries of factors, accounting officials, grain milling, manufacturing, procurement commissioners, utensils, losses at sea, averages, storage, interest on the funds that need to be paid in advance and countless other expenses that are incurred along the way'.[14] Playing in Mendinueta's favour were the factors of experience, family credit, family background, and alternative businesses, but he still needed the right opportunity to occur. All too often we historians tend to overlook the chance factor and in this particular case it was decisive. Mendinueta managed to muscle in and develop a large part of this business precisely because the political circumstances of the time favoured his endeavour.

In 1743 when Francisco Mendinueta made his first bid for the army victualling business, he did so, as we have already seen, backed up by past experience in state contracting and a long track record of crown service. Francisco Mendinueta, Knight

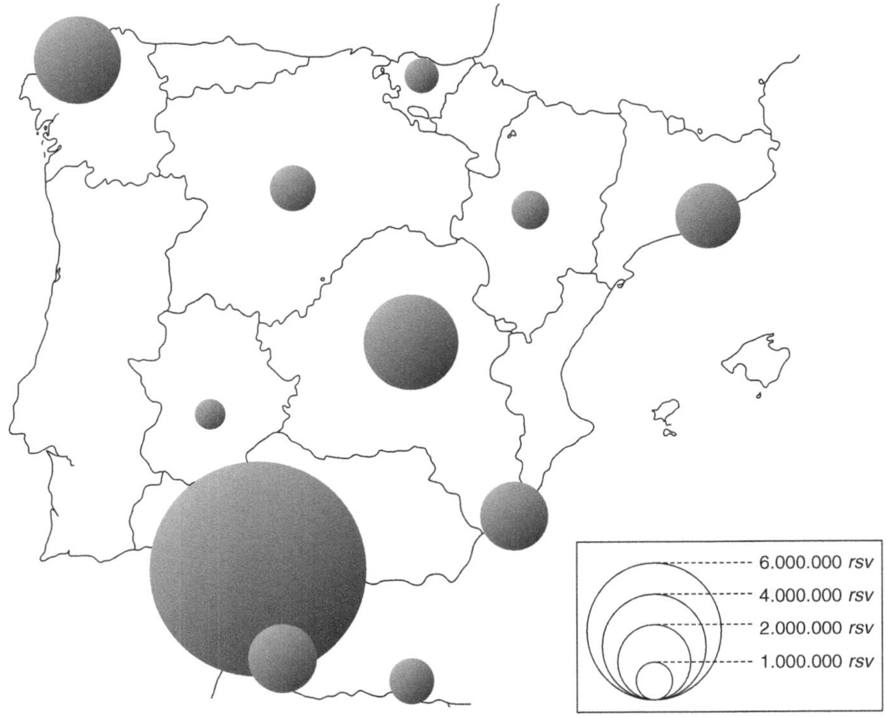

Map 4.3 Geographical breakdown of army victualling, 1778–83
Source: Author's own. Adapted from AGS, SSH, leg. 640–2.

of the Order of Santiago, in his very first communications with the minister, drew on all his tried and tested record as a crown servant, stressing that he was at that moment 'entrusted with the War Munitions *Asiento*'.[15] Moreover his first attempt to break into the national business was made in a new economic and political conjuncture that was particularly favourable to initiatives of this type. After the bankruptcy of 1739 the Royal Exchequer now needed fairly urgently to turn back to businesspeople but at the same time wished to change the roll call of names.

Prima facie it was purely an economic question. Mendinueta's asking price undercut all other comers and also lowered the victualling cost as compared with the previous years of direct *administración* by the Royal Exchequer. But the crown's readiness to do business with him must also have weighed heavily in the balance, together with the guarantees and influence wielded by Mendinueta himself and his friends. In fact, as Mendinueta himself confessed years later to the Secretary Marqués de Ensenada, with the sincerity and confidence allowed him after 12 years at the head of this military supply-contract, the final contracted price was not to be taken as gospel. Mendinueta acknowledged that it did not strictly reflect market costs; there was also a strong political component that only the minister and the contractor himself, according to him, could properly appreciate: 'I understand', wrote Mendinueta to the minister in 1756, 'that the bread ration including costs might be furnished at a cost of 19 *maravedis* and the *fanega* of barley at 27 *reales*, but to forestall any untoward surprise in the inexperienced, this latter price could be increased in the bread ration and lowered accordingly in the barley.'[16] In this case it was considered more important to 'forestall any untoward surprise' at the prices—in reality to avoid coming across to the rest of the economic elite as excessively favoured by the crown or whipping up grassroots opposition—than it was to reflect in *asiento* prices the sharp rise in the cost of barley over the last two years. In other words Mendinueta regarded his asking price as determined by a whole host of factors, not only economic.

Bearing in mind this way of acting and thinking, the fact that Mendinueta proposed an 18.7 per cent reduction in the prices of both the bread ration and the *fanega* of barley was an undoubted advantage, and an excellent starting point for negotiating with the Royal Exchequer. Such a price cut represented a significant saving for the royal coffers, about 3,700,000 *rsv*. He also tagged on a very attractive proposal. Mendinueta waived the advance payment that the Finance Ministry usually granted to oil the contractor's wheels in early procurements. This initial outlay by the Royal Exchequer had become the established way of offsetting surplus stocks received by military entrepreneurs from previous years. Mendinueta, for the good of the royal finances, publicly waived this right: 'although the custom is for the *asentista* to be given an advance payment, in view of the financial hardships of the government, he hereby applies for existing grain to be sold off and he be given the money arising therefrom'.[17] The contractor would take on the onerous task of getting rid of this surplus stock. In fact his task boiled down to writing off the value of the surplus products and rations. It had been the custom for some time now for the contractor to pass these stocks on directly to the troops rather than keeping them. For the state the crucial factor in any contract renewal was not the surplus stock itself but the advance payment to be made to the *asentista* for initiating new procurements, so the waiving of this right by the contractor practically freed the government completely from this expense.

The advance payment was a constant cause of haggling between the crown and *asentistas* due to the Royal Exchequer's chronic dearth of liquidity and because the contractor, furnished with this public money, stood in less need of credit from other private parties and partners. So important was it, in fact, that it usually became a crucial factor in choosing the contractor. Traditionally this advance payment was quite a hefty sum. In the times of Urbán Ruiz, the government pre-paid him 225,000 escudos, and the Marqués de Valdeolmos in 1740 would not shift downwards from a 3 million *reales* victualling advance payment. Mendinueta, though coming in from outside this structure, grasped the importance of the advance payment as a bargaining counter and agreed to waive it. This approach to negotiations spoke volumes about his creditworthiness. He kept up this offer in subsequent renewals over the following years until in 1750, now in a much stronger bargaining position vis-à-vis the crown, he changed tack. He asked for and got a 100,000-escudos advance payment, to be paid within eight days of the military supply-contract approval and to be paid back over the following 12 months. Subsequently, in 1755, he once more used the advance payment as a bargaining tool, waiving it anew to persuade the crown to grant him a new military supply-contract under circumstances that, as we will see later, were *sui generis*.[18]

Mendinueta's strategy for breaking into the army victualling business was thus, in effect, to moot a return to the pre-1730 situation, that is, before the switch to direct state management of victualling arrangements. And to do so he did not hesitate to copy and improve on the achievements of the contractor Urbán Ruiz Velarde in 1726, especially his proposal for moving towards a single military supply-contract. This amounted to a unification of the regionally based provisioning systems in a single *asiento* for the whole of Spain, and was in all likelihood an attempt to profit from the crown's chagrin at the chaos caused by partial victualling *asientos*, while also reacting to the political climate created by the general military supply-contract proposal of Marqués de Valdeolmos. The Finance Ministry was frustrated by the constant problems caused by juggling with a clutch of partial contracts signed in the years 1740–2. Each small victualling arrangement for troops in each region resulted in a plethora of time-consuming talks between local merchants and crown representatives. And this was a best-case scenario because sometimes no local businesspeople came forward at all, whereupon the state, terrified of leaving its troops unprovisioned, had to turn to the *intendentes* to whip up some interest from local businesses. Even this was no definitive or effective solution: experience had shown that these small local businessmen were often hard put to fulfil their commitments. They might be capable of handling a one-off, specific supply-contract but whenever any incident cropped up, either due to troop movements or new incorporations, these local contractors clearly revealed their credit limitations and also their restricted capacity for interacting with other commercial agents. The world of local business in Spain offered possibilities of extending the victualling business but also a host of risks that the state was not ready to run. An example of the risks and limitations of working with local businessmen can be found in the victualling of the troops of Mallorca in 1742 between the *intendente*, Antonio Horbegozo, and the local Palma merchant, Antonio Marcel. We know about this business due to correspondence between the intendente and Secretario Campillo. In this military supply-contract everything was problematic. The 40,000 *reales* advance payment asked for by that merchant was excessive. Madrid had permanent doubts about the merchant's solvency, since Marcel limited the delivery sites and refused to offer provisions outside the island. As if this were not enough, the merchant refused to be paid anywhere else except the city of Palma. Before the negotiations, however, the *intendente* Horbegozo himself had put forward this merchant as the best candidate, lauding him as: 'creditworthy and backed up by good connections'.[19]

Mendinueta was well aware of this local situation and the headaches and qualms it caused the state, and exploited them in his bargaining process. His bid was presented as a general military supply-contract, eliminating all existing partial *asientos*, with the aim, he argued, of 'avoiding contentions and disputes that hobble the Royal Service, whereby any partial victualling Military supply-contract should hereby be entirely discharged'. This proposal, in practice, implied a unification of the national victualling arena. It can by no means be ruled out that the contractor found a particular economic benefit in this unification, facilitating as it did his task of marrying supply and demand. This solution also offered the chance of harnessing economies of scale. Indeed, and this fact should be underlined, a Spain-wide victualling *asiento* under single game rules would be one of Spain's biggest national markets. Albeit artificially, this general and nationwide military supply-contract would favour contacts between distant locations and facilitate distribution and the flow of goods, thereby helping to integrate all the separate local markets of Spain. Despite the trend towards concentrating troops in the south of Spain, demand was still scattered rather than being focused on a single point, resulting in goods being distributed throughout most of the national territory. Such a national market still, of course, had to be increased in size and knitted together, but the very fact that goods were indeed being supplied nationwide speaks of its possibility. In the worst-case scenario a nationwide victuals market would at least stimulate local markets and their business worlds, forcing them to specialize and increase their output, and also boost the demand for transport, employment, and infrastructure. The last factor, distribution of provisions and development of the transport network, came increasingly to the fore during the second half of the eighteenth century. Witness the Banco de San Carlos's demand as contractor for an investment policy in public works in the interests of reducing victual distribution costs.

Mendinueta's subsequent performance seems to show that this contractor was certainly aware of the potential economies of scale in a nationwide military supply-contract. It was therefore a priority for Mendinueta to be granted duty-free transfer of supplies from one province to another, a concession he obtained in 1744 and held onto tenaciously thereafter. The sheer burden of duties impinging on local transport was a factor that might well cancel out any supposed benefit from a nationwide market. It was therefore undoubtedly a coup for Mendinueta to win this freedom from duties, even before the crown took it up as a rallying cry both at home and in the colonies, as occurred in the reign of Charles III.[20] Even so, Mendinueta's right to move army victuals around the country cannot be construed as a one-way imposition by the contractor on the state. Mendinueta's offer of a unified, singly conceived business was also useful for the state, whose ongoing supply management problems in the last decade were due mainly to the difficulties of wrangling with a herd of small contractors. In one way or another, the state certainly understood the advantages of negotiating with a single contractor. If the Finance Ministry had to negotiate only with a single businessperson it greatly simplified the whole process and improved chances of properly controlling the chosen contractor. Simplification and control of victualling arrangements was essential for the state. Exactly how this was done—in this case by negotiating with a single businessperson—was, for the state, a secondary matter. But the consequence was obvious: Mendinueta obtained a single nationwide contract and the state ratified a new way of understanding these relationships. From then on the contractor would hold onto an unchallenged position because the state granted a de facto monopoly. From now on monopoly and privileges would be key features of this business.

To shore up his proposal of a better economic deal for the state and a unified, nationwide conception of the business, Mendinueta added a more convenient payment system for the Royal Exchequer, an offer that was snapped up by the state. From now on the contractor would present victualling receipts at the Tesorería General as and when they accrued, the treasury then settling accounts with him every month. The really new feature here lay in the payment flexibility Mendinueta offered. Any sum owed him by the Royal Exchequer could be received by the contractor or his empowered agents at any point in Spain and by any means of payment; in cash, receipt of payment, or credit. This facility would help the Tesorería General to mobilize its economic resources. The advantage coincided with the Tesorería General's general tendency to move money about by accounting clearances between treasurers rather than physical transfer of funds. Along similar lines, Mendinueta even waived reimbursement of costs incurred in funding movements from distant treasuries. That said, Mendinueta did reserve the right of negotiating with the Royal Exchequer's receipts of payment to pay for procurements. In the hands of a businessperson trading on a nationwide scale this could prove an important source of profit and a secure way of strengthening the network of correspondents. Once more, therefore Mendinueta offered the Royal Exchequer an advantage: financial services with greater flexibility. With this last part of his bid Mendinueta really stood out from the crowd. In fact it was precisely here where the main difference resided between the biggest entrepreneurs and the other local financiers and merchants. Historians in the past have tended to dwell on the funds and capital these people could call on as the main distinguishing feature between bidders; besides this capital, however, due consideration has to be given to the services and facilities offered to meet the state's particular needs in each case. Mendinueta's family and business connections stood him in good stead to meet victualling obligations, outbidding other businesspeople with bigger fortunes and capital. This helps to explain why the major, eminently solvent Madrid or Cadiz financiers did not compete for this business.[21] What made Mendinueta different from them was his ability to offer the state just what it needed: nationwide supply, trustworthiness with less administrative involvement by the state, at a lower price and on a greater geographical scale, fleshed out with economic and commercial intermediation services and financial solvency. In other words Francisco Mendinueta knew how to offer the state the package it wanted: nationwide command of a victualling arrangement of strategic importance to the king at an appreciably lower price and much better financial facilities for the Royal Exchequer.

Francisco Mendinueta's negotiation strategy soon bore fruit. His bid was unmatchable qualitatively; indeed, there were in fact no other bidders, an unprecedented situation in any supply-contract since the start of the century. Mendinueta was appointed general army victualling *asentista* for Spain, Mallorca, and Oran for a one-year period. The crucial point though was not that he managed to convince the government of his initial arguments, but that he kept the state renewing his victualling military supply-contract for nearly two decades into the future. This was without any doubt his greatest success: it was highly unusual to remain so long in the saddle with this type of state business. Even though victualling demands were continually bucking and shifting beneath him, together with other variables like price and availability, Mendinueta and the government managed to ride the changes, resizing their relations and keeping up a business that both wished to succeed.

To alleviate the problems deriving from supply and demand changes, Mendinueta always advocated the signing of short-term *asientos*, 18 months at most, barring the final one, signed for three years from 1761 to 1763, and which in fact turned out to be one of the reasons for his ruin. These relatively short-term *asientos* allowed him to trim his sails to prevailing winds. Thus, on the basis of yearly contracts, Mendinueta managed in only five years, from 1744 to 1749, to raise his asking price by 53 per cent. The contractor's grounds for seeking the increases were nearly always the same: increases in the cost of grain and rising transport expenses, especially freightage and insurance, together with poor harvests. These claims, most of them true, left the state very little room for manoeuvre. One option was to cloak the real situation for fear of diplomatic observers, always on the lookout for these signs of the Spanish state's military and economic strength or weakness. Another option was to look for a new businessperson to replace Mendinueta. The search was made, but the state always balked at the final hurdle due to serious qualms about any replacement's trustworthiness. Indeed, after the end of Mendinueta's spell at the head of the military supply-contract in 1763, the state was hard put to find a new contractor capable of ensuring comparable provision. There was no lack of merchants and financiers in the business and a few actually came forward and participated, but there was a whole string of fiascos and bankruptcies before another contractor was found to match even in part the Mendinueta experience.[22] The third option was to renegotiate terms with Mendinueta. In the end the state preferred to come to the table, considering it at all times more important to secure victualling supplies than upset the complete business framework by abandoning this contractor.

The 1749 contract-renewal correspondence between Mendinueta and the Finance Minister and War Minister shows us the scale of this problem in a particularly significant year when Mendinueta persuaded the state to accept the biggest increase in the cost of the contract during the entire period while he was at the helm. In 1749 Mendinueta claimed it was impossible to ensure provision since market conditions had changed radically over the last year. The bottom line was always the same: 'checking one *asiento* against another, when grain is much costlier than last year'.[23] Ensenada asked provincial authorities for current grain price information to check the veracity of the contractor's claims. There followed a busy two-way traffic of price and cost statements. In the end the ministers saw that there really had been a cost increase but not sufficient to agree to his proposed terms outright; talks would continue to try to argue Mendinueta down. Muzquiz sent along a senior official with two proposals. The first proposal involved an increase in the advance payment, up to a maximum of 200,000 pesos (3,000,000 *rsv*). If, on top of this sum, Mendinueta 'should still want more', Muzquiz authorized his envoy to increase the proposed advance, on express condition that Mendinueta would then lower his overall contract price by one *maravedi* on each bread ration for each 100,000 pesos increase of the state's advance payment. The state negotiator's instructions were that, if possible, 'the price reduction should be the overriding concern'. The state, in other words, did not want to rack up the price per ration even higher because it feared the ratchet effect that this would have upon future military supply-contract negotiations. New interviews ensued, 'long conversations' according to later reports, in several sites in Madrid, but Mendinueta refused to accept any bid price reduction on the grounds that 'this vast business faces costs and hurdles that are not perceptible to most people'. The almighty secretary Ensenada himself then weighed into the affair, giving the most forthright and telling order 'that the *asentista* should not be pushed to breaking point'. Dragging out the talks was jeopardizing the continuity of supply; forcing the issue to the point where the contractor might back out was an excessive risk for the state. A compromise agreement was therefore reached. Mendinueta agreed to leave prices at 19 *reales de vellón* per ration and 19 *maravedis* per *fanega* of barley and the government recognized that more price trimming was difficult in the circumstances; in the words of the king's negotiator the best option was a contract renewal: 'the Royal Exchequer will benefit from a prolongation'.[24]

To cut this Gordian knot of short contracts and constant price haggling, and coinciding with an eventful political period of growing state interventionism in fiscal matters, the crown tried in 1753 to return to the direct administration of army victualling. The problem posed for Ensenada here was that, apparently, no one else knew the ins and outs of the business as well as Mendinueta and he also had an up-and-running network of factors and correspondents to work with. The option of ousting him and then trying to build up this information, knowledge, and credit network from scratch appeared extremely risky. The state was fairly confident of having things in place within a few years but again could not afford to run the short-term risk of a supply cut-off meanwhile. The urgency of military supply always trumped possible change in supply policies. In the end a surprising expedient was chosen, though logical from the point of view of state priorities. The government offered Francisco Mendinueta the chance of taking over this direct administration himself, that is, to become a civil servant: 'His Majesty hereby orders that Don Francisco Mendinueta be given such sums of money as he may request for defraying therewith such costs as may be incurred in the aforesaid two years in the army victualling contract, which commitment is to be assumed on behalf of the Royal Exchequer.'[25] This was a far-reaching change of status in two ways: first, in reduced liability, as the businessperson now receiving a commission on total expenses; and secondly, in relations with the government, since the entrepreneur now became a functionary in the king's service.

Mendinueta's performance during 1753, his first year at the head of this direct administration arrangement, was apparently judged by the government to be satisfactory, since the king renewed the post for the following year. Speaking of Francisco Mendinueta's post as new Army Victualling Director on behalf of the Royal Exchequer, the king was pronounced to be

> very satisfied with the zeal, dispatch and success with which you have handled said supply on behalf of the Royal Exchequer since 1 January 1753, securing this crucial service for the King without encumbering the people with new tolls, seizures and other such nuisances suffered in other less sterile years, despite the greater urgencies caused by the poor harvest of the current year ... continuing yourself therefore at the head of said provision your sworn reports, factors and commissioners.[26]

According to a report of 1758 from Cosme Bermúdez de Castro, head auditor of the Tesorería General, to the king, Mendinueta's work at the helm of this provisioning on behalf of the Royal Exchequer during 1753 and 1754 had been very meritorious: 'it is hereby acknowledged that Francisco Mendinueta's zeal and selflessness had achieved appreciable advantages in favour of the Royal Exchequer, he having managed, according to Bermúdez, such egregious efforts without enjoying any salary or gratification for his unstinting work'. The eulogies continued with such phrases as 'his selflessness, loyalty and zeal in the royal service, seeking and finding the most convenient and proportionate methods for bringing grain in from London, Marseilles, Sicily and other parts without the least waste and without enjoying any salary or gratification for his unstinting work', etc.[27] Such extolling of the virtues of this senior civil servant is more than suspicious and was no doubt overstated. Indeed, the figures given by Bermúdez clash tellingly with those furnished by the Tesorería General itself for the previous years. In the two years of 1753 and 1754 the Royal Exchequer paid for this same provision 17.6 per cent more than Mendinueta had been paid as private *asentista* in the two previous years. It is all too likely that this fulsome praise of Mendinueta was covering up a failure of the system. Indeed, in the very next year the state dropped this experiment and went back to the former contract system. For the state, continuing with the direct administration meant paying out more and tying up its economic resources in continual outlays to keep the whole procurement network up and running. In fact, in 1753 and 1754, the Royal Exchequer provided 57,413,723 *reales de vellón*. It is not clear whether this was a problem of financial liquidity as well as prices, but whatever the case in 1755 the state decided to return to the *asiento*-based victualling system.

Mendinueta once more won the business, this time from a very strong bargaining position. He racked up his asking price, took over stocks in warehouses and ovens, valued at about 10 million *reales*, and undertook to bring in half the necessary grain from outside Spain. The latter stipulation was vitally important in the career of any ambitious businessperson. As has already been seen, access to the international grain market proffered the chance of exporting silver legally, and no doubt illegally too. This is where his connections with Navarre traders in the French port of Bayonne came in, enabling Mendinueta to tap into their connections with other wool-trading Navarre merchants in the Dutch markets.[28] Mendinueta took full advantage of this chance, on the pretext of forestalling a rise of wheat prices at home, which would be driven up by the contractor's purchases of a significant percentage of the national wheat and barley output, and would therefore harm the general public. Playing this card for all it was worth he got royal authorization for buying wheat and barley abroad, with legal coverage for a host of other business on the side.

The following years up to the start of the 1760 decade were a veritable idyll between Mendinueta and the government. His backlog of debts owed him from previous *asientos* dealing with other military provisions were all paid off by the state, the most important being the 2.5 million *reales* owed him from the Eugui factory munitions military supply-contract.[29] His freedom from duties and taxes on the road was also broadened, becoming almost total. His greatest obstacles here were set by local authorities in the form of port duties, leading to a host of taxes from councils and local corporations of all kinds (guilds, hospitals, brotherhoods, and many others); the contractor was now claiming exemption from all of them. The general freedom from duties granted him under the first military supply-contract had in practice clashed with the interests and rights of those affected, who flooded the crown with suits. In the end the state decided that dealing with each individual case was just too complicated, so it ordered the contractor to be reimbursed his total outlay on these taxes and duties. This was officially recognized by the state as an *asiento*-linked privilege in 1756.

The reigning harmony between Mendinueta and the state prompted ministers to use this contractor often to act as their economic policy agent. In such a sensitive market for the grassroots economy as the victualling set-up, any massive grain purchase could affect the sales price. The state was chary of these sudden increases due to the possible domino effect on prices in general. It must therefore have sent out the recommendation that massive purchases should be spread out as thinly as possible. Mendinueta took these recommendations firmly on board and enforced them on his network of correspondents. In 1757, for example, Francisco Mendinueta duly informed Secretario Miguel Muzquiz, whom he addressed as 'amigo y señor' (friend and lord) of some big grain purchases and transfers from Aragon to Valencia and how they had been massaged so that they would not seem to have been made by a single purchaser. For this purpose, he explained, he had shared out total purchases among his various factors and several Catalan trading houses to make the corresponding purchases on their own account, each then shipping them from Tortosa, 'so that the many hands involved should account for the abundance of sellers'. He also reminded Muzquiz that this procedure had already been resorted to previously: 'this has already been done by me in various provinces at the behest of Marqués de la Ensenada'.[30] Without any doubt ministers had cottoned on to the impact of a single contractor in influencing the market; this would have been impossible with free competition among purchasers.

But even though Mendinueta's position now seemed stronger than ever, the tide was soon to turn. First, other entrepreneurs ready to offer the same service appeared on the scene. The very strength built up by Mendinueta was a lure to Madrid financiers, who were now more than ready to get involved in such an obviously profitable business. One of the most serious bids, in terms of the person involved and his previous roles in the market, came from Simón Aragorri, a silver exporter and head of one of the main Madrid finance houses.[31] In 1754 he made a bid for the victualling contract. Aragorri aimed to match Mendinueta's bid, asking only to be paid 15 per cent 'of the victualling sum to defray the costs of agents' salaries and fund interest payments'.[32] His professional interest in silver exports brought out even more clearly that one of the main advantages of this victualling military supply-contract was precisely the possibility of linking the two businesses. As will be seen, this link became even more evident during the second half of the eighteenth century, precisely when legal and illegal silver exports to Europe were booming.[33]

This competition to obtain the victualling contract was welcomed by the government. Without ever precluding Mendinueta, it was always on the lookout for the chance to replace him. Indeed, albeit undercover, it ordered *intendentes* to be alert to this possibility. Clear stimulation was given to the authorities of Catalonia, then accounting for the biggest share of military consumption. Repeated orders went out to the *intendente* of Catalonia, leaving no doubt about the state's interest in replacing their *asentista*: 'I hereby repeat to you,' wrote the minister to the *intendente*, 'that with the greatest celerity and guile you should seek out solvent candidates ... who at regular prices would be ready to take on this business for one, two, three years or more.' The financers who responded to these overtures included the Barcelona house of Milans: 'the strongest of those trading in this business', according to the *intendente*, who also took this chance to remind the minister that it had been achieved 'by dint of the most efficient persuasion'.[34] All this meant that the state was no longer against competition per se and was even seeking it. Nonetheless, the state's overriding concern was always to ensure supply. In the end it continued to shore up Mendinueta as the best way of ensuring continuity of such strategically crucial provisioning.

The only real possibility of modifying this relation came with a change of government. The advent of Charles III in 1759 and his new finance minister, Marqués de Esquilache, drastically changed the political status quo and therewith the relations between the state and military entrepreneurs. Mendinueta was one of the victims of this change. The new minister, the Sicilian Leopoldo di Grigorio had been army *asentista* in Naples from 1742 and was a connoisseur of this particular world. This activity brought him into contact with Carlos de Borbón and he ended up as Marqués de Esquilache and finance minister, first in the Kingdom of the Two Sicilies and then in Spain, when he accompanied him in 1759 after he had become Charles III.[35] It was this former military entrepreneur who took charge of redefining relations with Mendinueta. From the outset he made it clear that Mendinueta no longer enjoyed an unimpeachable position. In 1760 he drafted a royal order, which he insisted should be published throughout the whole realm, inviting victualling-*asiento* bids, with the new feature that bidding businesspeople should accept 'separate *asientos* for Kingdoms and Provinces'.[36] Esquilache here was directly threatening Mendinueta with the state's power in order to break the spiral of rising prices. By inviting market competition he was certainly bringing in pressure from other traders, mainly from Madrid, but there is no doubt too that he was altering the two-decades-long framework of relations between state and contractor.

The response from businesspeople was positive. In the first months of 1760 the Finance Ministry received an appreciable number of bids from merchants in various regions to take charge of local victualling arrangements. These were of all types, ranging from small contract bids for detachments of troops up to proposals for whole regions. Some of the most complete and plausible were those submitted by contractors from Navarre and Aragon. This was largely because the calculations of these local financiers and merchants took into account three salient factors: first, the proximity of the Aragon 'granary'; secondly, the possibility of river transport to Tortosa, much cheaper than overland transport; and thirdly, the proximity also to Catalonia, site of the biggest demand hitherto. The outstanding bids came from Juan Miguel de Zuasti, a Pamplona merchant, who offered to supply the troops of Navarre and Guipúzcoa on the basis that 'this kingdom of Navarre pools and stores the largest amount of wheat from ecclesiastical revenue farming such as the fruits of the *Mitra* (Bishop's Revenue) and others'. Another came from Pedro Puy, a Zaragoza merchant, 'temporary owner of the site of Tronzedo', who offered to victual the troops of Aragon, Navarre, and Guipúzcoa, and undercut Mendinueta by 6 million a year. Factors that favoured him were Aragon's abundance of grain and his offer of a fairly long military supply-contract of five years. Along similar lines Pedro Juan de Acha, from Pamplona, also offered a longish term, of four years, for provisioning the same territory covered by Puyo's bid.[37] As Esquilache anticipated, this measure put Mendinueta under considerable pressure and threatened his hegemony. If he wanted to maintain his position, Mendinueta would have to considerably better his terms. Indeed, he was forced to lower his asking price by 25 per cent, both in wheat and barley, and—an even harsher term—drop his stipulation of yearly terms and accept a longer three-year term from 1760 to 1763. Mendinueta thus recognized the state's stronger bargaining position, and bowed to its demands. The state, with the virtual help of the market, now achieved what a higher degree of intervention and military entrepreneur support had never achieved in the past.

This spelt the start of Mendinueta's decline and fall. Everything now began to conspire against him. Grain prices soared as never before; the crown protection he had enjoyed in earlier *asientos* to favour his purchases or seizures was now denied him and contract prices were way below market prices. Losses built up and the crown began to doubt his solvency. By 1763 Madrid was rife with rumours about Mendinueta's impending ruin. When the military supply-contract ran its term in 1763, in a last-ditch attempt to recoup his losses, he proposed a new *asiento*, whereupon Esquilache openly challenged him to prove his solvency. Mendinueta's protests and chagrin seemed to prove that Esquilache's suspicions were not wide of the mark: 'which would seem to cause mistrust in me,' wrote Mendinueta,

> to my uttermost vexation when I think of my 18 year tried and tested record that would seem to prove quite the opposite ... far be it from me to need endorsement or bond when I am owed so much from the harvest provision ... without counting the six million I have in the Americas and in other funds.[38]

For all these protests, Mendinueta's creditworthiness had been called into question, which was a very serious development in this business. To make matters worse the names of other financiers were now being bandied about the court; everything suggested his time was coming to an end. Nonetheless, Mendinueta had contributed hugely towards the strengthening of Spanish businesspeople in army victualling. He had in fact been instrumental in creating a veritable 'nationalization' of the business. His family connections and trading networks also meant that the business had by now become truly nationwide. After Mendinueta, it was very hard for foreigners to make any inroads into this field, as revealed by the stout defence of the national market put up by Mendinueta's successors.

DEFENCE OF THE NATIONAL MARKET: NATIONAL AND STATE CAPITALISM

Mendinueta's two-decade spell at the helm of army victualling showed that Spanish financiers and traders were more than capable of handling this business. This progressive establishment of Spanish businesspeople also occurred in other areas of military supply. It is without doubt the best reflection of the government's keenness to adopt and enforce a mercantilist policy, but the experience with other supplies shows that political will alone was not enough. As we will see in the case of the navy, ideally the contractor state would have liked all products to be manufactured and the whole supply system to be controlled at home, but in practice this proved a complex and problematic task. In its attempt to enforce its mercantilist ambitions the Spanish state was backed up by Spain's businesspeople. At least this seems to be the case judging from the way they fended off any foreign attempts to make inroads into the victualling business. Marqués de Esquilache's swingeing changes in the state's victualling procedures brought down Mendinueta and opened up the business to competition. Many Spanish entrepreneurs pricked up their ears at this, but so did some from France too. The upshot of this convulsion was that the Spanish army victualling contract was awarded in 1763 to a pair of French businessmen, the Dughes brothers. This has traditionally been taken to be an example of French dealers' stranglehold over the Spanish state's military supplies.[39] In fact, as has previously been indicated, it showed quite the opposite. The reappearance of French businesspeople on the scene sparked a serious clash with other Spanish traders. A continual stream of Spain's top financiers paraded through Marqués de Esquilache's office over the next few months; letters were sent and received revealing political and economic misdemeanours straying well beyond the business in hand; the French ambassador himself weighed into the affair, as did leading figures from Madrid's mercantile community and even legal experts. The situation was resolved in a few months but it reveals precisely how difficult it had become for any foreigner to break into the supplies business unless he had the support of Spanish capitalists. It illustrates the degree of control now wielded by Spanish businesspeople and their ability to fend off foreign interlopers.

In 1789 Juan Antonio Dughes, Conde de Cesseles, infantry colonel of the king of France's army and younger brother of Pablo and Francisco Dughes, claimed from the Spanish government everything owing to his brothers from their services for the king of Spain in the times of Marqués de Esquilache, when they were in charge of army victualling on the whole of mainland Spain and islands.[40] In a clearly laudatory tone the Conde de Cesseles shed unstinting praise on, in his judgement, the extraordinary services rendered for the king under this provision arrangement. According to this report Pablo and Francisco Dughes, originally from Perpiñán, had arrived in Spain after building up a fortune as military entrepreneurs of the French army during the Seven Years War. On the strength of this experience, according to the account given by the Conde de Cesseles, the Dughes brothers were personally invited by the Marqués de Esquilache to come to Spain and organize the logistical system of the Spanish army, which was assembling at that time on the Portuguese border.[41] This invitation from the Spanish Finance Minister was taken up by the Dughes brothers, who finally arrived in Spain in July 1762.

That the Marqués de Esquilache should invite these French military entrepreneurs to take charge of such an essential crown business makes perfect sense commercially, especially in view of the credit and experience they had built up in their years of service to the French state and also given the prevailing climate of political détente with France after signing the third Pacte de Famille. The Marqués de Esquilache himself, moreover, was partial to deals of this type. As a past military entrepreneur himself, he would have been well aware of the international scale of the credit and strategy needed, and the French brothers' experience in that world. He was also, as we have already seen, eager to put an end to the hitherto unchallenged hegemony of Mendinueta, as demonstrated in the renewal of his military supply-contract in 1761, when he exposed Mendinueta to competition from other financiers. The advent of the French brothers in Madrid the previous summer was probably not merely the result of their proven experience and solvency; it was also part and parcel of a ministerial manoeuvre to put paid to a long-held sway over the business by one man.

The Dughes brothers' first initiatives in Madrid must have fulfilled all the hopes of salutary change harboured by the Finance Minister, 'a minister of such enlightenment', in the words of Francisco Dughes.[42] The Dughes brothers offered Esquilache a variety of securities, most importantly a debt of over 5 million *reales* owed to them by the French king. They also demonstrated their experience and their technical skills and knowledge for the required logistical management. The reports sent by the Dughes brothers to the minister were full of technical details and brand new features that apparently justified his selection. They even proposed new production methods for soldiers' rations. The Dughes insisted that they had a new technique and procedure for increasing the yield of bread rations from each *fanega* of wheat. According to the narrative offered with hindsight by the Conde de Cesseles 'until they [the Dughes brothers] arrived a *fanega* of wheat produced 55 rations ... the experiments they carried out under the government's instructions showed that one *fanega* of wheat, deftly handled, could furnish 90 well-produced rations'.[43] This technical breakthrough must have been a big advance for the Spanish flour and bread-making industry. So much so that 20 years after its introduction in Spain, the Conde de Cesseles asked the Consejo de Hacienda to check that the Banco Nacional de San Carlos, at that moment in charge of army victualling, 'has enforced the production rules taught and followed by the Dugues brothers'.[44]

In 1763, therefore, there was certainly a political will for change and contact had been made with suitable persons; only one formality remained: a surety was now needed to begin the whole military supply-contract tendering procedure. According to the letters sent to Esquilache by Salvador Querejazu, general auditor of the Consejo de Hacienda and the person responsible for negotiations with the French, the Dughes brothers pulled out all the stops to achieve this surety. From this source we know that the main arrangements were made in Paris, where Pablo Dughes went 'to raise funds for preparation and performance of the contract'. Before going off to France Pablo had left his brother Francisco fully empowered to bid in the army victualling military supply-contract auction.[45] Francisco assured Querejazu that his brother Pablo would be furnished with the 4 to 5 million consignment in a few days, 'having gone to Paris to draft the money to Spain'.[46] Four days later Francisco turned up in Salvador Querejazu's house to inform him that he now had sufficient surety and a guarantor, namely one Cristóbal Partearroyo. Against all expectations, it was now apparently to be a Spanish businessman who was to endorse the French financiers' credit.

Who was Cristóbal Partearroyo and how had he managed to gain a piece of this business that seemed set to veer towards France? Cristóbal Partearroyo was a moneyed businessman, part of a mid-century Madrid trading community. His father, Francisco Partearroyo, starting out with a broadcloth shop in Madrid's Plaza Mayor, had knitted together a web of business interests and commercial and personal relations that eventually enabled him to take part in the royal revenue farming business in the reign of Philip V. Until his death in 1749, Francisco Partearroyo was head of the royal revenue treasury and *servicios de millones* (food tax) of the city and province of Palencia, farmed out to Pedro Azpeitia against a surety furnished by Francisco Partearroyo.[47] Cristóbal Partearroyo inherited these business interests and relations but brought fresh blood and impetus to the whole endeavour. By the middle of the century Cristóbal had become a benchmark and cynosure in Madrid's credit world. He habitually lent hefty sums to merchants of Madrid and its environs for purchasing colonial products in Cadiz (for instance, the 135,480 *reales* loan made on 10 September 1753 to Pedro Hualde, merchant of Alcalá de Henares; the 120,000 *reales* loan agreed on 1 January 1754 with Pedro Retes, apothecary; the 128,358 *reales* loan signed on 1 May 1754 with Gerónimo Arcipreste, all merchants of Madrid's Calle Mayor),[48] or for opening shops in Madrid.[49]

To a lesser extent he was also lender to many private businesspeople but his main business was the granting of sizeable loans to leading government officials and military personnel, who sought bridging loans while awaiting a new court appointment or taking up a new post, especially in the Americas, where huge debts were incurred in Madrid on expectation of even huger revenue to offset it in the near future. Witness the cases of Pedro de la Cueva, brigadier and colonel of the Dragoons Regiment of Sagunto, or Pedro Aguado Correa, captain of the Compañía Suelta de Castilla, to whom he lent the major sum of 126,300 *reales*, or Juan Vicente de Guemes y Padilla, colonel of the Queen's Infantry Regiment, to whom he lent 200,000 *reales*.[50] Credit facilities of this type granted to government officials and military personnel were the order of the day and represented a reservoir of top-up revenue from largely solvent sources for Madrid businesspeople.[51]

Cristóbal Partearroyo formed part of a Madrid-wide credit pyramid. Lending could be carried out as a business activity only if sufficient funds had been amassed beforehand, which could be done only on the strength of proven creditworthiness and business connections. Partearroyo habitually received loans from the Cinco Gremios Mayores or other local entrepreneurs; such loans were in turn secured against the deed of obligation of his own loans to local businesspeople. On 10 May 1754 the Cinco Gremios Mayores de Madrid lent Cristóbal Partearroyo 300,000 *rsv* to be paid back in two instalments over one year. On 7 August 1756 the Madrid merchant Pedro Esteban lent him 300,000 *rsv* and Julián Arozarena 1,000,000 *rsv*.[52] There was hence a chain of loans, mutually securing credit between them. The advantages of collective support were notable, but the system also ran the risk of domino-effect bankruptcies.[53] Partearroyo was in any case one of the keystones of this credit pyramid. The other way of raising finance was by managing collective funds, which offered liquidity and the possibility of granting new loans. Cristóbal Partearroyo had a finger in this pie too, winning himself the appointment as *síndico ecónomo* (bursar) of the influential Convento de San Francisco in Madrid, the Real Monasterio de Señoras Descalzas Franciscanas, and even as *síndico* of the Santos Lugares (Bursar of the Holy Sites) which proffered him the possibility of managing cash deposits, with all the concomitant advantages for a financier. Appointment to the post of *síndico ecónomo* of the Convento de San Francisco de Madrid had been obtained by his father, Francisco Partearroyo, in 1743, appointment as *síndico* of the Real Monasterio de Señoras Descalzas Franciscanas in 1756, and as *síndico* of the Santos Lugares in 1760.[54]

Cristóbal Partearroyo did not rest content with being a kingpin in Madrid's formal and informal credit markets: he spread his feelers much further afield and also sought diversification, looking for productive investments for the financial resources he managed outside Madrid. Here he brought all his influence to bear in order to obtain, for example, leasing rights over the revenues of the Duque de Medinacelli in various Spanish regions, ranging from the Kingdom of Valencia to diverse Castilian and Andalusian enclaves, holding on to these until 1768. Partearroyo's first lease on the revenue of the Duque de Medinacelli in Valencia was for four years, 1755 to 1758, the lease of the Gumiel ward of the Casa de Medinacelli ran from 1759 to 1768, and similarly long leases were attached to other territories such as Calatañazor, Dueñas, Villamizar, Ventosilla, and Sotopalacios.[55] Some of these revenue leases were subsequently subleased, thereby ensuring a safe source of income. These leases also extended to arable land held within *mayorazgos* (primogeniture and entail) of diverse cities or the leasing of the *encomienda* of Marqués de Croix in Aragón. Examples of these would include the four-year lease of the land of the *mayorazgo* founded by Antonio de Luzón in the town of Villaverde, or the lease of two farmsteads and public woodland of Antequera, or the five-year lease of the *encomienda* of Marqués de Croix.[56]

This search for investments outside Madrid probably also reflected a keenness to diversify from the traditional commercial financing business and also to maximize his range of credit, but there is no doubt that it was also part of his professional expansion, without which it is impossible to understand how he managed to plug into the lucrative military supply business. Significantly, most of the revenue in these revenue-farming arrangements was received in kind, mainly grain, an essential victualling ingredient, and even more so in the context of soaring wheat prices at the end of the 1750s.

With his professional expansion Partearroyo's business took on a whole new dimension. His Madrid offices had to cope with information from an increasingly wide network of correspondents, issue hundreds of deeds of empowerment and instructions to the most far-flung places, and regularly pay off the many charges on the leased land or the bills drawn against Partearroyo by his commissioners. His business horizon was shifting but, probably without actually anticipating it, he was building up the necessary wherewithal for taking on the 'stodgy business' of army victualling. Cristóbal Partearroyo now had the creditworthiness for raising financial resources; he ran a wide network of correspondents and also had farming products to place on the market. Army victualling could without any doubt be an excellent way of channelling all these new resources. Madrid's financial barons, moreover, were perfectly aware of just how much Francisco Mendinueta had managed to wheedle out of the state, the continual upping of his asking price, the commercial safeguard of prerogatives and privileges that enabled him to build up parallel business outlets and amass a huge fortune in Spain and the Americas.

At this point of Partearroyo's commercial development, therefore, it should come as no surprise to find him joining forces with another financier, José Florenza, in 1756 to take part in a victualling tender for the troops of the household guard, the only victualling arrangement that had escaped Francisco Mendinueta's grasp. José Florenza was entitled to bid as he wished and sign the military supply-contract in his own name and Partearroyo bound himself to defray it 'with all his property', for the provision of victuals from 1 July 1756 to 31 June 1757.[57] With Florenza he won the victualling military supply-contract for the royal household troop from 1 July 1757 to 31 June 1758, with Partearroyo putting up 120,000 *reales* as surety.[58] Partearroyo's keenness to switch some of his investments to this business was reflected by his stepping-up of land leasing investments in these years and, for example, the creation of a company to make specially designed grain-transporting carts based on a new invention. José Ibáñez y Gasía, from Fuentes Claras in the Kingdom of Aragon, had been granted ten-year manufacturing rights under a *real cédula* of 23 June 1762 for a cart fitted with barrels that he had invented. Cristóbal Partearroyo participated as sleeping partner in the company set up to exploit this privilege-protected invention. Later, in 1763, when Partearroyo was sure to move into the general victualling military supply-contract, his part was bought by José Ibáñez, who remained as principal.[59] Nonetheless, in the following years Partearroyo had to drop out of this military supply-contract in the face of fierce competition. The one big advantage that the provisioning of the troops at court had over any other victualling arrangement was that the contractor always knew beforehand the exact demand and delivery points; this greatly reduced the risk and uncertainty as compared with victualling troops on the move around the whole national territory, cutting down logistics and salary costs. Well-known figures of Madrid finances such as Bernabé Soto, Marcos Manuel Díez, and the Cincos Gremios Mayores locked horns with Florenza and Partearroyo, who were finally ousted from this *asiento* by the Cinco Gremios Mayores in 1759. The first Cinco Gremios Mayores contract was signed by its frontmen Francisco de Soria Zaldiba and Francisco Martínez de Vallejo on 1 August 1759 for the year to 30 July 1760, and was subsequently renewed.[60]

It is therefore understandable that when Madrid's trading community got wind of a change of tenure in Mendinueta's general army victualling military supply-contract and the advent of new French military entrepreneurs, Cristóbal Partearroyo saw his chance. We cannot be sure if it was Cristóbal Partearroyo who sought out the Dughes brothers or vice versa, but however their alliance came about, the French military entrepreneurs secured their bid with Partearroyo's surety rather than turning to the Paris financiers, as had been the previous and declared intention of the Dughes brothers. In early April 1763 Partearroyo and the Dughes brothers privately agreed to begin arrangements for winning this *asiento*. Cristóbal Partearroyo's condition was that the Dughes brothers should furnish a million *reales* guarantee, which would be kept in his house until the end of the military supply-contract. Through the Madrid bill broker, Martín Garate, the Dughes brothers raised the money for the private deposit, which was finally offered to them by the Madrid merchant of French origin, Pedro Larralde. This merchant had strong bonds with the Guipúzkoa and Navarre merchants who collaborated with French merchants in Bayonne.[61] Now only the bidding process remained, which in the end was unchallenged—eloquent testimony of what the rest of the mercantile community thought about what was going on. By the end of May it was all settled and the king granted the five-year victualling contract (1763–8) for the army of Spain, Mallorca, and Garrisons to the Dughes brothers 'and some other partner'.[62]

The following months were extremely busy. Everything had to be got ready by September of that year. According to the Conde de Cesseles, his brothers brought in about 500 French breadmakers 'to teach the Spanish' the new breadmaking and ration-packing technique for the troops. Both brothers, but especially Pablo, began to tour the whole country to check the state of victualling facilities and equipment, stores, ovens, and other support material and make them fit for immediate use, since under the contract they were bound to prepare an initial three-month supply. The reports sent by Pablo to the Marqués de Esquilache allow us to trace his comings and goings; they also reveal key details such as the poor state and insufficiency of the stores in Barcelona, one of the essential hubs of this business, and his growing concern about soaring grain prices and his repeated demands for the crown to step in and curb them; Pablo Dughes also complained about what was, in his judgement, 'excessive troop movements from one place to another'. In the report sent in to Esquilache on 1 July 1763 on the state of the Barcelona bread-baking facilities, Pablo Dughes concluded 'never would I have thought to have found so many defects in such a place as Barcelona'. As for the rise in grain prices, the Dugues brothers directly urged Esquilache to act against 'the rich harvesters and other grain holders keeping back their produce for sale on occasions of greater public need, [and to] force them to sell grain for the troops' current maintenance needs at market prices'.[63] Dughes's activity at this time was truly frenetic; he had to appoint agents and correspondents throughout the whole of Spain, some of them as payback for favours received, such as Juan Guillot in Coruña, who acknowledged some years later that he had been appointed 'at the behest of the Ambassador of France by the general contractors Dughes'.[64] At the same time the Dughes brothers were busy making purchases throughout the whole of Europe and North Africa, almost always through commissioned French merchants, and taking in a wide range of victualling products from canvas sacks in Languedoc to wheat in Algiers or Holland. In the case of Holland, due to its importance as a cereal entrepôt and procurement site, a permanent commissioner was set up there, the French merchant Bernardo Chebardet, who was commissioned 'to go to Holland and make due arrangements for the purchase of wheat from Poland'.[65]

By the end of the summer, according to a later estimate, the Dughes brothers had made purchases worth 6 million *reales*, which were duly defrayed by Cristobal Partearroyo back in Madrid. The Dughes brothers managed to input 4,800,000 *reales* from Pedro Larralde, who in turn pooled this sum from the Madrid trading community against the surety of monthly 1,200,000 *reales* advance payments that the Tesorería General began to pay *asentistas* in October. Negotiating with Royal Exchequer promissory notes was common practice at that time to flesh out credit and boost liquidity. In fact the Dughes brothers, as they subsequently recognized before the inspectors of the Consejo de Hacienda, assigned these *mesadas* to Pedro Larralde and partners on express condition that 'they were given not for cashing but for negotiating therewith'.[66]

Whether because the Dughes brothers did not really enjoy so much international financial back-up as they claimed or because a pretext was needed, Partearroyo did not limit himself to being the brothers' Madrid banker; right from the start he began to organize this same military supply-contract on the side and in his own right. The Dughes brothers' agents, spread about Spain, warned their French bosses that Partearroyo's commissioners were also buying up products for this same provision. Surprisingly, Partearroyo began to set up another network of correspondents, which could hardly remain undercover and in fact soon began to compete with the French commissioners for the same wheat output. Clashes between correspondents soon became much more than one-off confrontations and came to the attention of the *intendentes*, who duly informed Esquilache of this surprising rivalry, 'a struggle that was harming the Royal Service'. Finance Minister Esquilache immediately stepped in. The risks posed by this rivalry were much too great to leave it to be dealt with in the realm of private business. The Marqués summoned Partearroyo and Dughes to the court 'for a friendly alliance', but this came to naught. The Spanish partner soon showed his muscle. Partearroyo by this time knew he could control the military supply-contract single-handedly; it would suffice to reject the bills drafted by Dughes's agents and accept only those of his own commissioners, and he did not hesitate to do so. At the same time he unleashed the rumour, soon to be humming around Madrid, that the Dughes brothers could not meet any of their bills. Esquilache, stunned by events, asked for reports from Salvador Querejazu about what was going on and how the Dughes brothers, the prime contractors of the military supply-contract, were handling themselves. Querejazu's conclusions about what was going on were crystal clear. In Querejazu's opinion the Dughes brothers 'are not poor or financially weakened'—rather the opposite—'but they are unlucky enough not to have been recognised by any trading house in Madrid ... for creditworthiness in said business accounts for as much or even more than funds in hand ... and this creditworthiness works rather in favour of Partearroyo and his team'.[67] Querejazu argued that the problem was that 'Partearroyo and his team' had made capital out Esquilache's readiness to bring the French into the business but then had shouldered them out.

The last act in this veritable 'sabotage' by Partearroyo came from the Tesorería General itself when the Dughes brothers went to collect their November *mesada* and the treasury cashier, Francisco Arcaya, paid them in bills rather than cash, most of them falling due in December. Given their shaky credit and the rumour-fuelled cash flow crisis, this practically signed the Dughes brothers' death warrant as merchants. On the same day of 1 November the Dughes brothers protested to Esquilache about this form of payment, ostensibly only a footnote in dealings with the state and pretty common practice but crucial at their current juncture. It seemed obvious what was going on behind the scenes here. Partearroyo and his team had milked these French businesspeople to break into the business before destroying their creditworthiness and were now using all their influence in the Tesorería General to drive the final nail into their coffin. For the Dughes brothers the problem was not a falling-out between business partners but rather a fully fledged stand-off between French and Spanish financiers. The Dughes brothers wound up their complaints to Esquilache with crystal clarity: 'all this, sir, shows the scant affection we enjoy in this (Spanish) nation'. The treasurer general, Francisco Antonio Ibarrola, on instructions from Esquilache, asked the cashier Azcaya for explanations; the latter replied that paying in the form of bills was indeed common practice and that in any case everyone knew that the 'Frenchmen' were not upright people. Tellingly, he repeatedly used the word 'Frenchmen' to refer to the Dughes brothers. He concluded, rather redundantly in the circumstances but very revealing of the real underlying problem, that these Frenchmen's situation contrasted sharply with that of Partearroyo and Larralde, who were much more solvent and better reputed within the Madrid financial community. He ended, witheringly, 'I only rue having teamed up (as partners) with these Frenchmen and even more so on behalf of poor Partearroyo, and the whole of Madrid thinks likewise.'[68] The judgement of this chief cashier, coming down so clearly on the side of the Spanish, spelt doom for the Dughes brothers: it was not a problem of money but of credit, and 'the whole of Madrid' doubted the Frenchmen's creditworthiness. The market had spoken.

Where credit floundered, talk flourished. Esquilache accepted Partearroyo's claim against the Dughes brothers. It is interesting to note the growing tone of xenophobia with which Partearroyo, in his claim, resorts to the words 'Frenchmen' and 'foreigners' to bring out the full force of the infractions allegedly perpetrated by the prime contractors of the military supply-contract, the Dughes brothers. Among other things, Partearroyo accuses them of 'creating such a regrettable system, with rootless foreigners bearing no known attachments to the kingdom'.[69] The Marqués ordered that the proceedings be dealt with by the Sala de Justicia (Justice Chamber) of the Consejo de Hacienda and be solved 'with preferential treatment over all other cases'. The problem was of the utmost gravity for the state. The Chamber sat the very next day and, according to reports by Marqués de Someruelos to Esquilache, decided that the Dughes brothers should be removed from the military supply-contract in favour of Cristóbal Partearroyo and Pedro Larralde.[70] As the new prime contractors these two would then form the company 'Partearroyo y Larralde' with an initial capital of 1,800,000 *reales*, Partearroyo putting in the lion's share of 1,200,000 *reales* and Larralde chipping in with 600,000 *reales*. Later, in 1768, it came to light that Larralde's capital input also included a 300,000 *reales* participation from the cashier of the Tesorería General,

Francisco Arcaya, who had been so instrumental in undermining the creditworthiness of the Dughes brothers.[71]

The humiliation piled up on the French military entrepreneurs did not stop there. After the military supply-contract had been passed over to Spanish financiers, an order went out for seizure of the Dughes brothers' goods and their own imprisonment, as a precautionary measure until the debts had been paid off. As the assault on them was racked up to new heights, the Frenchmen took refuge in the French ambassador's house in Madrid. What had apparently started out as an internal problem between business partners became from that moment on a diplomatic incident. The French ambassador, well aware of the Spanish financiers' foul play and the xenophobic cast of the whole operation, protested strongly to Esquilache, arguing that this was no economic problem but a political and xenophobic attack. He openly accused the Spanish financial community of setting up the sting and complained of the treatment being received by the Dughes brothers, winding up his diplomatic complaint with a very clear conclusion: 'this has been such a scandal-mongering event that it fosters even in the best disposed a sort of public mistrust of the French businessmen trading in Spain'. He also gave a warning: 'Partearroyo may have funds and credit up to a certain point but he lacks the necessary know-how and contacts for procuring grain from abroad, all this funding and credit will run out within a year.'[72]

The French ambassador was quite right here. Partearroyo and his Spanish partners had exploited the advent of the Dughes brothers as a gilt-edged chance to break into a business that had been monopolized by Mendinueta for two decades. Esquilache had set the scene for the change by opening up the business to competition from the international financial and trading market, but there were some Spanish businesspeople who were not prepared to watch the situation slip back to what it had been a century before. Partearroyo's whole operation, his support, and connivance, even within the Tesorería General, outgunned the Finance Minister himself, who had to admit, almost certainly to fend off the ever-dreaded risk of leaving the troops unsupplied, that it was best to ditch the legitimate holders of the military supply-contract. All the apparent technical improvements that the Frenchmen had brought in and their international contacts counted for naught. The plain fact was that without Spanish support the Frenchmen were scuppered and this turned out to be the overriding factor in the end. The growing xenophobic tone in the criticisms might well have been a rhetorical ploy to widen the differences between the ostensible partners and stoke up rejection of the Dughes brothers, but there is no doubt that it was part and parcel of the Spanish financiers' successful attempt to block the entrance of foreign military entrepreneurs. Finally, the French ambassador's forecast of impending doom for Partearroyo in this business was a shrewd one. What could not have been predicted beforehand was that his fall would not in fact be bound up with his lack of business know-how but rather the rise of a powerful Spanish commercial and financial group, the Cinco Gremios Mayores, who set its sights on the victualling contract as one of the linch-pins of its whole business strategy.

5

Monopolist Entrepreneurs at the State's Service

The Cinco Gremios Mayores (Gremios) were Spain's most important industrial, commercial, and financial group in the second half of the eighteenth century.[1] Armed-forces victualling became one of the richest veins they mined during their business development, standing them in particularly good stead because it offered such a solid base for collaboration with the state. The rock-solid solvency and vast strength of this Madrid company offered Spain's fiscal-military state exactly the mainstay it had been looking for to guarantee one of its most crucial businesses of the second half of the eighteenth century. In return for this guaranteed supply, the state maintained the company's monopoly position and ensured it a privileged position in state business. That the state was ready to pay this price, to secure its victualling supply among other lesser advantages, had already been shown in the past, with Mendinueta. In this case it entered into alliance with a mighty private agent capable of coping with all the demands and urgencies of military provisioning and doing so rapidly and dependably, something that was almost impossible to achieve through the state's own resources and administration. The Gremios represent what we might dub the triumph of the monopolist entrepreneurs, growing up under the aegis of the state and more and more closely knitted into the state's own objectives and interests. The collaboration between the state and the Gremios was based on the mutual advantages that both obtained from this relationship, but the downside was the equally mutual dependency that was thereby built up and the risk of reducing business competition (see Figure 5.1).

The rise of the Gremios into the ranks of state business activity was based on one particular strand of armed-forces victualling: supplying the household guard. From the mid eighteenth century onwards this Madrid business group made the most of its closeness to the royal household in the court. These close bonds with the royal family had been forged by granting loans to members of the royal household. From 1774 to 1788 they granted diverse loans worth 14 million *rsv* between them.[2] Many members of the royal family were thus in debt to the company and found it a valuable source of credit without having to draw on the funds assigned to the royal household by the Royal Exchequer; this obviously brought the company into very close terms with the palace. The company, for its part, shrewdly exploited the change of dynasty to cement loyalty with the new monarchs. The

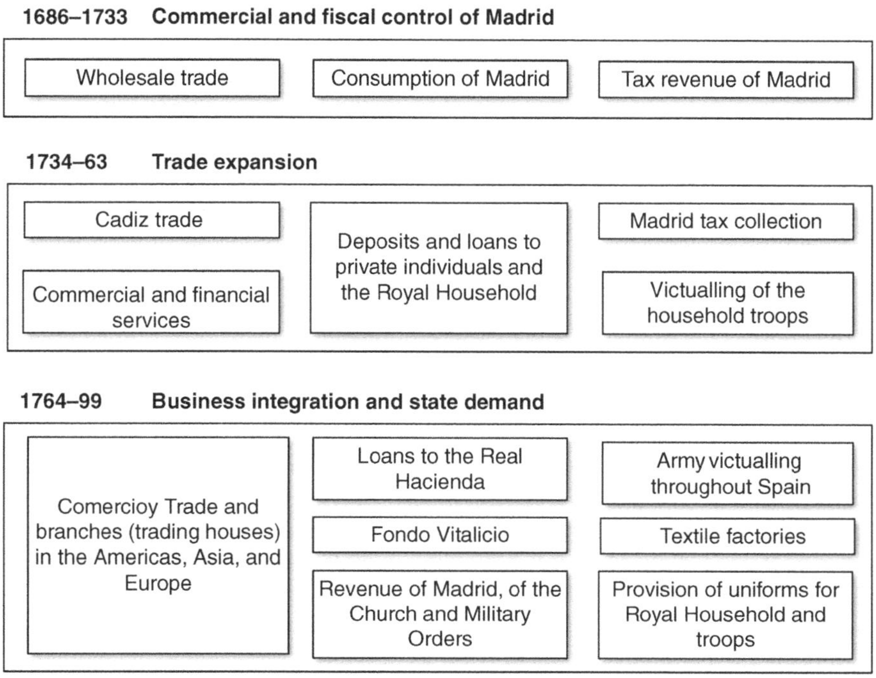

Figure 5.1 The business trajectory of the company Cinco Gremios Mayores
Author's own. Adapted from Miguel Capella and Antonio Matilla, *Los Cinco Gremios Mayores de Madrid* (Madrid: Cámara de Comercio de Madrid, 1957).

company thus played a leading role in the organization and financing of the public demonstrations of support for the new monarchs, starting with the accession to the throne of Ferdinand VI.[3] The company became closer to the throne than any other, a situation that was publicly recognized and highly visible during the reign of Charles III. The graces conceded by Charles III included one of an extraordinary symbolic value: the permission of kissing the king's hand in public ceremonies. This privilege was conceded to the company's representatives 'on the grounds of His Majesty's awareness of the company's ongoing success and zeal in carrying out the important business and commissions of his Royal Service and the public good'.[4] This context of proximity and privileged access to the royal household gave the Gremios a peerless base for offering the monarchs a new service and business that was of particular interest to them.

It was precisely the superior or political condition of the household guard that made the quality of their rations so overridingly important, feeding back into the very characteristics of this business. The authorities' constant concern about the quality of this particular troop's victuals made the government and even the king himself particularly sensitive about how and by whom this provisioning should be handled. The state's preferred option was to leave this victualling arrangement in the hands of the government itself, but the experience of the 1730s and 1740s brought out all the risks in this option. The officials in charge of this provision were, from 1733, Antonio Rubio and, from 1740 to 1743, Manuel García Villalobos.[5] The habitual inability to supply these victuals reliably, on time, and with the required quality was regarded as a serious political problem. During the years when provisioning of the royal household's troops was directly handled by the government these problems worsened. The traditional outlets for buying wheat, barley, and straw used by these public officials were insufficient and it was difficult to widen the trawl; in fact the net was never thrown wider than Castile. Broadening the purchase area would also increase the problems of meeting this particular demand properly. The officials, working from a scattered and patchy supply area, found it well-nigh impossible to respond quickly to any one-off surge in the court's demand for victuals. Any movement of the troops to royal estates or in transit through Madrid threw all these official's arrangements completely out of kilter. The farmers, for their part, were chary about selling their precious harvests to these public functionaries in view of likely payment delays or even outright defaults. The Royal Exchequer's payment inflexibility and its difficulties in shifting money quickly to the payment officials did nothing to lessen this distrust. The upshot was widespread discontent, even from the functionaries themselves who complained about transport difficulties and also about not being able to take proper advantage of seasons where food prices were low, undermining what they called the 'timeliness' of the business.[6] All these problems ended up affecting the volume, quality, and price of the provisions, generating a crescendo of complaints from the commanding officers of the provisioned troops and even from the royal family itself. It was precisely at this latter level where the monarchy's public image came into play and where all the above-mentioned limitations really came to a head, calling for special, individualized treatment by the government.

The poor showing in direct state administration of army victualling, and particularly of what we are here calling the 'household guard', that is, the troops guarding the court and royal estates, prompted the government to go for a private management arrangement. By the 1740s there was in general a clear political preference for wresting the management of the Royal Exchequer's revenue from private hands and bringing it back under state control.[7] Yet in the larger system of army supply, the crown was moving in the reverse direction, and accepting massive privatization. As we have already seen, the first years of the 1740s saw a stream of bids from Spanish businesspeople ready to take on the army victualling business for the state. Finally, in 1743, Mendinueta managed to break down the resistance of Verdes Montenegro and obtain an *asiento* for the whole army barring the household guard. In this general climate of privatizing the whole victualling business, therefore, it was thought equally appropriate to create and maintain a particular victualling contract for the troops guarding the royal family. In 1743 the government accepted the proposal of a Madrid trader and financier, Bernabé de Soto, to take on responsibility for victualling the court and royal estates under a contract. His activity hitherto had centred on tax farming in Badajoz and Murcia. He jumped at this chance of breaking into the military supply business since tax farming seemed to be falling on hard times and this new business could ensure his future. In fact Soto's business strategy was nothing new and had been practised since the War of Succession. But confirmation of this behaviour in other *asientos* and businesspeople would bear out a general desire to offset the losses to business and political influence caused by the state's growing control over its own Royal Exchequer and the consequent decline in royal revenue farming contracts. The military contract could begin to operate as a guarantee or rather as an alternative, loss-compensating business. His business strategy was clear: link both businesses. With the financial aid of Marqués de Villa López, Soto offered the Royal Exchequer a deal whereby payments would be offset between both activities: what Soto owed the crown would be set against what the Royal Exchequer owed him for victual purchases. This strategy turned out to be wise, since it unleashed an upward spiral of crown debt continually offset with new services, while also establishing an image of public service to the crown. The very next year, in his capacity of 'supplier of victuals for the court and royal estates' and to offset the growing state debts under this provision, he asked for leave to increase his salt tax farming business over a much large region, now taking in Murcia, Extremadura, and La Mancha.[8]

The important point is that this acceptance by the crown of private and exclusive management of household-guard victualling sparked off a fierce scramble among several businesspeople to win the business of victualling the court army. The next years were marked by clashes between diverse traders and financiers: Domingo García de Ortega, Eulalia Samper, Martín de Michelena, and José Florenza.[9] These confrontations, tellingly, were stoked up by the crown itself, fostering the competition to keep down the contract price paid by the Royal Exchequer, sometimes even levering it down from one contract to another. The crown did not hesitate to play the traders off against each other to bargain down their service terms: aspects negotiated included the unit price of the bread or barley supplied, the advance payment to be made by the Royal Exchequer to the military entrepreneur, the contract terms, the tax exemptions in the activity or even the possibility of seizing the necessary transport.

It was precisely this significant change in the state's attitude towards the management of military provisions, with a growing confidence in private management, that gave a foothold in this business to the Gremios of Madrid. In 1758 this company tendered for the troop supply-contract in the court and royal estates. To do so it pursued the same tactic as the other military entrepreneurs in the previous decade: undercutting the asking price elsewhere. The unit price of a ration of bread, standing at 16 *mrvs* in the previous contract, was cut to only 11 *mrvs*, while the *fanega* of barley was brought down from 16 to 13 *rsv*. This was tantamount to a 31 per cent reduction in the price of the so-called *pan de munición* and 18.7 per cent in the barley, a notable reduction in the price paid by the Royal Exchequer, especially if compared with the price paid at that moment in other army victualling *asientos* (20 *mrvs* and 20 *rsv* respectively).[10]

The Gremios also offered another condition that was highly favourable to the coffers of the Royal Exchequer: waiving the 300,000 *reales* monthly advance payment made by the crown to the military entrepreneurs against the final account. The Royal Exchequer leapt at this chance to avoid these payments. The Gremios declared themselves satisfied with four-monthly settlements of the goods supplied, the state then paying when it could with no set time limit.[11] There is no doubt that this would have come across to the Royal Exchequer as a very tempting offer.

The obvious question here is why the Gremios were interested in this business. Probably the various factors already mentioned came into the equation: commercial advantages, wooing the favour of the state and royal household, and changes in the government's attitude to its supply policy. Now, however, there was also a notable economic reason. The company's contract bid laid down a condition whereby the state accepted that the Gremios would be given tax exemption on all the transport arrangements for bringing in these supplies: 'free entry … of wheat, flour, barley, straw and firewood necessary for this *asiento*'.[12] This was tantamount to a privileged trading position. The company already controlled the Madrid customs and a sizeable chunk of Madrid's tax revenue too; this new condition meant that it could now add to that package the 'free' entry of goods. This all added up to a veritable carte blanche for transporting goods free of dues round the whole of Spain.

Over and above this economic advantage, the business also had an obvious political kudos, placing the company at the head of a service of crucial importance to the Casa Real. In a business world where many deals were forged in palace halls, as the Gremios themselves had understood in their expansion to the Americas,[13] sticking close to the royal family was a business strategy in its own right. What made the Gremios unique here is that over the following years they realized how to turn this political advantage into a larger strategy for growth and expansion.

By the time Charles III came to the throne in 1759, the Cinco Gremios Mayores had taken over part of the victualling business, but this as yet represented only 15 per cent of the state's total armed-forces victualling expenditure, and there were also other military entrepreneurs in the picture. Upping their share of this business was no easy matter. As we have already seen in other cases, ousting the current key entrepreneur was always tricky. Support from ministers, state debts, and alliances between business interests were all difficult knots to untie.[14] Further leverage was required.

The Gremios exploited a new political and economic development to expand their victualling business. Playing the dual card of business convenience and state service, the Gremios managed to present themselves to the government of Charles III as a sure and dependable way of tackling and solving the hornet's nest of problems created by the Marqués de Esquilache's policy changes. In fact the Gremios came across as the best option for overcoming the disorder sowed in this business by Esquilache's reforms. As we have already seen, the Sicilian minister, himself a military entrepreneur with Carlos de Borbón in Naples, brought sweeping reform to the contracts policy, reshuffling the military entrepreneurs and businesspeople involved; this was one of the many revolutionary transformations introduced or attempted by this minister.

The problems and uncertainty about the form that the military supply system should take was compounded in these years around 1760 by a major farming crisis, which raised the state's dread of a victualling dearth to a new pitch. The crisis was caused by poor harvests together with restricted access to the international grain markets, which had been upset and limited by the Seven Years War, and also by the liberation of the grain trade in Spain, which finally reduced the market and increased prices. Under these circumstances all the military entrepreneurs involved in the armed-forces victualling business were hard put to comply with their contractual obligations and some of them went to the wall.[15] The *asentistas* scoured everywhere for grain, but without success. In Spain, at first, the problem was not so much the price, invariably much higher than the contracted price with the crown, but scarcity and tactical stockpiling. The producers acted with the connivance of local authorities, who preferred to keep back grain for the local population. The problems were even greater abroad, where the military entrepreneurs found it hard to place their orders and no credit was on offer as a substitute for cash payments when losses were being run up on all sides. The result was a rash of bankruptcies, the most important being that of Cristóbal Partearroyo, who did not hesitate to attribute it mainly to the 'free grain trade, which has multiplied purchasers and raised the prices over the original contracted price of the *asiento*'.[16]

In this context of business losses and bankruptcies among victualling military entrepreneurs, the Gremios prospered. Their experience in provisioning the household guard and their growing political influence made them a sure bet to deal with all the ambient uncertainty. The Gremios managed to expand their victualling business because they knew how to exploit the crisis caused by Esquilache's policies and farming prices.

The company itself was in the middle of a transformation process, which laid down the base for its subsequent expansion and acquisition of the whole Spanish army victualling business. At this time the Gremios were increasing their financing sources. The firm found the Madrid lenders market to be increasingly lucrative. Over the previous years the Gremios had built up an important private banking function. They accepted interest-paying private deposits, including a life annuity service: Fondo Vitalicio.[17] They also granted loans to private parties. Madrid was in fact the hub of this market. At first the clients were the habitual court elites, these were soon joined in Madrid by the wealthy families running the livestock farming business. Since the middle of the century Madrid had become the main wool procurement centre for export, and the Gremios met these powerful livestock farmers' demand for loans.[18] The loan clientele soon swelled further to take in the officials posted to America. The increase in administrative control over the American colonies since the middle of the century meant that more officials needed to be posted abroad and most of them took out loans in Madrid before setting out on their voyage, in the hope of making a fortune in the Americas and paying off the loan on their return.[19] The Gremios thus managed to build up a sure and varied portfolio of private financing options. In fact, this banking activity was one of the main criticisms brought against the firm on the grounds that interest-bearing loans could be considered to be usury. The accusation of usury due to the loans and deposits extended to the premium-bearing business of changing *vellón* coins to silver or gold: in Madrid this premium was 1 per cent, while it was 2 per cent in Seville, and 3–4 per cent in Cadiz.[20]

This growing source of private capital enabled it to keep up a service to the crown at a time of widespread losses. According to the *intendente* of Guadalajara, only the 'hefty funds' of the Gremios could explain how this company could buy a *fanega* of barley at 17 *rsv* and then charge the Royal Exchequer 13 *rsv*.[21] Quite the contrary occurred with Cristóbal Partearroyo, who had a funding problem: 'because the funds were withheld in view of the known losses on the current *asiento* prices'.[22]

On the strength of this solid financial base plus a constantly expanding commercial network to service their growth in America,[23] and also exploiting the current juncture of transformation and confusion in the victualling business, the Gremios were able to win the victualling contract for the whole army. As the finance minister, Esquilache pointed out, the state could not afford to show compassion to military entrepreneurs who had run up losses at a time of soaring prices and poor harvests, or for any other reason, 'because the *asentistas* have resources for purchasing in other countries with lower prices and means unknown to the rest, and can moderate some costs, which in times of losses it is not logical for the state to pay'.[24] In the minister's eyes the military entrepreneurs' problems were entirely self-inflicted and the state was duty bound to seek the surest bet—at this time the Gremios.

The Gremios proved him right, turning out to have more loss-mitigating commercial and financial capacity than other military entrepreneurs. In the price crisis of the 1760s only the Gremios were able to support the financial activity of their correspondents, who bought on credit at various points in Spain and Europe, a *sine qua non* of performing the contract properly. The company's network of commissioners took in the whole of Europe and North Africa and its creditworthiness enabled it to buy up sizeable lots of grain in Holland, France, Sicily, and, above all, Morocco. It was precisely this capacity for trading in international markets that gave Gremios a clear edge over other *asentistas* (see Figure 5.2).

The Gremios also managed to draw on their political capital to achieve a regular source of supply. To do so they took over administration of the *excusado*, an ecclesiastical tithe paid partly in kind that became patrimony of the state in 1750. This tax was originally a grace conceded by Pope Pius V to Philip II for help in the fight against the Turks. It consisted in the state's right to receive the ecclesiastical tithe of every parish's biggest taxpayer. This privilege was renewed until it became crown patrimony in 1750.[25] The Royal Exchequer often found it hard to turn this revenue-in-kind into cash. The Gremios got the crown to grant them *asiento*-based administration and collection rights over the Excusado in exchange for a yearly payment of 12 million *rsv*. This sum was more than double the revenue of Madrid and nearly four times the income for victualling the court's army. This was the Gremios' real *pièce de résistance*, securing for the company the privileged future supply of victuals and mustering an extra revenue source with the management of the Excusado tithes, precisely at a time of soaring prices. All this would help to safeguard the success of their victualling business.

The first sign that the crisis was fuelling a change in the Gremios' business and bargaining power came when they managed to twist even Esquilache's arm

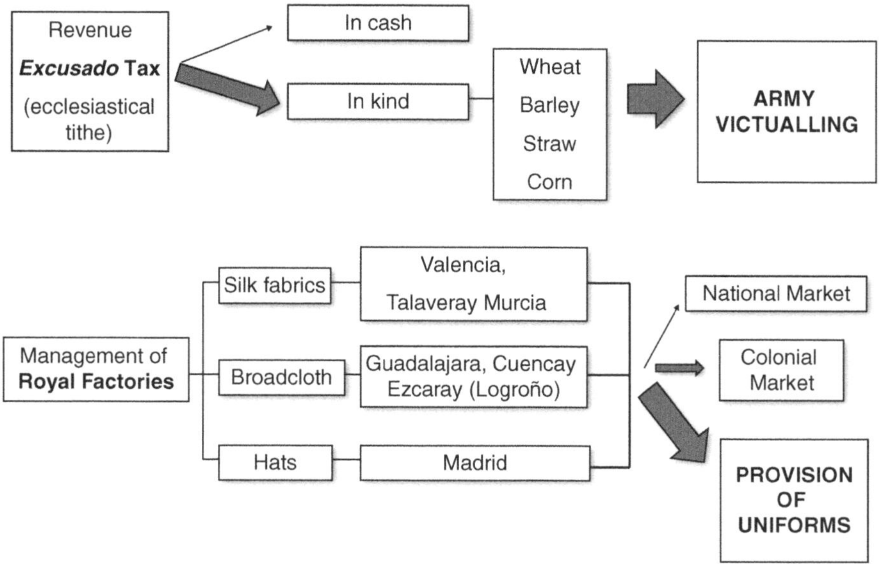

Figure 5.2 The Cinco Gremios Mayores' regular supply sources for its military provisioning business (victuals and uniforms)
Source: Author's own.

and revise the terms of their household guard contract. Although the Finance Minister systematically stood out against demands for protection and compensation for any *asentista*, he seemed, tellingly, to turn a blind eye for the first time in the case of the Gremios' victualling of the court troops. It is not known why this was, whether it was on his own initiative or under influence from the Gremios, or on the grounds that this was a supply arrangement that directly affected the Casa Real, but the fact is that the Gremios were clearly given preferential treatment in comparison to other military entrepreneurs. The Royal Exchequer accepted the company's proposal in 1764 to change the supply management terms. The Gremios got the crown to accept that the provisioning of the troops of the court and royal estates should be defrayed by the Royal Exchequer. This was a measure already taken by Ensenada with Francisco Mendinueta back in 1753, when the Marqués had wanted to take over direct control of victualling arrangements. This initiative failed and he had to turn back to the *asentista* and offer him a private administration arrangement but on the state's 'account'. In the same way in 1764 the company would continue to manage the provision, but all the business costs would be passed on directly to the Royal Exchequer: purchase of perishables, transport hire, insurance, chartering, and breakdowns and losses. Since the company ran the risk of future state payment defaults, the Gremios did not hesitate to remind the Finance Minister that they did so in return for continued favourable treatment: 'with no other advantage than the future offering and protection of Your Excellency (Esquilache)'.[26] Nonetheless, as immediate compensation for the loss of the contract, the Gremios persuaded the Royal Exchequer to grant a sizeable hike of the monthly advance payments: from 300,000 to 500,000 *rsv*. The change in the supply management method seemed to be very favourable to the firm. Judging from the accounts presented in 1767, the final price the Royal Exchequer had to pay the company for the victuals supplied from October 1764 to July 1766 was extremely high: the ration of bread came out at 24 *mrvs* and the *fanega* of barley at 25.4 *rsv*, and in the following two years the final cost for the Real Hacienda was 28 *mrvs* and 27 *rsv* respectively. In the last contract from 1762 to 1764 the fixed prices paid by the Royal Exchequer to the Gremios had been 15 *mrvs* per ration of bread and 13 *rsv* per *fanega* of barley.[27] In other words, by changing the modus operandi the company managed to pass on the cost of the crisis directly to the Royal Exchequer; no other *asentista* in any other type of military supply managed to do likewise.

This situation of privileged growth in a widespread crisis had two main consequences. First, the 1760s crisis had whittled down the competition and the number of bidders. In view of this alarming development, the Finance Ministry ordered the provincial *intendentes* to seek out and encourage businessmen to bid for new provision contracts. Secondly, the strengthened position of the Gremios made them more essential than ever to the crown. Whether or not military provisioning was a good business for the Gremios cannot categorically be established. What does seem to be clear is that the crown needed to turn to the firm more and more from then on. The price it had to pay for this dependence was a upward spiral of new services (such as troop transport, religious services, or purchases abroad), continually strengthening the firm's position in the Spanish business world. The Gremios began to be essential for the state.

The first sign of the new political-economic status reached by the Gremios during the crisis of the 1760s was an enlargement of their victualling contract. In late May 1768 the firm sought and obtained the victualling contract for the whole of Spain's land army. They also retained the victualling *asiento* for the troops of the court and royal estates so this important enlargement spelt control over victualling arrangements for the whole army. The contract terms made it clear that no one else could operate in this business; it even expressly excluded the Royal Exchequer itself, 'so that the whole supply should be our responsibility', as the directors concluded.[28] In other words the company had pulled off a de facto monopoly.

The Gremios victualling business boomed. The cost to the Royal Exchequer of the provisions supplied by them rose from about 4 million to about 24 million *rsv*. The terms and conditions of the contract also changed. The firm's growing negotiating strength emboldened it to ask for a sharp rise in the price of the victuals supplied. The new asking price was 24 *mrvs* per ration of bread and 24 *rsv* per *fanega* of barley, against the 11 *mrvs* and 17 *rsv*, respectively, paid in the last contract of the household guard back in 1760, but still less than the 28 *mrvs* and 27 *rsv* it had cost the state when run by the Gremios on the Royal Exchequer's account. Given the lack of other entrepreneurs to turn to, the crown accepted this new price without hesitation and the whole contract-awarding procedure went through in only ten days. [29]

In this new *asiento*, the Gremios included a condition apparently advantageous to the Royal Exchequer, namely the waiving of the crown's advance payment to the military entrepreneurs against the final settlement. As we have already seen, the Gremios had already used this ploy as a sop to win the victualling contract for the troops of the court and royal estates. This term was now extended to the general victualling contract for the whole army. The Gremios made much of their generosity on this point, stressing that this was done despite 'its having been common practice for *Asentistas* to be paid sizeable advanced sums by the *Tesorería General*'. What the company was really doing here was trading off the advance payment owed to it by the Royal Exchequer under this contract against the monthly payments owed by the firm to the Royal Exchequer on the revenue of Madrid and the Excusado tax. In all, the company ceased to pay the Royal Exchequer a monthly total of 1,413,905 *rsv* (970,833 for the *excusado* revenue and 443,072 for the revenue of Madrid). The implicit threat of this agreement was clearly indicated in the contract itself: should the government decide to take away the Gremios' revenue farming business it would then be bound to compensate the firm by a cash sum tantamount to the monthly advance payment: 'it being a condition hereof that should the two revenues be removed from the current military entrepreneurs, we should then be paid by the *Tesorería General* of Your Excellency the aforementioned 1,413,905 *rsv* in advance on the first of each month'.[30]

Well aware as they were of the chronic financial straits of the Tesorería General, they knew that this condition alone could be enough to dissuade the state from tweaking the agreed terms in any way. During these years the Gremios enjoyed a fluid relation with the treasurers general and had first-hand knowledge of the Tesorería General's bargaining leeway, its liquidity crises, and the possibilities offered by a close collaboration with the treasurers general.[31] The ostensible generosity of the Gremios thus ensured them two sources of income and privilege, both strategic for the ongoing viability of this business.

Another way in which the Gremios exploited this enlargement of the victualling business was to push for a longer contract term. This aspect had long been a tug of war between the government and the military entrepreneurs. The Royal Exchequer preferred to keep their contractors on a short leash, enabling it to keep conditions and prices under regular review and also helping to fend off dependence on a single *asentista*. The businesspeople, on the contrary, preferred to extend the contract term to limit renewal of the state's demands and curb competition from other entrepreneurs, often egged on by the government itself. The Gremios demanded a longer contract and the two parties eventually came to an agreement of three years and four months. This increase in the contract term was potentially crucial for the developing management of the business (see Map 5.1).

Up to then the Gremios had been working to satisfy a localized demand in Madrid and thereabouts, but now the troops might move anywhere throughout the whole empire. The greatest problem was no longer the procurement itself but the subsequent distribution of the product. There was now a need for a network of stores and buildings to deposit the purchases, prepare the victuals, and organize their distribution. Company directors expressly spoke of the need for setting up: 'houses,

Map. 5.1 Royal factories run by the Cinco Gremios Mayores

Source: Author's own. Adapted from AGS, SSH, leg. 640–2.

ovens, stores ... granaries, straw-storage rooms ... and to establish flour-grinding mills and bakehouses in towns and villages'. The necessary outlay for setting up and maintaining all this infrastructure was much more likely to be recouped over a long-term contract. Likewise, this longer term would help to sustain the wide-ranging network of correspondents, factors, and sales staff that the company needed in order to be able to provision the troops wherever they might be sent by the government. This whole network of agents could be sustained by a commission system with small local merchants, a system underpinned by the company's creditworthiness.[32] The Gremios were always keen to increase their correspondents' business turnover because this was the best way of guaranteeing their loyalty and hence the dependability, density, and accessibility of the network of correspondents.

Another incentive that greatly helped to bolster the loyalty of the network of correspondents was the privilege of *fuero militar*; this was usually granted to the contractors by the state, and the Gremios, well aware of its kudos, expressly claimed the right to be able to pass it on to the 'employees in this *Asiento*'. The *fuero militar* meant that the correspondents of the Gremios enjoyed the same status as military personnel, with the same rights, exemptions, and privileges of military jurisdiction. They were hence exempt from paying certain taxes, could opt for military rather than civil jurisdiction, and were also excused militia drafts and troop billeting obligations. Besides the economic incentive this privilege also offered social status and distinction.[33]

Over the following years and in successive contracts the firm kept up the same growth strategy based on monopoly and privilege, and its success was increasingly fuelled by the state's own need and dependency. It should be stressed here that control over victualling arrangements made the Gremios a vital factor in the government's handling of state affairs. In 1769, for example, it was commissioned to supply the German, Swiss, and Belgian settlers brought in by the crown since 1767 to repopulate Andalusia, drawing up a specific contract for this purpose in similar terms to those applying to military provisioning at that time.[34] Similarly, in 1770, the company was asked to organize the provisioning of the garrison of Cadiz,[35] while in 1771 and 1772 it provided provisions for the relief of the Canary Islands.[36] Charles III's governments found a resource of great political value in the Gremios's victualling skills and expertise.

The Gremios handled, with apparent success, not only the enlarged army victualling business but also all these one-off state commissions thrown their way. Everything seems to indicate that the crown's high degree of satisfaction with the firm's services gave it more leverage still for improving the terms of the victualling business. The government saw no problem in giving them privileged treatment to solve any dispute or controversy. Each time contractors ran into any conflict with local authorities, quite a frequent occurrence, the crown tried to weight the settlement in the formers' favour: 'because the *asentistas* have preference as providers of the royal service'.[37] Likewise, the government allowed agents of the Gremios access to the goods confiscated from the suppressed Society of Jesus on the grounds that 'since it is to be defrayed by the Royal Exchequer, the origin of the victuals is irrelevant'.[38]

The Gremios hence managed to build up a monopolistic and clearly privileged position against any other entrepreneurs. The company exploited this cloak of state protection to renew the general victualling contract over the next 15 years. Without varying the terms and conditions agreed in 1768 the Gremios hardly passed on the fall in farm prices during the 1770s. In this 15-year period the price of the bread ration fell only from 24 to 22 *mrvs*. At the same time the company managed to prolong the term of the *asientos*, raising it to five years. This constancy in the possession of the contract and the terms thereof reflect the sheer solidity of the Gremios' position by now. In other words, they were capable of successfully managing the leap from a partial victualling contract to a general one while simultaneously pursuing their own growth strategy.

The absolute control of the Gremios over army victualling arrangements came under attack on only two occasions, the common denominator being that both attacks came from financiers heavily involved in the silver trade. The silver price-spread in Europe and the pressing need for the precious metal in the European trading hubs made silver Spain's main export product and the main factor drawing Europeans to intervene in the Spanish economy.[39] Although it is as yet difficult to prove it outright, there are good reasons for believing that the military victualling contract offered cover for carrying out the silver trade with Europe. The need to make mass purchases in the European victuals market was sufficient reason for the crown to allow these legal exports. The company's correspondents in London, Paris, and Amsterdam could knit together a complex web of military supply purchases and silver shipments. These silver shipments also served in turn to sustain yet another appreciable business: dealing with bills of exchange. The illegal silver leaving Spain to defray victual purchases in Europe stemmed from the Gremios' trading activity in the Americas, where they had shown a marked interest in setting up shop near silver-producing zones. Since the 1760s the Gremios had upped their physical presence in the Americas, setting up their own factories in Veracruz and Arequipa, near the two main silver-producing regions.[40] It would seem to be no coincidence that the country's two main silver exporters, Simón Aragorri and Francisco Cabarrús, should show a sudden interest in army victualling affairs, and ultimately even dare to take on the all-powerful Gremios.

The first attack came from Simón de Aragorri, Marqués de Iranda, who already had experience of the huge advantages offered by the purchase of military supplies in Europe for his real interest: the silver trade. As from 1761, through the offices of Gerónimo Retortillo, he managed to win several supply-contracts for the navy and also the crown's concession for exporting the necessary silver for these procurements, tax free to boot.[41] It was precisely in 1772, however, when some European governments changed the price relation between gold and silver, that Aragorri turned his sights to the Gremios's army victualling contract and suggested to the Finance Ministry that it should be given to him. The Consejo de Hacienda acknowledged that Aragorri 'was a solvent person with sufficient funds for taking on any business', but in the end his proposal for taking over the contract came to naught, partly because the Gremios themselves agreed to undercut the price proposed by Aragorri and partly because the crown preferred the contract to remain in the hands of the Gremios, 'for it is a body worthy of protection for its commercial dealings in Europe and the Indies'.[42] Although the Gremios had to bend a little here, the government once more gave them the traditional privileged treatment in the end.

Even less successful was the next attack, made a decade later by Francisco Cabarrús. This Frenchman's glittering commercial and political career was also bound up with the silver business.[43] His extraordinary capacity for attracting French commercial and financial interest to the silver business enabled him to offer the government financial resources during the war against Great Britain, 1779–83, just at the point when the Gremios had proved incapable of meeting the government's war-swollen needs for credit. The conditions were by now, therefore, very different from those that had prevailed back in 1772 and the government accepted a good deal of Cabarrús's self-serving arguments. These included the skilfully worked and presented suggestion that his main creation, the bank called Banco de San Carlos, should be awarded a combined monopoly over silver exports and army victualling. Ostensibly, exporting silver and managing military supplies were two odd functions for a bank but Cabarrús insisted on the need for blending them with traditional banking activities. His triumph, however, was short-lived. Growing opposition from the country's economic and political elites to the business of Cabarrús, with the Gremios to the fore in this attack,[44] together with the bank's poor handling of the victualling contract, brought Cabarrús crashing down in disgrace in 1788; significantly, the victualling contract was specifically removed from the bank's duties, in the words of the Finance Minister Pedro de Lerena, 'because if it does not renounce this *asiento* the (bank) shareholders will be ruined, while they themselves had no intervention therein or notice thereof'.[45] The clash between Cabarrús and the Gremios clearly shows the need for support from the political powers that be. In any case Cabarrús's 'businesses' and his interest in army victualling lasted less than seven years. It turned out to be only a small blip in the hegemony established by the Gremios.

Despite Cabarrús's defensive arguments that the army victualling contract always turned out to be bad business for anyone handling it, the Gremios ran into fewer problems than did Cabarrús and did not hesitate to take the business back on board when the chance came. In 1790 the government indeed handed the army victualling contract back to the Gremios. Once more they were the banker option. The Gremios, however, took this chance to harden their stance. In some ways they had come out as an even stronger entity from the clash with Cabarrús and were also favoured now by the risky situation caused by the bank's poor management and the debts run up in the victualling business, even though it had been conducted mostly in times of peace. The Gremios took back the contract, but forced the Royal Exchequer to accept that the management should be through state administration this time, that is to say 'defrayed and costed' by the state, 'without being subject to losses', the Gremios holding a 10 per cent commission, and with incorporation of all state military supplies including those of the navy.[46] Cabarrús's mismanagement had taught the Gremios that they could afford to set harsher terms, less risky to them as businesspeople.

This was without doubt a great coup for the Gremios, but it turned out in fact to be a fleeting victory. In 1793 a war broke out that was to cause state bankruptcy and a huge backlog of debts. The Gremios saw all their economic bases quickly crumble away: American trade, silver exporting, and even their victualling sources in Europe. But above all the state itself floundered; Royal Exchequer payment defaults built up and dragged the company down to ruin in few short years. As Cangas Argüelles pointed out: 'the losses caused by the nation's wars from 1793 to 1814 have brought this famous firm down to the woeful state of having to suspend dividend payments to its shareholders'.[47] The return of Gremios to the contract brought out even more clearly their links to the state and their increased bargaining power. Their ostensible triumph was in fact their ruin and they were doomed to perdition by the state's insolvency and ultimate bankruptcy at the beginning of the nineteenth century. From here on in the state's debts with the Gremios could no longer be offset against new privileges or new business opportunities. The monopolist entrepreneur model had had its day. The trouble was that this important economic group's commercial credit leaked away as state debts built up. The decline became irreversible with the cut-off of American trade and dismantling of the credit-underpinning distribution networks between the Americas and Europe.

In short, the Spanish armed-forces victualling business changed over the century in line with the changes in the state's supply policy and, *ipso facto*, in its relations with its economic agents. In this process both the state and the suppliers tried to keep competing financiers and merchants out. The knock-on effects of this business could have benefited the whole economy a form of national capitalism. At first the state tried to manage the business directly but finally opted for trusting in a few, privileged suppliers. It never placed its confidence fully in free competition, preferring to ensure supplies by shoring up the military entrepreneurs and granting them monopoly status. The Bourbons' contractor state proved capable of rolling out a mercantilist supply policy and knitting the victualling expense more firmly into the national economy, but at the same time it ossified this economy by favouring a clique of monopolistic entrepreneurs and making them entirely dependent on its own credit.

In short, the state tended throughout the whole century to shore up the position of monopolist contractors. What is not clear is whether this was simply a product of a supposed absolutist ideology or rather the direct result of its pragmatic attitude, whereby the important point was to ensure dealings were done with a solvent and trustworthy contractor. In truth the problem was no different from those faced in other European countries. As Gordon Bannerman has quite rightly pointed out for the English case: 'The challenge for government was to find an array of contractors suitable for reliably supplying the army in a timely, consistent, and efficient manner.'[48] The difference resided in the chosen solution. Great Britain placed its trust in its pool of entrepreneurs, the state centring its own efforts on the administrative control of these military entrepreneurs and building up trust among contractors by paying them promptly. Spain, on the other hand, preferred to place its trust in an ostensibly solvent business elite rather than free competition and the associated uncertainty. The state did not impose monopoly per se; rather did it sidle into a monopoly arrangement as the best way of ensuring contractor solvency and contract performance. This would explain the strange paradox we have seen throughout the century. In the first half of the eighteenth century the state practised across-the-board absolutist policies and gradually encouraged, with advances and setbacks, the development of monopolist entrepreneurs. In the second half of the century, however, when absolutist policies were giving way to an increasingly free-trade stance, clearly so in the last third of the century, the state nurtured the monopolist solution to meet its demand for military supplies. To this extent the contractor state was not monopolistic per se but became so pragmatically.

PART III

BUILDING THE KING'S SHIPS

6

The Fiscal-Naval State

If army victualling has helped us to understand the relation between Spain's state and its military entrepreneurs, and their growing trend towards monopoly and mutual dependence, the navy side still has to be factored in. The strong eighteenth-century development of navies makes it essential to analyse how Spain's military entrepreneurs rose to the challenge of this arms race. The navy, moreover, offers possibilities of a richer and more varied analysis than the army, due to its intrinsic logistic and operational characteristics. From shipbuilding to hemp supplies, the navy offers up a whole universe of material needs and business possibilities; this makes naval supplies exceedingly complex to manage and control. At the same time, however, the economic effort required for its development makes the state keen to participate actively in its management and control. It is precisely the economic question that places most constraints on the mutual relationships between the state and naval supply entrepreneurs.

When Patrick O'Brien categorized England as a 'fiscal-naval state', he aimed to underline the close bond that existed between the navy and state during the eighteenth century. He argued, notably, that the construction of the British state and the development of Great Britain in the eighteenth century could not be grasped properly without first understanding the nature and intensity of this bond.[1] Nicholas Rodger, likewise, claims that if we wish to get beyond the 'military revolution' debate, then it is essential to understand the British navy as a whole. In his view 'the new concept of the "fiscal-naval state" seems to offer a much more convincing explanation of what really happened than we have yet had available'.[2] For Richard Harding the navy swallowed the lion's share of expenditure precisely because it was the hub around which revolved the most fluid and intense relations between the state and the political and economic elites that underpinned it. A sort of political and economic consensus was built up, guaranteeing that the state would be able to bring in more revenue and spend it mainly on military resources for the navy.[3] This state-society consensus was unique; other European states were hard put to match it. This was partly due to the sheer effort made by the navy itself. But as Roger Morris has recently pointed out, it was also due to the administrative effort made by the state and the active and effective participation of military entrepreneurs in coming up with the necessary naval supplies.[4] That the English navy should grow at such an unequalled rate and act with such an astounding degree of efficiency could be explained only in terms of a collective effort of the state and the military entrepreneurs, not only of the navy and its military capacity.[5]

The fiscal-naval state, as a concept, is no less useful for investigating the Spanish case, helping as it does to explain the nature of navy provisioning problems. The financing of the Spanish navy is not an exclusively economic question; it also differs structurally from army expenditure. At the start of the eighteenth century the traditional control over army finances was wrested from the military and vested instead in the Royal Exchequer.[6] In the navy's case, on the contrary, the changeover in financial control was a much slower process.[7] The idiosyncrasies of naval expenditure, especially the difficulties of forecasting and anticipating it, prompted the state to leave all documentation to do with what became known as 'the navy's money' in the hands of the navy officials. One way of overcoming this difficulty was to unite the state secretariats of finance and the navy in a single ministry, an expedient resorted to on various occasions during the eighteenth century.[8] But the navy and its officials tried at all times to retain a certain independence in terms financial control, giving them in practice a much stronger decision-making position than their army counterparts.

The navy's higher level of autonomy over its own expenditure was confirmed and ratified by Spain's navy financing system. This was a product not only of the administrative changes and thoroughgoing organizational reforms brought in by the Bourbons, but also of the new possibilities offered by Spain's brighter economic prospects and the firm political will to increase participation in the naval defence of the Americas. As the century wore on, the Bourbon state became increasingly aware of the need to increase the size of the navy, the number of seamen, and the fleet's operational capacity.

In the opinion of Olivier Chaline, throughout the eighteenth century there was a selection process at work between those European navies that were capable of projecting their power to far-off territories, and those that restricted their range of operation to regional seas such as the Mediterranean and the Baltic. Spain in particular managed to rank alongside Great Britain and France by this yardstick. Chaline concludes: 'unknown and above all misjudged, the Spanish Bourbons' navy was one of the three main actors of that time'. [9] Proof of this assertion is the naval capability built up by Spain by the end of the century.

In 1796 Spain boasted the world's second biggest fleet: 198 ships, including 76 ships of the line and 51 frigates (Great Britain had 220 ships of the line and France 35).[10] The increase in Spanish naval force throughout the whole eighteenth century called for a parallel financial effort; a specific naval finances management system also had to be set up (see Figure 6.1).

Financial management of the Spanish navy was essentially a question of managing expenditure. The revenue came almost wholly from the Royal Exchequer; throughout the whole century the navy did not establish a particular income source, at least not one that might generate a substantial proportion of its needs. In the case of privateering activity, for example, it was established that a percentage of the profits should be paid into the departmental naval treasuries. In each

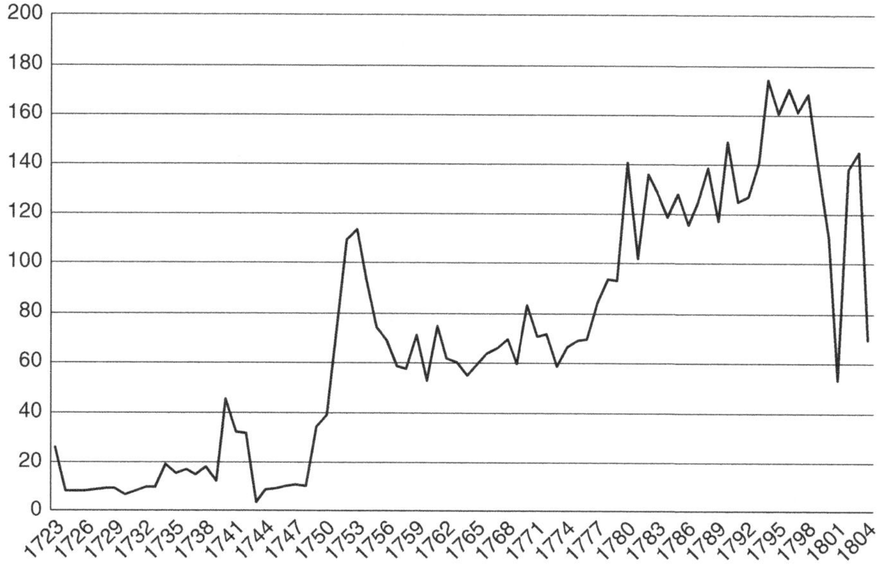

Figure 6.1 Total expenditure on Spain's home navy (millions of *rsv*)
Source: Author's own. Adapted from AMN, MS 471, AGS, DGT, Inv. 16, Guión 24, leg. 49.

of these treasuries a specific fund was set up to meet future expenditure on supplying privateering ships. This revenue became a permanent fund in each naval department, but in none of them did it build up to a substantial source of income, partly because privateering was an activity whose duration was strictly limited by political circumstances. Nonetheless, there were moments when privateering was very profitable, as in the war against Great Britain of 1739, or when any large convoy was captured, such as the British convoy captured by Córdova in 1780.[11] Another source of income outside the navy itself was the sale of supplies and products made in the shipyards. The navy did try to set up factories in the shipyards to produce specified naval supplies, such as rigging, sails, iron fittings, and glass; some of these factories were actually set up, but their output was always low, falling short even of navy needs, so there was seldom any left over for retail. The sale of products made in navy facilities never became a regular and substantial source of income. In fact, there were more chances of raising some income by retailing naval supplies and material thrown out by the navy as unserviceable, obsolete, or in a poor state.[12]

Apart from these income sources the rest of the Spanish navy's finances came from the Royal Exchequer. The critical point here is who determined the necessary level of navy financing in each particular year. In default of any parliament to discuss and approve a navy budget, the determination was made as the result of a complex series of negotiations between the navy and government. What complicated matters here was precisely the fact that their interests were sometimes at loggerheads, due to limited resources or different priorities. Throughout the eighteenth century there was a growing desire among the navy to control its own finances, that is, to determine the level of expenditure and manage the income received from the Royal Exchequer. Acceptance by the government of this pretension of the navy officials would run counter to the Royal Exchequer's overarching ambition to centralize the management of finances. The Bourbon state had been phasing in legislative and institutional changes precisely to boost the Royal Exchequer's control, endowing it with direct administration of tax revenue and a growing level of authority over the management of public money by means of institutions directly supervised by the government, such as the Tesorería General. For the Finance Ministry, which wielded control over the Royal Exchequer, the navy's ambition to achieve greater mastery over its own money bucked the trend of political priorities. The control achieved by the Finance Ministry over the army, whose treasuries were directly supervised by the Finance Minister and Treasurer General, was a feat that told against the navy's constant desire for a greater decision-making capacity.

Such confrontation between the government and the navy over the control of money rumbled on through the whole eighteenth century and even escalated. During the first half of the century the balance seemed to tilt towards the government and the navy had to bow to government impositions. Two main factors contributed to this. First there were various cases of ministers holding the double portfolio of Finance Minister and Navy Minister, such as José Patiño and the Marqués de Ensenada. This was conducive to a certain unity of action and a reduction of naval opposition to the minister's financing decisions. Secondly, the Finance Ministry put an *intendente* at the head of the navy departments and shipyards, who, by definition, reported to the Finance Minister rather than the Navy Minister. Indeed, his title was 'Main Minister of the Royal Exchequer of the Navy'. This coincidence of ministers and their direct control over the head of finances in the navy departments gave the government a much firmer grasp of navy finances.

The tug of war between government and navy flipped over in the second half of the eighteenth century. A succession of new ordinances and a greater degree of specialization and differentiation between the political heads of finances and the navy fostered an increasingly belligerent position by navy officials, enabling them to score notable successes in the direct control of navy finances. This conflict has been traditionally interpreted as navy infighting between navy administrators, the 'pen pushers' on one side and the front-line navy officials, 'the sword wielders', on the other, echoing the French experience both in names and postures. This should, however, be understood as in essence a conflict between the navy and government over the management of navy finances. Indeed, the milestones marking the victories of the navy officials over the government, or the Royal Exchequer, clearly show that the struggle was over management of navy moneys. At first timidly, with the ordinance of Montes in 1748 and the Matrículas de Mar or naval officials registration scheme in 1751, and then more forthrightly as from 1772, with the Ordenanza de Pertrechos, and finally with the ordinances of 1776, the navy's economic system was reshaped to the navy's benefit over the assertions of the Royal Exchequer. The main argument brandished by the navy officials to justify greater control over the navy's money was that it was conducive to greater military and economic efficiency. To achieve this change-over, economic authority was transferred from the *intendentes* to the respective Comandantes Generales de los Departamentos (General Department Commanders). In each navy department the *comandante general* would now govern with a *junta* made up by navy officials, who would now have all responsibility over economic matters. The *intendente* was now to report to the Comandante General and lost all his previous capacity for autonomous action, including the power of appointing his own employees and ministers in local *contadurías* and *tesorerías*. With this reversal of roles, the Finance Ministry lost its main leverage over navy officials (the navy *contadurías, tesoreros,* and *intendentes*), and the government now had to enforce its political priorities at the moment of allocating the funds. The navy's money-management triumph therefore served only to sharpen the century-long navy–state conflict (see Figure 6.2).

Against this background conflict the navy's economic system was built up on two mainstay principles: the main management instrument was the financial consignment granted by the government, and the basic unit of management was the navy department. Later on we will see how expenditure was controlled in the reign of Charles III, but the system was built up during the whole century and

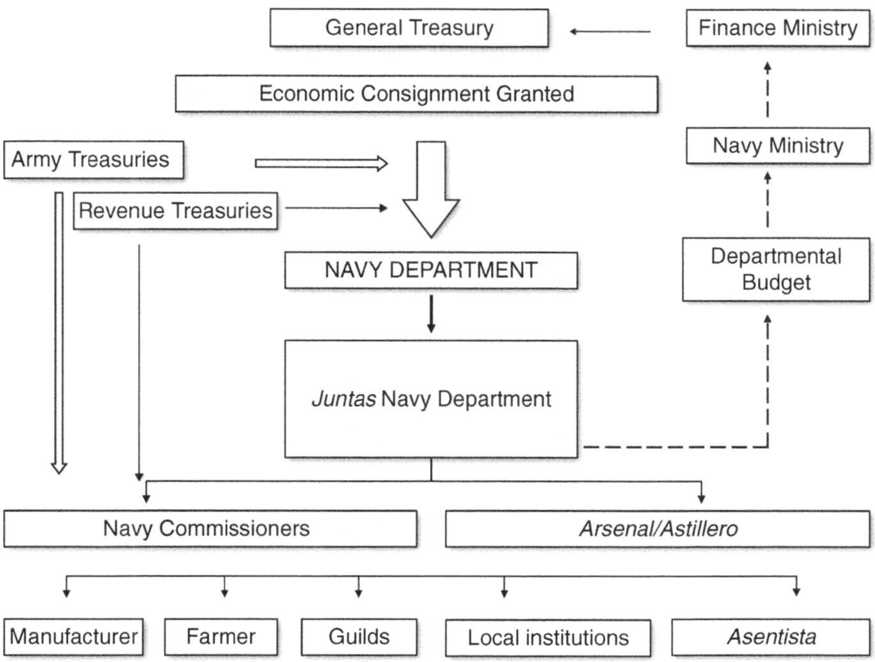

Figure 6.2 The navy's economic system

Source: Author's own.

was perfectly established by the 1770s. In general terms the system was fairly rigid. Each year, before August, the financial heads of the navy department—in the first half of the century, the *intendente* and, in the second half, the *juntas*—established the budget needed for the following year. The departments of Cadiz, Ferrol, and Cartagena, to which Havana was eventually added,[13] sent a budget proposal each year to the Navy Ministry, which discussed and amended it. With the changes ordered by the Navy Ministry it was then sent on to the Finance Ministry for discussion thereof and final approval by the king. Each department went through this procedure separately. Throughout the whole eighteenth century, therefore, the Spanish navy had no single budget, neither was there a single and uniform navy–government negotiation process, but rather a separate process in each department. The idiosyncrasies of each department, especially such features as unequal financing conditions, favoured maintenance of this structure of separate budgets, negotiations, consignments, and departmental autonomy in financial matters. All these factors worked against any unified navy-wide action.

Each department followed the same budget method as the basis for negotiation. This method was based on experience but was sanctioned by the ordinances. The essence of the whole process was to establish needs and expenditure for the following year. To draw up this budget each department had to conduct a complete inspection or review of all stores, buildings, and ships under its jurisdiction. Down the century some headway was made in the unification of information criteria, and increasingly complete and precise forms were established for conducting inventories and reviews. In each ship, for example, a distinction had to be made between all the different types of equipment kept in its particular store, but also those that corresponded to the specified ship but were kept in general depots such as mast and spar stores, sail stores, and the artillery depot. The aim, in this case, was to ascertain exactly how much equipment the ship had and how much it still lacked to be complete and become fully operational. In each case the calculation was adjusted to suit the ship's actual situation, either because it needed a hull, was in commission, was under construction, or in design stage. By adding together the information on crews, equipment and fittings, supplies, and construction work, separate budgets were drawn up and an assessment was made of its cost. To do so, the respective department established the prices they deemed fitting for each product. This freedom of each department to fix the value of operations and the price of products was justified on the grounds of their unequal economic circumstances, prices differing markedly from one region to another. To make matters worse the department authorities had to assign product and service prices over a wide-ranging jurisdiction, that of each navy department. As if that were not enough, the access conditions to naval supplies were also patchy, exacerbating the price differences from one department to another. The labour price, for example, was much cheaper in Ferrol than in Cadiz; wood was dearer in Cartagena than in Ferrol. This inconsistency of prices between departments prompted the government to keep up separate negotiations with each department, but it also hindered any attempt to set up a single nationwide naval budget. Another issue was whether the navy officials were capable of establishing the price of goods and services rigorously in each department. They found it particularly hard to glean up-to-date market information and tended to fall back on inertia, working as close as possible to historical prices. This made it hard to harness any short-term commercial opportunities and also tended to cement the different pricing schemes in each department.

The budgets of each department also had to include those drawn up by the navy ministers for their respective maritime jurisdiction. These were navy officials assigned permanently to sites where navy activity was important, such as ports and harbours or river mouths, or where specific commissions were carried out, such as woodcutting in Navarre or hemp-buying in Aragon or Granada. These navy ministers were also asked to draw up their budgets and forecasts of naval activity in their respective sites and for their respective commissions. The pooling of all this information scattered around the whole country was a complicated task, with many mistakes and accumulated delays. This made it almost impossible for all departments to fulfil their commitment of sending in budgets to Madrid by September of the year preceding the budget year.

Once the respective departmental budgets had reached the Navy Ministry, they were checked and, above all, cross-checked against previous years. Unless there was a clear political order to increase or reduce the number of ships in service or changes in the shipbuilding programme, the main remit of the Navy Ministry was to avoid any major mistakes in calculations, either due to unusual amounts of supplies, crews, or services or excessive prices. To that end, as in the case of the departments themselves, the main control instrument was institutional inertia. The prices and quantities of the proposals sent in were cross-checked against those of previous years before being given the go-ahead. The problem was that this system tended to be rigid and slow, reliant on continuity, and calling for unwieldy checks. The built-in inflexibility and backlogs ran counter to economic efficiency. The naval supplies market could not be effectively managed on a 'just-in-time' basis. As much anticipation of events as possible was essential but this system tended to delay the start of negotiations until it was too late.

The slowness of the departmental-budget system and the unwieldiness of the checks by the Navy Ministry were exacerbated by any unforeseen political events. The departmental authorities themselves often complained of having to budget blind, without any clear political guidelines about the following year's needs. By the time new political guidelines did appear, it was necessary to establish new budgets and reinitiate the whole process. To make matters worse, throughout the century the principle became imposed that no money should be swapped from one remit to another. This meant that after each new political instruction the whole budget had to be revised. The upshot was an overly bureaucratized system, reasonably efficient in times of peace but incapable of acting with any fleet-footedness in times of war.

When the whole departmental budget-checking process was over, almost always initiated a year late, a final consignment proposal was sent up to the Finance Ministry. The negotiation was then carried out between the Navy Ministry and

Finance Ministry. Contrary to what might be expected, the biggest corrections and changes to the departmental budgets were made in the inspections of the Navy Ministry rather than in the final rubber-stamping of the Finance Ministry. In general, Hacienda limited itself to approving the navy department consignment proposals almost verbatim. The Finance Ministry delegated to the Tesorería General the task of establishing the department payment procedure since it had access to all treasuries and revenue of the Royal Exchequer. The Tesoreros Generales could order that the money filtering into the treasuries of the respective royal revenues be sent on to the army treasuries, where it was placed at the disposal of navy treasurers. The authority acquired by the Tesoreros Generales, together with the exact information to hand on the funds of every treasury nationwide, enabled them to coordinate money circulation rapidly and efficiently and also make it available to the navy as expeditiously as possible. The Tesoreros Generales decided in each year and in each case which taxes or treasury they would take the navy's money from, ordering its transfer by the most suitable means, almost always as cash, exploiting the movements of troops or royal ships for that purpose. The option of sending bills of exchange instead of cash was resorted to less, because there were not always merchants and bankers available to deal with them, and also to avoid the interest paid on these credit instruments. In any case the regular habits of financial allocation tended to carve out fixed circulation channels for money over time, creating certain geographical catchment areas from which resources were habitually drawn to provide finance for each respective department, although there were important exceptions to this rule, as will be seen later. In general, the paid the corresponding consignment on a monthly basis, allowing departments to choose the payment site. Every month the Treasurer General sent a list of consignments paid to the Finance Minister to prove to the Navy Minister that the Royal Exchequer had fulfilled its remit, closing the budgetary circle. From this point on the money was available to be spent and managed (Map 6.1).

The need to negotiate the annual consignment tended to instil rigidity into the navy's economic system, but what made it even less flexible was the second factor alluded to above, that is, the principle that the basic management of the navy's money was in the hands of the navy department. The consignment system outlined above meant that separate accounting units had to be maintained. Each department had its own accounting arrangements and acted independently of other departments. Each seaman, ship, and fitting, therefore, was assigned to a particular department and departmental unit. This accounting assignation was maintained even when the money was actually spent in other departments and shipyards. Not even for expeditionary fleets was it jettisoned. At the end of September 1780, for example, the Spanish fleet operating in the Channel had to put into the port of Brest to take on victuals and have various repairs carried out. The Navy Ministry had to organize a complex administrative sleight of hand to provision and maintain the 20 ships of the line and five frigates, their crew and sick, for three months (costed at 6.2 million *reales*). The potential difficulties in sending the necessary equipment and fittings, and especially the million-and-a-half navy rations needed, meant it was considered more expeditious

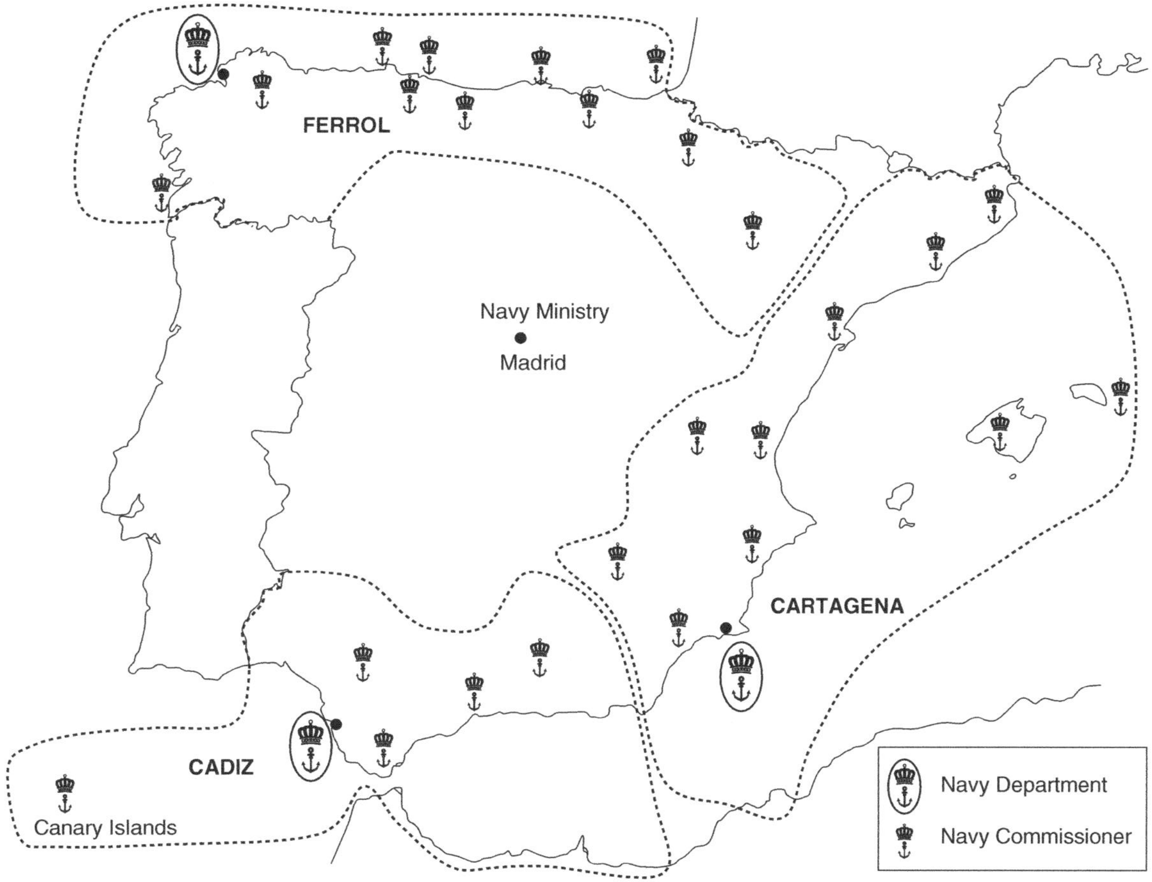

Map 6.1 Geographical jurisdictions of navy departments: navy commissioners of each department
Source: Author's own.

to buy up this wherewithal in the French port itself. The Real Giro of Paris and the Spanish ambassador of Paris were asked to procure and pay for the necessary supplies,[14] even though the whole support operation had ended up in the hands of the Finance Ministry, and the Navy Ministry ordered the Spanish fleet in Brest to maintain the departmental breakdown in the expenditure monitoring of ship and crew 'with the selfsame departmental formalities as are laid down in the shipyard ordinance for distribution within the units they belong to'.[15] Not even on this exceptional occasion was the principle of departmental accounting unity to be broken.

This principle of separate accounting created a plethora of problems. The constant flow of men, money, products, and services from one department or shipyard to another made it almost impossible to maintain. For example, the salaries of those employed in the Cartagena shipyard but sent in 1780 to the siege of Gibraltar had to be paid and recorded for accounting purposes from the department of Cartagena rather than the department of Cadiz where they had been sent prior to expedition. Even more crippling uncertainties then cropped up, such as where to record the cost of the victuals and clothing that were distributed in Gibraltar itself.[16] The confusion was worsened by the continual conveyance of naval supplies between shipyards and departments. Many of the products were procured in each department by means of *asientos* with private merchants but they might then be delivered in other departments or shipyards, where their allocated revenues then accrued. The revenues then had to be discounted from the receiving department, or offset against the consignment it was due to receive, or cleared against the department where the military supply-contract had originally been authorized.[17] To all this must be added the preferences of the *asentistas* themselves, who reacted to any increase in navigation risk by reducing the number of deliveries and avoiding the risk of cabotage. The result of this was a trend for the traffic in supplies to be concentrated in Cadiz, which had the knock-on effect of forcing other departments to offset the customs paid in Cadiz against goods received from there and going on to other ports. As if that were not enough, the financial situation of the three naval departments in Spain was, as will be shown, by no means the same. This meant that cash often had to be sent from one department to another. This was typically a one-off arrangement in urgent situations, but there was nonetheless a regular flow of money passing between the departments. The preferred means of conveyance in these cases was warships plying the route concerned.[18] The principle of department-based accounting was therefore significantly flawed, giving rise to a host of exceptions and irregularities and making it even more difficult to keep accounts separate.

Regional circumstances also ended up overlaying this principle. Not only was there no single naval budget for the whole country, but also there was no a single naval financing method for all departments and shipyards. The biggest difference arose between Havana and the Spanish shipyards and, within the latter, between Cadiz and those of Ferrol and Cartagena. Their particular features must be investigated in turn.

HAVANA

Havana was the main naval base outside Spain, and its shipyard was one of the most active during the whole century. Surprisingly, and as pointed out by Olivier Chaline, international historical studies have tended to underrate the fact that Spain was the only European power that managed to build up 'a true and fully operating shipyard outside Europe, capable not only of repairing but also constructing the navy of Havana'.[19] Its financing model was also the most idiosyncratic.[20] Yet for many reasons, the Spanish navy cannot possibly be understood without taking the Havana shipyard into account. In recent years, moreover, important pieces of research have confirmed the crucial role played by Havana in the development of Spain's eighteenth-century navy.[21]

One of the main events in the finances of the Havana shipyard came in 1748, when the Armada de Barlovento was disbanded and the Veracruz naval base was transferred to Havana.[22] This entailed a concentration of naval services and functions in Havana (naval defence of the Caribbean, protection of precious metal shipments and shipyards) and, consequently, a need for outside financing. From then on there was a reinforcement of the traditional flow of money from the rest of the Americas to Havana for the maintenance of the navy. The Havana shipyard became closely bound up with the development of colonial fiscal possibilities and especially those of Nueva España, which no longer had to finance the Veracruz navy. The second milestone was the relaunching of this shipyard after Havana had been briefly taken by the English. In 1763 the Intendencia de Marina (Navy Intendancy) was set up with the idea of reviving Havana's shipbuilding activity;[23] in 1765 the two navy treasuries that had existed hitherto, one for shipbuilding and another for coastguard and fleet maintenance,[24] were unified. The Navy Ministry thereby assured Havana a regular financing source.

Until 1772 control of the navy's money in the Cuban port had been regulated by an instruction of 1766, the purpose of which had been to set up a double entry accounting (*cuenta y razón*) system in the navy treasury. Subsequent orders laid down the obligation for a funding statement to be sent monthly to the Navy Ministry, accounting for income and outgoings made by the treasury and supervised by the Havana *contaduría*, following the same accounting procedure as Spanish departments.[25] This system tells us that slightly less than one-third of the navy's expenditure went towards payment of the wages of sailors of the Havana squadron; the rest was spent on the shipyard and maintenance of naval action in the Caribbean. As well as the ships of the main squadron, Havana also kept up a fleet of smaller vessels (*ganguiles*, two-sailed fishing boats similar to tartanes; pontoons; *lanchas*; *lanchones*, small and large port tugboats; feluccas) which were used for shipyard tasks to do with commercial ships, and, above all, for carrying wood. One of Havana's main advantages was Cuba's wood resources; the woods of Alquisar, Casigua, Matanzas, and Cayo supported a brisk activity in woodcutting, hauling, and conveyance.[26]

Havana also had to finance other model-changing expenditure items. As the main stop-over port between Spain and the Americas, it was forced to keep a good number of naval supplies for fitting out and repairing the ships stopping there, both military ships and merchantmen. Many of the goods stockpiled there could not be obtained on the island of Cuba itself and had to be brought in from abroad. Some of them were material naval supplies such as rigging or iron fittings,[27] but others were victuals. Havana also ran up a high foodstuff deficit and had to be regularly supplied from abroad. Flour, *menestra*, and meat were vital purchases for the Havana shipyard.[28] The most important in terms of volume was flour. It had traditionally been sent mainly from Veracruz; from the 1770s onwards, however, this source was gradually replaced by flour from the United States.[29] These purchases had a direct effect on navy expenditure since they formed part of the ordinary budget charged against Veracruz's financial contribution, which was no longer sent on to Havana (see Map 6.2).[30]

In the Havana shipyard the navy had to cope with unusually high hospital costs. Its status as a stop-over port after long sea voyages meant it often had to deal with sick and weakened crews. There were also the damaging health effects of the move from Europe to the Caribbean, with new diseases and contagions that became one of the main problems for the European expeditionary forces arriving in the Americas.[31] This inherent problem was exacerbated by war, as in the summer of 1780 when Solano's 12,000-strong expedition arrived in Havana. Another particular trait in Havana's expenditure model was the very low pension obligation. As a transit port it must have attracted mainly working-age sailors and few retirees would have stayed on to live in Cuba. Havana's pension expenditure was hardly one-tenth of that of any Spanish department at this time. In other words, the retirement cost of sailors, invalids, and widows was defrayed almost entirely by other navy departments. Likewise, Havana's rate for *asignaciones* was also very low: this term referred to the money that the navy officials ordered to be discounted from their wage for subsistence of their family for as long as their service lasted.[32] In navy departments in mainland Spain the cost of these *asignaciones* to relatives of onboard sailors could almost double the total pension cost; in Havana, however, they were not even recorded in accounts. In any case there is no doubt that Havana's expenditure on the sustenance of the 'other navy', comprising retired sailors and their relatives, was far less than that of the departments back in Spain.

Lastly, Havana also had to defray the navy's expenditure in other places. It regularly had to meet the cost of coastguards operating from their base on the island of Trinidad. The maintenance cost of this fleet was modest (*c.*300,000 *rsv*) and it had been achieving excellent results in the fight against contraband since it was set up in 1722.[33] Havana also had to help defray the increasingly frequent passage of ships and fleets through Cartagena de Indias. Studies to hand show that the military expenditure on garrisons and fortifications on that coastline left hardly anything for naval expenditure.[34] Everything suggests that this naval expenditure was bound up above all with the transfer of regiments from Spain. During the war, furthermore, it also had to cater for the passage of French ships and help out in their maintenance and the purchasing of victuals and beasts of burden on their behalf.[35]

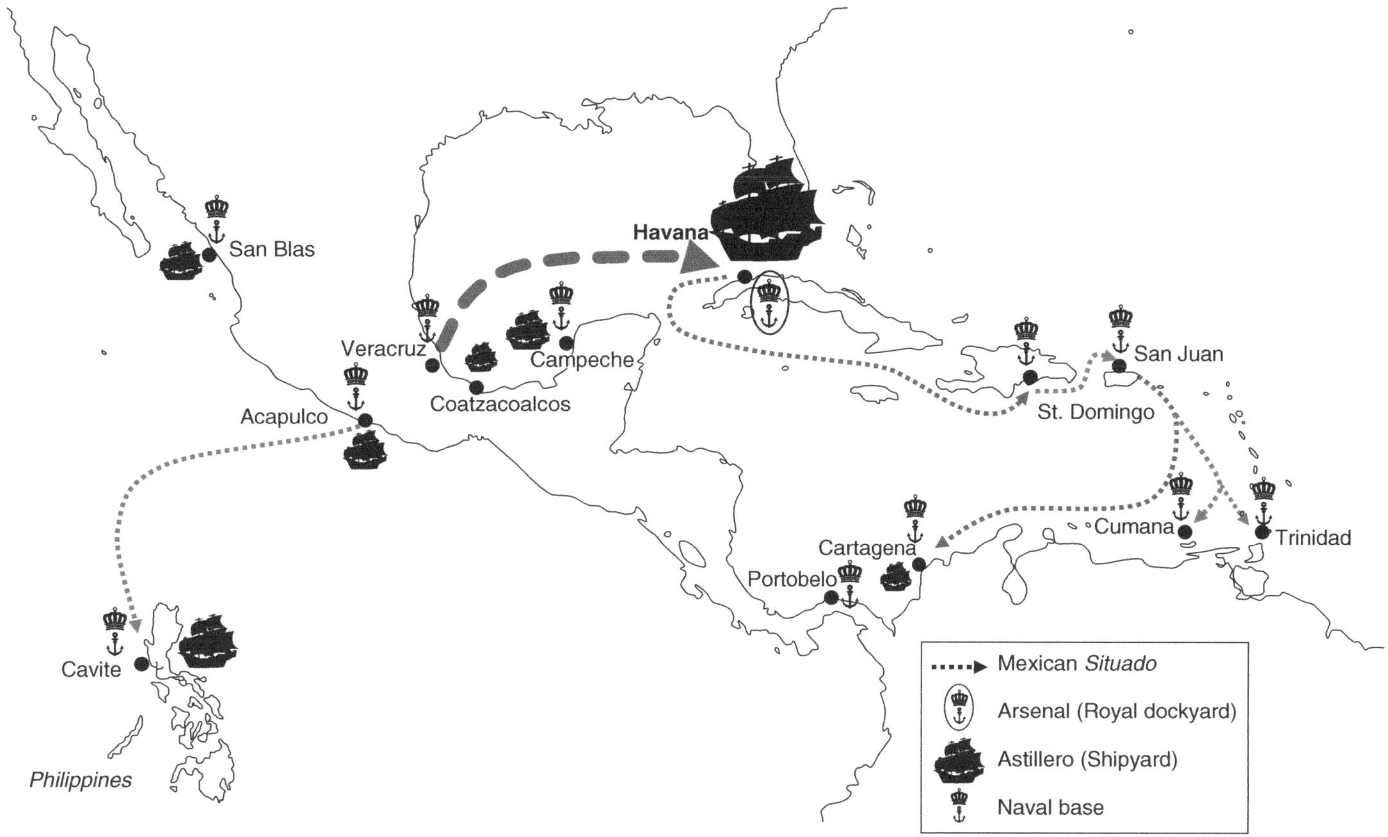

Map. 6.2 Navy bases, naval construction, and money remittances in the Caribbean in the eighteenth century

Source: Author's own. Adapted from Carlos Martínez Shaw and Marina Alfonso Mola, 'Los astilleros de la América colonial', *Historia general de América Latina* 3 (1999), 279–304. Carlos Marichal and Johanna Graffenstein, eds, *El secreto del Imperio español: los situados coloniales en el siglo XVIII* (México: El Colegio de México-Instituto Mora, 2012), 30. NB the pictogram size reflects the output.

To finance this expenditure the navy could tap into several income sources. All this made the navy financing model in Havana very different from the navy departments back in Spain. The main financing source was the flow of funds from Nueva España, known as the *situado*. From its very origin this particular funding arrangement had always been tied up with the maintenance of naval forces in the Caribbean, whether for the fight against pirates or the upkeep of the Armada de Barlovento. This model for consigning royal revenue to sustain military activity was not unique, and there were various *situado* arrangements throughout the Americas. What made the Mexican *situado* special was its notable growth during the eighteenth century. The Mexican mining boom and fiscal reforms in Nueva España midway through the century fuelled a big increase in income and prompted the Madrid government to harness the growing *situado* fund in many new ways. Since 1744 the Mexican *situado* had been annually financing the armed forces in Cuba, the navy and the purchase of tobacco to be sent to Spain. Although historians differ over the amount sent, everything seems to suggest there was a notable increase in remittances. According to Carlos Marichal, for example, in the 1750s the Mexican Cajas Reales sent 500,000 pesos a year. After Havana was regained, the naval reconstruction efforts called for an increase of the Mexican *situado* to 700,000 *pesos fuertes* in 1768, though even larger sums were sent on some discrete occasions.[36] During the war the remittances from Veracruz to Havana continued to grow, because Nueva España revenue was the lifeblood for the diverse expeditions organized in Havana; it also buoyed up the whole war effort in the Caribbean.[37] According to the figures of Johanna Grafenstein, from 1779 to 1784 the navy received from the Mexican *situado* slightly over 10 million *pesos fuertes* (200 million *rsv*). Nearly a third of the Nueva España input was spent directly on the navy, although there is also some evidence to suggest that other supplies of victuals, gunpowder, and even soldiers sent to the army and strongholds of the Caribbean also provided useful support for the Havana navy and its ongoing activity.[38] To this must be added the contributions from private merchants for the construction of two warships in Havana, which were never included within navy expenditure.[39] (See Table 6.1.)

Private financing was another source of income accessed by the navy in Havana. This recourse was sometimes also taken up by the domestic Spanish naval departments, but never to the same extent as in Havana. At home, private financing was sought only in cases of extreme urgency and nearly always, barring the case of Cadiz, with scant success. In Cuba, on the other hand, it became a regular and habitual navy financing recourse. This was due mainly to the financial possibilities on offer in the Cuban port, but it was also a widely used financing model in the whole of the Americas. In fact the model was also present elsewhere in Europe and was based on the idea that state money could serve as an incentive to private finances.[40] Merchants and financiers were ready to work with the state, to advance their capital and service capacity, always providing there was a firm guarantee of reimbursement. Some studies have shown that private financing of military expenditure was routine in the Americas. As Juan Marchena has shown, Cartagena de India merchants were interested in lending sums to the crown to meet its military needs against the surety

Table 6.1 Cash inputs used by the Real Armada in Havana, February 1778 to May 1783

Income	*rsv*	%
Situado	93,849,780	66.0
Private loans	29,140,100	20.5
Others	15,979,120	11.2
Sales	1,778,620	1.3
Currency exchange	1,404,280	1.0
Revenue	142,151,900	100
Expenditure	152,364,060	
Annual mean income	56,860,760	
Annual mean expenditure	60,945,624	

Note: Counting 34 months out of 55.
Source: AGS, Marina, legs 591, 592.

of future silver consignments. Merchants and financiers had a twofold interest in this activity: on the one hand the interest they could earn and, on the other, future access to silver currency, boosting their bargaining powers and building future profits on currency exchange.[41] There is evidence suggesting that this mutual interest between public finances and private financing was widely shared by American local elites in other spheres of state action.[42]

The Havana navy could therefore benefit from Cuban merchants' keenness to finance it. The *estados de caudales* (cash statements) sent monthly by the Havana *junta* to the Navy Ministry give us a good idea of the dimensions of this financing method. These show that about 20 per cent of the navy's funds in Cuba came from private sources. Private loans were commonly taken up. Nearly every month Havana's navy treasury received some loan input. The rate of these private loans, in comparison to the *situado*, suggests they were used as a top-up when the *situado* fell short of its needs. In the summer of 1780, for example, with the arrival of Solano's squadron in Havana, and without any increase in the *situado*, almost the entire navy treasury's income came from private loans. The sources give little information on the purpose of these loans but it can be safely assumed that they were used for financing the navy. In January 1779, for example, Havana's Contaduría de Marina informed that 'several individuals' had loaned 320,000 *reales de plata fuerte* plus 465,456 *reales de 'menuda'*, 'to defray urgent needs for the Navy until such time as it should be provided with new funds to pay it back'.[43] We do not know who the lenders were. On only a few occasions is any hint given about their identity: 'the bakers' guild' or 'the *regidor* Don Gabriel Peñalver y Cardenas, by way of a loan'. Some sort of indication was given that the funds used to pay back the loan would come from Veracruz or Nueva España. Or, coming to the same thing, the *situado* served as loan surety, guaranteeing moreover that it would be paid back in *pesos de plata fuerte*.

The Havana navy treasury itself took part in the money-exchange merry-go-round of Cuban businesspeople. Routinely, the navy treasury converted private parties' *plata macuquina* (hammered silver coinage of lower, or *menudo*, value) into *pesos fuertes* at a premium or interest rate ranging from 3 to 5 per cent, according to the instructions of the navy treasury.[44] The strong demand for silver within Cuba's trading community made the purchase of these *pesos fuertes* from the navy an attractive prospect and the navy itself needed the exchange currency for defraying the costs of many activities and salaries inside and outside the shipyard. The problem was that war, during which currency exchange revenue plunged, could wreak havoc with the navy treasury's exchange activity.[45] It was probably the build-up of urgent needs for the navy and the existing obligations for the repayment of loans that made the navy treasury loath to part with any *peso fuerte* that entered its coffers.

Lastly, another factor that set Havana's financing apart from that of the domestic Spanish shipyards was the revenue accruing from the retailing of navy supplies and goods. Back in Spain the sale of navy property involved mainly waste or unserviceable material; in Havana there seemed to be a clearer demand for useful shipbuilding goods. The list of naval supplies bears this out: 'wood, hawsers, cables, tar, artillery and other items furnished to various individuals from the stores of the royal shipyard'.[46]

Havana's financing model, therefore, was different from the navy departments back on the mainland of Spain. Havana depended on the *situado* for its financing but also tapped into the resources offered by its status as a commercial port and Cuban businesspeople's interest in any deal involving the navy's money as trade-off. Private loans, sales of merchandise, or currency exchange enabled the Havana naval treasury to top up its income by one-third and meet its needs when the *situado* did not arrive.

SPANISH NAVY DEPARTMENTS: CADIZ, FERROL, AND CARTAGENA

The financing arrangements of the three navy departments in mainland Spain, Cadiz, Ferrol, and Cartagena, were different from Havana's. First, their finances depended on the consignment system and, secondly, their regional circumstances were completely different. Factors such as creditworthiness, the scale and characteristics of the commercial activity, the presence of businesspeople, the availability of transport and communications, and the circulation of information all led to glaring differences in the financing arrangements of each navy department.

Cadiz was not Spain's biggest shipyard (Ferrol was) but it was the department with the best financing facilities and ended up as the most important. Several coincident factors conspired to make Cadiz the main naval base from a financial point of view. First, Cadiz benefited from the shift, throughout the eighteenth century, in the state's patterns of expenditure from Catalonia to Andalusia. During the first half of the century Catalonia accounted for the main deployment of armed forces, armies and navies, largely due to the deliberate policy of increasing central state control over Catalonia after the War of the Spanish Succession, and the use of Catalonia as the jumping-off point for Spanish military ventures in Italy.[47] During the second half of the century the reinforcement of the Atlantic strategy and the dwindling importance of European commitments tended to accelerate a shift in military expenditure to Andalusia. The upshot was that the Bourbon state ended up concentrating the bulk of its financial resources in the Lower Guadalquivir where expenditure needs were greatest. As the century wore on, the state therefore had an increasing number of reasons for concentrating fiscal and financial resources in Andalusian treasuries, from which it could meet the demands of the shipyard and all the activities organized from Cadiz. Secondly, Cadiz, as the capital of the navy department, also benefited from commercial expansion during the eighteenth century, especially after the Seven Years War with the commercial and public-finance reforms of the Americas. The Bourbon state channelled America's growing and regular revenue towards expenditure in Andalusia and above all the Contaduría de Marina of Cadiz. The treasury in Cadiz that received this American revenue, the Depositaría de Indias, remained at the disposal of the Finance Ministry and Tesorería General, and, through the latter, the navy department of Cadiz.[48] To this income the Royal Exchequer added the revenue streaming in from the rest of Andalusia and the city of Cadiz itself. As a result this *depositaría* became Spain's most important military treasury and the main financing source of the department and the Cadiz shipyard. Together with the army treasury of Andalusia, the second most important, it was the main treasury financing the navy department of Cadiz.

This greater availability of economic resources in the royal treasuries around Cadiz was matched by a higher level of naval activity in the department of Cadiz. As the war in the Atlantic progressively took priority over Mediterranean concerns and the Gibraltar blockade turned into a structural problem, naval activity in Cadiz picked up pace. This led to a higher concentration of ships and reception of naval supplies in the Bay of Cadiz, reinforcing this department's position in Spain's naval strategy.[49] Cadiz became the main departure point for maritime expeditions, especially after the Seven Years War,[50] partly because the possession of a greater resource mobilization capacity for any expedition helped to keep up a game of bluff and double-guessing about its purpose and destination. Such a red herring was deployed in the expedition to win back Minorca in 1780. At the same time the Cadiz shipyard acted as the main supplier of America's naval bases and shipyards.[51] Both factors had the effect of increasing expenditure, especially extraordinary expenditure. In other words, Cadiz was the navy department that boasted the strongest financing potential and the best chances of the Finance Ministry fulfilling the consignment commitment made with the Navy Ministry. It was also the department with the best chance of being able to increase expenditure rapidly to meet unforeseen circumstances. The upshot was that Cadiz, like no other department, had to cope with frequent and heavy borrowing needs and also had to seek new means of sustaining naval credit. Any payment defaults in Cadiz had more impact on the navy's operational capacity than elsewhere, precisely because it was here where most ships and supplies were concentrated. Failure to pay an *asentista* in Cadiz could become a serious problem for the navy, while in Cartagena or Ferrol it was an issue that could be cleared up by sending along the military entrepreneur to receive payment directly from the Tesorería General in Madrid (see Figure 6.3).

If the finances of Cadiz did not collapse it was precisely because one of the features that most differentiated it from the other departmental capitals was its fluid interactions with private business for the provision of naval services. The keeping up of large-scale, long-distance trading activity called for a wide variety of civil business. Ship construction and repair, fitting out, supplies, stores, specialist workers, information, and insurance companies and credit instruments constituted an active business world that the naval forces at Cadiz could draw on and exploit as in no other part of Spain.[52] The coexistence of all these factors sets it apart from the rest but it is also a crucial factor for understanding the central role eventually played by Cadiz within the navy as a whole. It was precisely this concurrence and collaboration with a private business world that historians have stressed as one of the main factors in the strength and success of the British navy.[53]

Cadiz offered the main advantage of a much more fluid commercial traffic than the other mainland departments. In Ferrol and Cartagena the lack of transport ships was a constant headache and, in times of war, a serious hindrance, whereas in Cadiz such services were always available, provided by a host of ships flying allied or neutral flags. This transportation advantage emboldened some Cadiz

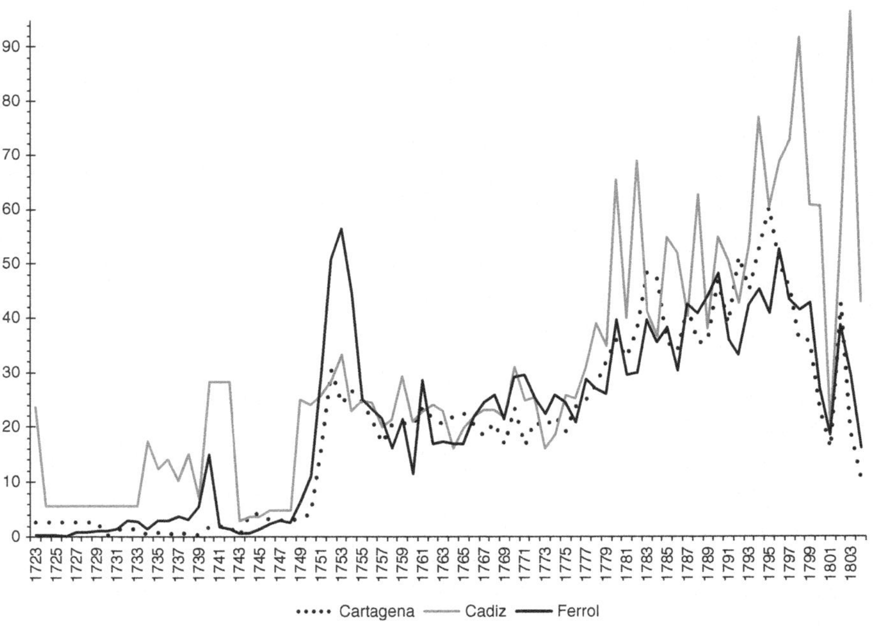

Figure 6.3 Total consignments paid by the Tesorería General to the three navy departments of mainland Spain (millions of *rsv*).

Source: Author's own. Adapted from AMN, MS 471, AGS, DGT, Inv. 16, Guión 24, leg. 49.

merchants to offer merchandise to the *junta*, even on credit and outside the *asientos* signed by the *junta* and approved by the Navy Ministry. This intervention of private merchants was especially important at times of war, when habitual suppliers were hard pressed to meet their contracted commitments. Although this aspect has not yet been studied, it would seem that, as on the River Thames, private business with the navy was a way of offsetting the loss of activity due to the closure of markets and the risks and increasing costs of navigation.[54] The attraction of *asientos* was key for such a bustling city as Cadiz. Any *asiento* auction there always attracted far more bidders than in other departments. Even a minor *asiento* such as the provision of lime for the 'Nueva Población' of Carraca attracted 14 bidders at the second time of asking.[55] This interest of the commercial world in navy business gave a real edge to the Cadiz navy department over the other departments.[56]

The existence of a core of major merchants in Cadiz offered the navy an invaluable source of maritime resources. What made this possibility really exceptional was the fact that many of these businesspeople were international merchants, trading in distant markets and backed up by excellent creditworthiness. Cadiz took up loans from entrepreneurs more often than any other navy department of mainland Spain. The navy *intendente* insisted that the navy always had to have money in the Cadiz treasury not only to deal with the many cases of expenditure that arose but also to guarantee credit for seeking loans from the Cadiz market, due to 'the importance of good faith in terms of finding these loans whenever needed'.[57] Cadiz, therefore, like no other department, could purchase supplies without cash down and at no specific interest rate, always providing there was a guarantee of future payment, and this depended on consignments guaranteed by the state.

Another particular feature that boosted Cadiz's adeptness in finding extraordinary financing outlets was easier access under better terms to credit instruments. Unlike the other departments, Cadiz could afford to accept or endorse bills of exchange or *vales reales*. This advantage was even exploited by the Finance Ministry, which, to pay national *asentistas*, offered them the sole option of collecting the payment directly in Cadiz.[58] Cartagena and Ferrol found it extremely difficult to bring in the use of *vales reales*, while Cadiz was able to convert this paper into cash and pay off part of its debts, with lower discounts even than Madrid.[59] The prospect of an inflow of funds from the Indies brought discount rates down instantly and the navy's credit back into balance. This situation contrasts sharply with that of Spain's biggest shipyard, Ferrol, which, according to the stocktaking in early 1784, did not hold a single *vale real* in its navy treasury.[60]

Cadiz's navy department, therefore, benefited from sounder financing bases, home as it was to the two main treasuries of the Royal Exchequer (Depositaría de Indias y Rentas and the military treasury of Andalusia) and backed up by the commercial activity and creditworthiness of big businesspeople to ensure the supply of naval wherewithal and credit for meeting payments. The problem was that this very financial advantage was accompanied by a higher concentration of naval forces and activity in the Bay of Cadiz. It is a moot point whether it was this financial advantage itself that skewed naval affairs towards Cadiz, but the result was that by the end of the eighteenth century, Cadiz was the only department capable of maintaining the navy.

The departments of Ferrol and Cartagena had fewer financing options, mainly because commerce and credit options were thinner on the ground.[61] Both Ferrol and Cartagena depended entirely for their income on the royal revenue assigned by the Royal Exchequer from bordering regions. The Tesoreros Generales organized the money transfers from the royal revenue treasuries to army treasuries, where it was made available to navy treasurers for the corresponding month of the approved consignment. Problems cropped up when there were any extraordinary expenses to meet, or when payments had to be made in a place other than the military treasuries. Both in Ferrol and in Cartagena the navy had few chances of turning to any other financing sources and hardly any possibility of raising credit from private parties. The limited trade in their ports stunted the size of the merchants' businesses and *ipso facto* the possibilities of furnishing the navy with products or services on credit. In the case of Ferrol, where the core of merchants was smaller and trading activity scarce,[62] the Royal Exchequer even had problems in transferring money by means of bills of exchange. Often, the only way of shoring up the finances of the shipyards of Ferrol and Cartagena was for the Royal Exchequer to make extraordinary financial remittances overland from neighbouring regions or by ship from Cadiz. Under these conditions the only *asentistas* and businessmen who came forward to work with the navy were strictly local in scope. They refused to accept any other form of payment than cash and in the shipyard itself, and it was not without difficulty that the navy managed to knit together wide-ranging credit and supply markets, an essential requirement for any mobilization of naval resources. Involvement in the *asiento* was therefore a parochial business, almost entirely linked up to staple goods, and any navy payment defaults could have devastating social and economic repercussions.[63] The biggest financing problems always cropped up in Ferrol, and that was where the most drastic remedy was adopted of paying national *asentistas* for the provision of such essential naval supplies as wood, tar, and hemp directly in Madrid and by the Tesorería General. The decision to take away this business from any potential Ferrol *asentistas* hemmed in their business options even further and stymied any chances of building up a more active financial and commercial market that might have helped to lessen the grave financial dependence of this department.

In conclusion, the ostensible organic unity imposed on the Spanish navy by the Bourbons during the eighteenth century cloaks the absence of any unique and national financing model. The navy–government tussle over the control of money prevented any definitive political solution and favoured the continuation of a naval financing system based on financing by departments. The basic element of navy financing and pecuniary management during the whole century was the navy department, a situation that the budgeting and consignment system helped to perpetuate. The Bourbon's navy financing system lacked the necessary flexibility for meeting naval demand. Regional circumstances imposed different financing models on each department and hindered implementation of any coordinated resource- and expenditure-management policy. In 1781 one Navy Minister, Marqués de Castejón, made the following boast about the Spanish navy: 'A navy the like of which is not to be seen in Europe, which can spend less or more promptly and flexibly, and meets and solves urgent needs of action and stockpiling in Europe and the Americas; neither is there any other part of the national economy that is better regulated.'[64] This fulsome praise in fact overlooked an excessively rigid financing system that was very hard to coordinate, just the opposite of what any navy organized on a war-footing really needed and running counter to what the British navy was doing at that time. The navy's control of the money and its managerial cost-cutting efforts tended to hard-wire inflexibility into the whole system, including the mobilization of naval supplies.

7
The Paradigm of State Intervention

A NAVY UPON WHICH THE SUN STILL DID NOT SET

At the beginning of the eighteenth century Spain's navy was in a critical condition, but remained operational day to day. Despite the growing list of military disasters since the mid seventeenth century, the empire handed on by Charles II to Philip V was still a global network upon which 'the sun never set'. Despite the dearth of resources, the navy continued to underpin part of the imperial defence. Historians, in fact, have recently been changing their positions about Spain's supposed exhaustion at the end of the seventeenth century.[1] Christopher Storrs, for example, has shown that Charles II's wide-ranging and well-oiled diplomatic network could still raise allies to assist with its naval commitments by emphasizing the growing French threat in Europe. In the final decades of the seventeenth century, Spain was able to muster Anglo-Dutch allied squadrons to help enforce its political will. The Spanish contribution to these joint operations was by no means negligible and could even account for the lion's share, as in 1692, when Spain's war fleet against Genoa pooled 17 warships, 19 galleys, and 3 fire-ships.[2]

Spain also summoned up the bogeyman of European rivalry to encourage shipbuilding at home. In the decade of 1610–19 Spain's shipyards turned out 32,000 tons of warships, then plunging to lower than 3,000 tons by 1650–9. From then on the trend turned clearly upwards, reaching almost 10,000 tons by the very next decade.[3] Although there are no figures to hand for the following years, everything suggests the recovery continued. It was precisely the alliances with Great Britain and, above all, Holland that expedited the transfer of shipbuilders to Spain, especially to the north of the country. It was there, on the Cantabrian coast, where shipbuilding in private shipyards revived strongly from 1650. Successive *asientos* were signed with the state for the construction and maintenance of warships: in 1662 a contract was signed with Pedro de Agüero for the construction of four ships of the line in the Guarnizo shipyard and another in 1676 with José de Iriarte for four ships of the line in the Colindres shipyard.[4] The main spur to this activity was the growing demand for ships for the Indies trade,[5] and the consequent need to provide naval protection for the Atlantic route. A stream of navy contracts for construction of over 20 galleons and warships fuelled a sharp increase in naval production capacity in the ports and beaches of Cantabria, Biscay, and Guipuzkoa.[6] The build-up of orders, both public and private, enabled these shipyards to cope even with the rapid increase in ship sizes. By 1681 large ships of the line were already being built; the 90-gun *Nuestra Señora de la Concepción,* for example, weighed 1,300 tons, while the 80-gun *Santísima Trinidad,* weighing in at 1,665 tons, broke the record. The resurgent navy seemed to have few problems in terms of technical knowledge or shipbuilding facilities;[7] neither was there any shortage of local businesspeople. The main problem seemed rather to be financial, with frequent payment defaults by the Royal Exchequer. The solution adopted was to grant privileges to shipbuilders and contractors, such as American trade permits or slave-trading rights.

The revitalization of shipbuilding in this final stage of the seventeenth century was performed partly at the cost of American output. Shipbuilding activity in the colonial territories was brisker than had traditionally been thought.[8] Colonial shipyards were capable of providing the necessary warships for protecting trade within the Americas, the essential routes between Mexico and Peru plus the overseas Philippine route, while also defending the coastline. But these remits grew with the American manufacture of large-tonnage ships for the Indies Run, known as *galeones de plata,* that is, the galleons charged with the mission of protecting the trade on the outward leg and then sending back the remittances of silver.[9] The main reason for this increase in American naval output was availability of naval supplies. The Americas and the Philippines between them ensured an excellent supply of wood, especially the West Indies, and also served as a viable fall-back option for tar, rigging, sailcloth, and copper, all in sufficient quantity to guarantee continued production of ships. The second reason was the creation of the Armada de Barlovento in 1635, with the special remit of Caribbean defence (the Caribbean was the most conflict-ridden zone and also of greatest strategic interest in terms of trade and communications with Spain), which served as a constant spur to American shipbuilding.[10] The Antillean shipyards of Havana and Campeche were able to meet the demands of this permanent squadron. This success was based on royal protection of the Caribbean naval industry as a whole: in 1638 Antillean ships were granted the same privileges as those built in Spain, and the shipbuilding industry there was given its own financing arrangements, the *avería* (a commercial tax) and the *situado.* The contributions of Mexico and Cartagena de Indias were enough to sustain the construction and maintenance of this navy.[11] Likewise, in the Pacific area, another navy spurred shipbuilding activities. The Armada del Mar del Sur created in 1570, was sustained exclusively with ships built in the shipyards of Guayaquil and Realejos. Its main purpose was to defend communications and merchant convoys between Peru and Panama; its finance came mainly from Peru, with sporadic contributions from Lima merchants with vested interests in keeping this armed force in operation. The most active shipyard was Guayaquil, employing 467 workers in 1690 and turning out several large ships of the line weighing over 1,500 tons, plus heavy artillery all the way up to 42-pounders, but many technical problems cropped up. In the Pacific shipyards, unlike those of the Antilles y Cantabria, shipbuilding was directly managed by the state; only one ship of the line, the *San Diego*, was built by *asiento*.[12] The monarchy's set of shipyards was completed with the creation in the Bay of Manila of the Cavite yard, which benefited from the 1679 ban on building galleons outside the Philippines; this meant that all galleons and warships maintaining the lines of communication with Mexico henceforth had to be built in the Philippines.

All of which shows not only that the Spanish navy was a strong and continuous presence in the late seventeenth century, but also had the capacity for expansion. The decadence of the European empire did not prevent efforts to boost Spain's own shipbuilding facilities, rather than depending exclusively on the purchase of warships from aboard or the adaptation of merchant ships for military use. During the second half of the seventeenth century a large shipbuilding zone had been created in the Cantabrian ports, with majority participation by local entrepreneurs and constructors. Even while this political cycle was drawing to its end, Spain also managed to graft the American contribution onto the shipbuilding effort. The Caribbean and the Pacific not only boasted their own permanent navies but could also set up shipyards and act independently to facilitate the production of naval supplies. The key to America's shipbuilding participation lay in the availability of its own financing arrangements and the participation of local magnates. Without any doubt Charles II's navy was not the navy of Philip II, but neither was it inconsequential; there was a real potential for regeneration.

THE WAR OF THE SPANISH SUCCESSION AND THE COLLAPSE OF THE NAVY

During the reign of the first Spanish Bourbon, Philip V (1700–46), the Spanish navy once more became an important naval force on the world stage, ranking third behind England and France. This naval resurgence has traditionally been explained as a consequence of the administrative and political reorganization of the Bourbon state.[13] The new ruler and his government applied to the navy the principles of uniformity, centralization, and intervention, ostensibly characteristic of their state, a state described as absolute and inspired by its new French ally. According to the classic reading this naval resurgence was the immediate product of the state's administrative expansion, of its political construction. The real picture may be more complex, and the causes may not have been exclusively administrative. Of the 110 ships of the line added to the *Real* Spanish Royal Navy during Philip V's reign, 12 were bought elsewhere in Europe and the rest were built in Spanish territory.[14] In other words, Spain proved able to fuel its naval resurgence by its own shipbuilding; this was without doubt a notable mercantilist feat. The interesting point here, however, is that only 10 of these 110 ships of the line were built in state shipyards and by means of direct state *administración*; the rest of the ships came from the private sector, built by entrepreneurs under contracts or bought from private individuals. By means of these private arrangements, Spain's shipyards provided 51 ships of the line and America's 34. There is therefore no doubt that the navy's resurgence was driven also by military entrepreneurs, and with an imperial input. To some extent the administrative changes brought in by Philip V's government tapped into the shipbuilding potential realized in the previous reign (see Figure 7.1).

It was not the legacy received from Charles II but the Spanish War of Succession that paralysed shipbuilding in Spain during the first decades of Philip V's government. From 1700 to 1713 the navy built only four ships of the line and three frigates. The paucity of this output can best be gauged from seeing this in terms of the number of cannons on the ships brought into the Spanish Royal Navy throughout the whole century, regardless of type and source. Using this yardstick is an effective way to reflect the larger development of warship construction. Later in the discussion the types of ship being built will also be considered. The cannons referred to in Figure 7.1 represent the number established by the navy itself for each new ship built and delivered. This list includes all ships considered to be of the Spanish Royal Navy, giving an overview and sidestepping the tricky problem of the precise terminology of each type of ship. It is true that within the same type of ship there was also a development in the number of cannons throughout the century, but it is preferable to maintain the single, shared criterion of the number of cannons regardless of type. Frigates, for example, ranged from 20 to 40 guns, but there were also smaller designs of ships, such as xebecks, which could

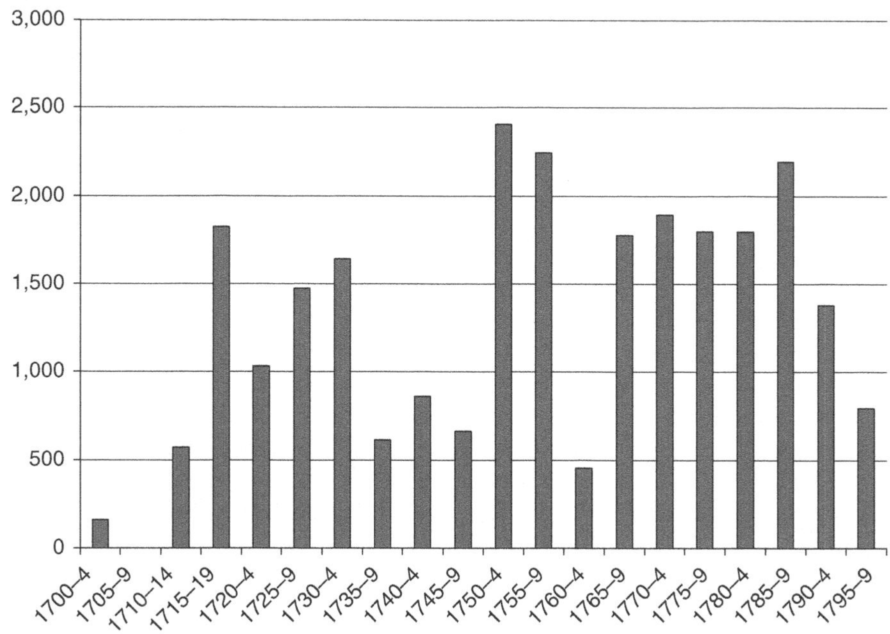

Figure 7.1 Number of cannons in the ships brought into the Armada Real

Source: Author's own. Adapted from: MS 471, AMN; Buques de la Armada, MS 8770, BN; and MS 2215, 12–17, AMN, and MS Almirante Vigodet, 'Relación de los navíos que formaron parte de la Armada Española, desde principios del siglo XVIII', in Gervasio de Artiñaño, *La Arquitectura naval española (en madera): Bosquejo de sus condiciones y rasgos de su evolución* (Madrid: Ateneo, 1914), 346–66.

carry over 30 cannons, hulks with 40 cannons, or corvettes with 20. So this first yardstick, counting the numbers of cannons, gives us an overview of Spain's total naval output capacity, not least because very few foreign ships were purchased at this time. Of the 610 warships brought into the Spanish Royal Navy from 1700 to 1799, only 69, or 11.3 per cent, were bought abroad. During the eighteenth century the total number of cannon mounted on warships grew on average by 256 guns each year. In Philip V's reign the average hit a century-long low, with 181 cannons a year. During the War of the Spanish Succession (1700–13) in particular, the yearly rate hit the rock-bottom figure of only 17 cannons.

The main reason for this drastic slowdown is that the Spanish navy did not have the wherewithal to continue shipbuilding; most resources had been siphoned off to defray the costly land wars. Projects such as those of Tinajero in 1712, for building ten 60-gun ships of the line by *asiento* in the shipyards of Cantabria and Havana, or Bergeyck's in 1713 for building another six 60-gun ships of the line in Basque shipyards, had to be shelved due to the costs of maintaining the siege of Barcelona.[15] Furthermore, the navy suffered severe losses from allied fleets, keenly targeting the colonial trading routes. Of the 99 ships lost in these years, 21 were warships.[16] One of the heaviest losses was suffered in 1702 in Vigo, where over 20 vessels were lost and the Armada de la Mar Océano almost disappeared.[17] Intense Spanish and French privateering activity[18] did not manage to shrug off the Anglo-Dutch fleet's stranglehold on Spanish coasts, choking off coastal traffic and even the movement of Spanish warships. Two ships of the line recently built in Guipuzkoa were captured in 1704 on their first voyage to Cadiz.[19] This paralysis of naval communications almost dried up naval supplies, further thwarting any attempt to renew construction. At the same time non-stop English and Dutch attacks on Spain's Atlantic fleet had the immediate effect of limiting trade and the circulation of American revenue, while also hindering movements of shipbuilding supplies between Spain and the colonies and also within the Caribbean itself. The 1705 launching of a ship of the line in Campeche was a banner event, reflecting the difficulty of keeping shipbuilding activities alive at this time.[20]

The collapse of the Spanish Royal Navy during the War of the Spanish Succession and the difficulties in renewing shipbuilding activities increased Spain's reliance on the naval support of its new French ally, seeking its own vested interests in the trade-off benefits of this collaboration. During the first decade of the eighteenth century French warships met the naval needs of Philip V's government, including the escorting of the Indies fleet. France's self-interested support and Philip V's financial straits tended to reinforce the general paralysis of shipbuilding, as in 1705 with the cancellation of the 20-frigate project for protecting trade with the Americas and the assignment of escort tasks to French ships instead.[21] Naval collaboration with France was so close that the French ministry even mooted the possibility of building ships of the line in France, in exchange for trading permits with the Americas.[22] Luckily for the Spanish navy, Louis XIV's financial crisis prompted him to withdraw military and naval support from his grandson Philip V and strengthened the hand of those in Spain who stood out against excessive French influence.[23] These developments were all conducive to a more independent naval policy.

The War of the Spanish Succession thus exacerbated shipbuilding problems almost to the point of deadlock. Neither did the return of peace in 1713 mean a return to pre-war shipbuilding activity, partly due to the conflict on the Catalan front lingering for another year. But the biggest problem for shipbuilding was the urgency. The navy was obviously severely weakened and political opinion had switched in favour of ending the French input. There was also a growing interest in restoring Spain to a position of diplomatic influence, and therefore rebuilding military power, especially as the political conflicts in Italy grew more intense. The immediate solution was to turn to international warship markets instead of relying on national production. From 1714 to 1717 the navy acquired 28 ships (12 ships of the line, 12 frigates, and 4 gunboats), a total of 1,074 cannons. Of these ships, 14 were bought from European markets, mainly in Italy, and another 4 bought from private individuals and incorporated into the navy as warships. This means that 64 per cent of the first great wave of naval reconstruction was fuelled by ships built outside Spain, cold-shouldering Spanish shipbuilders and entrepreneurs. A paltry ten ships were built in Spain (six ships of the line and four frigates), all by *asientos* with entrepreneurs; these were built in the shipyards of Havana and San Feliu de Guixols and, above all, Guarnizo, which produced four of these ships of the line. Several conclusions can be drawn from this. First, the state's reaction, both in form and intensity, was driven by urgency. As Allan Kuethe has pointed out, actual military or sabre-rattling activities determined the Bourbons' political decisions.[24] In this case the state did not set up any long-term, state-production policy in naval construction. It simply applied a pragmatic, short-term policy of acquiring the ships it needed as quickly as possible. Secondly, the priority given to purchases abroad rather than at home spells out the actual limits of an ostensibly mercantilist approach. In this case there was no attempt to harness naval demand for stimulating industrial production or even for serving the interests of any group of businesspeople. This wave of naval demand did not even stimulate the development of a naval supplies industry, partly because it had been seriously damaged during the war[25] but also because the state accepted that most naval supplies came from foreign markets, with Holland to the fore.[26] Thirdly, the appeal to national producers and entrepreneurs was made by means of the selfsame arrangement as before the war, that is, by way of *asientos* with military contractors and in the shipyards of Cantabria and Havana. To some extent the pressing urgency of naval reconstruction and the solution of turning to foreign markets prolonged the limitations from which shipbuilding had been suffering since 1700, forestalling any modification of the relationship between the state and naval entrepreneurs established in the times of Charles II.

ADMINISTRATIVE REORGANIZATION AND DIRECT SHIPYARD CONSTRUCTION

The shipbuilding model did not change substantially in the following years but there were important administrative changes, which had a mid-term, knock-on effect on shipbuilding opportunities and the participation of entrepreneurs.

Philip V executed a thoroughgoing administrative overhaul of the Spanish navy.[27] The reforms affected all aspects of naval management; their common denominator was an attempt at administrative centralization and unification. The diverse squadrons and fleets operating all around the empire were unified, together with their administrative structures.[28] At the cusp of this unification stood a minister established in 1717, the Intendente General de Marina (General Navy Intendant) who became the Navy Minister.[29] Unification of the Spanish Royal Navy enabled the whole naval procedure, from shipbuilding to operating the ships at sea, to be directed from the government and financed directly by the Spanish Royal Exchequer. From now on there would be only one arbiter, the Navy Minister, to establish and coordinate the state's naval needs. This facilitated the establishment of a true naval policy and, *ipso facto*, the possibility of standardizing shipbuilding designs and the terms and conditions imposed on builders and suppliers. Hereafter ships and naval supplies would not be so limited by regional constraints or the preferences of local authorities. It would be the Navy Ministry that would enforce technical and quality demands and characteristics. This is important because historians have traditionally taken it for granted that this enforcement of uniform standards of quality could be achieved only by way of direct state construction. This turns out to be false, both in other countries[30] and in Spain itself. As we will see later the state had no problem with enforcing its own contract terms or across-the-board quality standards. Drastically reduced were the previously large numbers of regional constraints on shipbuilding. Earlier, the state's naval needs had been largely hemmed in by regional possibilities, not only in terms of the availability of naval supplies but also of constructors, workers, entrepreneurs, creditworthiness, design capacity, and experience. Ironically, the only ships built by direct *administración* in Charles II's reign, those produced in the Guayaquil shipyard, were the most 'original', those most different from the rest of the ships built in the other parts of the empire, precisely because the construction process, in default of any standardized rules, was determined by local conditions. Designs, quality, and conditions were therefore all rather *sui generis*, and the results in fact turned out to be very disappointing.[31] From then on the regional influence was gradually overridden by the naval policy of the Navy Ministry.

Together with the administrative unification of the navy, there was another factor that impinged heavily on the future of Spain's navy, that is, the resurgence of Cadiz as a first-ranking naval centre. From the 1680s onwards there was a progressive transfer of naval affairs from Seville to Cadiz, culminating in 1717 with the transfer to Cadiz of the Casa de Contratación and the creation there of the Intendencia General de Marina.[32] The change of city represented much more than a mere geographical shift. The resiting of the main base of the merchant and warfare fleet of colonial trade sought to redefine the relations that had hitherto been woven between the state and the country's main business group, revolving around the colonial trading monopoly. Seville's colonial-trade businesspeople had managed to turn the Hapsburgs' dire financial straits to their own account, converting the state's pressing needs into a fountainhead of privileges and political influence, which they then harnessed to control the trading monopoly, the *Casa de*

Contratación, and even the fiscal policies of colonial trade.[33] The growing power of Seville's businesspeople gave them a stranglehold over naval policy, since the state was forced to turn to these entrepreneurs' financial and organizational capacity to cater for the naval defence of the Indies fleet. Their influence came to affect such fundamental questions as navy financing arrangements, naval equipment, the training of shipmasters and officers, and even ship design. Iván Valdez-Bubnov, for example, has shown how the Seville clique stood out against any increase in tonnage for the ships sailing to the Americas because it would hinder their navigation up the River Guadalquivir.[34] Under these circumstances the switch to Cadiz was highly expedient for the state, giving it the chance to adjust its relations with the country's main group of businesspeople. The state could now seek out new loyalties and spread its authority further afield, a considerable boon for any new dynasty but especially one whose legitimacy was questioned worldwide.[35] For Philip V the Cadiz option was a prime political stratagem that favoured its very survival and also profoundly affected its capacity to modify naval policy.

After the Cadiz move, further confirmation of this new state-driven relational framework came with the creation of the Intendencia General de Marina in the same year as the transfer of the Casa de Contratación, and unification of posts within both institutions. Indeed, the Intendente, as the main person responsible for the material organization of the navy, was at the same time president of the institution in charge of organizing colonial trade. Philip V's government was thereby merging naval policy and imperial policy. This represented a remarkable fusing of the different lines of government to serve a single interest. The link between them was twofold. First it was based on the need to fund the navy with colonial revenue by means of the Depositaría de Indias. In practice this was tantamount to ensuring that it would be the Royal Exchequer and not colonial trade and its related power groups that could determine the level of naval financing. Secondly, it represented an acknowledgement that the navy was the overriding strategic priority, meaning the Atlantic and the defence of colonial trade; this sharpened the need for a political organization of both spaces. For Philip V's government a logical concomitant of observing these two principles was keeping the Navy Ministry linked to the Secretaría de Indias in the same ministry, a union that was maintained almost without variation until 1776.[36] This ministerial union had important repercussions on the naval construction policy because it could expedite exchanges and develop complementary synergies in the shipbuilding process.

The physical representation of this administration unification and strengthening of Cadiz came with the 1717 Order for creating the *arsenal real* (royal shipyard) of La Carraca in Cadiz.[37] Shipyards in Spain were broken down into *astillero* (general shipyard) and *arsenal* (fully fledged state-run shipyard for naval warships and armaments), loosely comparable to the British distinction between merchant yard and royal dockyard. In Spain the two were distinguished by scale and functions. The *astillero* could be a temporary construction and its main objective was to harness the advantages of access to naval supplies or specialist labour; the *arsenal* arose as a permanent naval base with the object of ship maintenance and construction, based on possession of all types of naval supplies plus all the facilities, factories, and stores needed for the complete management of warships.[38] The *arsenal* was conceived as an authentic industrial complex, including shipyard, slipway, dykes, furnaces, and factories of all kinds. This approach was new in Spain, although the French inspiration was obvious. Its design and management was at all times subject to the state's desire to intervene directly in shipbuilding. The *arsenal* implied, in principle, complete state control of all shipbuilding affairs, extending also to naval supplies, since the state had to guarantee their production, preservation, and storage. The *arsenal* was, in short, the main lever for increasing direct *administración* and it was in theory off-limits to military entrepreneurs, the state's traditional recourse elsewhere.

Nonetheless, the sheer scale of the *arsenal* construction project acted as a constraint on the efficiency of the measure. Its construction called for a huge outlay and intense construction activity, which the state proved incapable of maintaining. The construction work of the Cadiz *arsenal* dragged on for several decades. Payment defaults and delays built up, at times jeopardizing the whole project. It was not until 1728 that construction work could start on the first ship of the line and it was 1735 when the first two frigates were built, and the whole *arsenal* construction project was by no means finished yet.[39] In fact it was not until the 1750s that construction work was completely finished and shipbuilding could begin in earnest. Results so far had been meagre. From 1717 to 1750 only eight ships of the line and two frigates had been built in the new Cadiz *arsenal*. If Cadiz stood for the political project of building a navy by direct state intervention these few ships of the line were undoubtedly a feeble result. New measures were now essential to meet the two overriding political objectives of imperial naval defence and ensuring international diplomatic influence.

One slew of measures revolved around extending the *arsenal* model to the shipyards of Ferrol and Cartagena. The idea was to set up three great royal *arsenales*, one each on the north, east, and south coasts, to meet the whole set of shipbuilding and maintenance needs while also serving as naval bases for organizing all administrative and operational tasks. In 1726 three Departamentos Marítimos (Maritime Departments) were created, each with an *arsenal* and jurisdictional district, dividing the coastline and also inland Spain into three regions for the purposes of naval affairs, mainly in terms of naval supplies or recruitment. These three departments were Cadiz, which took in the coast from Portugal to Almeria plus the Canary Islands; Cartagena, whose jurisdiction ranged from France to the strongholds of Africa taking in the Balearic Islands along the way; and Ferrol, which took in the Cantabrian coast as far as the Portuguese border. As in the case of Cadiz, the construction of the Cartagena and Ferrol *arsenales* took up a large part of the administrators' energies and the available naval construction resources. Construction of the Cartagena *arsenal*, up to then merely an anchoring point for the galley squadron, lingered on from 1731 to 1782.[40] It had no real construction capacity until 1750, when four xebecks were built and, tellingly, a recreational 'mini fleet' for navigating the River Tagus, at the behest of Ferdinand VI's wife Bárbara de Braganza. The first frigates and ships of the line were built in Cartagena in 1752 and 1753; up to then its main contribution to the navy was limited to important ship-maintenance and dry-dock work.[41] Delays were even longer in the Ferrol *arsenal* because the project underwent profound variations, the most important being the relocation of the *arsenal* within Ferrol's estuary. From 1730 to 1746 it was being built at Graña; in 1747 definitive construction work began at Esteiro.[42] Although four ships of the line were completed at the first site of Graña it was not until 1752 that systematic warship construction began. The upshot of all this was that the 1717 measures taken to increase direct *administración* and centralize naval construction in *arsenales* bore no clear result until 1750. In other words, Philip V could not rely solely on *arsenales* to rebuild his navy; like Charles II before him he had to fall back on entrepreneurs and businesspeople.

ENTREPRENEURS IN THE RESURGENCE OF THE ARMADA REAL: PRIVILEGE AND MONOPOLY

Philip V's navy was built up on the basis of contracts with entrepreneurs, in shipyards both in Spain and in the colonies. Returning to the yardstick of the number of cannons on the ships built for the navy, the figures are clear. In the home shipyards of Cantabria and the Mediterranean, the average number of guns was 52 per ship each year; in the colonial shipyards, mainly Havana, the yearly average was 50 canons, while the yearly average in the *arsenales* of Cadiz, Cartagena, and Ferrol up to 1749 was only 17 cannons. To put it another way, during the reign of Philip V, his *arsenales* supported only 14.4 per cent of naval construction, while contracts with Spanish and colonial contractors accounted for 85.6 per cent of the ships built throughout Spain's domains. The critical point here is how the contractors were able to meet the growing state demand and whether their business possibilities were affected for better or worse by their contribution to the growth of the Spanish navy (see Figure 7.2).

Any state wariness about *asiento*-based construction was swept aside for now by the pressing need to rebuild the navy after the War of the Spanish Succession. The work of private contractors had previously come under determined fire from government authorities. They were accused of all types of underhandedness, while supposedly astronomical profits were attributed to their contracting. Ships built by private contractors were said to be overpriced and the contractors were also accused of increasing ship tonnage to force the final price even higher. They were written off as shoddy and blithely unconcerned about any public benefits that might have accrued from a mercantilist supply policy. In the words of the Intendente General de Marina Patiño in 1717, 'to these excesses must be added the damage done by contractors in clear-felling our forests, wasting and rendering useless much wood and also using much green wood. Furthermore they buy all equipment and ship-building material abroad causing a drain on Spain's stocks of gold and silver and obviously provide no stimulus for the manufacture of these

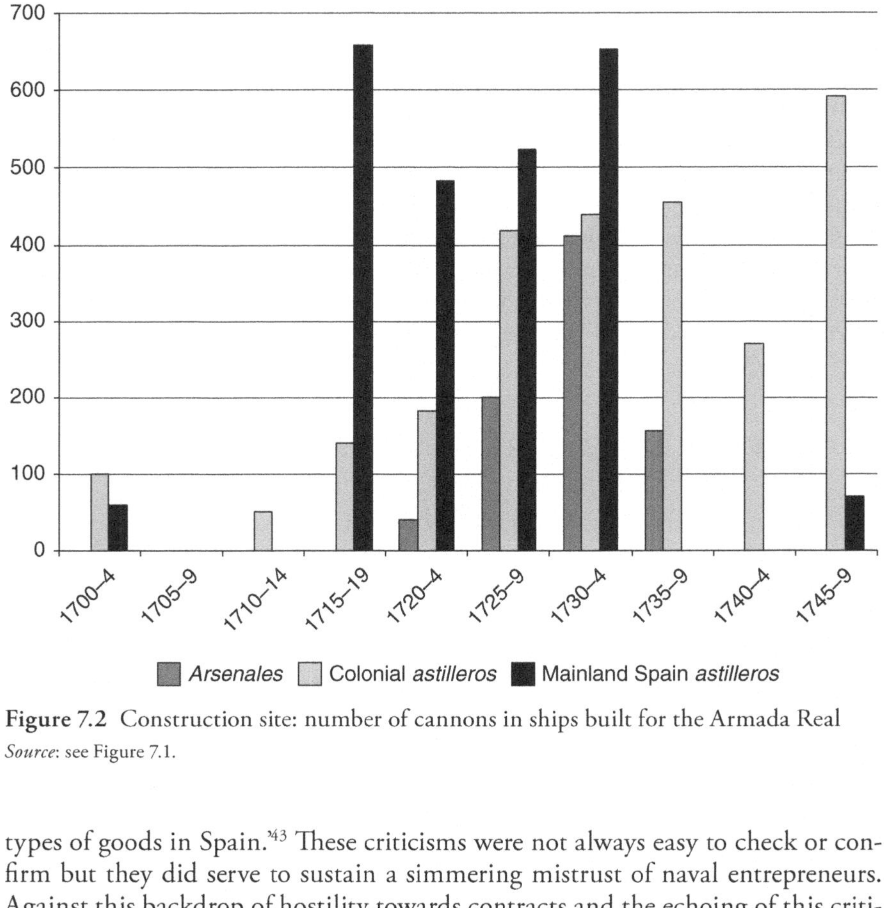

Figure 7.2 Construction site: number of cannons in ships built for the Armada Real
Source: see Figure 7.1.

types of goods in Spain.'[43] These criticisms were not always easy to check or confirm but they did serve to sustain a simmering mistrust of naval entrepreneurs. Against this backdrop of hostility towards contracts and the echoing of this criticism by the highest levels of naval administrators, it was all the more striking that the state should nonetheless turn to military contractors for reconstructing its naval force.

From 1717 itself, as soon as the war had ended, an ever-increasing number of shipbuilding contracts were signed with contractors. In these contracts the state laid down construction terms and conditions and an agreed price per ton built. The ships of the line had to be delivered to the navy in a seaworthy condition and completely fitted out, including artillery and spares. The state provided the slipways and enforced its terms on the constructor, and the *asentista* took on responsibility for finding the workers, materials, and supplies and managing the whole construction process. The state would intervene only to check the quality of the wood, sending along officials to make sure it was sufficiently cured.[44] With these contracts the state recognized the real possibility of finding entrepreneurs and shipyards capable of meeting the state's urgent shipbuilding needs. The *arsenales* were not a last-ditch solution to circumvent a lack of entrepreneurs and shipyards; they were a political option. Philip V's recourse to the market for rebuilding his navy offered several advantages. First it reduced the need to buy ships abroad, with the concomitant drain of silver, a factor much to the liking of Spanish authorities. The second advantage was speed. Within two years the contractors handed over the contracted ships. Thirdly, it expedited financing. The *asentista* in theory received monthly payments but in fact state debts often built up and the payment was made upon finishing the ship or even afterwards. The system therefore implied a certain financial flexibility for the state but this often served only to establish top-down rigidity into the whole production system, with knock-on consequences of financial default being felt by the contractors, and reaching right down to the shipyard workers. Prolonged payment defaults would produce an exodus of workers and the consequent need to reassemble them when payment was once more forthcoming. Despite this obvious downside, the state's financial advantages were obvious, especially at such times as the 1720s when the Royal Exchequer still did not have an extensive national network of treasuries capable of making payments and prepayments to the scattered supply-points of numerous shipyards (see Map 7.1).

There was another important advantage, which served to rebut an argument often brandished by the authorities to justify the creation of the *arsenales*. One of the commonest criticisms made by the authorities of *asiento*-based construction was its resistance to any standardization of shipbuilding procedures, a *sine qua non* of ensuring that the squadrons could all operate in similar conditions. A ground for the need to build ships in state *arsenales* was the argument that contractors were incapable of building ships with the quality and precision needed by the state; neither could they phase in quickly enough any changes in design or quality deemed essential for tactical and strategic requirements. Mainland shipyards showed during these years that this mistrust of *asiento*-based construction was ill-founded. For it was precisely during this time of contract-based shipbuilding in these mainland *astilleros* that the state made its great leap forward in terms of ship quality and standardization, especially for ships of the line (always the most complicated in terms of technology, construction, and supplies). As Juan Castanedo concludes, 'The definitive implementation of the ship-of-the-line in the Spanish Royal Navy started from 1720, with approval of the proportions of Antonio Gaztañeta and the experimental ships-of-the-line began in the shipyards of Guarnizo and Santoña under his direction and to the measurements laid down by him.'[45] In fact it sufficed for the state to approve some technical characteristics and for these to be phased into the successive contracts thereafter. For example Gaztañeta's shipbuilding specifications included the wording: 'whose proportions His Majesty has decided should be observed as a general rule in all the shipyards of Spain and the Americas'. Likewise, when an evident need for standardizing cannon dimensions, weights, and calibres in terms of poundage arose, there was no need to alter the contracting method; it sufficed to enforce these conditions in the cannon-casting contracts. As Iván Valdez argues, 'there is overwhelming evidence that the foundry contractors worked along these lines from 1718 to 1723'.[46] The *asentistas*' fleet-footedness in adapting to state conditions was such that, even when the navy deemed it fitting in the 1750s to bring in a radical change in the

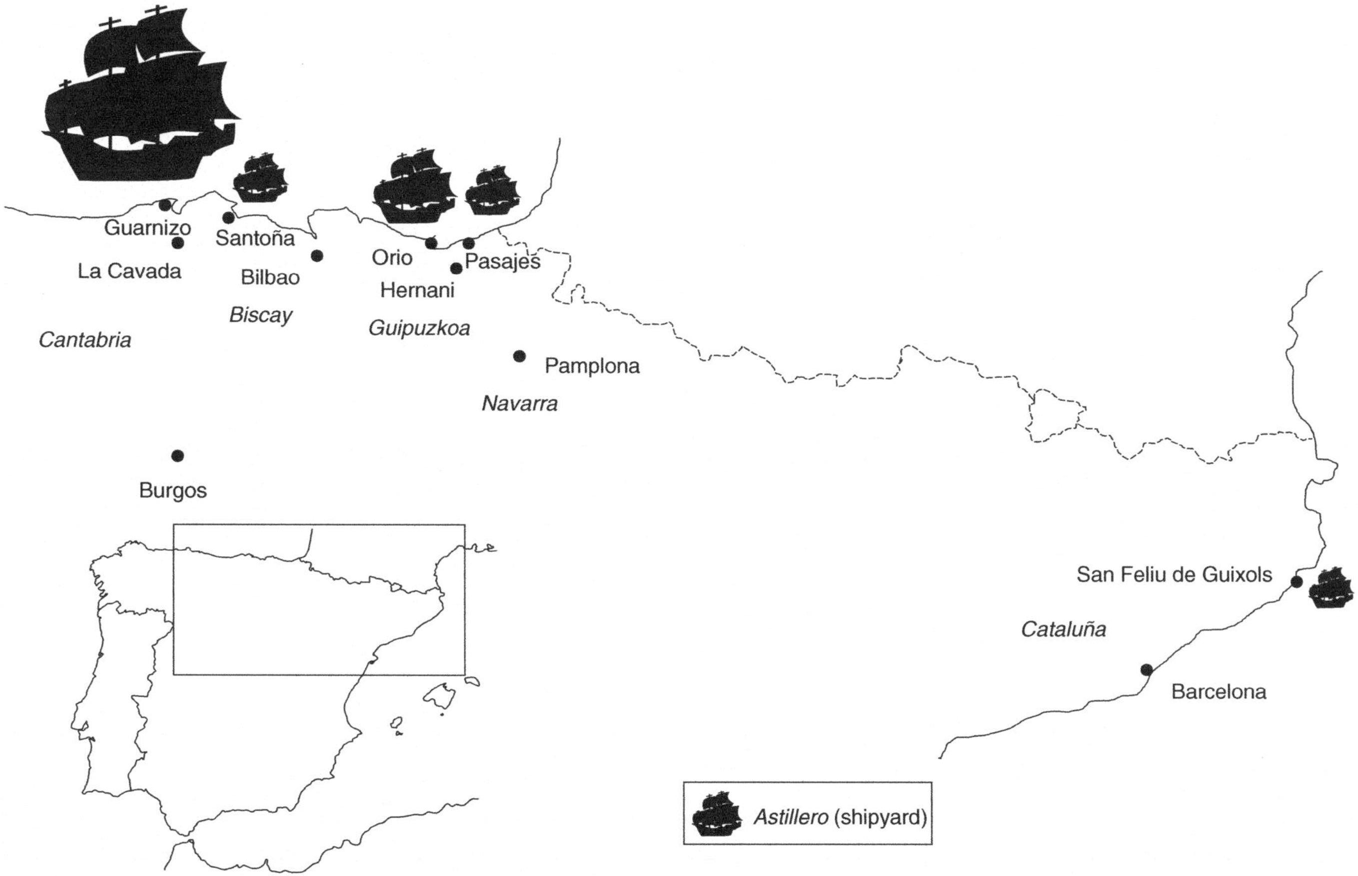

Map 7.1 Main navy *astilleros* (shipyards) in Spain
Source: Author's own. NB the pictogram size reflects the output.

principles of naval construction and to adopt the so-called 'English-style' system, the state continued to turn to contracts. When an order went out for four ships of the line to be built under the new system in *arsenales*, and it was then found that costs had built up and the ships were never finished, the Navy Ministry opted to build eight ships of the line under *asiento* 'in the English style' in Guarnizo, with the telling commitment of building them cheaper than in the *arsenales*.[47]

Asiento-based shipbuilding therefore offered the state several advantages of speed, flexibility, ease of financing, and technological adaptation, all of which gainsaid the government's traditional criticisms levelled at contractors. These advantages would help to explain why Philip V's state finally entrusted navy rebuilding to entrepreneurs.

Shipbuilding contracts with the contractors soon began to bear fruit. Six ships of the line were commissioned in 1717 from contractors Manuel de Guendica y Mendieta and Mateo Garthaing and three from Simón de Zelarain in Pasajes (Guipuzkoa). The same individualized contracting system was used in the Mediterranean, where *asentistas* Pedro Boyer and Bernardo Camby were contracted to build three ships of the line in the Catalan port of San Feliu de Guixols.[48] Although the Italian war arena might have been expected to spur shipbuilding in the Mediterranean shipyards, the bulk of the contracts were signed with entrepreneurs based in northern Spain. Their shipbuilding experience and tradition and ready access to construction materials resulted in demand being channelled to the shipyards of the Cantabrian coast. The north of Spain was better placed to tap into European naval supply markets, such as Holland, and also had an abundance of resources inland. Top-quality iron and wood, in particular, were close at hand, while the wood also served to fuel a traditional casting industry, both for artillery and anchors. Cantabria's shipbuilding cost advantages were complemented by a brisk seafaring activity, involving ship-based trade with the rest of Europe and deep-sea fishing. Only northern Spain, in other words, offered the right combination of shipbuilding tradition and human and material resources to meet naval demand.

Shipbuilding in Cantabrian shipyards fostered a concentration process, both of construction and management, often coinciding with the parallel trend towards entrepreneurial monopoly that has already been seen in army victualling. Shipbuilding demand and supply now focused on a single shipyard, Guarnizo. As in the rest of the Cantabrian shipyards, up to the eighteenth century its development was bound up with a long tradition of trading with Europe and Atlantic fisheries, further spurred on by shipbuilding demand for the Indies Run and the transport of troops for European military arenas. Seventeenth-century construction of large galleons led to the selection of convenient sites for continuous shipbuilding activity, consolidating some locations owing to the build-up of permanent infrastructure and completely abandoning the traditional model of construction on open beaches and the stockpiling of labour and materials. Guarnizo also offered the advantages of natural protection deep within an estuary, the existence of a commercial hub in the same estuary, Santander, and nearby *asiento*-run cannon-casting factories of La Cavada and Liérganes, the most important in

Spain.[49] Guarnizo's accumulation of shipbuilding experience and its constructive advantages over other ports and construction sites on the Cantabrian coast were largely driven by the state itself. From 1687 onwards the state sought to increase control over shipbuilding and it was in Guarnizo where it concentrated the establishment of officials and administrators.[50] This process was stepped up in 1717, with the arrival of Antonio Gaztañeta in Guarnizo under orders of enforcing standardized shipbuilding procedures on entrepreneurs. Gaztañeta, and his successor José del Campillo Cossió in 1725, acted as navy supply commissioners, living in the shipyard itself, with the commission of collaborating in the construction of permanent shipbuilding facilities. The state took on responsibility for constructing in Guarnizo the essential shipbuilding infrastructure, such as docks, stores, sheds, workshops, stores, and offices for custody of materials and goods. The state also undertook construction of necessary buildings for encouraging a permanent pool of workers, such as houses, residential districts, or common buildings such as stores or chapels. These state investments in Guarnizo, unmatched in other mainland ports or *astilleros*, had a double-edged effect, since the state was interested only in intervening in sites with state facilities. This policy also entrenched inequality with respect to other *astilleros* and distorted the traditional competition between Cantabrian shipyards. The most important shipbuilding contracts were granted on an ongoing basis to entrepreneurs to build the ships in Guarnizo. The entrepreneurs and *asentistas* benefited from these facilities in the management of their contract but they were also subjected to greater control and inspection by the authorities, who had to watch over the use of the king's facilities. To some extent both sides came out winning: with a minimum outlay the state managed to improve production conditions and control over the construction process; the *asentistas*' start-up investment was reduced and they could focus on the problem of finding materials and supplies and hiring skilled labour. The advantages were obvious, but so was the mutual dependence of both sides. The worst consequence was that this system put paid to competition and wiped out at source the multiplier effects that would otherwise have been passed on to other construction sites and businesspeople. Guarnizo thus came across as the veritable privileged *astillero* and its key shipbuilding role shines out clearly in any comparison with the rest of the shipyards in Spain (Orio, Pasajes, San Feliu de Guixols, Santander) (see Table 7.1).

The Guarnizo *astillero* provided 80.2 per cent of the ships built for the navy in mainland shipyards (as measured by the number of cannons). Of the 54 ships built in these shipyards, 83.3 per cent (45 ships of the line) were built in Guarnizo. Without any doubt this represents, once more, the triumph of an idiosyncratic form of management: trusting in the market and in entrepreneurs to meet military demand while at the same time increasing state control over the market and restricting it, in this case curbing potential competition among Spanish shipyards.

State-favouring of a privileged *astillero* also had a knock-on effect on entrepreneurs. Up to 1717 shipbuilding contractors offering their services from diverse Spanish ports had weighed in with seven newly constructed ships of the line despite the state's financial straits. This number now fell away with the rise of the

Table 7.1 Guarnizo, the 'privileged shipyard'

	Guarnizo *Astillero*			Other shipyards in Spain		
	Cannons	Ships of the line	Frigates	Cannons	Ships of the line	Frigates
1700–9	0	0	0	60	1	0
1710–19	290	5	0	368	6	0
1720–9	1,008	11	5	0	1	0
1730–9	593	8	1	60	1	0
1740–9	70	1	0	0	0	0
1750–9	574	9	0	156	0	1
1760–9	710	8	4	30	0	0
1770–9	0	0	0	168	0	0
1780–9	216	3	0	14	0	0
1790–9	0	0	0	0	0	0
TOTAL 1700–99	3,461	45	10	856	9	1

Source: see Figure 7.1.

privileged Guarnizo *astillero*. This change had a twofold consequence: on the one hand it severely pruned the entrepreneur market, slashing the number of entrepreneurs interested in participating in shipbuilding activities. Some of them continued, but restricted themselves to the construction of merchant ships of less tonnage thereby creating fewer infrastructure problems than naval ships.[51] On the other, the curbing of entrepreneurial competence worked to the benefit of the entrepreneurs cherry-picked by the state. This effect moved in parallel with that of the *astillero*. The chosen entrepreneurs were shielded from competition and enjoyed direct access to the Navy Ministry; this in turn prompted the state itself to protect and sustain them, shielding them even more from those outside the fold. As with the victualling military entrepreneurs, the shipbuilding *asentistas* in Guarnizo developed quickly under state patronage, building up positions of privilege and monopoly powers. This process did not consist so much of being granted *de jure* privileges; rather was it a case of being given a de facto position of privilege as the only entrepreneur and the only mainland *astillero* outside the *arsenales*.

The epitome of the state's determination to favour Guarnizo entrepreneurs was Juan Fernández de Isla. His first business involved iron foundries in Cantabria, growing in number throughout the 1720s in line with the increasing demand of iron for shipbuilding.[52] An insatiable entrepreneur, he continually grafted on other business lines such as grain milling, paper mills, or leather curing, but with a special leaning towards industries related to Guarnizo's demands, such as factories for the manufacture of rigging, sailcloth, or mooring ropes, or contracts for supplying construction wood from Asturias. Isla knew how to exploit the naval supply concentration trend to bolster his own business interests. In 1750 he won the century's biggest shipbuilding wood supply-contract. The interesting thing about this contract, besides its volume, was that it was gained on a monopoly basis, covering as it did practically the whole of the navy's timber requirement. Consequently, Navy Minister Ensenada's whole shipbuilding renewal contract and his aim of bringing in the English construction system depended for its wood on a single entrepreneur.[53] Relations with the state were necessarily intense, brewing a mutual dependence. Both parties, state and entrepreneur, reached a modus operandi whereby Isla practically took over construction activity in Guarnizo. Exasperated by the slowness of the shipbuilding project in the *arsenales*, the Navy Ministry opted to step up activity in Guarnizo and did so by turning to this entrepreneur alone. The contract laid down the terms of a complex state–entrepreneur relationship. Isla undertook to build four 70-gun ships of the line under the state's terms and conditions; he would deliver the ships completely fitted out and supplied with everything needed to take to the sea, 'with the express obligation of not charging more than the cost said to have been incurred for the other ships-of-the-line made in His Majesty's three *arsenales*'. The entrepreneur agreed to be paid the same as for a ship built in these other circumstances and even dropped the final price.[54] Without any doubt the state had managed to avail itself of, and even in part create, an entrepreneur to meet its needs. The state cut out the middlemen and set up a direct relationship: Ensenada summoned Isla to the court to discuss detailed contract terms or any variation in performance. The state had acquired the entrepreneur it needed but at the cost of piling up contracts and business for their favoured contractor. The tangled web of business, with offset profit and loss, might work to the state's benefit in the short term, but it could place the entrepreneur in a very tricky situation if there was any change in his political or financial support. This is what happened following the fall of Ensenada in 1754, whereupon Isla's business empire imploded. Both minister and entrepreneur epitomized the risks of channelling the whole of naval demand through a single outlet.

Privileged *astillero* and privileged entrepreneur were locked together and both fell with their ministerial patron. This ostensibly beneficial business arrangement in fact cramped the entrepreneur's style completely, leaving him very little leeway for diversifying resources into other business. Indeed, Fernández de Isla was not the only shipbuilding entrepreneur in Guarnizo who ended up bankrupt. According to Sobrón, with the sole exception of one entrepreneur, Donestebe, who replaced Isla, all the contracts signed with the navy in the Guarnizo *astillero* were 'the cause of ruin for their signatories in all cases' (see Map 7.2).[55]

This same trend towards privileged and monopoly entrepreneurs was echoed in Spain's empire. As in metropolitan Spain, the chosen option for strengthening the navy in the Americas was to turn to the market and military entrepreneurs, but here again there was a marked trend towards the concentration of shipbuilding contracts in the hands of a small number of entrepreneurs. Although the number of *apostaderos* (naval bases) increased throughout the eighteenth century, including some maintenance and even shipbuilding facilities, the truth is that their construction activity was meagre and spasmodic. To the shipyards inherited from the seventeenth century were added the Caribbean *apostaderos*, the most important being Campeche, together with the *apostadero* of San Blas and Callao on the Pacific coast, and the *apostaderos* of Montevideo Angostura and Paraguay

Map 7.2 Navy bases, naval construction, and money remittances in the Pacific in the eighteenth century

Source: Author's own. Adapted from Martínez Shaw and Alfonso Mola, 'Los astilleros de la América colonial', 279–304. Carlos Marichal and Johanna Graffenstein, eds, *El secreto del Imperio español: los situados coloniales en el siglo XVIII* (México: El Colegio de México-Instituto Mora, 2012), 30. NB the pictogram size reflects the output.

in Río de la Plata, plus the Filipino *astillero* of Cavite.[56] The common denominator for all of them was access to a close and plentiful supply of wood, but none of them managed to achieve stable growth.[57] As in Spain some of these shipyards were meant to be examples of state-managed shipbuilding—witness the case of the Coatzacoalcos *astillero* near Veracruz in Mexico.[58] Exploiting the abundance of timber resources, an order went out in 1730 for the construction of a 70-gun ship of the line. The management was a disaster; problems and costs mounted, and the state's will to continue shoring up this *astillero* broke. In 1735, the Viceroy of New Spain, mindful of the problems generated by this direct *administración*, decided to drop the *astillero* on the grounds that 'the *asientos* favour more the Real Hacienda than the direct *administración* system'.[59] After this failure of direct state management of shipbuilding there were no more attempts to repeat it or strike out along the path of *arsenales*. The preference was rather to repeat the Guarnizo *astillero* experience, which in the Americas meant strengthening the Havana *astillero* and a clique of businesspeople around it.

The port and *astillero* of Havana had already built up extraordinary importance as a shipbuilding and dry-docking centre for vessels of the Indies Run and the Armada de Barlovento.[60] To its strategic importance as a site was added the further advantage of an abundance of material resources in Cuba, especially top-quality wood that helped to lengthen the ships' useful life, and above all the possibility of obtaining finance from Mexico. This latter advantage turned out to be decisive in the end. But for the option of financing from the Mexican *situado*, the Havana *astillero* is unlikely to have been promoted by the state and is even less likely to have achieved its eventual output levels. Throughout the whole eighteenth century the Navy Ministry seemed determined to keep warship construction located in Spain. In fact Navy Minister Patiño did not even include Havana in his *arsenal* programme, neither was it considered when the three mainland *arsenales* were set up together with the three Maritime Departments in 1726. Probably a telling factor in the minister's decision was an archaic concept of mercantilism, stressing the advantages of construction in Spain while downplaying the value of an all-embracing vision of the empire as a whole, a vision taken up by later ministers.[61] Other factors fuelling qualms about Havana were fear of any disruption in Atlantic communications and Havana's dependence on the supply of some naval products from Spain, such as iron and cannons.[62] Nonetheless, Havana's financial advantages overrode political misgivings in the end, and the Cuban *astillero* was turned into a great shipbuilding centre (see Figure 7.3).

As Figure 7.3 shows, the Havana *astillero*'s importance remained constant throughout the century, building up to a level of 21.5 per cent of Spain's total shipbuilding output, measured by the number of cannons per ship. As with Guarnizo, its heyday came during the reign of Philip V, when it reached 26.9 per cent, although there were some decades when its input was even higher: 39.7 per cent in the 1730s and an all-time high of 56 per cent of all ships built in the Spanish monarchy in the 1740s. Unlike Guarnizo, however, Havana's importance did not fall away completely in the second half of the eighteenth century, holding steady at about 17 per cent. But it was in the construction of large ships for the navy that Havana came into its own. Havana shipyards built 68 ships of the line, while the most productive *arsenal*, Ferrol, turned out only 58. Havana's predominance in the construction of large ships of the line was complete from 1720 to 1750, precisely when the navy was being rebuilt (see Table 7.2).

Havana *astillero*'s extraordinary constructive feat was pulled off by following the Guarnizo model, that is, the state made the investment in the construction infrastructure (slipways, stores, factories, etc.) and then entered into contracts with shipbuilding entrepreneurs.[63] As in Guarnizo, the state laid down construction models and technical specifications in its contracts with Havana businesspeople; witness the contract signed with the *asentista* Manuel López Pintado in 1713 for building ten ships of the line in Havana, on the designs of Antonio Gaztañeta.[64] It was not as though Havana was the only option; there was no lack of shipbuilding

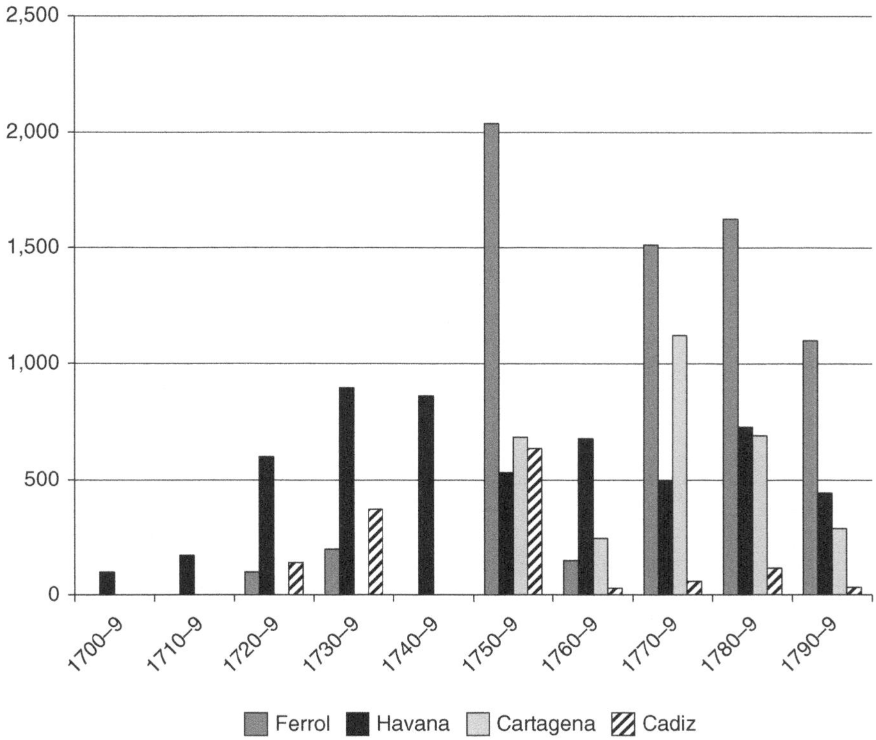

Figure 7.3 Havana shipbuilding as compared with the three *arsenales* in Spain: number of cannons in constructed ships

Source: Author's own. Adapted from AMN, MS 471.

offers from elsewhere in the Americas. In 1720, for example, Antonio de Echeverz put in a bid for building ships of the line by *asiento* in another bay of the island of Cuba, and Francisco Guiral, a prosperous merchant of the Indies Run proposed building one ship of the line and one frigate for the navy each year in Veracruz.[65] The projects were thrown out by the Navy Ministry on much the same grounds as we have already seen in Guarnizo: a preference for centralizing production in the location where the state was making its investments. Spanish ministers evidently did not see competition as an important factor in the shipbuilding strategy, and, as in Guarnizo, all naval construction was restricted to a single *astillero*.

The increase of state investments in the Havana *astillero* prompted the Navy Ministry to weigh up the possibility of bringing in direct *administración* in the Cuban *astillero*. In 1726 an order went out for building a series of four 60-gun ships of the line by direct *administración*. But the scheme once more ran into many problems and had to be completed by means of *asientos*.[66] The problems that emerged included confrontations between officers and Havana magnates interested in participating in the naval shipbuilding business. As Serrano has pointed out, the activity of the Havana *astillero* cannot properly be understood without

Table 7.2 Ships of the line and frigates in Havana and in mainland Spanish *arsenales*

	Ships of line					Frigates				
	TOTAL	Ferrol	Havana	Cartag.	Cadiz	TOTAL	Ferrol	Havana	Cartag.	Cadiz
1700–9	4	0	2	0	0	0	0	0	0	0
1710–19	26	0	3	0	0	39	0	0	0	0
1720–9	32	1	10	0	1	19	1	0	0	0
1730–9	32	3	14	0	3	7	0	1	0	2
1740–9	20	0	12	0	0	6	0	1	0	0
1750–9	51	27	6	5	4	24	2	4	4	12
1760–9	21	2	7	2	0	14	0	1	1	0
1770–9	20	7	5	8	0	32	11	4	9	1
1780–9	24	10	5	6	0	38	14	5	4	2
1790–9	13	8	4	1	0	18	0	3	8	1
1700–99	243	58	68	22	8	197	28	19	26	18

Source: see Figure 7.1.

factoring in the role of the Havana business elite.[67] These were moneyed merchants who found profitable business opportunities in supplying naval wherewithal to military entrepreneurs of the Havana *astillero*. Contracts for timber, victuals, iron fittings, and many more items tended to weave together a mesh of economic, social, and even family bonds between merchants and *asentistas*. These bonds were subject to alteration by any state decision to change the construction method. The Havana business elite did not act as a group; there was in fact much infighting amongst them, the results of which could either strengthen or weaken the *asentista's* hand. The important point is that, in Havana, unlike in Guarnizo, there was a wide-ranging and complex community of businesspeople interested and involved in the shipbuilding business, and changing the direction of this juggernaut, once in motion, was no simple matter. In the end the most logical option won out. The state finally grasped the fact that it was simpler and cheaper to give Havana's economic elite their head and allow them to tap into their connections with Mexican businesspeople, always providing they stuck to a given construction programme. For their part the contractors and collaborating elites obtained two extraordinary benefits: first, a complementary source of business which was paid for in the strongest and most universal currency, *pesos de plata fuerte*, and secondly a powerful military presence in Havana to increase the security for their business and the zone as a whole. This state–businesspeople alliance was very fruitful. During the 1720s and 1730s the state stepped up its investments in new construction infrastructure, including the construction under private contracts of a new *astillero* in 1734[68] and the signing of more contracts for building more ships of the line, achieving a century-long high point of warship production. The benefits of this alliance between Havana elites and the state stretched well beyond Havana. The lure of naval supply-contracts for the Havana *astillero* drew in businesspeople from other parts of the Caribbean, especially Nueva España, where there was a brisk and organized production of wood, rigging, and victuals. In the words of Andrade, 'a maze of vested interests' was woven in the Caribbean on the basis of the navy's demand.[69]

Nonetheless the definitive triumph of military entrepreneurs in the Havana *astillero*, in terms of both construction and military supplies, did not forestall the same development already seen in Guarnizo, with a trend towards entrepreneurial monopoly. In 1741 the crown decided to enter into an *asiento* with the Compañía de La Habana for construction of several ships of the line in the Havana *astillero*. This particular company was made up of a group of Spanish businesspeople, mainly Basque and Navarrese.[70] It had been set up the previous year with the express aim of controlling the supply of Cuban tobacco to Seville's royal tobacco factories.[71] The company had won the tobacco supply-contract on a monopoly basis, fighting off competition from other Cuban *asentistas*. The overriding importance of tobacco revenue for the Royal Exchequer gave this *asiento* a crucial strategic character. The Havana company inherited state-service and intermediation duties from the previous *asiento*-holding company, the Real Compañía Guipuzcoana de Caracas.[72] One substantial state service inherited was the strategically important *asiento* for supplying iron fittings from 1737 to the Havana *astillero*, plus other naval supplies from Spain. Working from these combined benefits of proximity to power, experience as a military supplier and with business interests in Cuba, and above all with the monopoly of tobacco supply *asiento*, the Havana company offered the state several services: developing the timber industry in Pensacola and Cuba; transporting military supplies and victuals to Cuba and other sites and strongholds in the Americas; the transporting of settlers to the Americas. The company therefore offered services of unquestionable economic and political value, contributing as it did to the development of the empire. However, the state was shrewd enough to exploit these business interests and impose a shipbuilding obligation on the company, which did not enter into its constitutional remit.[73] The result of these intermeshing interests between Spanish businesspeople and the state was a contract signed with the company to build four ships of the line per year in the Havana *astillero*.

As in the case of Guarnizo, this wide-ranging contract granted the company a de facto shipbuilding monopoly in the Havana *astillero*. The state restricted itself to determining how many ships were to be built each year, setting a price per ship, and imposing technical specifications, leaving it up to the company to decide how to manage affairs under the contract, including the hiring of employees and the procuring of materials. The Compañía de La Habana's input was the whole extensive and complex web of commercial logistics, opening up access to all types of supplies in the Americas, Spain, and Europe, including slave convoys. This logistical arrangement could be classed as pan-Atlantic because it spread from Holland to Venezuela and from Cadiz to Veracruz, enabling the company to respond with relative fleet-footedness to the state's growing and changing demands in terms of the number of ships of the line and their dimensions or numbers and weight of cannons. After the naval Battle of Toulon in 1744, for example, the Navy Ministry saw fit to increase the number of cannons, and all it had to do was to order the company to build three 70-gun ships of the line and two 80-gunners. The problem with these changes was the knock-on effect on the company's supply plans. In this case the company complained about the wastage involved in felling, carting, and preparing the wood for the 60-gun ships of the line that had originally been projected.[74] Under the contract, however, it was the state that established the type of ship and imposed construction rules. Without any doubt the company's construction monopoly could turn out to be onerous in this sense. The military context (the War of Jenkin's Ear) in which the contract was to be executed sharpened the relations between crown and entrepreneurs. The state needed more ships and more services from the company, while the company itself had to work with frequent trade cut-offs and incur extraordinary costs not provided for in the contract, such as dry-dock hull repairs of the navy's ships in the *astillero* or providing extra military supplies for ships in transit. The upshot was that by 1748 the company was on the verge of bankruptcy and threatened to drop out the contract, even offering the state compensation and ownership of company shares. The state had found significant advantages in working with these privilege-backed entrepreneurs and was not keen to see them go. The problem was to find a replacement; all the more so as the decision had been taken that year to close the *apostadero* of Veracruz and move it to Havana.[75] Negotiations dragged on until 1751, bringing out the full importance of the replacement problem. When an entrepreneur or company was so strongly shielded by privileges it reduced the number of other entrepreneurs who might otherwise have been interested in the business. In this situation any shut-down in the activity of the primary contractor would cause huge problems of replacement.

In this particular case the state found its escape card with the end of construction work in the three *arsenals*, providing a ready-made replacement, which limited the damage accruing from the end of the Compañía de La Habana's shipbuilding activity in that *astillero*. The company had performed the state's services impeccably. The 4 initially contracted ships of the line turned ultimately into 12 ships of the line and 1 frigate,[76] plus a range of services. This did not turn out to be good business for the company, although shipbuilding was never the company's top priority, but rather the tobacco business and, above all, the privileged relationship with the state. The end of the company's business in the Havana *astillero* and the turning of the state's interest to the *arsenales* could have spelt the end of the Havana *astillero* itself. Indeed, in the following years and up to the end of the Seven Years War, the *astillero* underwent its worst crisis. From 1752 to 1764 only 5 ships of the line were built, as compared to Ferrol's total of 27 in the same period. In the end the final crunch did not come, precisely because the state performed a new U-turn and decided to abandon reliance on the *arsenales*.

Guarnizo and Havana are therefore a good reflection of the state's naval reconstruction policy in the first half of the eighteenth century. Both royal shipyards benefited from state investments and built up a position of privilege over other shipyards where naval shipbuilding work had been carried out hitherto. In both shipyards the navy's ships were built by entrepreneurs on the basis of *asientos*. But the state's choice of a privileged shipyard policy tended to cut down competition, shoring up a single producer working close to the spheres of power on a monopoly basis. Without any doubt both shipyards, Guarnizo and Havana, played a key role in the revival of the navy during Philip V's reign. The three *arsenales* taken together provided only 9.4 per cent of Philip V's ships, whereas the two shipyards weighed in with 50.1 per cent of the total (measured as the number of cannons). The difference is glaring and the leading role of both shipyards unquestionable. So important was this role that, if we consider the century as a whole, these shipyards supplied 35 per cent of the ships built, whereas the three Spanish *arsenales* provided only 26.2 per cent (see Figure 7.4).

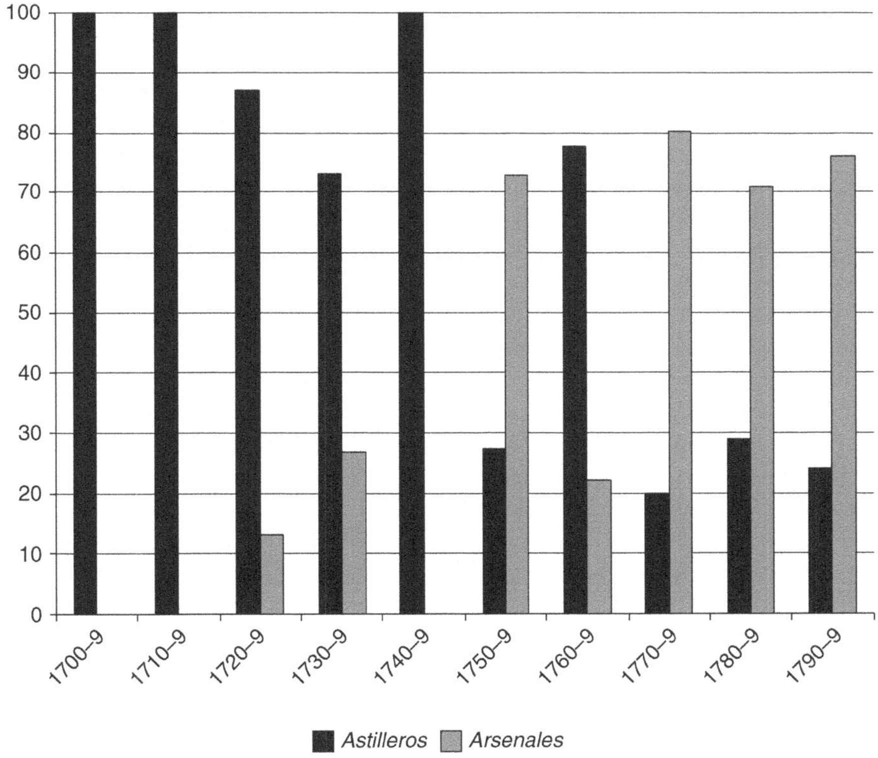

Figure 7.4 *Astilleros* as compared with *arsenales*: number of cannons in the ships built as a percentage of the total *Astilleros*: Havana + Guarnizo. (*Arsenales*: Ferrol, Cartagena, and Cadiz)

Source: see Figure 7.1.

THE TRIUMPH OF THE *ARSENALES*: THE LIMITS OF DIRECT ADMINISTRATION

The *arsenales* have been presented as the paradigm of state intervention in industrial production in general and shipbuilding in particular.[77] The state showed a steadfast political will to build the *arsenales*, first of all, and then to switch shipbuilding across from the *astilleros*. The 1717 Order for constructing the Cadiz *arsenal*, extended in 1726 to take in the *arsenales* of Cartagena and Ferrol, represented clear political determination to build up the navy by means of direct state *administración*. The *arsenal* was conceived as a world within a world, controlled directly by the state and concentrating there all the wherewithal for building and maintaining the navy. The ultimate aim of the *arsenal* was to ensure the state had direct control over maintenance and construction methods, the quality of the materials and the ships themselves, and also the supplies used. The control was also meant to respond with agility and flexibility to the navy's tactical and operational demands. As we have already seen, the construction itself of these great factory complexes was by no means easy and dragged on throughout the first half of the eighteenth century. At first their smaller output was offset by ad hoc recourse to the *astilleros*, but from the mid eighteenth century the question of whether or not to retain both systems, and therefore two construction methods, as complementary components was apparently resolved with the definitive triumph of the *arsenales*. From then on the policy of state intervention and concentration of shipbuilding activity in the *arsenales* overrode all else. Historians have long regarded this process to be proof positive of the state's will to construct its navy's ships directly. The moot point here is whether this political will was effectively enforced and how it might have affected the navy's global capacity, that is, whether concentration of production in *arsenales* was a spur or brake to the navy's growth (see Table 7.3).

From the mid eighteenth century there was a sea change in shipbuilding conditions within the Spanish monarchy. Output increased by 26.5 per cent, a sizeable increase but modest in comparison to Great Britain's and much too slow to close the gap on its English rival. While England built 261 ships of the line in the second half of the eighteenth century, Spain built 129.[78] Moreover, the fleets followed opposite trends. During the second half of the century Great Britain reduced the percentage of ships of the line built in its royal dockyards and increased construction in merchant yards. In the first half of the century only 29 per cent of the navy's ships of the line came from merchant yards while the percentage soared to 52 per cent in the second half.[79] In Spain the trend was exactly the opposite. There was a thirteen fold increase in the number of ships built in *arsenales* in the second half of the century. In the first half of the century only one ship in ten was built in navy *arsenales* (13.7%); in the second half this share soared to nearly seven out of ten (68.2%). The relative contribution of *astilleros* therefore plummeted, even falling 2.3 per cent in absolute terms in comparison to the first half. Nonetheless, and

Table 7.3 Shipbuilding in the Spanish monarchy (number of cannons in ships built for the navy)

	TOTAL	*Arsenales*	TOTAL *Astilleros*	Colonial *Astilleros*	Spanish *Astilleros*
1700–49	5,905	808	5,097	2,648	2,449
1750–99	15,641	10,663	4,978	3,110	1,868
1701–99	21,546	11,471	10,075	5,758	4,317
1700–49	100	100	100	100	100
1750–99	265	1,319.7	-2.3	17.4	-23.7
1700–49	27.4	7	50.6	46.0	56.7
1750–99	72.6	93	49.4	54.0	43.3
1701–99	100	100	100	100	100
1700–49	100	13.7	86.3	44.8	41.5
1750–99	100	68.2	31.8	19.9	11.9
1701–99	100	53.2	46.8	26.7	20.0

Source: see Figure 7.1.

rebutting the received idea of a total success of the *arsenal* construction model, shipbuilding continued in the a*stilleros*. Although construction did indeed fall away in Spanish *astilleros*, Havana's continuing output was sufficient to keep the *astillero* share at one in three ships overall. If the political objective was to switch shipbuilding wholesale to *arsenales* under direct *administración*, this was only partly achieved.

The primacy of *arsenales* was based on exclusivity, not on complementarity with merchant yards as occurred in Great Britain. In the Spanish case attempts were even made to head off any competition between *arsenal* and *astillero*. This would seem to be the thinking behind the decision to shut down the Guarnizo *astillero* in 1754. It was apparently the fall of Secretary Marqués de Ensenada, and therefore the end of business relations with the powerful entrepreneur Fernández de Isla, that prompted the decision to end construction of ships of the line by *asiento* in Guarnizo. This decision meant that all Cantabrian shipbuilding could now be concentrated in the Ferrol *arsenal*. The result was disappointing, and Ferrol's output fell. During the 1750s Ferrol turned out a total of 27 ships of the line, 12 in the first five years and 15 in the second five years of the decade. In the next 20 years, however, even with competition from Guarnizo removed, only nine ships of the line were launched. Exclusivity did not allow the construction rate to be increased, not even enough to offset the loss of production from Guarnizo. The irony here is that Ensenada's policy itself was a repudiation of exclusivity, showing that *asiento*-based construction and direct *administración* could complement each other. During the 1750s, under Ensenada's construction programme, the Ferrol *arsenal* and the Guarnizo *astillero* between them produced no fewer than 26 ships of the line, a decade record for the whole century.

Table 7.4 Trend of the ships brought into the Spanish Royal Navy

	Artillery	Total ships	Ship of the line	Frigate	Xebec	Gunboat	Brigantine
1700–9	160	4	4	0		0	
1710–19	2,394	69	26	39		4	
1720–9	2,504	53	32	19		2	
1730–9	2,255	41	32	7		2	
1740–9	1,522	26	20	6			
1750–9	4,650	92	51	24	14		1
1760–9	2,230	53	21	14	6		
1770–9	3,690	106	20	32	16	5	2
1780–9	3,991	107	24	38	10		4
1790–9	2,173	60	13	18	1		5
1700–49	8,835	193	114	71	0	8	
1750–99	16,734	418	129	126	47	5	12
1701–99	25,569	611	243	197	47	13	12

Source: see Figure 7.1.

The systematic favouring of Ferrol not only watered down competition but also changed the construction ground rules and possibilities. As we have seen from the financing point of view, Ferrol presented the biggest drawbacks for costing shipbuilding activity. Not only was the commercial and financial community smaller, reducing the possibility of withstanding navy payment defaults and delays, but the dockyard was also further from the commercial networks of Cantabria and the naval supply markets. Guarnizo's big advantage was precisely its access to resources of timber, iron, anchors, munitions, cannons, and lime, with the added possibility of tapping into European networks through the offices of Basque merchants. Ferrol's case was just the opposite, and all this wherewithal had to be shipped in from the Basque country or Navarre. This not only boosted the transport costs but also increased the risk of a breakdown in supply lines during wartime and the consequent danger of a construction shutdown, as occurred with the French dockyards that depended on Baltic supplies.[80] The main reason, for example, for the 1781 order for the construction of a 74-gun ship of the line in Pasajes (Guipuzkoa) in the midst of war with Great Britain was, in the words of the Navy Minister, Castejón, 'due to the proportions of that port and the cut wood in its vicinity, the conveyance of which to Ferrol is very time-consuming and costly'. Such was the build-up of cut wood that a later directive went out to order 'making a frigate at the same time to make use of this timber'.[81] And all this with easier financing, obtained by the Royal Exchequer at no great effort in the Basque provinces and through the customs of Burgos and Navarre.

The disappointing results of the concentration of production in Ferrol prompted the navy to do a U-turn. In 1763, right in the midst of rearmament after the Seven

Packet boat	Quarter galley	Hulk	Corvette	Schooner	Bilander	Quechemarin	Galley
2							
	8	4					
4	1	17	5	4			
3	2	1	3	10	1	1	10
9		4	1	3	3		3
18	11	26	9	17	4	1	13
18	11	26	9	17	4	1	13

Years War, the state turned back to a private entrepreneur, the Bilbao merchant Manuel Zubiría, for the construction of six 68-gun ships of the line. His success in this commission then encouraged new bids from other businesspeople. In 1766 Gerónimo Ceballos, a resident of Santander, proposed building another six ships of the line by *asiento* under the same terms and conditions; like Zubiría he too accepted the contract term of defraying 'all the costs of this enterprise'. In the same year another merchant called Esteban Martinez de Cosío also offered to build another six ships. The navy authorities accepted the bid, but the price seemed excessive to the Navy Ministry even though it was only slightly higher than the one contracted with Zubiría.[82] The interesting point here is that, had it wanted to, the state could have revived the Guarnizo *astillero* and other Cantabrian shipyards, thus building up a pool of entrepreneurs to complement the output of the Ferrol *arsenal*; but this probably ran counter to the political objectives bound up with the whole Ferrol *arsenal* project.

The *arsenales* were by no means a resounding success. The state harboured serious doubts, largely due to the direct-*administración* construction cost. As María Baudot has pointed out, in 1756, the Navy Minister, Arriaga, ordered navy *intendentes* 'to sound out shrewdly' among shipbuilders and entrepreneurs whether it might be a good commercial idea to build ships by *asiento*, 'to weigh up which option best suits the Real Hacienda'.[83] These state doubts lingered on throughout the whole century and were still being voiced right at the end.[84] In times of pressing need these doubts seemed to formulate themselves into outright rejection. Hence the surprising decision to offset ship losses in Havana during the Seven Years War by resorting to new *asientos* and overseas purchases: from 1762 to 1764

13 new ships of the line were brought in (12 by *asiento* and 1 purchased outright).[85] In fact, of the 19 ships of the line built in the 1760s, only 4 were built in *arsenales*; the rest involved a significant return to *astilleros* and contracts: 15 ships of the line (7 in Havana and 8 in Guarnizo). As at the start of Philip V's reign the state turned back to entrepreneurs and *astilleros* to rebuild the navy.

The resurgence of the Havana *astillero* in 1763, after a decade-long shutdown, is another factor that argues against the vaunted success of the *arsenales*, signifying as it did a renunciation of the political project of concentrating shipbuilding in the *arsenales* at home. There were three main reasons behind Havana's revival: first, the urgent need to reinforce military power in the Americas; secondly, the financing advantages offered by the Mexican *situado*; and thirdly, the keenness of Havana's elite to participate in shipbuilding and financing arrangements. But the revival of Havana was at the same time a recognition of the impossibility of forging on with the shipbuilding plans at home using Cuban wood, as demonstrated during the 1750s. The ambitious Carraca and Ferrol shipbuilding plans depended, among other things, on Cuba's role as wood supplier to Spain's *arsenales*. This timber, paid for by the Mexican Viceroy, was of better quality and lengthened the ships' useful life. But the state was not capable of guaranteeing this supply, and in the end the Navy Minister, Arriaga, preferred to move shipbuilding operations directly to Havana.[86] Havana's subsequent shipbuilding rate suggests this move was shrewd; in the following decades up to the end of the century the *astillero* turned out 21 ships of the line plus 13 frigates, almost all of them by *asiento*. Once more, as had occurred in the first half of the century, Havana's elite was keen to take part in shipbuilding operations and several business houses succeeded each other in the contracts signed with the navy. And they did so at a time of greater technical complexity and more standardization. In 1783 Romero Férnandez de Landa laid down and standardized the new ship-of-the-line model, which could be enforced in the Havana contracts without problems,[87] even when it became necessary to introduce the big ships of the line with three bridges and 100 cannons. This proved to be impossible in the Carraca *arsenal*. In other words the Havana contracts showed that the navy could meet its quality and standardization needs outside the *arsenales* (see Table 7.4).

The triumph of the *arsenales* also involved a notable change in construction quality. Since the 1770s competition with the British navy had made it essential to build large ships of the line, but *arsenales* such as Cadiz and Cartagena were unable to meet this demand. There were also other ways in which the *arsenales* found it hard to keep up with the tactical requirements of naval warfare. The navy's growth in the second half of the eighteenth century was largely accounted for by ships with lower firepower. Ships of the line increased by only 13.6 per cent whereas frigates and smaller craft did so by 77.5 per cent, that is, exactly the opposite trend to the one demanded by the tactics of warfare in naval squadrons. The interesting point here is that it was the *arsenales* that played the leading role in this trend, since it was there that most of the smaller craft were built. In some cases there was even an authentic specialization process; witness the xebecs, which increased by 47 units overall, of which 18 were built in the Cartagena *arsenal* and another 7 in the Mahón *arsenal* after the conquest of Menorca. Gunboats, quarter galleys, or packet boats often completed the *arsenales*' roll call, while big ships of the line were built by *asiento* in Havana.

Arsenales therefore determined both the location and the majority shipbuilding method of the navy in the second half of the eighteenth century. This trend ran in exactly the opposite direction to that of the English navy, and involved seeking exclusivity rather than complementarity. As it turned out, however, state support for *arsenales* was not set in stone. Financing limitations and production difficulties meant that entrepreneurs and contracts remained a fall-back option right to the end of the century, running counter to official policy but often taken up to meet urgent needs or to suit temporary convenience. The gravest problem is that there was no complete and consistent direct *administración*, and neither was any systematic complementarity sought between *arsenales* and contracts. The triumph of the *arsenals* in terms of the concentration of shipbuilding behind their walls was not as resounding as historians have frequently argued. This was largely because there was a tighter relationship between state and naval entrepreneurs than had previously been thought. As a corollary of this, the *arsenal* walls were not as impervious to these entrepreneurs as they might otherwise have been.

8

The Spanish Naval Contractor State and Entrepreneurs

BREAKING DOWN THE ARSENAL WALLS

Under the general heading of shipbuilding methods lay a complexity of state–entrepreneur relationships that are hardly understood at all. They are traditionally presented as isolated worlds, almost always confrontational, but this is an overly narrow and simplistic view. In fact both state and entrepreneurs found good reasons for collaboration and mutual support. The intention here is simply to look at the characteristics of this relationship and weigh up the motives that brought them together.

The starting point should be the *arsenales*, ostensibly representing the triumph of direct administration and hence least accessible to entrepreneurs. From the outset it would not seem to be true that *arsenales* were home only to organized, navy-run activities. A perusal of the documentation of the Navy Ministry shows a motley universe of entrepreneurs and companies working jointly with navy workers and officials.

Shipbuilding in the *arsenales* did not always imply the construction of new state factories inside the military precincts. In some cases, existing private companies in the neighbourhood were brought into the *arsenal*. This is what happened with the manufacture of rigging and canvas, one of the most important *arsenal* activities. During the first third of the eighteenth century these naval supply needs had been met by *asientos* from existing private centres of Sada (Galicia) and Cadiz.[1] To control output the state tried from the 1740s onwards to take over direct management of these factories, finally ordering their transfer to the nearby *arsenales*. This measure came up against surprising opposition from navy *intendentes* themselves who were in charge of enforcing the order. 'If it ain't broke, don't fix it' seems to have been their basic argument. In 1754 Julián Arriaga, *intendente de marina* in Cadiz (and Navy Minister to be) stood out against the transfer of the private rigging firm in Puerto Real (Cadiz), eulogizing it as 'a useful factory almost to the point of perfection'.[2] These warnings, notably, turned out to be realistic, and it was only when the private rigging and canvas factories were nonetheless transferred to the *arsenales* that the true scale of the consequent problem came to light. The Navy Ministry soon discovered that the transfer to the *arsenal* meant that it would then be the navy's remit to take on the whole production process. Other *arsenal* products had also run into problems deriving from a disparity and mistiming between raw material supply and the required pace of manufacturing. In the case of rigging and canvas these timing problems were exacerbated by the difficulty of bringing together the huge amount of labour needed into one production centre. Coordination between raw material availability and labour became the *arsenal* officials' main headache. From the *arsenales* came a stream of pleas for necessary workers to be mustered by provincial *intendentes*.[3] Persistently low wages by no means helped to solve the timing problems in the production of rigging and canvas and the forced transfer of workers to the distant *arsenales* only served to worsen the performance of these factories.

Under such circumstances the only real option was to turn back and ask private entrepreneurs to fill in manufacturing gaps, in other words to remove the rigging and canvas factories from the *arsenales*. After barely two decades of activity in the *arsenales*, therefore, production reverted to outside factories. In the 1770s, while the number of workers employed in the *arsenal* factories fell, navy demand from factories outside the *arsenales* rose. This demand fuelled a veritable boom of companies in Granada and Aragon. Some of them achieved huge growth, outnumbering the workers employed in some *arsenales*. The Granada entrepreneur Gómez Montero was running a 2,000-strong workforce by the start of the 1780s, matching the number employed in all the rigging and canvas factories of the three *arsenals*.[4] The state, finding this makeshift arrangement to be convenient or essential to meet pressing demand, was reneging on its own ambition of managing and controlling rigging manufacture in the *arsenales*. The debate about whether the state should completely relinquish the rigging and canvas factories in the *arsenales* simmered on in following years. An 1803 report concluded that rigging manufacture should definitively be taken out of the *arsenales* on the grounds that 'under the sure conviction that His Majesty should never be manufacturer or craftsman ... the Navy Departments are asked that the effort they have hitherto exerted in stockpiling hemp and mustering workers be henceforth spent on stimulating production by private parties under acceptable terms and conditions'.[5]

The rigging and canvas case is by no means unique. During the 1760s the navy began to contract out an increasing number of *arsenal* tasks. These could include works of civil engineering bound up with the construction of the *arsenal* itself, but also navy shipbuilding and maintenance work: iron forging and smelting, blacksmithing, glasswork, carpentry, and so on. The key point here is that much of this work had hitherto been carried out directly by the state and it was later that the idea was mooted of contracting it out to firms and entrepreneurs outside the *arsenal*. The navy *intendente* of Cadiz, Juan Gerbaut, suggested to the Navy Ministry that the method should be changed, 'given the advantage that would accrue to the Royal Exchequer by contracting out iron forging work in lieu of the direct administration resorted to at present'.[6] This top executive for the navy's management of resources based his case largely on finance: entrepreneurs would represent a saving for the Royal Exchequer. The argument for economy came into its own over the following years but until that time it had played second fiddle to the safety, control, and production-quality reasons that had previously been utilized in favour of moving factories, companies, and workers into the *arsenales*. The *arsenal* bosses themselves (first the *intendentes* and from 1770 the *juntas departamentales* (Navy Department Boards)) soon grasped the importance of the financial argument, partly because they were in charge of a budget that, once approved by the Navy Ministry, was, as we have already seen, tied in with a set of stipulated commitments. Any managerial saving could provide greater leeway for dealing with unforeseen costs cropping up elsewhere, but also for corruption. *Arsenal* bosses found it useful to offload some of their production problems (labour organization, supply of raw materials, or pace of production) onto private parties and entrepreneurs. Thus, the Junta del Departamento de Cartagena's justification for its 1774 decision to transfer hemp spinning tasks from its arsenal's canvas factories to entrepreneurs left no doubts about the complexity of the problem: 'acknowledging the propitiousness of doing so by *asiento*, not only due to the lower price but also the concomitant benefit of avoiding the prejudicial consequences of allowing women into the *Arsenal* on the hemp and flax supply days for spinning same'.[7] Sexual mores may therefore have been another factor spelling the end of *arsenal* factories.

It was in all likelihood the very success of outside production that encouraged *arsenal* bosses to increase *asiento* take-up for naval production. From the 1760s onwards private *asientos* weighed in with an increasing amount and variety of *arsenal* production. The list of these contracts with companies became a very long one, showing the scale of this increasing devolvement to private companies. The contracts ranged from large-scale civil engineering work (port cleansing, construction of buildings and canals) to maintenance work and accessory work such as ship painting, construction of navigation lights, ports, and windows, cleaning of pipework, mast assembly, and many more.[8] There were even *asiento de bueyes*, whereby an entrepreneur undertook to bring together and then maintain in the *arsenal* the *juntas de bueyes* (ox teams) needed by the navy and to pay all the employees and also defray necessary food and stores. In each one of these contracts with entrepreneurs the same formalities were observed as with the large state *asientos*, regardless of the value of the business contracted out, including the same prerequisites and performance bonds. The terms and conditions laid down in these contracts, and also by the *asentistas'* guarantors and bondsmen, tell us how these entrepreneurs fitted into the society of the time. There is a clear link between contractors and local merchants, with a large role played by companies comprising both contractors and merchants. Another notable presence, however, is that of big landowners, many of them noble, whose properties could generate supplies of naval interest such as wood, iron, hemp, lime, or fodder. The contractors, therefore, acted as middlemen between state demand and the production, financing, and supply capacity of the rest of the economy.

The persistence of *arsenal* bosses in this gradual shift to private contracts expedited a new feature in this procedure: that is, incorporation of *arsenal* workers themselves. This factor has been little studied hitherto. *Arsenal* masters and wage-earning workers were bold in proposing contracts to the *arsenal* authorities. Such initiative almost always came from masters and skilled craftsmen within the *arsenal*, now offering to carry out specific work as a private firm. The necessary workers were also recruited from within the *arsenal* or from outside, but to all intents and purposes they ceased to be *arsenal* workers and were now offering services as a separate firm. Sometimes the two facets of worker and entrepreneur could hardly be disentangled. Francisco Pozo, for example, a Cadiz resident who formerly worked as master carpenter in the Carraca *arsenal* of Cadiz, offered to carry out under *asiento* 'the carpentry of gun-carriage seatings'. The trouble was that he did not wish to give up his status as *arsenal* wage earner, arguing that this could still be compatible with his entrepreneurial pretensions. The solution could not have been more pragmatic: 'always providing that he should not be employed in the shipyard on making carriages, he should be employed with the corresponding wage on maintenance and construction work ... making sure he receive no wage payment for work carried out under the *asiento*'. As bond he offered his property, a house and 'as special mortgage the value of my tools', giving us a good idea of the small value of this commission. But its modest value did not at all dampen the aspirations of this inspired new entrepreneur, probably spurred on by the entrepreneurial *arsenal* ambience; he did not hesitate to lay down the condition that: 'all skilled workmanship in this production should be supervised and approved only by myself'. Equally telling are the cases where wage-earning *arsenal* masters even contracted work out to other outside masters and workers, although the actual work would be carried out in the *arsenal*. Manuel de la Torre, master and *asentista* of navigation lights in Carraca, for example, declared that 'he had a private contract drawn up' with a master lead worker who 'had worked in the Cartagena *arsenal* and was now working for his company'. The master tinsmiths Tomás and Carlos Batellin accused the master lantern maker José Urso of a breach of contract, claiming that 'he had exploited his contractual position' for winning a 1772 *asiento* in the Carraca *arsenal*.[9]

The striking feature is that these private contracts did not involve activities that the *arsenales* were incapable of carrying out themselves. On many occasions, in fact, the work had previously been carried out in the *arsenales*. It would therefore seem to have been a conscious choice of the *arsenal* authorities, running counter to previous procedure. In some cases this measure was adopted because it seemed more in keeping with the *arsenal*'s own past experience. This at least would seem to be the conclusion to be drawn from a very significant shipyard *asiento*. Construction of the first-ever dry dock in Spanish *arsenales* ended in 1754 in Cartagena. Its construction had been a matter of hot debate in the Navy Ministry over preceding years. The unprecedented nature of this construction and its cost concentrated the attention of senior naval administrators. Merino detailed the continual squabbles sparked off among the authorities (Antonio de Ulloa, Sebastián de Feringán, Jorge Juan, and Arriaga) as a stream of technical, labour, and economic problems emerged. In the end the dry dock was built and its final cost amounted to 6,712,780 *rsv*, but in the judgement of the navy authorities it was a relative failure, calling for the corresponding debriefing council to pinpoint errors and decide on remedies.[10] The experience built up in this first dry-dock construction then proved to be decisive for construction plans for future docks in Ferrol and Cadiz, and also raised questions about the way they should be built. This idea was reinforced in following years with the example and apparent success of docks built outside the *arsenales*. According to Merino, there are records of at least two docks having been built by private contractors, one in Pasajes, in 1766, by the Compañía de Caracas, and another in Cadiz, by the merchant and shipbuilder Jacinto José de Barrios, for dry-docking merchant ships. This dock was hired by the navy in 1779 and then bought outright in 1784. When, 30 years after construction of the first dry dock in Cartagena, the navy was mulling over construction of another in Cadiz's Carraca *arsenal*, the option finally chosen was to do so under a contract with private constructors and entrepreneurs. Past experience suggested that the best scheme was to delegate construction to a navy-supervised entrepreneur.

The dock construction was broken down into several different contracts. The biggest contract was for 'excavation of the drydock and building dock'.[11] The bidding and final knockdown of this *asiento* is illustrative of the scale of the activity to be carried out and state policy towards entrepreneurs. The contract attracted many Cadiz businesspeople. Eight bids were put in for the second auction. The final bid-winner was Lázaro Fernández Miranda, a Cadiz merchant backed up by the surety of the Cadiz trading company, Constante Albertini, which offered a 100,000 *reales* bond and four of its houses in Cadiz as collateral. The *asentista* undertook to carry out all the digging and earthmoving work and also to provide the necessary tools and wherewithal. The Royal Exchequer, in exchange, granted military jurisdiction rights to him, his workers, and his dependents, and forwarded such goods as he might need from royal warehouses, to be paid for by Fernández Miranda at the set price.[12] All the workers would be paid by the entrepreneur, but the Royal Exchequer reserved the right to enforce an increase or decrease in the number of employees, and 'they [*asiento* workers] will be given, on the Royal Exchequer's account, water, a room or dwelling for ironworking and rigging tools and covered stoves for cooking'. To exploit the *asentista*'s workforce to the full, the Royal Exchequer laid down that if Fernández Miranda's workers 'should suffer any considerable downtime, they will be employed for such hours as this downtime might last on *Arsenal* tasks so as not to forfeit their wage entitlement for that time'. The whole job would be finished by a fixed date and this deadline was actually met. In other words the docks began to be built by direct administration and ended up, on the navy's own initiative, being built by entrepreneurs.

It was not only as a complementary measure that external entrepreneurs and companies were deployed. They also built ships of the line inside the *arsenal*. Although it is no longer easy to tell if they were built by direct administration or by *asiento*, we do know these were more than isolated episodes.[13] The common denominator in all of them was that the entrepreneur also dealt with the wood supply problem. As has occurred earlier in Guarnizo, with the entrepreneur Fernández Isla, or in Havana with the Compañía de La Habana, wood supplies were guaranteed for *asiento*-based ship construction. Examples of this modus operandi are the contracts signed by several Italian trading houses for providing, first, Italian oak from 1761, and afterwards with contracts for building and completely fitting out six 68-gun ships of the line and several 30–40-gun frigates in Cartagena *arsenal*.[14] The main Italian trading house was that of Monticheli, of Genoa, which had inherited a wood provisioning contract from José Marcenaro, but other Genovese and Venetian houses were also lured in, playing a complementary part in diverse *asientos* for supplying wood and sundry material; they also provided Italian dock workers and brought them to Cartagena *arsenal*. There was even a certain competitive edge between the entrepreneurs, a factor welcomed by *arsenal* authorities as it boosted their own bargaining power, as occurred with the Genoa company of Baltasar Castellini y Cia. The way these contracts actually played out showed the complexity of all the interests at stake. Each *asiento* renewal brought the fraught relationship between the Navy Ministry and these entrepreneurs to a head. The Italians, sponsored by several Madrid financial houses (the most important being that of Juan Bautista Rossi), used the *asientos* as leverage to win silver export licences, which they justified in terms of the need to buy wood and other supplies abroad. As also occurred with the army victualling contracts, the lucrative business of silver exportation, legal and illegal, was an additional incentive for businesspeople to work with the Spanish state. Whether silver was in fact the main lure of working with the navy we will never know, but there is no doubt that it was a crucial factor in the desire to enter into shipbuilding contracts. In fact, the main reason for turning down Castelini's shipbuilding proposal was not the technical conditions, the price, or deadlines but the excessive number of silver export licences he asked for.[15] The wood–shipbuilding–silver triumvirate wove a tangled web of business that fell within the scope of international capitalism, bringing out the fact that international businesspeople too were sometimes capable of breaking into the *arsenal* business.

A progressive reversion to entrepreneurs for building ships of the line also occurred in Havana where output had fallen off sharply after the ships of the line built by the business group of the Compañía de La Habana: from 1751 to 1764 only five were constructed. It was in 1766 when the decision was taken to activate production of the Havana *astillero* and it was the navy authorities themselves who advised doing so by means of contracts with entrepreneurs. That year Lorenzo de Montalvo, Cuba's general navy *intendente*, informed Julián Arriaga about Havana's shipbuilding plan and concluded 'with the ongoing fervent desire of saving His Majesty's shipbuilding expenses for the Royal Exchequer in this port and having thought long and hard about how best to achieve this end, the repeated past experience tells us that the best option is to continue with the various *asientos* for all the corresponding work involved in the perfect construction of each ship'.[16] From then on and up to 1796 Havana turned out ships at a healthy rate: 19 ships of the line and 13 frigates. Havana thus snatched back part of its unquestionably leading role of the first half of the century, largely due to increasing state leniency about building outside the home *arsenales*. The *asiento* method and the colonial *astillero* came to the fore again as its construction potential and, above all, its financial resources (Mexican *situado* and the Havana business elite) gradually broke down the previous opposition.

At the same time as the state discovered growing possibilities and advantages in working with entrepreneurs its confidence in them was also shown to have certain limits. An analysis of the contracts signed by the state with entrepreneurs in a host of different activities shows a telling trend towards an increasing ring-fencing of the functions and activities to be performed by entrepreneurs. The state, in other words, seemed to accept the occasional convenience of working with entrepreneurs, but in exchange for a greater control over their activity. In 1784, for example, the state entered into a contract with a local entrepreneur, José Ortega, for the construction of two pontoons and four barges in the Carraca *arsenal*. In this contract the state saw fit to define the terms and conditions so strictly as to almost organize Ortega's firm. In the past the workforce had normally been provided by the contractor but in this case 'to forestall shutdowns due to lack of workers or materials' they would be provided by the *arsenal*. Likewise, the necessary construction materials, which had traditionally been left up to the entrepreneur, were now to be purchased perforce in the *arsenal*, furthermore at a higher price, since they were raised by 15 per cent 'to cover transfer and storage costs'. The contractor even lost significant control over labour matters: 'the *asentista* being bound to dismiss such workers as the work Supervisor [also appointed by the *arsenal*'s department board] deems to be unfit for the task in hand, and to increase the staff to ensure the work deadline is met or even finished early if this could be done at no damage to the *asentista*'.[17] The state was ready to allow entrepreneurs to take part in *arsenal* activities but with greater control over them. This was without doubt the price to be paid for greater state flexibility.

The state, moreover, gradually found it to be more convenient and less onerous to control production at the point of delivery in the *arsenal* rather than trying to organize the whole production procedure. This development came out clearly in the 1772 and 1776 Ordinances for the Military and Economic Governance of its *arsenales*, which regulated the responsibilities of engineers. These regulations tended to reinforce the Junta del Departamento, increasing its flexibility and powers for agreeing and controlling *asientos* and relations with entrepreneurs, and also engineers, who were given the important task of supervising the *asentistas*' work and delivery. Should *arsenal* authorities decide henceforth to stop producing a certain naval supply themselves, they would be able to work with a ready-made ordinance to unify and improve quality control arrangements. From here on in the *arsenal* authorities would be able to contract any product they needed and assure its quality. The procedure was very simple: the entrepreneur was given a copy of what was needed and another exact copy was kept in the *arsenal* to check against the products delivered by the entrepreneur. This method was now extended to all naval supplies. An example of this procedure is given in a contract for supplying tools to the Ferrol *arsenal*, signed with José Roger y la Cruz from A Coruña for the years 1776–9. Both parties agreed

> to forestall all doubt and any appeals or misgivings at the moment of checking and delivery into the general warehouse that the *asentista* hereby be provided with a

> model of each part required, whereby the presence and dimensions thereof should serve as yardstick for all production, in due cognisance of the fact that said models will remain in the general warehouse for this purpose. All parts will be checked by the engineer, without whose approval none will be accepted. Furthermore any parts that prove to be discrepant with the samples or are rejected for any defect will be withdrawn from the *asentista* at the latter's cost ... Due monthly certification will be given of all accepted parts for payment thereof under the same terms as have been agreed with the other *Ympresarios* [entrepreneurs].[18]

The state was without doubt beginning to realize that the quality problem could be solved by means of clear game rules together with the will or financial capacity to enforce them.

The *arsenal* therefore is far less of the closed world under the direct, cast-iron control of the state. *Arsenal* walls were apparently more porous than has traditionally been thought. Private companies and entrepreneurs dealt with many aspects of naval construction, including shipbuilding. But the important point here is that it was the navy itself, its *arsenal* authorities, that found it convenient to let entrepreneurs into the *arsenales*. This was either because the authorities found it difficult to coordinate the factors of production, raw materials, and labour, or because they saw an opportunity for cutting costs; the fact is that the three home *arsenales* ended up delegating part of their activities to entrepreneurs. It is difficult now to gauge the implications and ripples of this delegation because such a host of entrepreneurs was involved, ranging from international businesspeople down to masters working in the *arsenal* itself who jumped on the entrepreneurial bandwagon. There is no doubt, however, that direct administration learned to live with this arrangement.

THE RELATIONS BETWEEN THE STATE AND NAVAL ENTREPRENEURS

Insisting that the crown did not clearly come down on either side in its eternal buy-or-produce dilemma, not even within the state-generated world of the *arsenales*, also underlines the fact that state demand for industrial military products must have had a bigger knock-on effect on entrepreneurs and private companies outside the *arsenales* than might appear at first sight. The navy's requirement for industrial goods that was not directly covered by the *arsenales* themselves must have had a ripple effect on private production centres, thereby generating changes in the wider economy. What were the repercussions of this state demand when it was channelled outside the *arsenal* towards the external world of private companies and entrepreneurs? Three main factors are of significance: first, how information about the navy's demand reached these companies and entrepreneurs; secondly, whether the state was able to enforce changes in their production methods; finally, whether the state had any means of boosting their operational capacity. In the previous section the ability of private business to break down the *arsenal* walls was examined; now, conversely, the capability of the state, from the *arsenal*, to impinge on the external companies and entrepreneurs is studied. This is without doubt a vast, largely uninvestigated field with very few features as yet sketched in. The approach will be to examine the phenomenon case by case, looking at some examples of the possible implications and complexity of this extension of activity.

The first question is to find out how private companies came to learn of the state's naval demand. In eighteenth-century society this information would have run through fixed channels; it was not available on equal terms to all potential producers/suppliers. The crown's relationship with privileged companies is well known. As main shareholder and patron it could make its demands known directly. On other occasions this privileged interlocutor was missing and then the state auctioned the contract for the product it needed to the best bidder. This is where the information began to run through different channels. *Asiento* auctions followed a watertight procedure kept unchanged by the Bourbons throughout the whole century, 'otherwise experience shows that bidders' greed will dream up no end of suits and remedies'. This procedure was managed and controlled by the Navy Ministry.[19] There were two important barriers to filter out bidders. One was the need for support from a solvent guarantor or bond-giver. The state never showed any discretion here because this was the main guarantee of *asiento* performance. Thus, when the *ympresario* (*asentista* or entrepreneur) was not either known or well heeled, the authorities called for all types of surety as well as certifications of the assets of producers and guarantors. It did not hesitate to ask *intendentes* for reports, 'in secrecy', about the condition of the *asentista* and its readiness and ability to fulfil the remit required. This first barrier filtered out all producers and entrepreneurs bereft of resources and collateral, or a guarantor to answer for them. The guarantor was crucial, since one of the state's conditions was that the producer should defray transport costs; this often turned out to be the biggest expense of all and the most complicated operation to carry out. Simple production capacity, therefore, did not suffice on its own; it was also necessary to attract someone to guarantee distribution arrangements or even take on responsibility for them itself. The Carraca *intendente* could not have expressed this more clearly in giving his opinion on an *asentista* before beginning the auction: 'he is known to be a right-thinking man … Andrés Morales built up expertise in this business by helping García, who owns goods in the Country, is the owner of useful waterborne craft for transport purposes and is backed up financially by Juan José Santibañez, a Cadiz merchant'.[20] From the Navy Ministry's point of view, he fulfilled all the auction eligibility requisites.

The second barrier filtering out applications was the circulation of information. The state tapped into its military organization as the main way of making direct contact with producers and entrepreneurs who might be interested in the business. The orders went out from Madrid to the top military authorities in each zone that might serve a given production need, always with the prerequisite of finding 'well secured and capable subjects'. When there were several candidates their intervention was usually called for again, to help obtain the best terms and conditions. These arrangements, made before going to auction, have left some documentary evidence in the case of important products. In 1750, for example, the Navy Minister, Ensenada, asked the Bilbao *corregidor* to shortlist the entrepreneurs to be told of the crown's interest in providing, under contract, iron, nails, and fittings for building 20 ships of the line. Even before the *asiento* terms and conditions were published, Ensenada urged the *corregidor* to make all necessary arrangements for improving the contract: 'calling on all your astuteness as well as wit to seek the best conditions for the Royal Exchequer in this contract in terms of the advance payment made to the *asentista* and punctual payment of all provided'.[21]

The demand did not always have a specific addressee; the state often had to fall back on the publication of edicts. These announcements were not published throughout the realm; the state shortlisted appropriate publication sites, depending on the type of product to be contracted in each case, seldom more than four or five localities. The court was one of the most frequently selected sites because edicts there made more of a splash. The concentration of financial and trading houses in Madrid meant that bid invitations spread more quickly and brought more people into the bidding. Expressions reflecting this propinquity often crop up in documentation: the important naval supply entrepreneur Gerónimo Retortillo wrote, 'I have seen in the Consejo de Hacienda the invitation to bid for the mast-and-spar contract currently being bruited abroad.'[22] The state and the Navy Ministry were familiar with the locations hosting the main production centres or where they might find people capable of raising enough capital for organizing production and distributing the product. This meant that it was the state itself that shortlisted the locations and chose the individuals to be notified. To suit each particular production need a network of veritable 'catchment areas' was set up where the state knew the trawl would be biggest. In a locksmithing contract for the Ferrol *arsenal*, for example, the order went out for the bid-invitation edicts to be published in the cities of Ferrol, Coruña, Santiago, Bilbao, San Sebastián, and Ribadeo. Whether or not proximity was always the main grounds for the state's choice is not always clear. But this decision could nonetheless have major repercussions, helping in practice to build up a regional pool of specialist skills and either facilitating or hindering access by interested parties. This is a crucial aspect. We are speaking here about a factor that could help to knit together the whole economy. State demand brought distant production centres into contact; this could favour interregional integration but it could also disrupt the internal coherence of local or regional economies with no national market capable of replacing them. To take one example: the Bilbao merchant Tomás St Aulari, after resounding success in the export of wool and iron, managed to win several *asientos* for supplying iron to Ferrol *arsenal* in the 1750s and 1760s. The stability and size of this demand enabled him to build up a very active and densely related trading network centred on Cantabria. This trading network, through which flowed merchandise of all types for the *arsenal* while also supplying cargo for its ships and credit and information for other businesspeople, helped to knit together the whole Cantabrian coast, where prices and markets tended to converge. In this case the driving force was *arsenal* demand, but these benefits were passed on to the local economy as a whole by this entrepreneur's trading network (see Map 8.1).[23]

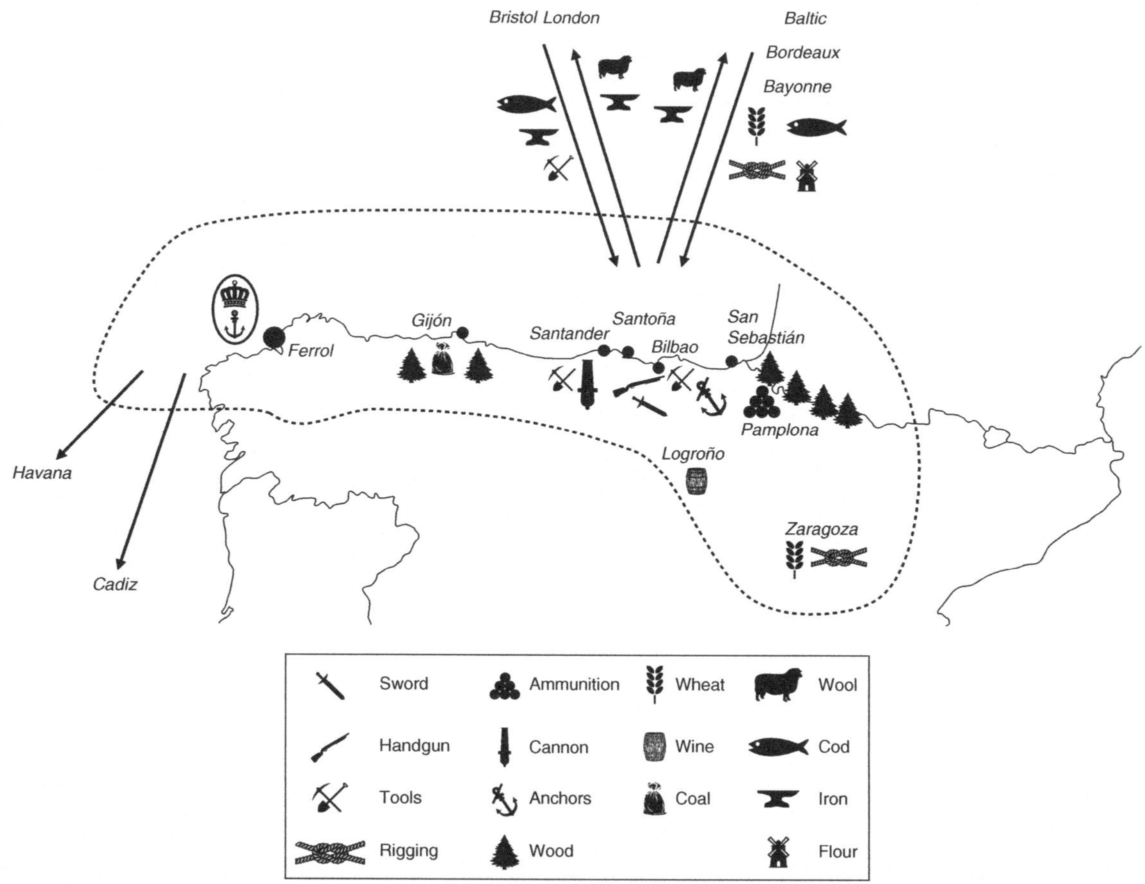

Map 8.1 Commerce, military supplies, and geographical integration: the businesses of the entrepreneur Tomás St Aulari, 1750s and 1760s

Source: Author's own. Adapted from Rafael Torres Sánchez, 'Comercio y *asientos* militares. Hacia la integración comercial del Cantábrico en el siglo XVIII', *Cuadernos de Investigación Histórica* 17 (1999), 81–108.

Nonetheless, geographical integration was by no means the state's main target in passing on information about its naval demand. For the state the problem boiled down to getting someone to accept established terms. Failing that, the bid-invitation edict could always be sent on to other localities and the whole process certainly helped to improve information systems, to an appreciable extent in some departments: 'in *asientos* of this type [transport of wood from Cantabria to Ferrol] it might be best not to confine their publication to the ports of that coast [Cantabria], since publication thereof in Barcelona, Cartagena, Ferrol and Cadiz is likely to attract other bids to improve the *asiento* terms'. At least the state was aware that each information-giving process was not a self-contained event but could help to build up a more finely tuned network for communicating future military demands.

It stands to reason that the continuity and persistence of the *asiento* system throughout the whole century brought a growing number of individuals into contact with state demands, often lifting them completely out of their daily routines and affairs. We know of some examples in which knowledge of these contracts was crucial in prompting them to take part in the first place and then remaining on the qui vive for future state business thereafter. In the 1770s there were two major contractors of Asturian coke for Ferrol, Juan Bautista González, who supplied the factories of Liergánes and La Cavada, and Matías Abadiano, who directly supplied the Ferrol *arsenal*. One of the most important sources was the mines of Avilés. In 1774, José de las Alas y Valdés, deputy of the Principado de Asturias, with a *mayorazgo* (entailed estate) in Santa María del Mar de Avilés, put himself forward for the *asiento*. A rural grandee, ostensibly far removed from these questions, he had spotted the business opportunity and took the plunge. The grounds he argued in support of his taking over of the contract were, paradoxically, 'to restrict the excesses of the *Ympresarios asentistas*, and the advantages that would accrue from the management of a landowner'. Apparently he was driven by the desire to end the problems stoked up by current coke entrepreneurs in the area and in its 'country workers', but the truth is that this noble rentier-landowner was offering the state an appreciable business venture. Acting from good will or a wider-ranging economic strategy, or both at once, he was moved to set up the necessary infrastructure and venture his own capital for running the mine and distributing the coke to the *arsenal* gates.[24] Jumping to the conclusion that this noble acted merely from a knee-jerk reaction to the existence of military entrepreneurs near his land would perhaps be over-hasty. Other reasons may have encouraged him too. There is little doubt that the simple presence of these contractors and the acquired knowledge of their modus operandi and organization egged him on, making it viable, at least in his mind, to take the step from grandee to entrepreneur working for the state.

This sort of copy-cat effect was part of an imprecise and complex set of sociological reasons related to status and prestige, quite apart from any business logic, that might encourage people to put in bids. In 1761 the navy minister of Santander complained to the Navy Ministry about the ongoing problems of finding 'capable *ympresarios*' for organizing the felling and conveyance of timber. Many put in bids but, in the words of the minister 'they do not do so to win but rather to feature therein ... and they look not on whether it may turn out well but simply undercut other bidders for the kudos of the contract even at the cost of exhausting their funds'.[25] This example shows that taking part in a tender for a navy contract could be a form of social ostentation or upward mobility rather than strictly a business opportunity per se. But it was still a way of bandying about the notion of 'entrepreneur'. Be it a grandee who decided to become an entrepreneur or a moneyless man who bid as though he were moneyed, each was one facet more of this universe of entrepreneurs, or would-be entrepreneurs, but was also the product of the state's system of communicating its naval demands. It was largely because of the lack of control at this first level of contact that the state preferred to make direct contact with potential entrepreneurs as a known quantity with direct court access. As was seen when looking at army victualling and shipbuilding procedures, the inherent risk of this procedure was the nurturing of a few monopolist entrepreneurs shielded from all competition as a way of exerting direct control over them.

Prima facie, the first consequence of state demand should be to stimulate production. Some examples can indeed be found of industries in which this incentive was decisive. Witness the state's demand for anchors to equip its warships. Guipuzkoa's traditional anchor industry had fallen on very hard times in the seventeenth century, due to difficulties in adapting to the new demand for large anchors now needed by Europe's navies for ships of ever-increasing tonnage.[26] At the start of the eighteenth century the Spanish navy had to import its anchors, and the Basque foundries were limited to meeting the demand of merchant shipping. Everything changed, however, in the 1730s when the need for new anchors began to soar. Ignacio María Carrión debunks the traditional theories that put this industrial resurgence down to an industrial espionage assignment carried out by a master anchor-maker, arguing instead that it was the positive effect of strong demand on a production structure that had not been wholly dismantled precisely due to the ongoing anchor needs of merchant shipping.[27] The upshot was that, in a few short years, Guipuzkoa's foundries turned out enough anchors to equip Spanish warships. In fact, from 1739 the importation of large English anchors was abandoned, and in the following decades there were no great problems in meeting urgent needs and even exporting anchors to France, Portugal, and England itself.

The potential growth of this output did not escape the notice of the Navy Minister, Marqués de Ensenada. In 1744 the state planned to set up a Royal Anchor Factory in Arrazubia (Guipuzkoa); this meant imposing direct administration on production currently in the hands of private entrepreneurs. In the end the project foundered, among other reasons because it clashed with local vested interests when the state tried to force towns and villages to supply the state factory with firewood.[28] The state's intentions of breaking into anchor production did not stop there. A few years later there was an even more ambitious state intervention project. The idea was to set up a great anchor factory in Renteriola (Guipuzkoa) under exclusive state supervision and control. In 1749 the king approved the construction project of the Royal Anchor Factory of Renteriola-Olalde.[29] The bid to centralize production called for construction of an authentic 'industrial complex', in the words of María Lourdes Odriozola.[30] Constructed buildings for this project included warehouses, foundries, a mill, a dam, workers' houses, and offices, plus various facilities to give 'prestige' to the site. Surprising as it may seem, the construction work for the Royal Anchor Factory also included a 'basilica, gardens, theatre, *pelota* court and hunting woods'.[31] All this created a higher demand for land than previously planned and engendered no end of lawsuits with local landowners and authorities, partly because this land was acquired by expropriation rather than purchase. Nonetheless, as in the previous attempt to set up a state anchor factory, the true problem was how to procure a firewood supply to feed the furnaces. The *intendente* had to negotiate wood provision, its quantity and price, with the representatives of each nearby local authority. The sheer diversity of jurisdictions in local woodland complicated these negotiations, undermining any possibility of establishing fixed supply rules. Factory managers' inability to achieve targets of flexibility and timeliness exacerbated the problems, eventually crippling the factory completely.

State abandonment did not spell the end of production. In 1750, during this shutdown phase, the town of Hernani, one of the fiercest opponents of the Royal Factory project, offered to take on an anchor-production *asiento*. As in the case of the Guarnizo *astillero*, therefore, ownership remained royal but management was privatized. To carry out this *asiento*, Hernani could draw on three large foundries, with which it aimed to meet the navy's total demand.[32] The state had to drop its intervention and centralization project but found an entrepreneur, albeit an institution, possessing respectable guarantees. The owners of the three foundries taking part in the *asiento* undertook to make all the anchors the navy asked for. Their experience, expertise, and access to fuel distribution channels enabled them to solve the firewood-supply problem rapidly. To do so, Hernani, as *asiento* tenure holder, set up 'concords' with nearby local authorities to ensure the necessary fuel. The state delegated production but managed to cover its demands without taking on logistical problems or having to deal with local infighting. On the contrary it stimulated local production and brought local magnates into the fold, interested in supporting the crown and its naval demands. This essential step in strengthening the monarchy has not always been given appropriate attention.[33] The important point about this alliance is that the navy got the anchors it needed, produced to the required standards of quality. It had only to appoint two inspectors, one ship captain and one master anchor-maker, to check that the finished and delivered anchors met the rules laid down by the Navy Ministry; if they failed this quality control they were rejected without payment.

We know something about how this contract unfolded thanks to the diary of the captain, Francisco Antonio de Oquendo, who recorded the criss-crossing correspondence during its performance. These letters tell us the problems that cropped up. The biggest snags were payment delays by the navy authorities for the finished anchors, often fraying nerves, and once almost to the point of provoking an open rebellion. Nonetheless, Hernani, as entrepreneur, had to deal with complex management problems, being obliged as it was to enlist other entrepreneurs and workers. The owners of the foundries, in turn, had to hire other master anchor-makers, paying them not by means of wages but by profit sharing, making them de facto entrepreneurs who then had to hire their own workers. But the biggest problems of all were logistical. As the entrepreneur, Hernani had to convey the manufactured anchors to the boarding port in San Sebastián, where they were received by the navy authorities. Hernani promised huge wage rises to any transporters willing to get involved 'regardless of the past customs of this town', but this still failed to lure in enough of them. At one time Hernani even considered drawing up a specific transport contract with other entrepreneurs but preferred in the end to seek state support, forcing all local transporters to collaborate on pain of a fine. Hernani therefore began to act as a privileged entrepreneur, with the familiar two-way dependency between state and company.

Despite these snags, the contract with Hernani was satisfactory and the anchors were produced and distributed punctually and of acceptable quality. The interesting point is that the persistence of navy demand encouraged local businesspeople and commercial capital to intervene in the production and iron forging. Their advent coincided with a wider phenomenon of employing Bilbao merchants in Basque industrial output.[34] The progressive insertion of the Basque mercantile bourgeoisie in international circuits awakened their interest in iron production.[35] By means of the system known as *socorrer ferrones*, international traders advanced money to the foundries for the purchase of materials and provisions and the foundries then paid back this loan in iron or in cash with 6 per cent interest. This practice and the excesses committed by these capitalists came in for a lot of criticism at the time.[36] At the head of this moralizing debate stood the clergyman Calatayud, who accused them of usury, of forcing foundry craftsmen to return the loan in products, of valuing the finished products at sub-market prices, and tampering with the pesos used to buy and sell them. All these underhand practices were said to win them exorbitant profit margins. This moral debate and divided public opinion did not worry the state, which was more interested in the benefits accruing from the advent of these businesspeople in a production procedure that was essential for naval construction purposes. Their participation in the *asientos* assured high levels of performance for the state, which could then be enforced in the event of any breach by the entrepreneur. This avoided direct dealings with the master anchor-maker and transferred distribution costs to the middlemen, a huge boon in economic and organizational terms. From the 1760s onwards, one of the terms laid down in the contracts signed by these contractors, now often expressly recorded in the documentation as *empresarios* (entrepreneurs) was the following: 'it will be the entrepreneur's obligation to defray all costs stemming from manufacture of the anchors and their transport by land and sea'.[37] It thus became the responsibility of the *asentista* to coordinate all *asiento* phases until the anchors turned up at the *arsenal* gates.

The state looked gladly on these improved terms and conditions and the growing competition among businesspeople. Meanwhile, in a 1765 *asiento*, Juan Fermín Guilisasti, who presented himself as 'first founder and promoter of the Anchor Factory', offered to convey the anchors at his own cost to San Sebastian; this was already an advantage over the Hernani *asiento*. Moreover, Tomás Santa

Aulari, an important Bilbao businessman, offered to transport the anchors at his own cost, in times of both peace and war, to the various *arsenales*, and also agreed to be paid wheresoever and howsoever the Royal Exchequer should decide.[38] The arrival on the scene of commercial capital had without any doubt improved contract terms for the state, especially in terms of distribution and financial flexibility.

Killing yet another bird with the same stone, these *asientos* also solved the state's vexing quality-control problem. Some years beforehand the seaman and scientist Jorge Juan warned the state to look out for the quality of the anchors and the output of the master anchor-makers: 'it would be a good idea,' wrote Jorge Juan, 'for a right-minded man, standing in for the King, to oversee this manufacture and answer for the soundness of said anchors'.[39] The advent of these businesspeople solved all these quality-control problems at a stroke. The anchors would be checked in the *arsenales*, with rejection of all substandard products. The Navy Ministry, of course, recommended that all master anchor-makers should sign their anchors 'enabling the *Ympresario* to lodge a claim against the maker of any defective anchor'. This detail is important because it meant that the state offloaded the quality problem onto the manufacturer-entrepreneur, with the navy on the sidelines. Under these conditions of healthy competition and secure supply it is no surprise to find that, for the rest of the century, the state should drop its original intention of centralizing and intervening directly in production, placing its trust instead in private industry for its anchors. This shows that, under the right conditions of competition and security, the state was prepared to renege on its own direct administration policy. The trouble was that the state's procedure of favouring the entrepreneurs involved ended up stifling competition and thereby thwarting too the certainty of the product being delivered to the navy.

Such an example might be dubbed a case of positive adaptation between state demand, private production capacity, and the aspirations of commercial capital. But these three factors did not always come together so neatly. In many cases their interests did not coincide; sometimes the entrepreneurs did not exist or commercial capital was not lured in, but the certain thing is that the state had to intervene directly with the entrepreneurs to ensure performance of the contract. The question is how the state could intervene. The dearth of entrepreneurs, the lack of any economic fabric, and the damaging effects of a restrictive state relationship with entrepreneurs all tended to convince the state that the best way of intervening was to shield the entrepreneur with privileges. The state's main form of intervention was thus to grant privileged rights over a given manufacturing process. This policy, however, introduced changes in the production structure and its economic context, stoking up social tension and introducing unwanted rigidity into the whole system. Some examples make this point clearly.

Quicklime production in Asturias was a household industry to help poor farmworkers eke out a living. Habitual use of quicklime along the Cantabrian coast kept up a traditional demand fed by the towns and villages of Asturias, Cantabria, and Galicia. The Ferrol *arsenal*'s demand for lime in large quantities upset the delicate balance between farming, land revenue, and quicklime production in the Asturian region of Castropol.[40] The amounts sent in to the *arsenal* were insufficient and, above all, too sporadic. The *intendente* of Asturias could do little to organize and control such an atomized and scattered production structure. As demand soared the locals tried to increase the output of their lime kilns, often employing all household members on the task. According to the description given by the *intendente* Antonio de Perea, some farmers with lime kilns on their properties went so far as to mortgage their property to be able to work full time on lime production. The output was taken by the producers themselves to the coast and sold off directly to boat masters who then shipped it along the coast and sold it to the Ferrol *arsenal*.[41] The constant growth in state demand and the fickleness of this supply procedure prompted the state to contract lime supply with an *asentista*. The results were far less positive than in the previous example of anchors. The *asentista* tried to corner the whole output and, drawing on the privilege of military jurisdiction rights conceded by the state, 'forced [according to the producers' account] manufacturers to up their lime output ... without any legal right to do so'.[42] The quicklime producers' protests centred on the fact that the contractor acted without the authority of ordinary justice, the contractor retorting that he acted under the orders and carte blanche of 'the king's service', issued by the Navy Commissary of Asturias. The producers also accused him of seizing the lime at a much lower price than paid hitherto. They also claimed that the entrepreneur had mopped up the whole supply, leaving none for traditional use as fertilizer: 'the supply of this lime creates a dearth for fertilising farmland'. The state's reaction was telling. It rejected the producers' complaints and continued to support the *asentista* on the grounds that 'its supply [of quicklime] was crucial'.

Steadfast state support still did not flag as protests swelled over the following years. Lime kilns quickly dried up and, above all, firewood ran out in the nearby areas, whereupon the lime output plunged. Small producers were not willing to commit to the purchase and transport of wood from ever more distant sites, especially when the fixed price then ate into their profits. The solution they suggested was that the *asentista* should hire them as journeymen: 'that the *Asentista* should buy it [the lime] on his own account and then defray them as journeymen for the work carried out'. But the contractor, shielded by crown privileges, saw no reason to make a change that would be to his own financial disadvantage. The end came when lime output fell so much that the *asentista* had to abandon the whole *asiento*. State privileges and support for the entrepreneur had served only to worsen production problems, finally spelling doom for the whole undertaking. State demand could spur industrial production only up to a very limited point if the urgent supply was ensured only by wrapping the middleman in cast-iron privileges rather than looking out for the interests of the actual producers. The irony here is that even while turning to the market the state was curbing its proper operation by setting up privileged cliques.

The problem, however, was not who enjoyed these privileges—producer or middleman—but the state's very use of privileges as an instrument of its economic policy and the effects of these prerogatives on the beneficiaries. When it was producers who were shielded from all comers, then they effectively acted as *asentistas*. State-granted prerogatives allowed them, among other things, to co-opt workers at will, buy up raw materials without competition, and likewise exercise pre-emptive rights over all available transport arrangements, which distorted any potential competition with and from other producers. Take the case of Antonio Raimundo Ibáñez and his blast furnace of Sargadelos.[43] From the outset his output went mainly to satisfy military rather than civil demand and was therefore protected by navy jurisdiction. Ibáñez was given priority access to the abundant supplies of firewood needed for his blast furnace, a vital resource in that economy. He was also entitled to call on his neighbours for transporting coal or other wherewithal during 40 days every year and also for fixing the roads used by the *asentista*, with the total support of ordinary justice, which was called upon to proffer 'all necessary aid to overcome the fierce competition among local carters'. Any potential ripple effect of state demand was therefore smothered at source by the state itself and even became an unexpected source of social tension.[44]

It was precisely the stubborn persistence with the prerogative policy, regardless of the decisions taken in the overarching make-or-buy dilemma, that most curbed the potential knock-on effect of state demand. Priority access or political prices agreed for a given activity, to ensure supply of a product desperately needed by the state, could rack up costs in other dependent activities, passing on these costs as a form of surcharge generated by the policy of granting privileges to those chosen producers. Such were the effects of the subventions paid to the biggest and most privileged *asentista* of all, the Banco de San Carlos. To ensure the Banco was able to perform its iron-fittings contract in 1780, it was authorized to raise prices. The bank's huge orders from the Basque foundries produced, among other effects, a rise in the cost of iron fittings, finally affecting the manufacturing costs of other iron-consuming products such as anchors.[45] This seriously hindered the sector, just at the time when the Basque foundries were beginning to become less competitive in foreign markets.[46] It was turning out to be dangerous and one-sided to consider only the positive effect of privileges without also considering their damaging downside for related products.

Even when shielded by state support, private producers whose main client was the state were seriously hobbled in their business strategies by the very rigidity of the state's administrative system and, above all, by fickle demand, as shown by Agustín González and the case of artillery munitions.[47] State demand was unforeseeable, soaring in moments of military urgency and then nose-diving at the end of a conflict or when hit by a shortfall of funds. This fickleness pre-empted any proper business strategy and often spelt the entrepreneur's doom. From the organizational point of view any sudden surge in state orders was just as bad for private producers as a sudden slump. A different example can illustrate this mismatch between the navy's demand and private industry's response capacity: the case of a major contractor, ostensibly stable and working with foreseeable demand, providing cut stone blocks for construction of the Cartagena *arsenal* in the mid eighteenth century.[48] At that time these stone building blocks were being supplied by *asiento*, but the navy decided to increase the construction rate of the *arsenal* and therefore needed to speed up the supply of masonry. It was decided to meet this increased demand via another *asiento*. In 1750 the decision was taken to procure over five and a half million cubic feet of stone by *asiento*. The navy stipulated that it would be the *asentistas*' responsibility 'to open the quarries, equip them with tools, workers and carriages ... and deliver the stone building blocks to the construction site'. This was therefore a large-scale operation and a correspondingly big performance caution was asked for. The auction drew in several businesspeople and companies keen to win the contract. In the end it was awarded to Miguel Carrer y Cía, whose partners included the monarchy's hospital *asentista*. This is where the first snag cropped up. The person who up to then had been the stone-supply *asentista*, whose contract was still in force, complained about the competition from the new contractor in terms of mustering both labour and carts, and also the fact of working in the same quarries. In the end, and despite the numerous warnings and pleas to the authorities from this *asentista* about his dwindling economic capacities, he went bust. The state had solved its problem of soaring demand by accumulating new contracts but persisted in its line of granting privileges, stifling any competition among the various producers. The problem was never competition per se; quite the contrary, the problem was rather the exclusive privileges, which closed off access to any new competitors. In fact, after the bankruptcy of the former *asentista*, the new ones, following the protection logic, claimed new privileges to be able to keep up with the pace of demand. These included privileged access to the wood required for making the charcoal to feed the quarry and *arsenal* forges. The solution, once again, was to grant more exclusive privileges. The trouble was that these privileges were already in the hands of other military entrepreneurs, who protested about losing them and invoked the risk of their own ruin. Much the same happened again a bit later as the demand for new construction work in the *arsenal* continued to grow. The company therefore needed to recruit more workers, mainly quarrymen and stone dressers. Attempts to call them in from further afield, especially from Catalonia, were unsuccessful, and they once more turned to the state. They were given the privilege of being able to force workers to move to the *arsenal*, on a simple state-backed order from the company: 'in the event of resistance not to accept any excuse whatsoever, paying them on my [the contractor's] behalf a fair wage and travel assistance'.

When, after many mishaps and a hefty outlay, the contractors finally managed to set up the firm and build up to the planned output, they came up against the fickleness of demand and *arsenal* administration. In 1766 the shipyard engineer decided to slash the number of building blocks sent because it exceeded the initially planned consumption capacity and there was physically nowhere to store so many in the *arsenal*. The military entrepreneurs complained that they could not just turn off the tap and cancel distribution and logistics arrangements already in full swing. The intransigence of *arsenal* authorities forced them in the end to lay off many workers and carters and partly dismantle the firm itself. Only a few months later the *arsenal*'s demand soared again due to a new navy edict, whereupon the contractors were ordered to increase output anew with some urgency. Logically, the contractor's response capacity was by now limited. Inactivity had forced them to expel many workers and cut others down to half-day working on half pay; many of the latter then simply downed tools and fled. The same went for most of the carters. *Arsenal* demand for building blocks remained pressing because other work was grinding to a halt. The contractors explained that, despite having considerably boosted wages, they were still short of carts and workers and were now unable to meet the requested output. The navy *intendente* wrote to the *corregidores* and governors of neighbouring regions, ordering them to requisition carts for the military entrepreneurs. This expedient was largely unsuccessful too, and open threats directed at the *asentistas* availed little either. The *intendente* then decided that the army should take charge of transport using its own human and material resources, the cost thereof to be defrayed by the contractors against payments due and their performance bond. This left them precious little leeway to develop their businesses. The very privileges that had enabled them to build up their production thus far now locked them into a captive, rigid, and unforeseeable market.

Relations between state and entrepreneurs were thus shaped by the way state demand was fed through to the entrepreneurs. The bidding system was hosted in different parts of the country according to the criteria of the *arsenal* authorities in each case. This scatter-gun information system had the advantage of stimulating the participation of local elites, but with its consequent downside of doubts about the economic and financial solvency of the contractors. In view of this situation the state preferred to intervene as much as possible and stick as close as possible to the entrepreneurs. To this end the preferred procedure was to work with a small clique of entrepreneurs. The trouble was that this cut down competition, locking the state into a vicious circle of granting new privileges as the potential pool of entrepreneurs dwindled. This vicious circle was apparently broken only when the state gave some leeway to commercial interests and competition. This enabled entrepreneurs to knit together geographical markets and bring production outlets into a working relationship with each other. The problem was that this optimal solution was by no means a frequent development in the Spanish monarchy.

PART IV

THE CONTRACTOR STATE IN ACTION

9

National Market versus International Market

The Limits of Mercantilism

It seems clear that the relations between the state and entrepreneurs were determined by broader economic policy. At this time economic thought throughout Europe was dominated by ideas that historians have later come to dub 'mercantilist'.[1] At that time there was a widespread consensus concerning the need for more state intervention in economic matters, with the aim of favouring the activity of national agents and achieving the widely shared objective of increasing national wealth and fortifying the state itself. But in fact, in all European states regardless of their political form, the most coveted and sought-after objective of mercantilist practices was authority.[2] Rather than speaking of mercantilist policies governed by a rational project of state construction, the real picture was a constant government effort to increase its sovereignty, a *sine qua non* of sustaining law and order and setting up secure frameworks for social and economic coexistence.[3] Mercantilism represented an opportunity to cut costs previously generated by a host of clashing sovereignties and political and economic claims, all hemmed in by vested interests. Mercantilism, therefore, strove to set up an unimpeachable authority and security that would increase the state's range of action and enable the country to increase its wealth. This led to the overriding governmental desire to protect the national market and national entrepreneurs.[4]

Our analysis of eighteenth-century army victualling procedures showed how the state's policy and its relations built up with military entrepreneurs were shaped by overarching mercantilist thought. The state exploited its need for military supply to reinforce the national market, while also favouring national entrepreneurs over foreigners. Army victuals produced and supplied on an essentially local basis favoured the achievement of these objectives. Naval supplies, however, were a different matter: they often had to be procured abroad using the commercial networks of transnational entrepreneurs. The state therefore had to call on private business spheres outside the limits of its sovereignty. What this chapter aims to do is to look at how the Spanish state managed to square its mercantilist ideas with the need to turn to external markets and entrepreneurs outside its sphere of control. This will be examined utilizing a clear example of where the state turned to international markets: hemp. In this case there is also the telling and thought-provoking fact that it would in fact have been possible to manufacture this product in Spain. A key issue here is to show how Spain's military entrepreneurs were affected by their relations with a state driven by mercantilist principles but forced at the same time to deal pragmatically with the limits of this mercantilism. [5]

THE MERCANTILIST PROJECT

The supply policy for such a strategic policy as hemp was shot through with mercantilist criteria right from the start of the eighteenth century. The prime Spanish thinkers of the early eighteenth century had already laid down the basic principles that were to govern the supply of this product. Jerónimo de Uztáriz, in 1724, clearly mapped out the problem. In his opinion Spain had no limitation on growing and making all the hemp it needed. The plant could be grown perfectly easily in many Spanish regions, and production in Spain had many advantages in its favour. First and foremost this policy would ensure regular supply of a strategic product for the Spanish navy. Uztáriz was keen to free this product from the yoke of imports; at that time the lion's share came from the Baltic and secondly from Italy. Furthermore, the manufacture of rigging and sailcloth would also encourage the development of the merchant navy and stimulate trade, a *sine qua non* in Uztáriz's economic thought. Lastly, national production offered another clear advantage: it would avoid import payments, the 'main drain on our economic resources'.[6] In other words, the main driving forces behind these ideas were national security and the stimulation of the national economy.

Uztáriz's solutions of encouraging national hemp growing, limiting imports, staunching the silver drain, and boosting national trade and industry were the pivotal ideas of a clear mercantilist school of thought, which saw in the state's demand for hemp, sailcloth, and rigging a means of promoting national wealth. The ideas were not radically new; in fact, Uztáriz himself referred at times to the benefits that, in his judgement, were already accruing from the application of the ideas and principles that he championed: 'thereby eschewing the drain of a great deal of money to cover the value and traffic thereof, and also of masts and planking, and of rigging, tar and pitch ... in view of the great importance of strengthening in Spain the manufacture and provision of all these goods, which are equally conducive to useful trade and assurance by Your Majesty of dominion over both seas ... as is only to be expected by the special attention to be paid by Your Majesty to the importance of the Navy'.[7] This writer echoed the state's attempts to whittle down the Dutch monopoly on hemp supplies and the Junta de Comercio's efforts since the 1670s to stimulate private initiative, mainly by Dutch entrepreneurs, to spread the farming and production of hemp in Spain.[8] Uztáriz, in fact, drew on and plugged into the changes in Spain's political and economic thinking that had now been in train since the last third of the seventeenth century.[9]

So important were Uztáriz's political ideas on hemp that they were maintained almost unmodified during the rest of the eighteenth century.[10] Spanish politicians and thinkers echoed and endorsed Uztáriz's arguments up to the end of the century as the best way of solving the hemp supply problem and also the most efficient means of boosting economic development. Bernardo de Ulloa and José del Campillo faithfully churned out Uztáriz's ideas during the first half of the eighteenth century. Both insisted that the best way of ensuring such an essential navy provision was the adoption of a national policy in which the state would make sure that the product was grown and made in Spain.[11] This policy was also extended further afield to Spain's colonies. Ward and Campomanes pointed out the need for encouraging this production in the Americas to avoid the high cost of buying it from European merchants in American ports.[12] Campillo, who was also a member of the government, even argued that hemp growing in the Americas was more beneficial than cotton farming.[13] It was not only the main writers and thinkers who stuck close to the ideas of Uztáriz. Senior military officials and the decision-makers of Spain's naval policy similarly repeated throughout the whole century the mercantilist principles laid down in Uztáriz's magnum opus *Theórica*. From 1755 to 1772 the mariner and scientist Antonio de Ulloa laboured on a prolix work in which he compared the European navies, their forces, institutions, and supply arrangements. Here he set out once more an authentic mercantilist project for state intervention and promotion in the national production of hemp, rigging, and sailcloth. Ulloa once more used Uztáriz's ideas, but this time insisting on demonstrating the advantageous quality of Spanish hemp; Uztáriz in fact had himself touched on this advantage when he argued that rigging and sailcloth produced in Spain were superior to the European product 'due to the forwardness of our Hemp'.[14] Ulloa, like the good scientist he was, conducted a series of experiments and compared the properties of the products made with hemp from various parts of Europe. He came to the conclusion that the rigging and canvas produced from 'national' hemp were superior because they were 'more resistant'. His recommendation left no room for doubt about the mercantilist approach, 'which should not allow the use in Spanish shipyards of ... rigging and canvas made from other than national hemp, which, albeit more expensive, will always come out cheaper in the long run due to the greater security and longevity of the masts and rigging'.[15] The quality seemed to justify a projectionist supply approach. Ulloa also argued that hemp cultivation would pose no problem, even going so far as to argue that enough raw material could be obtained 'for supplying the whole of Europe'.[16]

It was this naval thinker, Antonio de Ulloa, together with Jorge Juan, who urged politicians most forcefully to try to spread hemp production to the Americas, particularly in Cuba, from the mid eighteenth century onwards. The all-powerful minister Ensenada left no doubt about the mercantilist principles inspiring attempts to promote hemp cultivation in Havana: 'to ensure reliable hemp supply for all the ships of the Royal Navy and merchant fleets and thereby enough rigging to fit them out at a much lower cost to the Real Hacienda'.[17] The same mercantilist principles lay behind the attempt to extend hemp cultivation and production to Mexico in 1777, when the Indies Minister, José de Gálvez, justified it on the grounds that it was the 'Crown's express will to spread production thereof to supply the royal shipyards back in Spain'.[18]

Examples of the enduring imprint left by Uztáriz's mercantilist principles are rife right up to the end of the eighteenth century. In 1781 the Navy Minister, the Marqués de Castejón, told the Finance Minister, Miguel Múzquiz, that the optimal supply policy was to buy in Spain as much hemp as possible, for the simple reason that it was useful 'to sustain our Navy, national trade and avoid in the future the drain of so many millions outside of the kingdom'.[19] These mercantilist ideas were yet again endorsed by the next Navy Minister, Antonio Valdés, when he called for more promotion of hemp production on the grounds that any state expense in hemp farming would turn out to be useful for the national economy: 'the initial outlay remaining within the national money supply and eventually making its way back to the treasury by way of taxes as would any expense abroad in the longer term'.[20] This mercantilist school of thought eventually filtered down through the whole society. In 1778, Juan Tomás Pezzeti, a Granada merchant, sent to the state a report drawn up in the Economic Society of Seville, asking the government to support hemp farming in Andalusia. His arguments could hardly be more mercantilist or closer to the ideas of Uztáriz and the naval thinkers and senior politicians that had preceded him throughout the century. He encapsulated this way of thinking with his final conclusion that, if Spain obtained this supply, 'What a glut! What a blow against the nations of the north.'[21]

There is no doubt about the eighteenth-century consensus in Spain over the political and economic advantages of intervening in the navy's hemp supply. All the examples we have found tackle the problem from a markedly mercantilist viewpoint. It behoved the state to intervene in the promotion of hemp cultivation and the stimulation of the production of rigging and canvas, doing so on a national scale that would incorporate the nation's colonies too. This long and enduring consensus cloaks an ongoing failure. If the arguments had to be repeated ad infinitum this was mainly because they had never been properly implemented. Although everyone advocated the cultivation and use of 'national hemp', it never became available in sufficient amounts to supply the navy. In 1767 the Navy Intendant of the Cadiz Maritime Department pointed out to the Navy Minister, Julián Arriaga, that it could not eschew hemp imports from Europe because 'the Cadiz rigging factories need hemp and there are no prospects of supplying it from the harvests of Spain'.[22] Along the same lines, the Marqués de Monteverde expressed to Arriaga his opinion that 'the rigging and even canvas factories should always be supplied with hemp from the north, since the product is more resistant and cheaper than the home product'.[23] When national production is examined in detail it is clear that it could not possibly cater to the whole demand. The evidence is overwhelming. At a moment of high hemp demand for the navy, such as the outbreak of war against Great Britain in 1779, the Junta de Marina (Navy Council) of the Department of Cartagena set out its detailed hemp budget at 25,045 *quintales* to produce the necessary canvas and rigging, but recognized that Spain would be able to produce, 'on a prudential calculation', no more than 9,000 *quintales.*[24] According to the budget set out by the Junta de Cartagena, the complete sail area of a 70-gun ship of the line called for 19,000 *varas* of fabric made from hemp while a frigate needed 13,100 *varas*. In all, to make the 140,237 *varas* of fabric needed by the department for the coming year, it would be necessary to buy 2,804 *quintales* of hemp, which, at a price of 190 *rsv* per *quintal*, came out at 532,760 *rsv*. Likewise a completely fitted-out ship of the line needed 2,400 *quintales* of rigging, and a frigate 1,200 *quintales*. In all, Cartagena needed to produce a total of 22,241 *quintales* of rigging for 1779; this involved purchasing the same number of *quintales* of hemp, which, at 162 *reales*, came out at 3,603,042 *rsv.*[25] Similarly, the national hemp that the navy thought could be mustered for Ferrol in this same year was only 3,500 *quintales*, from Aragon, against the 20,000 *quintales* that had to be bought in Riga.[26]

The main reason for this yawning chasm between what was envisaged in theory and what was finally possible in practice is the way these mercantilist ideas were applied to Spain's actual situation. Although Uztáriz laid out the objectives clearly, the supply policy pursued during the first half of the eighteenth century had more to do with inertia than change. Everything seems to show that the much-vaunted 'Bourbon reformism' did not substantially change the methods handed down by the Hapsburgs for obtaining hemp, rigging, and sailcloth. The state continued to fall back on a set of private military entrepreneurs for supplying specific shipyards under fixed-term contracts. Díaz Ordoñez's studies have shown that the *asientos* for supply of hemp, rigging, and canvas followed each other in an unbroken sequence up to the middle of the century.[27] The only significant new development was the greater presence of Spanish businessmen in these *asientos*. This particular supply in fact followed the general trend in military supply arrangements as a whole, with its steady replacement of foreign entrepreneurs by Spanish ones. The Treaty of Utrecht trimmed Spain's European empire and deterred foreign entrepreneurs, mainly Dutch and Flemish, from taking part in the business for the provisioning of Spanish troops. The state continued to turn to private contractors to ensure the supply of hemp, rigging, and canvas, but the switch in the imperial geostrategy and the war-forged loyalties between the crown and Spanish contractors favoured a systematic change in the origin of the entrepreneurs. To some extent the change did represent a mercantilist triumph, in terms of the 'nationalization' process, but the supply system itself did not change.

The Bourbon state continued to turn to private *asentistas* as its first-resort naval hemp suppliers, even though they were now Spanish. The only exception to this predominance of Spanish hemp military entrepreneurs was the *asiento* signed by the state with an English merchant, John Burnaby, for the provision of hemp and rigging in the Cadiz shipyard, 1732–8.[28] The system was also maintained in the Americas where the state preferred to entrust the provision of necessary rigging for the Havana shipyard to Spanish companies, the Compañía Guipuzcoana de Caracas and the Compañía de La Habana.[29] Although all these Spanish companies and entrepreneurs at some moment presented the state with projects and ideas for promoting hemp cultivation in Spain or the Americas and for the manufacture of sailcloth and rigging, the truth is that they all ended up buying most of the products they needed in the European markets. The military entrepreneurs who supplied the shipyards of Ferrol and Cadiz resorted mainly to the Baltic and Holland; those who supplied the Cartagena shipyard, to Italy, and the Havana shipyard suppliers to France and Holland. To give only one example, in 1740 the Compañía de Caracas was asked to supply 12,000 *quintales* of rigging for Havana's 20-ship fleet; the company responded by mobilizing its correspondents in France to meet the demand.[30] The entrepreneurs fitted in with the mercantilist ideal but the product was still procured and made outside Spain.

If the advantages were so patent, why were no firm measures taken to promote national production at home or in the colonies? The answer may lie in the *asientos* system itself. The military entrepreneurs often won the contracts on the strength of a complex intermeshing of various state services. Take the case of the Goyeneche *asiento*. After the end of the War of Succession, Juan de Goyeneche's hemp military supply-contract, as with the concession of other military supply-contracts, was clearly a way of fobbing off this entrepreneur for state debts run up in other *asientos* or services he had provided.[31] An authentic spiral of mutual dependence was built up between the state and this military entrepreneur, leading to the joint award of military supply and revenue-farming *asientos*. The contract awards were justified on the grounds that the state thereby managed to stretch its credit facilities while also ensuring that the supply objective was still achieved. Under these conditions of mutual dependence the state was incapable of reining in the military entrepreneur to a national arena or steering the business activity towards a promotion of national industry. The state had to settle for the hemp or rigging being made available in the corresponding navy store without being able to set better terms and conditions. Likewise, for the contractors themselves, these contracts were a lucrative business because they enabled them to continue working, sustain the whole set of their activities, extend their business abroad, by means of a network of correspondents, and branch out into other areas, including the illegal exportation of silver, justified now on the grounds of the need of making purchases abroad. Under these circumstances, the military entrepreneurs did not hesitate to buy hemp and rigging at the lowest prices, and these were always to be found in European markets, as pointed out by Ulloa himself halfway through the century, and borne out by other studies.[32]

The system brought in no substantial changes in terms of implementing mercantilist ideas. The situation changed in the mid eighteenth century when a shipbuilding plan was roughed out, showing, among other things, the urgent and strategic need to secure a national supply of hemp and sailcloth.[33] Navy demand was obvious, but why now, given that back in the 1730s there was already a brisk Patiño-promoted shipbuilding programme and the hemp supply policy could have been overhauled to meet it? The answer lies not so much in the navy's demand but the state's mid-century chance to break the mutual dependence spiral between state and military entrepreneurs. From the late 1740s onwards the state made considerable progress in its control over its revenues by bringing in direct administration of the Real Hacienda's most important tax sources. From then on the state ceased to depend on the services of businesspeople to collect the state's taxes

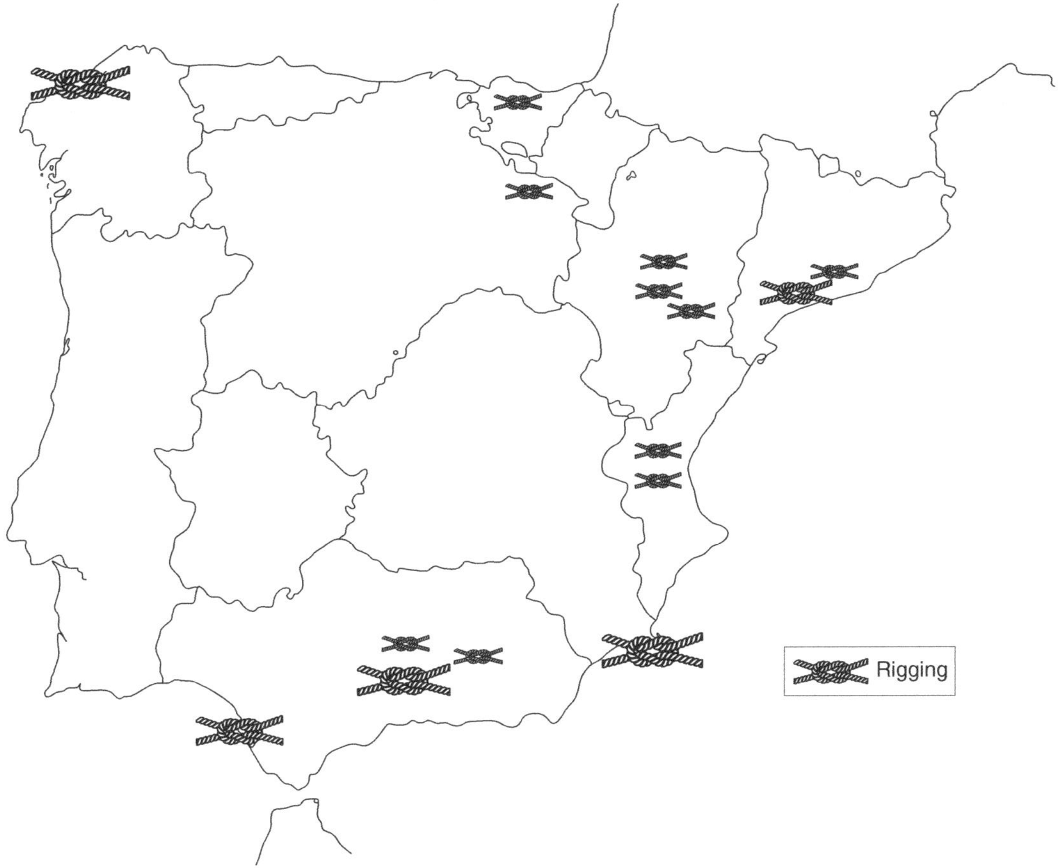

Map 9.1 Production of rigging and canvas.

Source: Adapted from AGS, Marina, legs 592, 593, and 613; AGS, SSH, legs 48, 49, and 51. NB the pictogram size reflects the output

and therefore no longer had to offset its debts and payment defaults by granting military supply-contracts. The state had broken the vicious circle. The state was now able to launch itself as an entrepreneur and provide itself directly with the supplies it needed. This also enabled it, at last, to implement its firmly held mercantilist ideas (see Map 9.1).

From the mid eighteenth century the Spanish state took two crucial measures in terms of the supply of hemp, sailcloth, and rigging: it set up rigging and canvas factories in the shipyards and promoted hemp farming in the Spanish regions most apt for the crop and with the longest-standing tradition: Granada, Catalonia, Aragon, and Valencia. The setting up of the factories inside the shipyards was a simple step but it threatened ruin for the few private factories previously existing in the hinterland. We know about the case of Cadiz, for example, where in 1754 even the Navy Intendant of Cadiz himself came out in defence of these private factories, for fear of limiting even more a scarce resource. The Intendant opposed the idea of bringing one of these factories inside the shipyard, classifying it as a 'useful factory, that could almost be said to be perfect as it is'.[34] Despite the Cadiz Intendant's gloomy forebodings, the state-sponsored factories functioned and performed with no great problems for the rest of the century. The navy's problems did not stem from the factories themselves but rather the lack of flexibility in coping with demand surges, an essential factor for any navy. The factories in the three departments almost cornered the complete production. With the dismantling of the existing private factories there was now no real leeway for dealing with any surges in demand to meet changing military circumstances. The manufacturing monopoly also extended to the Americas. When it was decided in 1777 to set up hemp farming on a mass scale in Mexico, Venezuela, and Louisiana, this was done with the idea of producing a supply of raw material for the shipyard factories back in Spain. The outbreak of war with England forced the government to allow rigging and canvas production in the Americas. A great factory was set up there but on the express condition that, 'at the end of the war any flax and hemp bought on account of the Real Hacienda should be sent back to Spain'.[35] What was actually done at the end of the war was to close down the factory, despite the high cost of setting it up and its potential to provide for civilian demand.[36] In this case a 'perfect monopoly' was sought, in which the colonies would supply the necessary hemp for the shipyard factories.

The trouble with a 'perfect monopoly' is that any variation in the production conditions of the state factories had disastrous effects on the navy's operational capacity. Take the following example. In summer 1779, soon after the outbreak of war with Great Britain and faced with the urgent need to fit out a fleet to launch an attack in the English Channel, the Navy Council of the Department of Cadiz recognized that it could not produce any more canvas or rigging due to a lack of workers. The *junta* could come up with no solution to the manpower shortage in order to increase production and meet the demand, neither were there any other private factories to turn to. Abandoning any attempt to make policy, the *junta* left it 'up to the will of Your Majesty to procure the manufactured rigging'. The requirement added up to 25,400 *quintales* of rigging and 'the department's factory, due to lack of manpower, can produce no more than 14,000 *quintales* a year ... 94,000 *varas* of canvas that can be made only in the department due to lack of workers',[37] which in practice meant buying sailcloth and rigging on the international markets, in this particular case massive fabric purchases from Amsterdam.[38] The navy officials were unable to produce the necessary goods in their shipyards, and recognized that they had no way of making up the deficit elsewhere in Spain or her colonies. Or, what comes to the same thing, they showed a notable incapacity to respond flexibly to the navy's fluctuating demand. In fact, this incapacity forced them to change tack and from the 1770s onwards the shipyard activities where gradually hived off to private firms outside the shipyards.

Despite these risks of production rigidity, the true problem for the factories, the navy, and finally Spain itself arose in obtaining the necessary hemp for producing the rigging and sailcloth. All the mercantilist approaches worked from the assumption of a national hemp supply to head off the need for buying abroad. To this end the state, in fact the navy, organized a system for encouraging the growing and purchasing of hemp in the regions with productive capacity. A system of navy commissioners was set up, one for each navy department, to make all the necessary purchases for supplying hemp to the factories of the corresponding shipyards. The commissioners would take on responsibility for boosting hemp growing in the assigned zone, paying the hemp farmers, and transporting it to the shipyard factories. The whole system, from purchase to manufacture, thus remained under the direct control of the navy administration.

The system, once set up, did not have the desired result. Antonio de Ulloa himself, the naval thinker who had most explicitly championed greater state intervention in the hemp farming enterprise, had to acknowledge in 1773:

> to this end hemp was planted [in] Granada, Valencia, Murcia and other provinces from the 1750s onwards and a sailcloth factory was set up. One and the other made notable progress at first; but afterwards, having valiantly met the propositions of the contractors—who only seek their own vested interests, at the treasury's cost—the hemp plantations have decreased, undermining the whole manufacturing process.[39]

This naval thinker, with an unrivalled grasp of the Spanish navy's real situation, was in no doubt that the party to blame for this failure was the self-seeking *asentistas*. According to Ulloa, the state was balked in its mercantilist plan of ensuring a reliable national supply of rigging and canvas because it clashed with the vested interests of the military entrepreneurs, who, from Ulloa's viewpoint, failed to understand that the state's interests should be paramount. This type of reasoning, public interest versus private interest, was very much to the fore among Spanish political thinkers of the 1730s, frequently denouncing the profits creamed off by the military entrepreneurs at the Real Hacienda's expense.[40] This was without doubt an idiosyncratic view of mercantilism, in which national wealth should be created mainly by the state instead of the sum of private and public interest, as would seem to be the case with English mercantilism.[41] Despite Ulloa's direct indictment of the contractors for the failure of the state, we believe that part of the blame should also be laid at the navy's door for the way it acted as 'contractor state' in its goal of ensuring the hemp supply.

The obvious point here is why the navy commissioners failed to achieve their remit of encouraging hemp production and its purchase for the navy. Everything seems to suggest that the advent of the navy commissioners in the fields of Spain sparked off opposition from the private merchants who bought up hemp for the private factories and the guilds that used this raw material. Merino describes the conflict that arose between the navy and the Ropemaker's Guild of Castellón in 1759.[42] The conflict could be construed as a consequence of the public and private competition for a resource as yet little developed. But in fact this conflict was caused by the navy's attempt to corner the whole harvest. The trouble was that this was no mere teething problem in the new policy; it became a habitual event over the next decades. Words such as 'embargo', 'rate', and 'fixed prices' began to crop up more and more in the commissioners' reports to the Navy Ministry. The cause of the problems was not so much the increase in demand in itself but rather the way the commissioners turned up in the fields to requisition the whole harvest in exchange for a fixed below-market price. Small wonder, then, that the farmers 'should be loath to increase the area sown with hemp and prefer to sell what they did produce to private merchants'.[43] The correspondence of these commissioners with the councils of the navy departments gives us a better idea of the real nature of the problem.

The navy commissioner's management of this issue was always a tricky affair due to the hornet's nest of problems that was being stirred up on the ground and the differences in the regional conditions under which each commissioner operated. Nothing could be regulated in a single, across-the-board manner and each purchase called for a certain flexibility, which a merchant might understand and exploit but not commissioners who were severely shackled in their way of working. The simple activity of transporting the hemp was also subject to huge regional variations. The Aragon hemp for Ferrol, for example, was cheaper to convey by sea via the Mediterranean than from Bilbao. According to an appraisal of 1768, 'Aragon hemp, although conveyed through Bilbao on commission to Ferrol, proves very expensive; shipping it through the Mediterranean turns out much cheaper.' It is estimated that freightage to Ferrol increased the price by between 9 and 12 per cent.[44] That said, the commissioners' main problem was always with the economic side. The hemp-buyers had to go to locations well off the beaten track, or at least well off the commercial circuits, where it was difficult to draw a bill of exchange or find any type of credit facility. They worked with suppliers, farmers, or farmworkers (journeymen or labourers) who accepted nothing other than cash payment. The hemp purchasing commissioner in Catalonia told the Intendant of the Maritime Department of Cartagena that he needed money in cash 'because neither the farmworkers, carters, workers or craftsmen are people who can work or hand over their fruits without receiving first their respective stipends'.[45] The money was needed at the point of sale but the navy's financial mechanisms operated in precisely the opposite direction, that is, concentrating all economic wherewithal and payment capacity in the department capitals of

Cadiz, Ferrol, and Cartagena. By restricting naval treasuries to the departments alone and conceding greater managerial responsibility over these to the councils of the Maritime Departments, the state aimed to increase the navy's control over its own economic resources. The trouble was that this made the navy commissioners dependent on the money supplied by the departmental treasuries. The pretext given was to prevent any embezzlement by the commissioners, but in practice it meant that the commissioners were forced to channel all their payments through the departmental treasuries, and this was totally inappropriate for the sellers they had to deal with. Very few of those who sold hemp to the commissioners were prepared to traipse off to the departmental capital to be paid for their services. They belonged to a world of small producers who lived on cash not credit.

If the commissioner turned up cash in hand, the farmers did not prove loath to sell their hemp harvests. In fact they jumped at the chance because it was a source of ready money in a cash-poor local economy and helped to pay their taxes. The Granada hemp commissioner pointed out that the producers will always sell, for 'the owners [of the hemp] need the money urgently to pay their royal taxes'.[46] This was echoed by the navy minister of Barcelona when referring to the readiness of Catalan farmers to sell their hemp 'because they can thereby pay off their taxies and levies'.[47] But the farmers needed to be paid on the spot and in cash, not with bills of exchange or in some far-off city. The option of middlemen merchants might have been explored as a solution to this situation, to pick up the money in the naval treasuries and pay it on the farms but the spirit of direct administration ruled out the idea of paying extra commissions to local merchants.

Although the commissioner's lack of liquidity was the most glaring problem, the government never tackled it at all and even exacerbated it with the wrong makeshift solutions. For example the government once tried to pay for its hemp purchases with currency that had been withdrawn from circulation, *moneda de vellón*. Francisco Cantos, the hemp-purchasing commissioner of Aragon expressed in no uncertain terms the huge scorn of the 'public' [farmers] for this currency and he predicted that if hemp farmers were finally paid with *moneda de vellón* the 'farmers will then refuse to sell their hemp harvest to the king rather than accept the currency'.[48] Much the same happened when an attempt was made to pay hemp farmers with *vales reales*, interest-bearing public-debt securities of a high face value for any farmer. The navy hemp-buying commissioner in Granada acknowledged that no farmer would accept *vales reales*. Under this plan the only places in which they could be cashed were Málaga or Cadiz, with the caveat that they would lose 'over twenty percent'.[49] The government rejected this solution because it would not only represent a loss but would also increase public scorn for *vales reales*, and the navy commissioner was forbidden to discount them. The result was that the hemp commissioner now had a hemp-buying means of payment that he could neither use for that purpose nor cash in. He naturally had serious problems in his remit of supplying Cadiz with hemp.

As well as the serious liquidity problem, hemp purchases had their own expenditure timetable, bound up with the seasonal pattern of hemp harvests in terms of production, processing, and transport. This did not necessarily tally with the pattern of funding availability within the Maritime Departments. The hemp purchasing commissioners were continually asking the navy officials for massive injections of cash before beginning to collect the harvest, 'because this helps greatly to drive down the price and stockpile the harvest'.[50] Experience had shown that the best way of working was for the commissioner to draw up a harvest-buying contract with the greatest possible number of farmers, otherwise the product would become more scarce and would then have to be 'bought at double the price'.[51] In some cases, to convince farmers to reserve their whole harvest for sale to a shipyard, it was even suggested that the whole supply should be bought regardless of the quality: 'having pledged in the king's name to take all the hemp offered'.[52] In practice a veritable purchasing monopoly was the aim, on the strength of the promise beforehand of immediate payment. The commissioner Esteban Gaztambide asked for more money to buy the 1781 Granada hemp harvest because he believed that 'if we let only a small part of the harvest be sold elsewhere due to lack of funds this will set a terrible example in price terms; to avoid this I have bought up the whole harvest down to the poorest quality'. He was buying at 58 *reales* per *arroba*, and had to avoid showing any 'weakness or allowing owners any leeway to sell to outsiders, which has surreptitiously been done already (with) some batches at 85 *reales* per *arroba*'.[53] The same stance was taken by the navy minister of Barcelona, Agustín de Navarrete, who, like the rest of the commissioners, asked for hemp-purchasing funds to be forwarded beforehand because 'not having the funds now means paying more in the future', and he also claimed that he had to do it 'because it avoids the crop being sold off to other merchants from whom we would eventually have to buy it back at a higher price'.[54]

The hemp-buying commissioners needed cash, and to be delegated enough flexibility to be able to outmanoeuvre any other purchaser in the farming areas. When neither cash nor flexibility was forthcoming, the problems began. The navy's financing system had evolved in the direction of leaving it up to the shipyards' Juntas de Marina to manage most of their fiscal resources. Each maritime department worked with a fixed budget, approved by the Navy Ministry, which the Finance Ministry then simply rubber-stamped and enforced. Any modification of this budget was a long-winded business that was unlikely ever to be quick and flexible enough for the commissioners on the ground. This cramped the commissioners' style and they fell increasingly out of sync with the shipyards. Despite the strategic importance placed on the purchase of Granada hemp by the Cadiz Junta de Marina it had to bow out, declining to fund 'the necessary amount for purchasing hemp in Granada due to ignorance of the portion that might be stockpiled'.[55] The surprising result of all this was that the shipyards no longer knew how much national hemp they could work with. Worst of all, this uncertainty accelerated the last-ditch solutions of harvest embargoes and seizures. The main reason for this mess was undoubtedly the purchasing policy bereft of cash or flexibility but the navy's demand also became a problem for Spanish hemp producers. A telltale sign here is the clearly negative assessment of this state intervention in the national hemp market made in the early nineteenth century by the Finance

Minister, Canga Argüelles: 'the spread of hemp farming in Granada has been outrageously hampered by our own royal navy. Not content with forcing farmers to sell all their produce at a fixed price, it also laid down the farming and processing method and vexed them in many other different ways.'[56]

If we return to Antonio Ulloa's indictment of the contractors, blaming them for the state's failure to ensure navy supplies of hemp, sailcloth, and rigging, our analysis of how production and purchases were run shows that part of this blame must also be laid at the door of the state and navy. The practical result of all this was an inability to ensure supplies from national sources and the need to continue buying in from abroad. But the irremediable need to maintain the *asientos* system did not spell a complete return to the early eighteenth century. The state also introduced some changes here, though these once more led to increased monopolistic tendencies.

THE MERCANTILIST UTOPIA

Despite the mercantilist project of achieving a national or colony-based supply, the Spanish navy's supplies continued to depend on far-off countries during the second half of the eighteenth century. Masts, spars and rigging, wood, hemp, iron, and tar of adequate quality could still not be produced in Spain, but had to be bought in the Baltic by means of *asientos* with private businesspeople, Spanish or foreign. The problem with this trade was not only logistic, there was also an important strategic and political factor. Since the Baltic had become such a crucial area for most naval powers, the European states had made access to this market a top-level diplomatic affair. The result was a complex interplay of clashing interests. The English wielded control in the naval supply business during the second half of the eighteenth century but inroads were being made by the other northern powers and now the French and Spanish were trying to muscle in too.[57] This all added up to a complex and turbulent international provisioning market.

Everything seems to suggest that the Spanish government stepped up its involvement in the Baltic naval supply trade. Another option would have been to tap into the continual and copious flow of goods through the nearest port to each department for its supply of northern merchandise. This expedient was never taken up as a naval supply method by the government of Charles III. Only in cases of extreme urgency were orders given for any cargo passing through the port to be snapped up. It seems that the very opposite happened; trade was steered towards direct procurement of naval supplies from the Baltic, in an increasingly monopolistic, Madrid-centred form.[58]

Until the beginning of the 1760s Baltic hemp was supplied by means of partial purchases offered by Spanish traders from Spain's north coast, who drew on their network of contacts in northern Europe, mainly Amsterdam but also the Baltic, to buy the merchandise. Marcelo Ramón de Uribarri, a resident of Bilbao, put forward as his purchasing surety 'the long-standing correspondence and knowledge I have in the main trading cities of the Baltic, such as St Petersburg, Riga and Danzig'.[59] The usual trading arrangement here was for merchants to bring in small amounts of hemp at their own risk and then offer them to the provincial navy ministers or directly to the shipyard *intendentes*. Some of them used this as a pretext for getting silver out of Spain, legally or otherwise.[60] In other cases the hemp business underpinned a much wider-ranging commercial network of goods and services and helped to make the whole trade more profitable, as in the case of Tomás de Santa Aulary with the supply of Baltic hemp in Bilbao and Ferrol.[61] This relatively open and competitive model, involving also the participation of foreigners, gradually evolved towards a more monopolistic model in which the final purchasing decision switched from the Juntas de Marina of the Maritime Departments to the Navy Ministry. The sales proposals were still received by the *intendentes* but were dealt with in the Navy Ministry and, increasingly, by 'means of reserved affairs for the Hacienda'.[62]

A watershed moment in this trend of centralizing the supply in Madrid came with the advent of Felipe Chone, a Bilbao merchant, who managed to corner the entire business of Baltic hemp supplies. To do so he offered to make massive purchases for all the state's shipyards over a long period of time (five years) on the express condition that 'for such time as the *asiento* lasts no northern hemp should be bought from any other *asentista*'. He undertook to supply 12,000 to 16,000 *quintales* of hemp a year, all from St Petersburg. This amount could be increased if necessary but only via orders of over 4,000 *quintales*.[63] What this merchant was offering the state, in other words, was a de facto supply monopoly, converting his own massive purchases into an exclusive business between the Finance Ministry of Madrid and the entrepreneur. The purchasing monopoly option was being increasingly taken up in other areas of military supply, but in this case of Baltic provisions it was a way of ensuring a complex supply arrangement made essential by the puny development of national hemp farming.

Felipe Chone's supply monopoly was maintained despite attempts by various foreign merchants to take over the business. The sternest challenge came from Juan Federico Brandenburgo, consul of Russia. His trading house, Casa Rey-Brandenburgo, was well known to the navy; for some time it had been offering cargoes of hemp and other northern produce to the ports of Ferrol and Cadiz and was deemed to be very trustworthy due to its 'trading credit and its business base in St Petersburg, making it eligible for preferential rights offered by the Russian empire to patricians of that city in terms of quality and prices'.[64] The house itself invoked a wide range of services to the crown: 'SS. Rei, i Brandemburg, established now for many years in the trade of the city of Cadiz ... with proven experience in nearly all the troop transports to America, and Regular Fathers of the Society of Jesus to Italy and others of greater scale, which it has undertaken, well known to the Departments of Cadiz'.[65] With this track record behind him, Brandenburgo offered to take on Chone's military supply-contract for the departmental council of Ferrol, undercutting his price. The *junta* sent the proposal on to Madrid, where it was analysed by the Navy Minister and Finance Minister. The government decided to turn down the bid, despite the cheaper price, since it was seen as unfitting 'for a foreign consul to become involved in a business that might reveal the failings of the shipyards or armament plans, especially when they are considerable'. The government preferred to stick with Chone, protégé of Conde de Clonard, who was, it was expressly stressed, a Spaniard and 'vassal of Your Majesty'. In other words, there was a whole compendium of strategic and mercantilist reasons.

To keep this king's subject at the head of the *asiento*, the government did not hesitate to give reserved orders to the Treasurer General, Marqués de Zambrano, for the Real Hacienda secretly to sustain the entrepreneur Chone 'albeit at the cost of making him some sort of secret payment'. In exchange for this financial support the government asked Chone to make some reduction in his hemp military supply-contract prices, 'in the assurance that he will be duly paid by the Real Hacienda'. The whole negotiation was conducted in Madrid and it was expressly decided not to pass on the fine detail or political reasons to the councils of the maritime departments, on the grounds, in the Finance Minister's words, 'that these (navy departments) should not become cognisant of the reserved condition in which the intervention has been made. The only means is for the aforementioned excess to be met by Your Excellency [Marqués de Zambrano] in separate payments apart from the main sum.' These reserved agreements between contractor and the Navy Ministry were the source of many problems for the Treasurer General, who then had to account for the extra expenditure. As Zambrano complained to Múzquiz, these reserved payments to Felipe Chone and other military entrepreneurs of the north, like Carlos María Marracci, were not easy to account for before the Tribunal de la Contaduría 'where many eyes pore over the sums paid'. He proposed, his suggestion duly taken up, that it be accounted for under 'the name of secret expenditure, the certifications of the main department comptrollers then being collected in the Ministry under your charge'.[66]

The Baltic hemp purchases thus became an affair of state, sidestepping the managerial arrangements of the councils of the maritime departments and at times even of the Navy Ministry itself. The government seized the option of one monopolistic entrepreneur to guarantee the supply and confidentiality required by such a strategic product; once that decision had been made it did not hesitate to support the contractor even by underhand methods, such as officially agreeing one price and actually paying another.

State intervention in this Baltic hemp supply increased in the following years, in line with the growing needs of the navy as war broke out and escalated, with a concomitant increase in European rivalry for access to the Baltic. The need for greater state involvement in this business cum affair-of-state became patent as from 1774. In this year Miguel Soto, Conde de Clonard, a resident of Cadiz and trader with America, bondsman to Felipe Chone, notified the minister Arriaga of his trading house's problems in procuring Baltic hemp. Judging from the reports of his commissioners in the Baltic and in Holland, working in this market was becoming distinctly complex and expensive. The sudden surge in demand from the Northern European navies drove up prices and also produced clashes with the Dutch merchants, who had traditionally acted as middlemen and were now bearing the brunt of the increasing competition from the rest of the European merchants. This information tallies with that given by the French consuls to their government at this time.[67] Everything suggests that the Dutch feared losing their main middleman function in the Baltic trade, both for making the purchases and also for dealing with the payment arrangements in Amsterdam. Their reaction, according to Clonard's commissioners, was to drive up the financial charges connected with their mediation. This commissioner informed Clonard of the letters of its agents in the Baltic, warning of the Dutch manoeuvres to drive up the price of their mediation services:

> for even the commissioners we have in Riga, Danzig and other ports where purchases are made, goaded by the rest, have completely changed the credit conditions and sums of the cargoes, doing this so brusquely and with such dramatic rises that our correspondents in Amsterdam, to meet these payment obligations, have drawn huge sums on this city, at much shorter terms than hitherto.[68]

Clonard was perfectly familiar with the keys to Spain's foreign policy and the state's aspirations in that area, and knew perfectly well how to broach the problem in the most suitable language. In 1772 Clonard himself had sent Múzquiz a report, asking him to send it up to Grimaldi, showing the coincidence of the state's and Clonard's interest in that area, particularly the project that then sought royal protection for the Baltic trade 'to ensure the best possible reception of these frigates and a leniency in the duty levied by the Crown of Denmark on the passage through Oresund Strait'.[69] He directly contacted the Finance Minister rather than the Navy Minister, couching it in terms of an affair of state directly impinging on the mercantilist principles upheld by his government. What was at stake here was not the hemp itself but rather, in the entrepreneur's own words, 'the happy success with which His Majesty's flag is allowed to trade in the northern seas and the very subsistence of the Spanish house of *Chone y Soto de San Petersburgo*'. At that moment Clonard claimed to be employing 26 ships on this hemp provision trade with a back-log of losses now adding up to over 70,000 pesos. Clonard proved that he had shown the highest dedication and made the greatest possible effort in promoting the public interest, but also claimed that his ruin was inevitable. That being so, he asked only for state protection, or in his own words, 'the greatest patronage of your excellency [Múzquiz] to counteract these rival powers, bringing to bear all the power of the king ... with an indefatigable zeal to continue with an undertaking so beneficial to the state'.[70] Clonard's strategy worked. The government decided to support this entrepreneur unconditionally. The Finance Minister ordered an immediate payment of 40,000 pesos to the military entrepreneur, advising the Navy Minister 'that he be conceded this grace because the *Asentista* is owed a greater sum'.[71] In other words, the state took on the contractor's losses as its own and showed a clear will to keep him at the head of his business. Contrary to the claims of Antonio Ulloa, public and private interests could be merged in a common venture and mercantilism could facilitate this union.

Several concurrent factors weighed heavily in the government's decision to pitch in behind this northern hemp contract and stick to this policy in subsequent years. First, there was the prevailing sabre-rattling mood at that time; secondly, the state's mercantilist-driven keenness to increase Spain's direct presence in the Baltic; and thirdly, in all probability, its mistrust of the ability of the national hemp supply alone to fuel a wholesale naval rearmament programme. There are many examples of government aid given to this hemp contractor, although it is not always so easy to ascertain the nature of this support, for example when Castejón asked Múzquiz to pay Chone 'the bonus stipulated by secret agreement with regard to the provision of 77 [which] comprised only 13,850 quintales of Riga hemp, when it should have been 16,112 *quintales*'.[72] The important fact is that this increased interaction between state and the monopolistic *asentista* favoured the awarding of other navy-provisioning *asientos* with goods from the Baltic to the company of Chone and Clonard, such as the contract of masts and spars and planking from 1772 or bitumen from 1773.[73] The front man for this transaction was Manuel Martínez, resident of Coruña. They took on responsibility for the supply of all the northern bitumen for three years. It was renewed for another four years (1774–7). The main source of tar was Sweden, 'which is now the biggest supplier for France, England and other countries'.[74]

When we also factor in that Clonard himself financed other navy provisioning *asientos* in Spain, such as those of Carlos María Marraci, standing as bondsman for any replacement merchant in the event of bankruptcy, we see that this entrepreneur's hand was continually strengthened in an upward spiral of state support. The shadowy presence of the Conde de Clonard can clearly be discerned behind some military supply-contract changes. Take the case of Ignacio José Haedo's bitumen provisions for navy shipyards, guaranteed by Clonard under a contract beginning in 1 February 1777. Haedo asked to be 'relieved of the obligation because of growing losses run up since that date for unforeseeable reasons'. He was replaced by Felipe Abancido, a Madrid merchant also guaranteed by Clonard, taking over on 1 April 1778. It could even be safely claimed that it was the state that contributed most to the development of this monopolistic entrepreneur. Once more private and public interests went hand in hand.

Naval supplies could no longer be allowed to stray outside the decision-making spheres closest to the government. This trend was confirmed and strengthened by the escalating scale of warfare, making state intervention even more necessary. The first consequence of the sharp demand for hemp was a soaring increase in the asking price. Carlos María Marracci, on behalf of Clonard and Chone, informed Castejón that the price of hemp and other Baltic goods had increased considerably in Riga 'due to the naval rearmament taking place in Europe since 1775'. In October 1777, Clonard presented the king with an ultimatum: unless the price difference was made up they would renounce the contract. The government once more caved in to the military entrepreneur's demands, paying outside the contract the cost increases for the provisions over the previous two years. It did the same in the two following years in which 'the same price increases continued'. His last contract was in 1778, lasting two years and supplying three naval departments.[75]

The monopoly-based mutual dependence spiral was a risky ploy because any contractor bankruptcy checkmated the state. As with the manufacturing monopoly, it proved difficult to fall back on the market to make up for any *asentista* shortfall. The only solution was to shore up the military entrepreneur even more, that is, a new escalation in the spiral of dependence between state and contractor. The government had to sustain the military entrepreneurs not only with secret and underhand payments and agreements, as we have already pointed out, but also with flagrant political exceptions, such as tax benefits. Thus, the Navy Minister had to support Clonard's company when the Ferrol revenue farmers, in observance of a general order for all contractors to pay taxes, demanded payment of the taxes levied on the supplies of northern goods for the Ferrol shipyard. The reasons given by the minister were telling: 'it seems unprecedented for duties to be demanded in such exceptional circumstances when the risk is being taken of bringing them in neutral ships'. His conclusion and recommendation was that 'this is not the time to weaken them [the contractors]'. The Finance Minister Múzquiz therefore ordered that a fiscal exception be made for shipments of hemp and other Baltic provisions.[76] In other words, while hemp purchased by a navy commissioner in Catalonia paid duty on entering the Cartagena shipyard, the hemp bought in Riga was duty free upon landing in Ferrol or Cartagena. The growing state-*asentista* dependence was now beginning to jeopardize the government's own mercantilist principles.

This tightening spiral eventually meant that the government became increasingly enmeshed in the financial arrangements of these *asentistas*, and might eventually even be forced to replace them. As we have already pointed out, one of the problems faced by these contractors was the use of the Dutch houses as middlemen between the Baltic ports and Cadiz or Madrid. The government's solution was to make the Real Hacienda's overseas offices, the Real Giro, available to the military entrepreneurs to help them finance their naval supply purchases. As from 1776, therefore, the treasury of the Real Giro de Amsterdam recorded an unusual spate of activity. Its treasurer, Juan Manuel de Uriondo, and the Minister in The Hague, received a continuous stream of requests for a host of financial services bound up with an increasing range of naval supplies. These services involved not only the financing of hemp purchases but also large fabric orders in Holland 'for the Royal Navy'. Vizconde de la Herrería was furnished with 2,100,000 *reales* to make these fabric purchases. The objective of this massive fabric purchase was 'to stockpile this useful shipbuilding element and head off much higher costs if bought later'.[77] The treasury of the Real Giro de Amsterdam even sometimes took out loans in Holland to endow itself with liquidity until such time as funds arrived from Spain.[78] The whole system was coordinated from the Treasury General of Madrid. For example, should it arise that 'the Treasury (was) low on funds', Uriondo had been ordered to pay Vizconde de la Herreria 920,000 *reales* 'which it will have raised on loan to pay military entrepreneurs on time in the past'. According to one estimate made by the Treasury General in 1784 over 11.5 million *reales* were paid out in 1779 alone to defray these naval supply purchases.[79]

All the state support doled out for contractors proved insufficient to sustain them in the end. Baltic navigation was becoming an increasingly risky business due to the presence of English ships and the soaring prices of raw materials, insurance, and freightage. The result was a rapid withdrawal of *asentistas* from the northern naval supplies business. The de facto monopoly conditions that now obtained made the fall and Baltic withdrawal of Chone and Clonard in 1780 an especially grave event.[80] The problem the government faced now was how to replace these military entrepreneurs. The monopoly had reduced the fold of entrepreneurs working with the state and the climate of uncertainty prevailing at that time dissuaded other potential entrepreneurs from chancing their arm. The solution once more was political: it could not be dealt with at the level of shipyards, councils, or maritime departments so the state itself had to tackle it as a political problem. The Navy Minister, the Marqués de Castejón, had to acknowledge that it was not a problem that could be solved by navy officials in the departmental councils; once more it was an affair of state. As Castejón explained to the Finance Minister, 'now that the northern passage is practically closed, the hemp and mast-and-spar military entrepreneurs have fallen well behind in their obligations and there is now an urgent need to replace them either by means of national goods or bringing in goods from the Mediterranean if need be'.[81] In other words, it was the government that now had to guide the search for the supplies that were no longer arriving, either from inside or outside Spain.

Castejón was quite right about the naval supply business being an affair of state and also that the contractors running this business had fallen heavily into debt. But he was not entirely correct about the Baltic market now being closed off. Whether to make up for the deficiencies of national outlets or to make the best of the previous shift of naval financial affairs to Amsterdam, the truth is that the Spanish government continued to seek solutions in 'the North'. The government snatched at the opportunities offered by neutral countries for purchasing naval supplies and transporting them to the Spanish shipyards. Russia played a key role in these supply arrangements. It also proffered the advantages of state capitalism in which the Russian government itself offered its war frigates for transporting the hemp to Ferrol. Payments were made in Madrid to Patricio Joyes, in this case for two war frigates costing 1,337,955 *rsv*.[82] The government therefore began to make the purchases directly in the Baltic. The Baltic hemp supply had thereby changed from an *asiento*-based system run from Madrid to a direct administration system strongly controlled by the state but carried out by private commissioners.

The system was centred on a St Petersburg businessman, Pedro Normande, who bought the goods ordered by the Secretary of State locally, charging a commission for the service. In other words it was no longer the departmental councils or Castejón or even Múzquiz who intervened directly in the hemp supply business but the Secretary of State himself, the Conde de Floridablanca, on a diplomatic basis. Normande had received from Floridablanca 'a commission as the king's chargé d'affaires in St Petersburg'. This remit mainly involved the purchasing of goods of all types for the navy. Although later documents referred in detail to this commission, who ordered it, and the reason behind it, we do not know the exact date upon which the commission was given, though evidence seems to suggest that it would have been in late 1780.[83] Normande liaised directly with the Secretary of State and kept him abreast of how the business was going. His purchases were paid for in bills drawn by Antonio Colombi, a Spanish trading house based in St Petersburg, who was to become Spanish consul in Russia against correspondents in Amsterdam or Madrid;[84] in the latter case nearly always on the bankers Patricio Joyes, Agustín Queneau, and Esteban Drouilhet, who then presented them for payment to the Treasurer General.[85] There are numerous examples of these payment arrangements; so Pedro Normande informed Floridablanca of the bill drawn in favour of Antonio Colombi, who endorsed the credit of Patricio Joyes to the value of 20,000 *ducados de plata* for masts and spars ordered for the Royal Navy, which the Treasurer General paid against the budget consignment of the department of Ferrol. Another, was with the same merchant and of the same value but for planking and hemp. The choice of these banking houses as receivers was probably because they were known, were solvent, and had good relations with the commercial networks linking Cadiz with Europe. In any case it all formed part of the same clique of mutual trust and interchange of information and business. There are sometimes express references to the link between the network participants. Thus, Esteban Drouilhet referred to Pedro Normande as his 'friend from Petersburg ... who needed these funds to meet various obligations he has undertaken on our behalf'. It was sometimes Normande himself who drew the bills, mainly against the Treasury of the Real Giro de Amsterdam.[86]

The Treasurer General then recorded all these expenses in the corresponding navy department, charged against the budget consignment for that year or directly, that is, the same procedure as would be used by a navy commissioner buying hemp in Aragon or Granada. The selfsame procedure was used with the insurance and freightage of the neutral ships bringing in goods procured in the Baltic. Whether procured in Amsterdam or the Baltic, reports on the management thereof were sent up to the Navy Ministry 'as reserved state information' under the supervision of the Treasury General.[87]

The upshot of all this was that Baltic hemp was still the most widely used raw material in the shipyards' rigging and sailcloth factories. Its purchase was coordinated from the State Secretariat as a diplomatic matter, carried out by private merchants who acted as navy commissioners and were paid directly by the Real Hacienda in Amsterdam or Madrid. National hemp played second fiddle. The navy's typical eighteenth-century demand surges called for more flexibility and rapid responses than the national market could provide, forcing the government to turn to the overseas markets. Mercantilism was without doubt the pet theory of Spanish politicians and thinkers, but its application did not produce the desired results. The Spanish contractor state was only partially successful in passing on the potential benefits of the demand for hemp, sailcloth, and rigging to the national economy. Despite the Spanish state's will to harness this naval supply to boost the national market, things turned out very differently. Strong state intervention in the production and purchase of national output ended up demotivating the wider national market and therefore increasing dependence on supplies from abroad. Moreover, when the state finally had to turn to these overseas markets, it mistrusted the free competition of merchants and chose instead to channel demand through a handful of trading houses in a last-ditch effort to increase its intervention, shielding these chosen few with privileges and protecting them from any competition. Monopoly once more became the chosen modus operandi, and along the way mercantilism showed all its shortfalls and was reduced to mere lip-service.

10

Monopoly versus the Market

Urgency and Flexibility

The relations between the state and military entrepreneurs were defined by the policy pursued in the procurement of military supplies, but this analytical approach can become too hidebound. More often than might be thought, everything could change in a very short—sometimes surprisingly short—time-span. A rumour spreading through diplomatic circles, for example, sufficed to create a sense of urgency and the need rapidly to adopt measures that often conflicted with previous procedures. The contractor state adopted a short-term outlook, and this implied switching and changing the ground rules and relations with entrepreneurs. To complete our view of the Spanish contractor state, therefore, we need also to analyse this fickle, short-term dimension. An analysis of the ad hoc and flexible nature of the contractor state provides a clearer understanding of the true nature of the relations between the state and military entrepreneurs.

This aspect will be considered through examination of a specific moment, when the Spanish contractor state had urgently to solve a problem of military supply in the face of impending military action. Of all military activities one of the most complex for any state was undoubtedly an amphibious expedition. It was in this scenario that the state had to show all its efficiency and rapid adaptability to mobilize the huge variety of supplies and resources needed.[1] What made an amphibious expedition so complex was precisely the need to coordinate and manage a host of supplies, command hierarchies, warfare resources, and military entrepreneurs operating in different markets.[2] The problem became even more acute when the expedition had to be supplied in enemy territory and from sources abroad.[3] Supply lines were longer and more complex while supply times were tight. Urgency and complexity make amphibious expeditions an excellent exemplar of the timing problems a contractor state might have to face.

These issues will be examined in detail through the particular case of the amphibious expedition organized by Spanish armed forces in 1781 and 1782 to conquer the island of Minorca.[4] The state had to mobilize and sustain a 10,000-strong expeditionary army while at the same time setting up a wide-ranging network of army and navy supplies that extended throughout almost the whole of the Western Mediterranean. Of particular interest here are such factors as the character of the supply policy, the government's working expectations, and the reasons for changing this policy. It is indeed these fluctuations that give us the best idea of the changing relations with the military entrepreneurs involved.

An amphibious expedition, from the state's point of view, was a source of business to be offered to entrepreneurs. On 29 July 1781 Miguel Múzquiz, Secretary of War and Finance, informed the Conde del Asalto, Captain General of Catalonia, that an expeditionary force under the Duc de Crillon had just passed the Strait on its way to win back Minorca. The purpose of this missive was twofold: first, to reveal the destination of a naval expedition that had hitherto been kept in the strictest secrecy and, secondly, to muster as much support as possible for this expeditionary force from Catalonia. Del Asalto's reply conveys a hand-rubbing glee at the trade bonanza in view for the region's victuallers: 'upon learning of its arrival I shall bring home to the locals just how propitious to their interests these new circumstances might be, it falling to the island and the place where the army is quartered to victual and provision the individuals thereof, all on the assumption that the seas are cleansed of corsairs and enemies'.[5]

Indeed, the Captain General of Catalonia had quickly and clear-sightedly recognized the trade-boosting aspect of this expeditionary force, especially in view of the fact that the escort ships of the fleet carrying de Crillon's army would necessarily create a swathe of secure waters in the area. The victualling operation looked as though it would be on a grand scale, and these bright business prospects were confirmed and even enhanced by the news filtering into the Captaincy General of Catalonia over the following days. The army that originally landed on the island was 8,048 strong, with more troops being phased in over the following months, reaching a total of 10,610 Spanish plus 3,901 French soldiers. The number of allied soldiers on Minorca at the moment of the English surrender, on 5 February 1782, was therefore 14,511.[6] If amphibious warfare implied complex mobilization of resources, the provisioning of an army corps on this scale could become an almost inexhaustible fountainhead of opportunities.

Unlike the previous expeditions to Algiers and Sacramento, this expeditionary force was heading for a well-provisioned territory. The Junta de Estado (State Cabinet) was perfectly informed of Minorca's supply potential. Several factors had come together to make Minorca such a richly provisioned island. First and foremost, the islanders themselves, by dint of a considerable commercial effort, had managed to eliminate the Balearic Island's chronic cereal output deficit.[7] Minorcan merchants had woven together a wide-ranging web of cereal production and consumption areas, taking in a large part of the Western Mediterranean (Barbary, Sardinia, Sicily, Spain, and Italy). Notwithstanding Minorca's longstanding mercantile tradition, Joan Hernández Andreu traces the real start of the trading boom to the creation of Mahón dockyard by the English in 1724.[8] Other driving forces behind this trading activity were the protection offered by the English to this trade, the good relations maintained by Great Britain with North African regencies, and the free port status granted to Mahón by the English.[9] The grain trade became the mainstay activity of Minorcan merchants and also an efficient way of ensuring the provisioning of Minorca. So resounding was their success that they even managed to muscle into the Majorca cereal supply while also playing a leading role in supplying the Spanish Mediterranean coast, especially Catalonia. In the 1770s, therefore, the island of Minorca was the most active market with the best cereal supply of the Western Mediterranean.[10]

Secondly, the Junta de Estado was perfectly aware of the fact that the island's stockpiles had grown even during the first years of the war against Great Britain. The espionage network organized since late 1779 in Minorca by the Majorcan Marqués de Sollerich kept Floridablanca abreast of the heavy concentration of victuals and supplies of all types in Mahón. The Spanish Secretary of State knew that, on top of the two relief convoys received in Minorca from Great Britain, the English were making purchases all round the Mediterranean to shore up Minorca's resistance against any future blockade. The first provisioning convoy sailed in late February 1780 under Admiral Rodney. After supplying Gibraltar he sent 17 ships to Minorca. The second convoy got to the island in April 1781, with 13 ships carrying victuals and military supplies. According to Desmond Gregory, the first convoy consisted of seven ships and carried only munitions, not victuals.[11] The English government had also involved Minorca in the Gibraltar relief effort. Lieutenant-General James Murray, Governor of Minorca, bought these provisions with funds from the Victualling Board, through the British consuls in Genoa and Leghorn,[12] or turned to Minorcan merchants who procured them in Barbary, especially livestock and wheat. These mass purchases by Minorcan merchants in Barbary even prompted the king of Algeria to protest against the British authorities on the grounds that the ostensible purchases for Minorca would in fact be sold to their Spanish enemy.[13] The Board of Ordnance tripled the Minorca provisioning budget during the war years to ensure the continuity of these purchases, and the English set up a regular supply of funds from Italian ports carried on neutral ships. According to the Spanish spies, 'the troops [in Minorca] are well paid and assisted, receiving funds via Genoa and Leghorn, like the sealed orders from London, and a few days ago a Russian frigate said to be carrying money anchored in that port'.[14]

There is little doubt that the bulk of these purchases were to end up in Gibraltar. English eyewitnesses of the Gibraltar blockade reported a high number of small Minorcan craft managing to bypass the Spanish naval blockade and reach Gibraltar. On some occasions these relief supplies were sizeable, like the 24-ship victual-carrying convoy that put in to Gibraltar on 27 April 1781.[15] For their part the spies working for the Spanish confirmed Minorca's role as a relief store for Gibraltar: 'there are frequent shipments of wines and comestibles from Mahon on xebecs and light craft, sailing along the coast of Africa to bring these stores to Gibraltar, where they are said to make hay from the high prices being charged there'.[16] From 1779 to 1781, therefore, Mahón became a huge, well-stocked storeroom, with the wherewithal to withstand a three-month siege and enough left over to give constant relief to Gibraltar.

Minorca's plentiful supplies were one of the sharpest goads to heavy Corsair activity in the years running up to the arrival of Crillon's army. In these years the English governor granted Letters of Marque to 55 Minorcan vessels, crewed by

3,000 men and armed with about 535 cannons. This veritable war fleet was further swollen by Greek, Italian, Berber, and English privateers. The corsair fleet operating from Minorca captured a total of 262 ships in these years.[17] Minorcan privateering became an endless source of business at that time, also spawning a thriving market for buying and selling the captured booty. These eventually caught the eye of foreign merchants, mainly from Genoa and Leghorn, who came to Mahón to take part in the auctions of captured ships. The difference from the privateering of earlier wars resided not only in the scale of it but also in its better organization and widespread support by Minorcan society and economy.[18] Governor Murray tapped into the privateering market to top up the supplies stockpiled in Minorca. Majorca's bad harvest in 1779 drew in cereal from Minorca to fill the vacuum and there was a parallel increase in shipments to the Spanish coast. This prompted the governor to decree that any wheat- or barley-carrying vessels captured by corsairs of any nationality should be obligatorily brought to Mahón.[19]

The connections between privateering and the level of Minorca's supplies did not go unnoticed by the Spanish spies, who informed the Spanish authorities of the rapidly increasing number of captured ships being brought in and the widespread acceptance of their legality by the English authorities: 'A vast number of prizes have been deemed to be legitimate and five neutral ships have been arrested';[20] 'the corsairs are very abundant, bringing in as many as 20 prizes some days. Be it known to Your Excellency that the number of corsairs in this island is increasing daily, in view of the growing number of prizes they bring into the ports ... and unless Your Excellency thinks otherwise, it would be well to take Minorca before Gibraltar because fresh provisions are continually being sent by this island to that town.'[21] Another informant said:

> the island (Minorca) is well supplied with victuals. Each day prizes laden with wheat for Spain are brought into the port, others with oil or wine. It has recently been published that over 15,000 *cuarteras* of wheat have entered the port, plus 100 oxen and 100 rams which have arrived from Barbary on the recommendation of the governor, with another 200 being expected of each species.[22]

Worthy of note here is that some of the ships laden with wheat for the Spanish troops in Campo de Gibraltar were finally taken by Mahón privateers and ended up being sent to the English troops in Gibraltar; such was the case for some purchases made by the Five Major Guilds in Marseilles through the Bellón e Hijos house and sent to Algeciras.[23]

The Spanish Junta de Estado, therefore, was of the opinion that Minorca had become a well-provisioned island that could work as a very active market and warehouse, thereby jeopardizing trade in the area and preventing the isolation of Gibraltar. As the Conde de Floridablanca explained to the *junta*, it was essential 'to pull the rug of Mahón out from under Gibraltar, which it has served as storehouse for some time past, whereby, without the many ships and relief supplies sent from Mahón to Gibraltar, the latter could hardly have withstood the blockade'.[24] The Spanish authorities were also mindful of the worth of such a well-supplied island as Minorca as a storehouse of pre-prepared resources for the expeditionary force. So important was this advantage that the strategy for the assault on the island was largely based on preventing the English from destroying or removing from the Castillo de San Felipe the many victuals and supplies that were supposed to exist in Mahón. The Duc de Crillon himself explained to Ventura Moreno, head of the fleet conveying his army, that his plan to land simultaneously on two fronts offered the singular advantage 'of catching the English by surprise and preventing them from removing from Mahón all their troops, stores and effects, therefore leaving them to our mercy'.[25] Months before the invasion, the Junta de Estado had even received from a 'Ciutadella merchant' the serious proposal to 'buy the Prizes and other stores in Minorca of all possible grains and victuals, to set them aside for the army', a proposal that found great favour with the *junta*.[26]

Subsequent events proved the Spanish *junta*'s appreciation of the island's supply possibilities to have been well founded. The hasty flight of the English to the San Felipe fort left a treasure trove of supplies in the hands of the Spanish. This was described by an eyewitness thus: 'the enemy has abandoned vast stores to us, full of many and varied riches and there is no doubt that the English loss on this occasion is tantamount to that suffered by the Dutch in Sint Eustatius'.[27] The worth put on the goods left behind by the English, including the captured ships and the items stored in the Castillo de San Felipe, amounted to over 5 million *reales*.[28] This wealth attracted many merchants to the island, ready to bid for these supplies and even buy them lock, stock, and barrel: 'all the more so with the arrival here of a representative sent by a Rich and Solid Company who offered to buy all the goods outright'.[29] Over the following months the Finance Minister, Miguel Múzquiz, would continually refer to the supplies taken on the island to defuse any requests for new victuals. In reply to Crillon's application for more meat, for example, Múzquiz pointed out that 2,450 barrels of salted meat had been inventoried in diverse stores of the English, adding up to 19,600 *arrobas* of meat, Múzquiz concluding that 'so great a quantity cannot possibly have been used up already'.[30]

The Junta de Estado was therefore confident that the victualling of the expeditionary force would pose no problem, first because of Minorca's own bounteous supplies and secondly because of the opportunities that might be harnessed on the Spanish coast for additional supply. These sanguine hopes were dashed in the following months. The supply system was too rigid, leaving hardly any leeway for the initiative of private merchants, throttling all the positive prospects for further contracts, and turning the victualling of Crillon's army into a major problem.

THE EXPEDITION PROVISIONED IN CADIZ

The troops and supplies for Crillon's expedition were stockpiled and mustered in Cadiz and Seville from early May 1781 to mid July of the same year, when the fleet finally sailed. The expedition's provisioning strategy was governed by the need to keep the destination secret and the aim to get an army up and running within four months.[31] The arrangements for putting together an 8,000-strong army could hardly have gone unnoticed to British espionage, so it was bruited abroad that the expedition's purpose was to reinforce American garrisons. To lend credibility to this red herring the ships had to be chartered as if they were going to the Americas, at a much higher freightage cost, while the provisions shipped on board also had to bear out this deceit. The Casa de Contratación de Indias, responsible for these freighting arrangements, charged 10 to 11 pesos per ton, while the going rate for ships sailing the Mediterranean was 3.5 pesos. Several sources bear out these figures: 'and always reducing the freightage to the going rate for the Mediterranean, which is one half of the price for the Americas', or 'the advantage of chartering national ships and others as may be needed, both because of their medium size, making port entrances and exits easier, and for the freightage price of three and a half pesos per ton'.[32] In victualling terms there was a notable difference between army supplies, called *ración de pan* or *ración de munición*, and the provisions for the navy and the troops that might be carried on its ships, called *ración de armada*. The navy allowance had a greater variety of ingredients and was hence much more expensive: 96 *mrvs* as against only 22 *mrvs* for the army's allowance. The navy victualling was contracted to the *asentista* Nicolás Ambrosio Garro, with payment of Luis Manuel Quiñones and Josefa María Arizcun, for the period 1777–83. The army victualling contract was awarded to the Gremios at this time in a contract signed by its empowered managers, Juan Manuel de Baños and Isidoro del Castillo.[33] The loading up of a very low number of rations would have been a giveaway for the English spies. To throw them off the scent, therefore, the Spanish had to ship navy rations sufficient for the ostensible journey to the Americas. The benchmark for such an expedition was the convoy that took Cevallos's expeditionary force to Sacramento in 1776. Back then 4,300,000 rations were shipped on board for an 8,210-strong infantry force and a total crew of 17,000 and a time-frame of six months.[34] When Crillon's army set sail, according to the navy's purveyor general who provided them, 'it took 3.5 to 4 million rations'. To make 3,500,000 rations, the following ingredients were needed: 37,800 *quintales* of hardtack, 157,500 *arrobas* of wine, 899 *quintales* of meat, 6,000 *quintales* of pork fat, 1,500 *quintales* of cheese, 9,000 *quintales* of pulses, plus oil, vinegar, garlic, and firewood.[35]

The superior navy rations augured well for supplies on the trip but also implied a future risk, since no more provisions were included for staying at the destination (this allowance had been made in the case of Sacramento). Quite possibly the inflated cost of shipping navy rations made them over-keen to economize elsewhere by direct victualling in Minorca, but the truth is that no provision was made for the stay on the island. The *intendente* and Finance Minister of the expedition, Pedro Montenegro, complained to Múzquiz about his ignorance of the expedition's purpose. 'I'm groping in the dark because I don't yet know the destination of the undertaking ... a prudent calculation has only been made of the navy rations.'[36] He was therefore unaware of the conditions under which the supply would be carried out, once 'the landing has been verified (whereby) I have taken it upon myself to make a provisional purchase corresponding to a month and a half on the basis of the prudential calculation of sundry items'.[37] Montenegro complained about this impromptu way of working and the sky-high prices being asked by the navy victuallers in Cadiz, who, 'knowing that the King is paying, hike up their asking price'.[38] However laudable might have been his initiative of making purchases in Cadiz on his own account to fill up the voids he detected, this was still a highly personal procedure that flew in the face of the normal victualling system based on official contracts or *asientos* regulated directly by Madrid. As if this were not enough, Montenegro also lacked any allocated resources to defray these purchases. In fact, when he asked the *intendente* of Andalusia in Seville to send 2 million *reales* to Cadiz for these purchases that he intended to make (mainly for victuals and utensils for field hospitals), he was told in no uncertain terms that this was not his remit 'for your offices in Cadiz not even a maravedi'.[39] In equally clear terms he was told that the preparatory provisions were the responsibility of the Conde de O'Reilly, that 'the exercising of your excellency's functions should not begin until after boarding, until which time your excellency does not have to spend so much as a maravedi, nor should you do anything else than check the effects and provisions going on board'.[40] As minister responsible for the financial side of the expedition, however, Pedro Montenegro was allocated 4 million *reales* 'in gold and silver' to cover expedition costs, mainly for wages and purchases to be made in Minorca, and he was ordered not to spend this money until the fleet had entered the Mediterranean. By Royal Order of 28 June 1781 it was decreed that the funds currently at the disposal of the Treasurer General, Marqués de Zambrano, in the Depositaría de Indias in Cadiz should pass on to the expedition paymaster in Cadiz, Julián Pastor, 4 million *reales* in gold and silver, which would then be at the disposal of the expedition minister.[41] This allocation was topped up, before the fleet had reached Minorca, by a consignment of 500,000 *reales* to be sent monthly by the army treasury of Catalonia to the expeditionary force.[42]

These funds gave the expedition minister a certain contracting and procurement capacity; this was a crucial factor because the fleet was headed for an area that, from the Spanish authority's point of view, should not be considered as a territory to be won back but rather as part of Spain. The Junta de Estado's strict instructions to Crillon were that a scrupulous respect be shown to the Minorcan population and its property, treating them with 'kid gloves, not demanding any contribution from the population or encumbering them with any charges'.[43] In due compliance with this order Crillon instructed his force to treat the Minorcans exactly as though they were 'in the very heart of Spain' on the grounds that they were 'natives of Spain'. This meant that 'all dealings had to be by way of voluntary agreement and nothing would be demanded or received without payment'.[44] Thus, Crillon's fleet was sailing well provided with money to a region with rich provisioning potential, which had to be considered as an integral part of Spain. Nor was this all: further support was to be forthcoming from all the *intendentes* of the Spanish Mediterranean coast, who had been instructed to encourage the merchants of their regions to contribute towards the expedition's supplies. All seemed to be plain sailing for the coming campaign.

Finally, the invasion fleet set sail from Cadiz on 20 July 1781 and got to Minorca on 20 August. After picking up reinforcements from the naval base of Cartagena, the invasion fleet that arrived at Minorca comprised 105 vessels, 27 of them warships and the rest merchant ships being used for troop transportation.[45] The invasion plan was to launch a direct attack on the two main cities, Mahón and Ciudadela, with the political objective of taking possession of the island as a bargaining lever for future peace talks. The rapid withdrawal of the English forces, almost 3,000 strong, to the island's main fortress, San Felipe, about 3 kilometres from Mahón shipyard, favoured occupation of the island and also gave Spain access to all the supplies stored in Mahón, left behind in the hasty flight. Complete occupation of the island gave Crillón the chance of increasing the scope of his ambitions and planning a formal siege of the castle. The government accepted this new proposal. After agreeing on siege plans, it was found that the squadron's supplies were insufficient, even when factoring in the supplies taken from the English and also those that might be procured in Minorca. Siege tactics, with the construction of siege batteries and trenches, called for a great amount of supplies, especially artillery, gunpowder, and draught animals, plus men and ships; this therefore increased the supply logistics. Crillón's army took from the end of August 1781 to January 1782 to finish the artillery batteries and begin an intense bombardment, leading to the surrender of the English garrison by 4 February 1782.[46] Throughout these months the expeditionary army's supply problem worsened, testing the mettle of the Spanish contractor state. If its efficiency is gauged by the urgency and flexibility of its reaction capacity, the supply of the siege army in Minorca clearly brought out the problems deriving from the chosen provisioning methods.

THE FIRST REACTION: A MONOPOLY FROM MAHÓN

By the time Crillon's army landed on Minorca (20 August 1781), the expedition's finance *intendente*, Pedro Montenegro, had changed tactics. Montenegro declined to set up in Mahón or elsewhere a centre for procuring the supplies offered by Minorcan or Spanish merchants to the expeditionary force, preferring instead to obtain most of the victuals needed by Crillon's army from a Majorcan merchant, Gerónimo Rivera, on a monopoly basis.

Múzquiz had chosen Montenegro as expedition finance *intendente* because of his first-hand knowledge of the social and economic circumstances of the area, having served as treasurer of the Majorcan army. He had been treasurer of the army of Majorca before becoming army treasury of Extremadura in 1778.[47] Montenegro must have met Rivera at that time, since he was later to present him as 'a private merchant well established in Majorca, whom I met and had dealings with when I served on that Isle'.[48] By the 1770s Gerónimo Rivera had become an important Majorcan businessman, carrying considerable weight in the island's finance and trade circles. In 1770, for example, Rivera was the official farmer of Majorca's spirit taxes[49] and in the following years he habitually featured as shareholder in the island's insurance companies.[50] Where he really predominated, however, was in olive oil exports, an activity accounting at that time for 70–80 per cent of all Majorca's overseas trade. In 1768 he was Majorca's third biggest exporter of oil and by 1787 he had become the number one.[51]

It was this leading Majorcan merchant that Montenegro summoned two days before the actual landing in Minorca. Montenegro made his summons when he was still aboard the flagship San Pascual, sailing past the island of Cabrera. According to the later account given by Rivera himself, the message instructed him that 'on the first news of the happy landing of the army and the taking of the Island I was to present myself at his lodgings (Montenegro's) to serve Your Majesty in the victualling of the troops'.[52] When they at last met up they agreed, without drawing up any formal contract and only 'on the word of honour of Gerónimo Rivera', that this merchant would take on exclusive responsibility for victualling Crillon's army for a four-year period 'in the event that the British Army leaves the island and it comes under the control of Your Majesty or otherwise for such time as the expedition should last'. The whole deal was done by word of mouth, but we know the details of the agreement because Múzquiz subsequently asked for them in writing. This contract after the event tells us that Montenegro gave Rivera responsibility for supplies of flour, barley, straw, coal, firewood, and beds for barracks and hospitals, a commission that, tellingly, Rivera himself admitted that 'I have already started upon (orders given)'. The quantities in the first order were significant: 4,000 *fanegas*, 30,000 *quarteras* of flour, 3,000 *arrobas* of oil, 50,000 *arrobas* of straw, 10,000 *arrobas* of coal, 30,000 *quintales* of firewood, 4,000 beds for barracks, and 400 beds for hospitals.[53] Montenegro granted him generous economic terms. The price accepted by Montenegro, without holding any type of auction, was 26 *mrvs* per ration of bread, this being 4 *mrvs* more than the state paid the Five Major Guilds for an identical ration. Montenegro also conceded him all the typical privileges granted in *asientos* of this type: exemption from duty, military jurisdiction, and the power to embargo carriages and boats for transporting the goods, with the added promise that in 'urgent cases it will be the expedition minister who will furnish the carriages, making such embargos as may be necessary to suit the urgency of the case'. In short, Montenegro gave a victualling monopoly for a whole army to a merchant he had previously contacted and without drawing up any sort of formal contract. This was obviously an irregular way to go about allocating such an important *asiento*, and Montenegro was later to invoke the pressing urgency of that moment to justify his behaviour to Múzquiz: 'reiterating to Your Excellency that a drowning man clutches at any straw and without the advent of Rivera the army would ultimately have run out of its daily bread, which I now have fully assured'.[54]

The monopoly granted to Rivera left little leeway for other merchants; neither did it ensure the expeditionary force's supplies, which began to run out in the following months. Montenegro himself, even though Rivera was his protégé, described the situation in graphic terms barely a month later: 'officers cannot afford good shoes, at two pesos the pair, meat costs 28 *cuartos* a pound while the bread is dearer than in Madrid'.[55] Several factors caused the scarcity and rising prices. In a later report from Crillon to Múzquiz it came to light that Rivera, with Montenegro's permission, had begun to suck Minorca dry, reducing its previously healthy stocks to perilously low levels. From Crillon's complaint we know that Rivera had made massive purchases of grain and livestock on the island for the army's consumption, jeopardizing the supplies of Minorca's own population. In view of this, the general recommended that things should be set up on the 'military principle' of 'never consuming any of the products that are necessary for the island's subsistence, such as wheat and livestock'. Crillon felt that this principle was a *sine qua non* anywhere but it was particularly crucial in Minorca because its stocks could help to stave off the consequences of any future English blockade. The general was surprised that Montenegro should allow Rivera to make these purchases when he had already warned him not only of the strategic importance of these stocks but also about the poor harvest of that year:

> I have been shocked to see this method entirely varied by the *intendente* (Montenegro), who, although instructed that this year's harvest had produced only 76,000 *cuarteras* of wheat (instead of the 100,000 needed for the supply of the island's 30,000 inhabitants, without counting foreigners), has taken all the wheat from this harvest instead of having distributed to each district the necessary amounts to make up for the shortfall.[56]

So great was the havoc wrought by these purchases that the army soon ran short of supplies and the Minorcan population itself began to complain openly about the dearth. Crillon wound up his own complaint by stressing how dire the Minorcans' situation might become in the following months: 'the 30,000 inhabitants have no sure supply of meat or wheat for three months'.[57]

Rivera's purchase strategy had been topped up by other goods ordered in Majorca. Although Majorca's victualling potential was limited, Rivera made wheat purchases there, sparking off protests from the Majorcan authorities, especially the *intendente* and the Audiencia (court of justice). These protests escalated when Montenegro told Rivera to buy up the draught livestock, needed for transport and siege duties: in this case 160 mules that this merchant bought in Majorca 'at cost price'. Rivera's modus operandi here had the devastating effect of driving up the prices of the mules bought and the freightage of the vessels to transport them (23 boats). The army treasurer of Majorca complained to Múzquiz about Rivera's way of making these purchases and of an alarming lack of economy and control in his contracts. The *intendente* did not turn down the purchase but did try to head off the price rise, stipulating that the mules 'be appraised and paid for at fair values'. Everything seemed to be out of control and Montenegro was directly blamed for the losses caused by Rivera's method of rifling Majorca's stores, on the grounds that 'only he who has given the order, and knows why, should be held responsible'.[58] Rivera's provisioning system had thus been set up on the basis of a monopoly over local resources. In Minorca he imposed his privileged status and in Majorca he milked his advantage of being in the king's pay. Paradoxically enough,

Rivera was now perpetrating in the Balearics the very abuses that Montenegro himself had so bitterly complained about in Cadiz, where the profligate *asentistas*, 'knowing that the King is paying, hike up their asking price'.[59]

As if the leeway for other private merchants were not already narrow enough, Montenegro tightened the screws even further with his policy of raising prices. When some supplies began to run short he set up a system of public shops with higher prices, set and monitored by his officers. In these shops the army and the public at large could buy staple products offered by other merchants. This was a way of trying to head off the black market but it also shackled more tightly any private merchants who might sell their wares there. Many merchants, especially Catalan ones, found that it was no longer worth their while taking victuals to Minorca because the selling prices did not cover shipping costs.

The Catalan merchants' protests about this price intervention in Minorca rose in crescendo and finally came to the ears of the Captain General of Catalonia, who reported the problem to the Finance Secretary. The Conde del Asalto, visibly angered by the situation, felt himself to be in a cleft stick, pressured on one side by Múzquiz who asked him to speed up the victualling process, and on the other by Montenegro who asked for his help in coping with the dearth of supplies in Minorca. Sharing their chagrin, therefore, he passed on the Catalan merchants' protests with heartfelt empathy: 'I did all I could to encourage the locals to supply victuals, even offering a prize from my own Pocket to the first comer, but the first to come forward with wines, pulses and liquor soon withdrew upon seeing that their products were unlikely to make them any profit, in light of the prices offered.' In the opinion of the Captain General of Catalonia, the main problem here was the artificially established prices of the Minorcan market, flying in the face of all commercial logic: 'particularly in terms of the prices, wherein I consider any established rate to be harmful, for by my way of thinking abundance is what we should be seeking rather than authority in an isolated location, where victuals have perforce to be brought from some distance, running a gauntlet of risks along the way'.[60] Montenegro, therefore, had undermined the basic principles of trading in this context, and frittered away the initial advantages offered by Minorca and its demand-driven supply.

THE SECOND REACTION: A MONOPOLY FROM MADRID

The difficulty for Montenegro and his monopolist entrepreneur in establishing a firm and secure supply base prompted the government to consider a very significant change. Negotiations began in Madrid to seek another entrepreneur near the court who would offer more guarantees of solvency and a greater logistical capacity. In practice this meant continuing to rely on monopoly as the supply method but with a crucial twist: now the monopolist would be in Madrid, near the government and with the back-up of all state machinery. Little did it seem to concern the government that this spelt doom for Rivera and his contractual commitments. In one way or another the government was reacting to the problem, and it did so on a grand scale during the second half of the century: the aim was to cut down the number of middlemen and work only with known entrepreneurs with a proven track record of state service. The business group chosen by the finance minister for this new monopoly was the renowned company Cinco Gremios Mayores.

The Gremios had held a pre-war army victualling monopoly and during the war were asked by the government also to take on responsibility for the extraordinary victualling of the army besieging Gibraltar. It was a very complicated provision arrangement and the state had to accept compensation agreements and favourable treatment for the future: 'in as many cases as may occur henceforth they will be looked upon with all benignity and protection as befits their sterling service rendered in the past, which His Majesty will always be mindful of'.[61] The upward spiral of state demand, state payment defaults, and the uncertainty shrouding this business forced the state and the Gremios towards mutual support. For the state it was the only way to put off payment for services already provided, an essential factor in times of war, and for the Gremios it was the only way to ensure that payment would finally be forthcoming. The state imposed new contracts but the Gremios set ever harsher terms. The main condition was that the goods should not be supplied at a set price, but rather by *administración*, that is, against the Royal Exchequer at 'cost price' plus commission. In other words the Gremios would take on the necessary supply arrangements but would not run the normal business risks involved therein, such as a sudden increase in the prices of the products bought, contracted freight, or possible ship captures.

The state and the Gremios were locked in this pragmatic embrace of mutual support when Múzquiz turned again to the Gremios for the victualling of the expeditionary force that had landed in Minorca. By late August 1781 Múzquiz had reached an agreement with the Gremios and communicated this to Crillon. Montenegro's reaction on hearing this news was swift and defensive, painting a dramatic picture of the supply shortfalls then being suffered by the expeditionary force: 'in Minorca I have nothing substantial to fall back on for sustaining the troops'. Montenegro claimed that the lion's share of the supplies left behind by the English had been gobbled up by local looters and the Spanish army: 'nor will I receive what the English have left behind in a number of houses, which have been looted by local people and used up as supplies for individual soldiers',[62] and that the rations brought would be needed by the fleet itself for the return journey and such tasks as they might be asked to perform. In any case there was no place on the island to store the landed goods and they were rotting away, 'so that only the ship's biscuits could be used'. Montenegro also claimed to have received clear orders from Madrid not to accustom the army to these navy rations, 'for if too long allowed to enjoy army rations and wine they would be spoilt and feel the lack more keenly thereafter'.[63] Faced with this situation, Montenegro insisted he had had no option but to turn to 'a private and eminently solvent Majorcan merchant who came to my aid at my bidding'.[64] According to this *intendente*, therefore, the agreement with Rivera had been the fruit of sheer necessity and it would be very dangerous to drop it now because all the orders and purchase arrangements were already underway.

The situation was tricky, especially for the state. On the one hand, dismantling Rivera's monopoly might jeopardize the whole operation of laying siege to the Castillo de San Felipe, just getting underway at that time, especially if, as Montenegro insistently claimed, there really was no other way of obtaining the supplies. On the other hand the Gremios had been promised in the king's name that they would take charge of this supply on a monopoly basis; leaving them out now would raise the cost of this particular operation and seriously undermine the state's other business with them. In the end a compromise was struck between these two antagonistic demands: the government 'praised the zeal' shown by Montenegro in contracting Rivera and the latter was thanked for his willingness and generously compensated for his effort, but the monopoly agreement with the Gremios was regarded as overriding on the grounds that they were the 'general purveyors' and also offered 'the advantage that they would not stand out for immediate payment in the current emergency situation'.[65] In other words the state–Gremios tug of war would enable them to put back the payment deadline and this would be impossible in dealings with Rivera.

Rivera was fobbed off with a series of exceptional advantages. The Royal Exchequer would pay him for everything already supplied, at the price agreed by Montenegro, with no type of discount, and he would be paid for all surplus provisions at cost price plus a 2 per cent commission. Furthermore, he would be allowed to continue supplying straw, firewood, coal, and beds on a monopoly basis and without the intervention of the Gremios.[66]

Montenegro was loath to accept the granting of the monopoly to the Gremios, even though it was a royal decision. He argued that, until the Gremios could take over supply arrangements, a crucial time would pass for the survival of the army, and also that the proposed arrangements would turn out to be more expensive than those made by Rivera: 'not only do I fail to descry any advantage whatsoever in this submission to the *Gremios Mayores* but I am sure they will always add the cost of freightage and expenses to their *asiento* price'.[67] He then tried to play for time, stalling the arrival of the Gremios's commissioner on the island and hindering the setting up of a Gremios factory in Minorca. The factor appointed to organize this factory was Manuel Cabriada, previously in charge of the provision of the Gremios in Catalonia. His correspondence with the managers of the Gremios in Madrid gives us a blow-by-blow account of all the obstacles that Montenegro put in his way.

Manuel Cabriada landed on Minorca on 25 September to take charge of the provision, bringing with him all the necessary logistical personnel and wherewithal for setting up the factory, including bakers, utensils (kneading troughs, bolting machines), 1,500 *fanegas* of pre-prepared flour, and money.[68] Montenegro's response was to oppose the setting up of the factory and advise him to return to Barcelona, leaving the flour and money behind, recommending that the 'measures be suspended'. Cabriada acknowledged that he had walked into a difficult situation: 'we found ourselves in something of an awkward affair, and I for one did not know how to get out of it'. He did not know whether to press on regardless or suspend the orders of victuals from other factors, but a decision had to be made quickly because winter was looming up and any arrangements would then become much more complicated: 'neither have I been able to write to the factors for them to continue the shipments, which need to be considerable for an army of this size, and before the winter comes upon us, for the strong easterlies would prevent some shipments from coming and ruin others on the sea'.[69] All the above problems were exacerbated by the fact that the port of Mahón had not yet been brought under control, so the landings had to be scattered around in Ciudadela, Fornells, and other coves, taking on afterwards the grave problem of the transport to Mahón. All this increased the price and depressed the trade:

> until such time as the fortress falls and the port is opened up to us ... this is why there is a shortage of meat and victuals of all types here, and since the Masters bringing them from other provinces, such as Catalonia, find no help with the beasts of burden, either the goods are lost or have to be taken back with heavy losses to their points of departure.[70]

Cabriada's reports back to the Gremios were the last straw. The Directors urged the Finance Secretary to solve this problem forthwith, because big issues were at stake, namely the 'conservation of your excellency's decorum and powers and of our own reputation and the name of the *Cinco Gremios Mayores* that we represent'.[71] Múzquiz's reaction was swingeing. He informed Montenegro of the king's disgust at his having granted a monopoly to Rivera—'your commitment to Ribera in this remit runs counter to the king's intentions'—and also at his opposition to the Gremios's factors, 'it being entirely unreasonable to mete out such treatment to men who had gone to that destination on a mission of His Majesty and to carry out a commission of his Royal Service'.[72] He was then unceremoniously sacked as the expedition's finance *intendente*. This was an unprecedented step, showing that the state had come down heavily on the side of the Gremios even at risk of jeopardizing the sustenance of the army on Minorca.

STATE SUPPORT IN THE VICTUALLING PROCESS

The uncertainty hovering over the whole victualling process in the last three months had seriously worsened Minorca's supply position. The state therefore had to step in, and did so on several fronts. First, emulating the procedure at the very start of the expedition, the Finance Secretary again turned to the *intendentes* of Spain's coastal regions, urging them to encourage the merchants of their respective areas to send products of all types to Minorca. The net was now spread wider, throughout the whole Mediterranean area. The government even used the glitter of Spanish silver, otherwise severely restricted, as bait to attract foreign traders.

The Secretary of State, Floridablanca, ordered 'that the consuls of Bordeaux, Marseilles, Sette, Nice, Genoa, Naples and Sicily be instructed by the state to publish in their districts the opportunity for local traders to enrich themselves by bringing back gold and silver as payment for everything they take and sell in Mahon'.[73] This diplomatic ploy was especially important for obtaining fresh meat in Marseilles. Montenegro had already warned that fresh meat was in short supply 'along the whole of our Mediterranean coast'.[74] In fact the traditional market sources had been Barbary and France. In Catalonia the acute meat shortage had engendered an active legal and illegal trade with the south of France. The difficulty in ensuring supplies of fresh meat had already been amply demonstrated by Rivera's purchases in Minorca and Majorca and the exhaustion of Barbary's supply, which had previously been stockpiled by the English on the island. The only option left was thus the diplomatic ploy. The idea was the brainchild of Crillon himself who, unbeknown to Montenegro, ordered oxen to be bought in Marseilles to supply the army. The Spanish consul in Marseilles, Juan de la Rosa, had to set up a complex oxen-purchasing operation in several French regions, including the safekeeping of the animals until ships were ready to transport them, the storing and sending of vast amounts of fodder, and a formerly unheard-of payment system by means of bills drawn against the Real Giro, the foreign-debt bank in Paris. In all a supply of 500 oxen was ordered.[75]

Secondly, the state was forced to become an auxiliary contractor of the Gremios. The government decided to procure by commission all victuals that the Gremios were not in the end obliged to supply. To do so it turned directly to the Marqués de las Hormazas, the navy victualler. This was by no means a straightforward task because this *asentista* was snowed under with work. To make matters worse the Navy Secretary, Castejón, objected to the siphoning off of supplies that were equally crucial for the Cadiz fleet, which had to prevent the English from entering the Mediterranean. Finally the Navy Secretary buckled under the heavy pressure exerted on him and agreed that the navy purveyor could also work for the Minorca army, on condition that the navy 'be correspondingly redressed' whenever possible. The important point here was that he was contracted not as an *asentista* but rather as a private merchant on a commission basis. He was therefore ordered that 'in all these dealings you are to act as though it were your own business ... proceeding as though you were acting on your own account, never mentioning the name of the *Real Hacienda* for fear of driving up the prices'.[76] The duplicity here was obvious: on the one hand the authorities were encouraging the merchants to trade while on the other they were hiding the fact that the whole demand was in fact to be channelled through a single purchaser. The state commission prompted the Marqués de las Hormazas to organize massive purchases of broad beans, rice, beans, chickpeas, and pork fat. The quantities involved were huge: '1200 *quintales* of broad beans, 300 of rice [later raised to over 1,000], 4000 *quintales* of beans, 250 of chickpeas, 400 of pork fat'. All these purchases were made on the Spanish east coast, mainly Valencia, Alicante, and Murcia, and must have had a considerable domino effect on the local economies whilst also discouraging other merchants of the area from making new shipments.

This model of state commissioning of private merchants was repeated with the Valencia merchant Antonio Galaber, in this case for buying diverse comestibles, especially meat and pork fat from Italy: 'Be it known that Antonio Galaber, resident and merchant of Valencia, was commissioned through the offices of Francisco Cabarrus'.[77] The important thing about this commission is that this merchant was the father-in-law of Francisco Cabarrús, who was at this time the most important financier of the Madrid court and the right-hand man of Múzquiz and Floridablanca in seeking warfare financing schemes.[78] All this seems to show a government mistrust and scorn for free market initiative. When it decided to step in and help to rectify the problems created by Montenegro in Minorca, it might well have done so by trusting in the merchants' unfettered ability to trade. Instead of this it fell back on the cliques and power elites, such as the navy purveyor and the financier Francisco Cabarrús. The consequences of this new state intervention would soon be felt.

THE MARKET OPPORTUNITY

Neither the monopoly of the entrepreneur Rivera nor even that of the Gremios, backed by total state support, turned out to be enough to meet the growing demands posed by the siege. The reports filing into Madrid in late November 1781 warned that the whole siege operation might be jeopardized by the lack of supplies. In this context the government once more reacted with a knee-jerk change in its supply policy. This change was eminently political, centring on a replacement of the responsible *intendente*, but it also brought out the need to explore other arrangements besides monopoly. The consequence of all this was his replacement in December 1781 by the *intendente* Pedro López de Lerena, future Finance Secretary and champion of free trade and tax reforms.[79] The advent of this new *intendente* meant a radical change in the Minorcan army's supply situation, mainly because he took a number of trade-stimulating measures.

En route to Minorca Lerena stopped over in Barcelona to meet up with Conde del Asalto and discuss how to coordinate and improve the supply situation. Both agreed that the problem was how to ensure the provisions not only of the army laying siege to San Felipe Castle but also of the island's civilian population.[80] Crillon's reports on the Minorcans' supply problems showed that the problem was no longer purely military, particularly when dealing with a population that had been living on a well-stocked island beforehand. In early December Crillon himself had mooted trade stimulation as the only way of solving the problem. In the general's view the solution would involve supporting the traders' interests: 'encouraging and favouring trade and leaving it up to the merchants themselves to seek the best supply lines, with no more duties on the comestibles that those that might naturally be imposed by abundance or scarcity'.[81] This line of thought was shared by the Conde del Asalto, who, as has already been seen, had complained vociferously about the harmful and disruptive effects of Rivera's monopoly and Montenegro's price-fixing on the Catalan merchants who had tried to sell their wares in Minorca. Lerena, for his part, echoed these deregulatory proposals and was also firmly convinced of their usefulness and the need for putting them into practice.

Lerena's first measures, even before the English surrender, were designed specifically to remedy the scarcity of meat, the most serious shortfall he detected. He published several edicts throughout the island encouraging the Minorcans themselves to renew meat trading. He scrapped the duty on meat imports, a move that Montenegro had always systematically opposed on the grounds of 'the abuses that the private merchants might commit'.[82] He implemented Crillon's idea of giving a doubloon reward to any merchant that imported livestock; the aim, in Lerena's words, was to 'encourage the merchants to import fresh meat into this island on their own account ... the reward was one gold doubloon per head of cattle weighing over 400 pounds, then falling in line with the weight, 6 *reales* per head of sheep or goat weighing 30 pounds'.[83] He sought a price reduction to encourage the consumption of meat that had arrived by direct purchase of the Real Hacienda and was sold in the three butcher's shops set up by Montenegro. This price cut meant that the treasury would in fact be trading at a loss since 'it will not be able to get back even one half of the cost price to the king', but it was the only way of getting the meat onto the market quickly and steadying consumption patterns. Lerena's objective was none other than to 'kindle in this way competition and hence favour the purchasers' interests'.[84]

The results of this policy were felt immediately. The trading activity of the Minorcans themselves soared and they were soon joined by Catalan, French, and Italian traders, no less keen to get in on the act (see Map 10.1). Judging from the correspondence between Lerena and Múzquiz, the main problem now was the arrival of the purchases made by the government in the previous months, just when trade was getting off the ground and supplies were steadying. This hardly spelt a glut, but it did create a sizeable price difference between the products shipped in on the king's account and those that now came on sale in Minorcan shops and markets. Lerena quoted the example of the Marqués de las Hormazas's rice shipments from Valencia, a telling example because it was a product not grown in Minorca. The final price of the rice placed on the Minorca market by Hormazas was much higher than that of the rice that Lerena could now directly buy there himself. The same price differences obtained even in comparison to the retail rice market: 'it is being sold at a much higher price than the retail rice on sale in many houses of the town ... with a difference of over 12 *reales* per *quintal* on the rice shipped in easily from France and Genoa'. He also warned of more rice-laden ships on the way from Cullera, also on the orders of Marqués de las Hormazas.[85]

The rest of the products soon ran into the same problem. Any cargo of wheat, barley, meat, beans, broad beans, wine, rice, or vegetables unloaded on the Real Hacienda's account would be undercut by the same products that Lerena could now buy directly in Minorca. The *asentistas* continued to bring in their products on a monopoly basis and with no fixed price; likewise, the government's

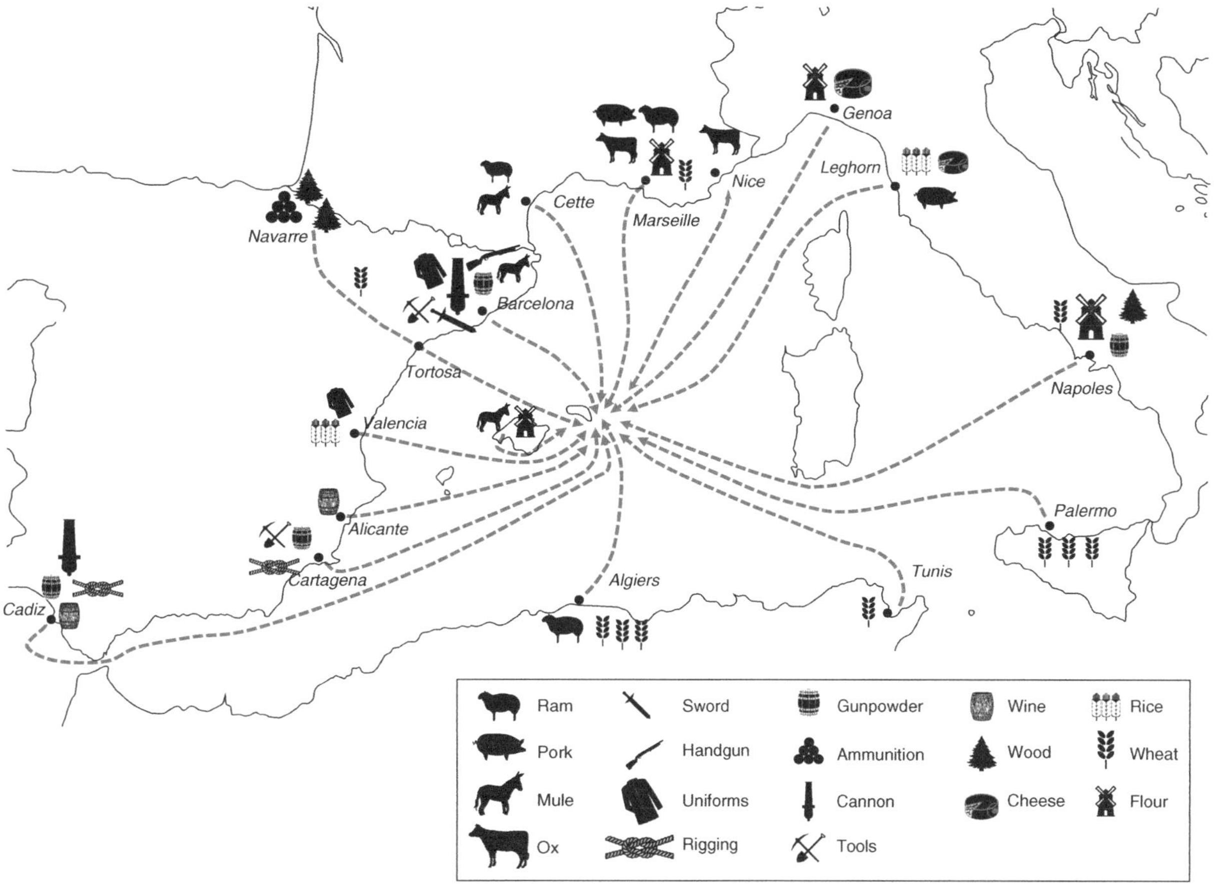

Map 10.1 Supply of the Minorca-occupying Spanish expeditionary army, 1781–2

Source: Adapted from AGS, Guerra, legs 3762 and 3763; AGS, SSH, legs 748 and 749.

directly managed products, on the Real Hacienda's account, continued to arrive on the island. All these products could now be bought in Minorca at a lower price. Everyone, *asentistas* and merchants, was doing his job well, but Lerena's problem was now becoming seriously intractable.

Lerena's solution was to try to stem the state-managed orders, but this did not turn out to be easy or cheap. Lerena was aghast at the price of the oxen still being sent to him by the Spanish consul of Marseilles. The Real Hacienda paid for the purchase itself, the animals' keep until they were boarded, and fodder and freight until they reached Minorca, and all this inflated the price paid by the king well above the price of the livestock on sale in Minorca. For example, the retail ox-meat price from a shipment sent by the Barcelona merchant Juan Vidal worked out at 5 *reales* per pound, whereas the consul's shipment cost the Real Hacienda 11 *reales* a pound. Lerena had no choice but to ask for the purchase to be suspended, but this was easier said than done because Rosa now saw no way of annulling purchases that had already been effectively carried out: 'it is no longer possible to dismiss them because the livestock have been brought from another province under a formal deed of purchase'. In the end he was ordered to get rid of the cattle in Marseilles as best he could, even if this meant selling at a loss: 'suspend the rest of the purchases in any way you can and try to sell them off, dead or alive, as best you might, because the freight cost and overheads greatly inflate their basic cost'.[86]

The same occurred with a meat shipment that the government had agreed with an Alicante merchant José Portes, in the previous months. In late October this merchant had agreed with Múzquiz to buy livestock, mainly rams, in Valencia and Albacete. The purchase cost would be defrayed by the Real Hacienda against the tobacco revenue of Alicante or Valencia, the state also taking on transport costs and a 2 per cent commission for the merchant.[87] In the following months he sent three meat shipments to Minorca and the authorities accepted them without qualms. The problems cropped up when cheaper meat from elsewhere began to arrive at Minorca. Then, as with the Marseilles transactions, it was decided to suspend the purchase operations and new shipments because, Portes was told, 'meat comes out so expensive in that destination that it can hardly be sold at half its cost price'. But the state paid little heed to the effects of its reneging on this dealer's business; he was merely thanked for his efforts and urged to continue trading with Minorca, with the caveat that it would henceforth 'be at his own risk, selling there at the prices he deems most fitting'. Finally he was reminded of the continuing duty-free status of imported comestibles and the ease of removing the earnings from the island afterwards, whereby 'this business has bright prospects for those who take it up on their own account'.[88] The commission of the Valencia trader Antonio Galaber was cancelled in the same unceremonious fashion. His purchases had been made mainly in Tuscany and Marseilles but, as in the case of Portes, the pork fat brought directly by Minorcans and Italians to Minorca turned out much cheaper and obliged Lerena to break off the arrangement.[89]

The situation had clearly changed and Lerena now preferred to tap into Minorca's traditional trading advantages. His way of thinking was forthrightly expressed when he complained to Múzquiz that excessive intervention from Madrid had only made the supply problem worse, squandering Minorca's bounty as a well-supplied island that could even cater for Spain itself:

> I declare to Your Excellency that it was indeed thoughtless reckoning to send here so many shipments of sundry goods when this is traditionally a well-stocked region where our country could surely find a good supply of pulses and wheat if the locals were only left to trade freely. They are especially keen to resume their trade with Barbary, which, diplomacy permitting, they should be allowed to do, whereupon the coasts of Spain would want for little at any time.[90]

Without any doubt it was the state's fleet-footedness in modifying its supply policies that enabled the amphibious expedition and the expeditionary army to be adequately supplied with its wherewithal. It clearly shows the tight time-scale it worked to and the fluctuations it experienced, but also the consequences for the military entrepreneurs. This example shows that the Spanish authorities involved in the process did not trust the market as the main channel for supplying that expeditionary force, preferring to fall back on monopoly practices. As in so many other contexts, they opted to clothe certain merchants with garments of privilege, thereby disrupting the commercial advantages that the island had boasted hitherto. The exhaustion of local resources and disincentives to traders exacerbated the shortfalls; the government then tried to solve the problem by price fixing, curtailing trade even more. The only way the state could see to cut through this vicious circle was to commission massive purchases from the clique of merchants close to the uppermost echelons of power, without looking at the cost or weighing up other alternatives. This interventionism was a cumbersome parasite of trade. It was not until the *intendente* was changed that trade was stimulated once more and competition encouraged, whereupon the local merchants themselves, now unfettered, managed to improve the supply situation and bring down its cost. Tellingly, the troops that returned to Campo de San Roque to try to end the siege of Gibraltar brought with them more victual-laden ships than those that had gone with the Minorca expeditionary force. Lerena, in short, had shown that there was another way of tackling the supply policy even in a situation as complex as that facing the expeditionary army. Lerena indeed showed how an opening up of the Minorca market might offer better business opportunities. In the opinion of the future finance minister, it was preferable to run the risk of market uncertainty rather than fall back on the specious security of monopoly. The supply of the Mahón army showed the difficult of changing the supply policy and, *ipso facto*, the rigidity of the Spanish contractor state. But it brought out its pragmatism too, showing how the system could be modified in an extreme situation. The greatest weakness it showed, on the other hand, was the fickleness with which the state could change the ground rules, undermining the confidence of both the state itself and its contractors and changing the opportunities for one and all.

11
Conclusions

The Spanish contractor state managed to procure the military supplies it needed to meet the increasing size of its armed forces during the eighteenth century. This could safely be dubbed a success because it was done without running up much debt and also while ensuring that most of these supplies came from Spanish entrepreneurs and were managed by Spanish officials. Unlike in earlier periods, the gains from this state demand remained largely within the national economy. Problems come to light only when we focus on the relationships between the state and military entrepreneurs. This is when the established system shows all its complexity and shortfalls, to the point of curbing the beneficial effects that would otherwise have been generated by this state demand for military supplies.

The Spanish contractor state held one thing dear above all else throughout the whole century: the desire to produce and manage all the military supplies it needed, on the dual grounds of mercantilism and the upholding of authority. This proved to be a pipedream, however. The reasons for this failure were not strictly incapacity. As we have seen, the *administración–asiento* dilemma was partly a false dichotomy. In the end the two options were not so radically different. Such political aspirations were relegated into second place by the factors of urgency, cost, or timeliness. The state was pretty much ready to switch back and forth from one method to the other and the political debate was still raging at the end of the century with very similar arguments being brandished in favour of both options. In fact, if one system did not definitively win out over the other it was precisely because the differences between them were not so great. This was partly because Spanish military entrepreneurs shared most of the state's objectives, such as strengthening the home economy. Indeed, the biggest success of the military supply system, its completely national character, was due largely to the participation of Spanish military entrepreneurs. It was not so much a question of the Spanish state setting up barriers against inroads by foreign entrepreneurs but rather the Spanish entrepreneurs themselves putting up their own fierce defence of the home market.

The state and military entrepreneurs not only shared mercantilist ideals but also continually revamped their relations to suit their mutual interest. Both found advantages in collaboration and both were ultimately victims of the determined effort to shield the system from competition. Chosen Spanish entrepreneurs found obvious advantages in the state's preferential, privilege-granting, and open-handed treatment of them, fending off free market competition by entrepreneurs and products. At the same time the state itself benefited from direct access to a pool of known, solvent, and creditworthy entrepreneurs, who were ready if need be to act with the utmost discretion and reserve. However, this relation was at the same time perilous for both parties. First and foremost it created a very risky dependence. Secondly it excluded other would-be entrepreneurs from the supply business. Dependence and exclusion ended up as part of the same tangled web. The state and military entrepreneurs were capable of meeting demand, but at the cost of reducing opportunities for other entrepreneurs, other production systems, and the national economy as a whole. Monopolies and privileges were the ultimate consequence of the interaction and increase in demand. The mercantilist policy shared by state and entrepreneurs alike managed to strengthen the national production of military supplies but failed to increase business opportunities or drive the economy.

At the same time as these structural problems cropped up, there was also great opportunity for progress and development. One of the most positive consequences of the activities carried out by the contractor state and the *asentistas* was an improved integration of the Spanish economy. Spain's military entrepreneurs made a huge contribution in this way, helping to knit together geographical areas, integrate activities, and make the whole arrangement more complementary and synergistic. Regions historically isolated from each other by tolls and institutional borders saw some of the products and services melded into a nationwide, entrepreneur-planned distribution arrangement. This was especially notable in the north of Spain, but ended up affecting the south too due to the state's strategic priorities in the lower Guadalquivir (Cadiz and Gibraltar). As the nature of war changed during the eighteenth century, some of these product and service networks were even set up outside Spain in the Americas, especially to sustain the defence of the Caribbean and shipbuilding in Havana. This geographical integration went hand in hand with the participation of business groups from outlying areas of Spain in the national and imperial military supply markets, such as the Basque and Navarre businesspeople and also Catalan merchants for the supply of uniforms. Integration of the military supply markets, in other words, fuelled a new, growing national economy coordinated and sustained by a business elite that sloughed off its parochial outlook in favour of a nationwide business policy. Indeed, one of the most upfront results was a growing participation and identification of the outlying elites with the new Bourbon dynasty, not only as a business opportunity but also as a means of social promotion. This in turn led to a greater collaboration between them and recognition of the monarchy's authority and of the exercising of state power by the elites of the outlying regions of Spain.

This integration process picked up even more speed after the state managed to get most of its military supplies produced in territories under its control. During the eighteenth century, unlike the situation under the Hapsburgs, the economic resources mobilized by Spain's renewed fiscal military state circulated mainly within territories under its sovereignty, thereby avoiding the massive outflow of funds that had occurred in previous centuries. This domestic and colonial circulation had multiplier effects that are difficult to quantify, but undoubtedly beneficial nonetheless. A more effective redistribution of income within the national economy offered opportunities to local sectors and areas, offsetting the traditional deficit that the Hapsburg's imperial policy had engendered in home taxpayers. Both the state and the *asentistas* of the eighteenth century contributed towards this national redistribution of income. The state did so by means of an active policy of investments in the production of military supplies, mainly in textile and iron-and-steel factories and shipbuilding; the contractors did so by prioritizing the purchase of supplies within the national and colonial territory. As we have already seen, however, this mercantilist policy could sometimes be overridden by other concerns, especially the growth of its armed forces. The national production policy could more or less be kept up in the first half of the century, but as wars and sabre-rattling picked up pace among European powers, especially in the naval scenario, demand could then no longer be satisfied at home alone. The state and *asentistas* had no choice but to look abroad. It was then that the chickens came home to roost in terms of the stunted development of Spain's entrepreneur market and international trade outlets. Once more the state's solution to this problem was to place its trust in only a few of these entrepreneurs capable of working with solvency and creditworthiness in international markets. Even so, the wholesale nationalization of Spain's military supply arrangements in the eighteenth century was without doubt a notable feat, marking a big advance on previous centuries.

Integration of the national market was not the only benefit of this policy; strengthening of the business elite was another plus. The prime aim of the state's business monopoly policy was to ensure contract performance. It was not simply the result of a supposed state ideology, also supposedly absolutist: rather was it the most obvious product of the state's short-term pragmatism. The state's overriding aim was to secure the military supplies it needed; everything else played second fiddle, and it was always prepared to switch its supply system to suit. Hence the supply-method fickleness in all military supplies throughout the century; the case study of the amphibious expedition to Minorca showed that the state was much more interested in the ends than the means. This would explain the apparent paradox we have already seen in the first half of the century, whereby, together with construction of a clearly absolutist state, there was also a growing presence of monopolist entrepreneurs, while in the second half of the century the state phased in more free-trade policies at the same time as it encouraged monopolist solutions to meet the demand for its military supplies. In other words, in the relations between state and entrepreneurs, monopoly was not so much the result of an ideology but rather the practical consequence of the state's perceived need to ensure quick and immediate control over entrepreneurs. The upshot was an increasingly fortified business elite. The benefited entrepreneurs thus managed to improve their bargaining position and authoritativeness in the activities they carried out. The growing trend of subcontracting local *asentistas*, peaking in the last third of the century under the Cinco Gremios Mayores, is a faithful reflection of this fortification.

The strengthening of the business elite tended to bring them into line with state priorities but also promoted a sense of identification with the society they lived in. Witness the example of Juan Goyeneche, investing his profits in the creation of a new settlement, Nuevo Baztán, fitted out with factories, services, and town-planning of a clearly enlightened inspiration, illustrating the desire of this business elite to participate in national development. The Cinco Gremios Mayores, likewise, and many other *asentistas*, expedited a whole host of state services, shoring up public creditworthiness while at the same time investing their capital in financial and commercial activity, whether this be sugar production, as with Mendinueta or Aragorri, or insurance companies, like the Gremios. The activity of these military entrepreneurs also created opportunities, thereby stimulating the development of Spain. Without doubt this mixture of limits and possibilities lies at the very crux of the relation between the state and military entrepreneurs; it is also a *sine qua non* for understanding the growth and sustenance of Spain's imperial monarchy during the eighteenth century, and also its rapid collapse in the first years of the nineteenth.

This book began by asking whether the state 'would go further' by involving military entrepreneurs in its military supply needs, on the English model. The answer for the Spanish eighteenth-century state was no. The state's day-to-day relations with military entrepreneurs and its overall policy ended up hobbling both. The state proved incapable of ousting military entrepreneurs completely from the picture and ended up turning to them anew. But the state did not want, or was not able, to use its demands for military supplies as a galvanizing force for building up a dynamic and competitive market of entrepreneurs. It preferred instead to create competition-cramping policies based on personal and monopolistic relationships. Military entrepreneurs in Spain dwindled as a result, becoming more and more dependent on state finances. This approach was risky and shaky. In the end, the political management of military supplies during the eighteenth century made the state, military entrepreneurs, and the Spanish nation as a whole weaker and less developed than it might have been.

Notes

CHAPTER 1

1. Marqués de la Corona to Miguel Múzquiz, Madrid, 10 Feb. 1767, AGS, SSH, leg. 1997.
2. Michael Mann, 'Putting the Weberian State in its Social, Geopolitical and Militaristic Context: A Response to Patrick O'Brien', *Journal of Historical Sociology* 19 (2006), 364–73; Douglass C. North, John J. Wallis, and Barry R. Weingast, *Violence and Social Orders: A Conceptual Framework for Interpreting Recorded Human History* (Cambridge: Cambridge University Press, 2012).
3. Philippe Contamine, ed., *War and Competition between States* (Oxford: Clarendon, 2000); Jan Glete, *War and the State in Early Modern Europe: Spain, the Dutch Republic and Sweden as Fiscal-Military States, 1500–1660* (London: Routledge, 2002).
4. An example of the historiographical evolution of one of these concepts, that of the fiscal-military state, in Rafael Torres Sánchez, ed., *War, State and Development: Fiscal-Military States in the Eighteenth Century* (Pamplona: EUNSA, 2007), 13–44.
5. Martin Daunton, *State and Market in Victorian Britain: War, Welfare, and Capitalism* (Woodbridge: The Boydell Press, 2008), 61.
6. Charles Tilly, *Coerción, capital y los Estados europeos, 990–1990* (Madrid: Alianza, 1992), 57 (*Coercion, Capital and European States: AD 990–1992*, Wiley-Blackwell, 1993).
7. Douglas W. Allen, 'The British Navy Rules: Monitoring and Incompatible Incentives in the Age of Fighting Sail', *Explorations in Economic History* 39 (2002), 204–31.
8. An analysis of the problem in Stephen Conway and Rafael Torres Sánchez, eds, *The Spending of the States: Military Expenditure during the Long Eighteenth Century: Patterns, Organisation and Consequences, 1650–1815* (Saarbrücken: VDM, 2011), 9–30. See also Richard Harding, 'Parliament and the British Fiscal-Military State: Ideology, Consent and State Expenditure in Britain, 1739–1748', in Conway and Torres Sánchez, eds, *Spending of the States*, 31–50.
9. Peer Vries, 'Governing Growth: A Comparative Analysis of the Role of the State in the Rise of the West', *Journal of World History* 13 (2002), 67–138, esp. 110.
10. Stephen Conway, 'Public and Private Contributions to the Mobilization of Manpower and Resources for War in Mid-Eighteenth-Century Britain and Ireland', in Huw V. Bowen and Agustín González Enciso, eds, *Mobilising Resources for War: Britain and Spain at Work During the Early Modern Period* (Pamplona: Eunsa, 2006), 37–58.
11. David Parrott, *The Business of War: Military Enterprise and Military Revolution in Early Modern Europe* (Cambridge: Cambridge University Press, 2012).
12. John Brewer, *The Sinews of Power: War, Money and the English State, 1688–1783* (New York: Cambridge University Press, 1989), p. xxiii.
13. Rafael Torres Sánchez, ed., *War, State and Development: Fiscal-Military States in the Eighteenth Century* (Pamplona: EUNSA, 2007), 13–44.
14. Peter Earle, 'The Sinews of Power: War, Money and the English State, 1688–1783', *Economic History Review* 43 (1990), 142.
15. Chester Dunning, and Norman S. Smith, 'Moving beyond Absolutism: Was Early Modern Russia a 'Fiscal-Military' State?' *Russian History* 33 (2006), 19–43 at 44.

16. Max Edling, *A Revolution in Favor of Government: Origins of the U.S. Constitution* (Oxford: Oxford University Press, 2003), 220.
17. Mark Dincecco, 'Fiscal Centralization, Limited Government and Public Revenues in Europe, 1650–1913', *Journal of Economic History* 69 (2009), 48–103.
18. Richard Bonney, ed., *The Rise of the Fiscal State in Europe* (Oxford: Oxford University Press, 1999); Bartolomé Yun-Casalilla, Patrick K. O'Brien, and Francisco Comín, eds, *The Rise of Fiscal States: A Global History, 1500–1914* (Cambridge: Cambridge University Press, 2012), 2.
19. Patrick K. O'Brien, 'The Nature and Historical Evolution of an Exceptional Fiscal State and its Possible Significance for the Precocious Commercialization and Industrialization of the British Economy from Cromwell to Nelson', *The Economic History Review* 64 (2011), 408–46.
20. Jan Glete, *War and the State in Early Modern Europe: Spain, the Dutch Republic and Sweden as Fiscal-Military States, 1500–1660* (London: Routledge, 2002), 29.
21. Guy Rowlands, *The Financial Decline of a Great Power: War, Influence, and Money in Louis XIV's France* (Oxford: Oxford University Press, 2012).
22. Philip Harling and Peter Mandler, 'From "Fiscal-Military" State to Laissez-Faire State, 1760–1850', *The Journal of British Studies* 32 (1993), 44–70; Joanna Innes, 'The Domestic Face of the Military-Fiscal State: Government and Society in Eighteenth-Century Britain', in Lawrence Stone, ed., *An Imperial State at War: Britain from 1689 to 1815* (London: Routledge, 1994), 96–127; Christopher Storrs, ed., *The Fiscal Military State in Eighteenth-Century Europe* (Burlington: Ashgate, 2008); Martin Daunton, 'The Fiscal-Military State and the Napoleonic Wars: Britain and France Compared', in David Cannadine, ed., *Trafalgar in History: A Battle and Its Afterlife* (London: Palgrave Macmillan, 2006), 18–43; Frank Tallet, and D. J. B. Trim, *European Warfare 1350–1750* (Cambridge: Cambridge University Press, 2010); Erica Charters, 'The Caring Fiscal-Military State during the Seven Years War, 1756–1763', *Historical Journal* 52 (2009), 921–41; Gunner Lind, 'Beyond the Fiscal-Military Road to State Formation: Civil Society, Collective Identities and the State in the Old Danish Monarchy, 1500–1850', *Balto-Scandia* 18 (2012), 1–11.
23. Conway and Torres Sánchez, eds, *The Spending of the States*, 31–50.
24. Roger Knight and Martin Wilcox, *Sustaining the Fleet, 1793–1815: War, the British Navy and the Contractor State* (Woodbrige: The Boydell Press, 2010), and Roger Knight, *Britain against Napoleon: The Organization of Victory, 1793–1815* (London: Penguin, 2014).
25. Knight and Wilcox, *Sustaining the Fleet*, 214.
26. Fritz Redlich, *The German Military Enterpriser and His Work Force: A Study in European Economic and Social History* (Wiesbaden: Franz, 1964).
27. Bernard Pool, *Navy Board Contracts 1660–1832: Contract Administration under the Navy Board* (London: Longmans Green, 1966); David Syrett, *Shipping and the American War* (London: Athlone, 1970); Norman Baker, *Government and Contractors: The British Treasury and War Supplies, 1775–1783* (London: Athlone, 1971); Christian Buchet, *Marine, économie et société: un exemple d'interaction: l'avitaillement de la Royal Navy durant la guerre de sept ans* (Paris: Champion, 1999).
28. Gordon Bannerman, *Merchants and the Military in Eighteenth-Century Britain: British Army Contracts and Domestic Supply, 1739–1763* (London: Pickering & Chatto, 2007).
29. Along the same lines, the thought-provoking works of Aaron Graham, 'Auditing Leviathan: Corruption and State Formation in Early Eighteenth-Century Britain',

English Historical Review 128 (2013), 806–38, and 'Public Service and Private Profit: British Fiscal-Military Entrepreneurship Overseas, 1707–12', in Jeff Fynn-Paul, ed., *War, Entrepreneurs, and the State* (Leiden: Brill, 2014), 87–110.

30. Bowen and González, *Mobilising Resources for War*; Torres Sánchez, ed., *War, State and Development*; Christopher Storrs, ed., *The Fiscal Military State in Eighteenth-Century Europe*; Conway and Torres Sánchez, eds, *The Spending of the States*; Richard Harding and Sergio Solbes, eds, *The Contractor State and its Implications, 1659–1815* (Las Palmas: Universidad de Las Palmas, 2012); a study of the Contractor State Group in *International Journal of Maritime History* xxv: 1 (June 2013); Jeff Fynn-Paul, ed., *War, Entrepreneurs, and the State* (Leiden: Brill, 2014).
31. Irving A. Thompson, *Guerra y decadencia, gobierno y administración en la España de los Austrias, 1560–1620* (Barcelona: Crítica, 1981); *War and Government in Habsburg Spain, 1560–1620* (London: Athlone, 1976).
32. N. A. M. Rodger, 'From the "Military Revolution" to the "Fiscal-Naval State"', *Journal for Maritime Research* 13 (2011), 119–28.
33. Roger Morriss, *The Foundations of British Maritime Ascendancy: Resources, Logistics and the State, 1755-1815* (Cambridge: Cambridge University Press, 2011).
34. Patrick K. O'Brien, 'The Formation of a Mercantilist State and the Economic Growth of the United Kingdom 1453–1815', United Nations University, Research Paper n.2006/75.

CHAPTER 2

1. On the overriding importance of Thompson's thesis, see Antonio Espino López, 'La historiografía hispana sobre la guerra en la época de los Austrias. Un balance, 1991–2000', *Manuscrits* 21 (2003), 161–91.
2. I. A. A. Thompson, *War and Government in Habsburg Spain, 1560–1620*. Trans. into Spanish as *Guerra y decadencia, gobierno y administración en la España de los Austrias, 1560–1620* (Barcelona: Crítica, 1981), 315.
3. I. A. A. Thompson, *Guerra y decadencia, gobierno y administración en la España de los Austrias, 1560–1620* (Barcelona: Crítica, 1981), 344.
4. Jan Glete, *War and the State in Early Modern Europe. Spain, the Dutch Republic and Sweden as Fiscal-Military States, 1500–1660* (London: Routledge, 2002), 29.
5. This historical research is weighed up in Rafael Torres Sánchez, 'The Triumph of the Fiscal-Military State in the Eighteenth Century: War and Mercantilism', in Rafael Torres Sánchez, *War, State and Development: Fiscal-Military States in the Eighteenth Century* (Pamplona: EUNSA, 2007), 13–44.
6. David Parrott, *The Business of War: Military Enterprise and Military Revolution in Early Modern Europe* (Cambridge: Cambridge University Press, 2012). His thesis also applies to the eighteenth century, with a strong reinforcement between both spheres, as demonstrated by the works of: Gordon Bannerman, *Merchants and the Military in Eighteenth-Century Britain: British Army Contracts and Domestic Supply, 1739–1763* (London: Pickering & Chatto, 2007); Roger Knight and Martin Wilcox, *Sustaining the Fleet, 1793–1815: War, the British Navy and the Contractor State* (Woodbridge: The Boydell Press, 2010); Roger Knight, *Britain against Napoleon: The Organization of Victory, 1793–1815* (London: Penguin, 2014); and Aaron Graham, 'Public Service and Private Profit: British Fiscal-Military Entrepreneurship Overseas, 1707–12', in Jeff Fynn-Paul, ed., *War, Entrepreneurs, and the State* (Leiden: Brill, 2014), 87–110.

7. Antonio Jiménez Estrella, 'Asentistas militares y fraude en torno al abastecimiento de pólvora en el reino de Granada (siglo XVI)', *Investigaciones históricas: Época moderna y contemporánea* 30 (2010), 11–30, and Alicia Esteban Estríngana, 'El suministro de pólvora en el ejército de Flandes. Sobre la gestión directa y delegada del aprovisionamiento militar (siglo XVII)', in Enrique García Hernán and Davide Maffi, eds, *Guerra y Sociedad en la Monarquía Hispánica: Política, Estrategia y Cultura en la Europa Moderna (1500–1700)* (Madrid: Fundación MAPFRE, Ediciones del Laberinto, CSIC, 2006), ii. 473–522.
8. Carla Rahn Phillips, *Seis galeones para el rey de España: la defensa imperial a principios del s. XVII* (Madrid: Alianza Editorial, 1991).
9. Juan Miguel Teijeiro de la Rosa, *La Real Hacienda militar de Fernando VII: el cuerpo administrativo militar* (Madrid: Ministerio de Defensa, Secretaría General Técnica, 1995), 44.
10. H. O'Donnell, 'Luis María de Salazar, capitán de navío, ministro de Marina', *Cuadernos monográficos del Instituto de Historia y Cultura Naval* 54 (2007), 115–28.
11. Luis María Salazar, *Juicio crítico de la marina militar de España dispuesto en cartas de un amigo a otro* (Madrid: D. Miguel de Burgos, 1814), 5 (Letter III, January 1814).
12. Salazar, *Juicio crítico*, 149 (Letter XXV, June 1814).
13. Salazar, *Juicio crítico*, 120 (Letter XXIV, May 1814).
14. AGS, DGT, Inv. 25, leg. 14. On this attempt see Rafael Torres Sánchez, 'Cuando las reglas del juego cambian. Mercados y privilegio en el abastecimiento del ejército español en el siglo XVIII', *Revista de historia moderna* 20 (2002), 487–511 at 491–4.
15. Salazar, *Juicio crítico*, 176 (Letter XXV). Salazar himself confirms that 'for nearly the whole century victuals were supplied by *asiento*', 175.
16. Sergio Solbes Ferri, 'Contracting and Accounting: Spanish Army Expenditure in Wardrobe and the General Treasury Accounts in the Eighteenth Century', in Richard Harding and Sergio Solbes, eds, *The Contractor State and its Implications, 1659–1815* (Las Palmas: Universidad de Las Palmas, 2012), 273–93 at 283.
17. Marqués de Castejón to Miguel Múzquiz, Madrid 8 Sept. 1776. Reference is being made to the Order of 2 Sept. 1763. In 1777 the previous system was restored whereby each battalion procured its uniforms on its own account, including the expense thereof in the item called *Gran masa* (bulk items) and added to the annual budget of each navy department. In 1771 there were 12 navy battalions: AGS, SSH, leg. 50. The state expense from 1763 to 1777 is in AGS, DGT, Inv. 46, leg. 5.
18. Sergio Solbes Ferri, 'Campillo y Ensenada: el suministro de vestuarios para el ejército durante las campañas de Italia (1741–1748)', *Studia historica. Historia moderna* 35 (2013), 201–34 at 210.
19. Francisco Andújar Castillo, *El sonido del dinero: Monarquía, ejército y venalidad en la España del siglo XVIII* (Madrid: Marcial Pons, 2004). See also Francisco Andújar Castillo, 'Guerra, venalidad y asientos de soldados en el siglo XVIII', *Studia historica. Historia moderna* 35 (2013), 235–68.
20. Thomas Glesener, 'La estatalización del reclutamiento de soldados extranjeros en el siglo XVIII', in Manuel Reyes García Hurtado, ed., *Soldados de la Ilustración: El ejército español en el siglo XVIII* (A Coruña: Universidade da Coruña, 2012), 237–61, quotes at 238 and 239.
21. Saltpetre accounted for 75% of the gunpowder, Enrique García-Torralba Pérez, *La Artillería Naval Española en el Siglo XVIII* (Madrid: Ministerio de Defensa, 2010), 572.

22. Covadonga Villar Ortiz, *La renta de la pólvora en Nueva España (1569–1767)* (Seville: CSIC, 1988); Miriam Núñez Torrado, 'Estudios de costes en la renta de la pólvora de nueva España ante la implantación de un nuevo sistema de gestión (1766–1785)', *Revista española de financiación y contabilidad* 111 (2002), 47–74.
23. Contract with the house of Cabarrus and Lalanne, 1779, in AGS, SSH, leg. 1048. With Juan Gil de Meester (from Amsterdam) on 1 Jan. 1780 in AHN, Hacienda, Libro 6731. With Meester the state had also contracted gunpowder provision in 1776, AGS, SSH, leg. 269.
24. We analyse this question in Rafael Torres Sánchez, 'Producir o comprar, la demanda de la corona española de productos industriales en el siglo XVIII', in Luis Antonio Ribot and Luigi de Rosa, eds, *Industria y Época Moderna* (Madrid: Actas, 2000), 95–131 at 118–23.
25. José Patricio Merino, *La Armada española en el siglo XVIII* (Madrid: Fundación Universitaria Española, 1981), 99.
26. Merino, *La Armada española*, 281–6. See also Rafael Torres Sánchez, *La llave de todos los tesoros: La Tesorería General de Carlos III* (Madrid: Sílex, 2012), 254–5.
27. Rafael Torres Sánchez, 'La política de abastecimiento de cáñamo a la Armada en la segunda mitad del siglo XVIII', *Revista de historia naval* 116 (2012), 47–71. See also the excellent study by Manuel Díaz Ordóñez, *Amarrados al negocio: Reformismo borbónico y suministro de jarcia para la Armada Real (1675–1751)* (Madrid: Ministerio de Defensa, 2009).
28. Torres Sánchez, *La llave de todos los tesoros*, 237.
29. Cadiz, 18 Feb. 1760, AGS, Marina, leg. 609. This majority *asiento* arrangement in transport was also the case in production lines that had passed into the hands of the state, such as the bronze cannons of Seville. Antonio Aguilar Escobar, *Cañones de bronce para el Ejército: Historia de la Real Fundición de Sevilla en el siglo XVIII* (Madrid: Adalid, Ministerio de Defensa, 2010), 168. An example of transport by *asiento* in Agustín González Enciso, 'La renovación del asiento de transporte de municiones y armas en 1793 y el protagonismo de una familia navarra', *Memoria y Civilización* 15 (2012), 51–69. See also the thought-provoking reflection in Agustín González Enciso, 'Estado militar y empresarios de industrias militares', in Agustín González Enciso, ed., *Un Estado Militar: España, 1650–1820* (Madrid: Actas, 2012), 423–47.
30. Expression used by Francisco Andújar Castillo, 'Guerra, venalidad y asientos de soldados en el siglo XVIII', *Studia historica. Historia moderna* 35 (2013), 251.
31. Agustín González Enciso, 'Del *contractor state* al Estado fabricante. El cambio de propiedad en la fábrica de municiones de Eugui en 1766', *Revista de historia de la economía y de la empresa* 7, BBVA, 455–84.
32. An analysis of the practical consequences of switching to state cannon production in Rafael Torres Sánchez, 'Velas sin Cañones. La eficacia de las reformas artilleras tras la Guerra de los Siete Años', in Francisco Morales Padrón, ed., *Piratería, Corso y Guerra Marítima. XVII Coloquio de Historia Canario-Americana* (Las Palmas de Gran Canaria: Cabildo de Gran Canaria, 2008), 1717–28. An example of the return to private *asientos* in Xán Carmona, 'Antonio Raimundo Ibáñez, un empresario en el filo de dos épocas', in Joaquín Ocampo, ed., *Empresa y empresarios en el norte de España (Siglo XVIII)* (Oviedo: Trea, 2012), 69–90.
33. Ricard Martí, *Cataluña armería de los Borbones: Las armas y los armeros de Ripoll, Barcelona, Manresa, Igualada … de 1714 a 1794* (Barcelona: Salvatella, 2004), 51–70.
34. Merino, *La Armada española*, 359.

35. This idea has already been forthrightly expressed by María Mestre in an insightful article that has unfortunately never been followed up. María Mestre Prat de Padua, 'La construcción naval de guerra en la España del siglo XVIII. El marco legal de los procesos de financiación', in Carlos Martínez Shaw, ed., *El derecho y el mar en la España moderna* (Granada: Universidad de Granada, 1995), 299–322. For more information on the shipbuilding *asientos* in Guarnizo and Havana see Juan Manuel Castanedo Galán, *Guarnizo, un astillero de la Corona* (Madrid: Editorial Naval, 1993), and José Manuel Serrano Álvarez, *El astillero de La Habana y la construcción naval militar (1700–1750)* (Madrid: Ministerio de Defensa, 2008).
36. Iván Valdez-Bubnov, *Poder naval y modernización del Estado: política de construcción naval española (siglos XVI–XVIII)* (Mexico: Iberoamericana, 2011), 365.
37. Quoted by Klemens Kaps, 'Entre el servicio estatal y los negocios transnacionales: el caso de Paolo Greppi, cónsul imperial en Cádiz (1774–1791)', in Marcela Aglieti et al., eds, *Los cónsules de extranjeros en la Edad Moderna y principios de la Edad Contemporánea* (Madrid: Ediciones Doce Calles, 2013), 225–36 at 232.
38. Castejón to Miguel Múzquiz, Madrid 8 Sept. 1776, AGS, SSH, leg. 50.
39. The reasons for this failure are given in María Lourdes Odriozola Oyarbide, 'La Real Fábrica de anclas de Renteriola: un intento fallido', *Boletín de la Real Sociedad Bascongada de Amigos del País* 46:12 (1990), 41–78.
40. A list of these anchor *asientos* is given in AGS, Marina, leg. 606.
41. Germán Luis Andrade Muñoz, *Un mar de intereses: La producción de pertrechos navales en Nueva España, siglo XVIII* (México: Instituto Mora, 2006), 83.
42. Quote of 1752 by María Baudot, 'Barcos para el rey', in Manuel Reyes García Hurtado, ed., *La Armada española en el siglo XVIII. Ciencia, hombres y barcos* (Madrid: Silex, 2012), 316.
43. AGS, DGT, Inv. 25, leg. 14. Rafael Torres Sánchez, 'El gran negocio de la época, la provisión de víveres al ejército por Francisco Mendinueta (1744–1763)', in Santiago Aquerreta, ed., *Francisco Mendinueta: Finanzas y mecenazgo en la España del siglo XVIII* (Pamplona: EUNSA, 2002), 101–34 at 127.
44. The proceedings in AGS, SSH, leg. 644.
45. Pedro de Lerena, 3 Sept. 1789, AGS, SSH, leg. 647. The problem is analysed in Rafael Torres Sánchez, 'Los Cinco Gremios Mayores y la provisión de víveres al ejército español en el siglo XVIII', *Studia Histórica. Edad Moderna* 34 (2012), 407–32 at 430.
46. Roger Morriss, *The Foundations of British Maritime Ascendancy: Resources, Logistics and the State, 1755–1815* (Cambridge: Cambridge University Press, 2011). See also Gordon Bannerman, *Merchants and the Military in Eighteenth-Century Britain: British Army Contracts and Domestic Supply, 1739–1763* (London: Pickering & Chatto, 2008) and Roger Knight and Martin Wilcox, *Sustaining the Fleet, 1793–1815: War, the British Navy and the Contractor State* (Woodbridge: The Boydell Press, 2010).
47. In the original texts, dating from October 1814, 'general principle' is in italics. Roger Morriss, *Foundations of British Maritime Ascendancy*, 113 n. 117. For more information on the way the Victualling Board worked, see Janet Macdonald, *Feeding Nelson's Navy: The True Story of Food at Sea in the Georgian Era* (London: Chatman, 2006), 45–71.
48. The advantages for the government of being able to ascertain the real cost were obvious because 'an actual examination can be made of the cause of the alteration', determining whether it is due to a change in the prices of raw materials, labour, production, distribution, 'or carelessness or embezzlement by the Administrator'. Miriam Núñez Torrado, 'Estudios de costes en la Renta de la Pólvora de Nueva

España ante la implantación de un nuevo sistema de gestión (1757–1787)', *Revista española de financiación y contabilidad* XXI (2002), 72.

49. AGS, SSH, leg. 641.
50. As expressed by Fermín Folch, because 'directors are the *Intendentes*, main *Contadurías* serve as accounting officials, treasurers are those of the army while *comisarios de guerra* (War Commissioners) could cover other offices', Madrid 22 Sept. 1740, Report by Fermín Buenaventura Folch to Fernando Verdes Montenegro on the provision of victuals made by Manuel Santos, administrator of the house of the Marqués de Valdeolmos, AGS, SSH, leg. 640.
51. The study was carried out in Havana in 1792 and the comparison of costs between both systems showed that *asiento* was the cheapest option: 8% for ships of the line and 40% for frigates, Valdez-Bubnov, *Poder naval*, 423.
52. Gabriel de Arrieta, *Alphabeto y cartilla militar* (Cadiz: Imprenta Real de Marina de D. Manuel Espinosa de los Monteros, 1757), 465 and 447.
53. Marqués de Castejón, 1774, AGS, SSH, leg. 50.
54. Belderrain, Cadiz, 11 Aug. 1760, AGS, Marina, leg. 610.
55. Marqués de Ensenada to Andrés Marver y Vera, Madrid, 12 Sept. 1750, AFB, Judicial, Corregidor/Civil, 694/23.
56. Miguel Múzquiz, 3 Oct. 1771, AGS, SSH, leg. 645.
57. AGS, SSH, leg. 641.
58. Miguel Múzquiz to Cinco Gremios Mayores, 4 Oct. 1772, AGS, SSH, leg. 645.
59. Aguilar Escobar, *Cañones de bronce*, 93.
60. The Consejo de Hacienda declared that this was the cause of fraud: 'In this procedure of the D'Hugues the *Consejo* has unearthed two frauds, for, having agreed to pay the *mesadas* into the coffers of Partearroyo, they were assigned thereafter to Larralde, and then asked for and in fact received the October *mensada*, leaving the two overdrawn', Madrid, 12 Nov. 1763, AGS, SSH, leg. 642.
61. The *mesadas* were 25,000 pesos (375,000 *rsv*) to be received from 1768 to 1772. It was used as an indicator of the sum agreed in the former *asiento* of Manuel Zubiría, Arriaga, Madrid, 23 Oct. 1766, AGS, Marina, leg. 607.
62. Morriss, *The Foundations of British Maritime Ascendancy*, 107–8. Several examples in Norman Baker, *Government and Contractors: The British Treasury and War Supplies, 1775–1783* (London: The Athlone Press, 1971), 56–7.
63. Report of Fermín Buenaventura Folch to Fernando Verde Montenegro on the victualling proposal made by Manuel Santos, administrator of the house of Marqués de Valdeolmos, Madrid, 22 Sept. 1740, AGS, SSH, leg. 640.
64. The union between revenue farmers and military entrepreneurs during Philip V's reign should not be construed exclusively as a political imposition on the state by businessmen; in the author's view a more pragmatic reading is equally valid, whereby the state obtained the necessary liquidity to ensure military supplies without forfeiting any royal authority, since it was the state that finally decided which *asentista* to use and which advance it would pay. The best work on this is still Manuel Ibáñez Molina, 'Rentas Provinciales, administración real y recaudadores en el reino de Felipe V (1700–1739)' (Granada: Doctoral thesis, microfiches, 1985).
65. Consignación Departamento Marítimo del Ferrol, 1777, AGS, SSH, leg. 50.
66. Rafael Torres Sánchez, 'In the Shade of Power. Monopolist Entrepreneurs, the State and Spanish Military Victualling in the Eighteenth Century', in Jeff Fynn-Paul, ed., *War, Entrepreneurs, and the State* (Leiden: Brill, 2013), 260–84.
67. 'Informe reservado', Madrid, 5 Nov. 1771, AGS, SSH, leg. 645.

68. Kenneth Morgan, 'Mercantilism and the British Empire, 1688–1815', in Donald Winch and Patrick Karl O'Brien, eds, *The Political Economy of British Historical Experience, 1688–1914* (Oxford: Oxford University Press, 2002), 165–91.
69. This thesis is in Patrick O'Brien, 'Taxation for British Mercantilism from the Treaty of Utrecht (1713) to the Peace of Paris (1783)', in Rafael Torres Sánchez, ed., *War, State and Development: Fiscal-Military States in the Eighteenth Century* (Pamplona: EUNSA, 2007), 295–356. A more detailed development of the thesis is in Patrick Karl O'Brien, 'The Nature and Historical Evolution of an Exceptional Fiscal State and its Possible Significance for the Precocious Commercialization and Industrialization of the British Economy from Cromwell to Nelson', *The Economic History Review* 64:2 (2011), 408–46.
70. Castejón to Múzquiz, 2 Oct. 1781, AGS, SSH, leg. 51.
71. Diego Gardoqui, 1792, AHN, Estado, leg. 232.
72. Guillaume Garner, 'Caméralisme et territoire. Ètat, espace et économie dans le discours économique allemand au XVIIIe siècle', *Revue du Nord* 85 (Oct.–Dec. 2003), 729–45 at 730–1.
73. Salazar, *Juicio crítico*, 78 and 122 (Letters III, January 1814, and XXIV, May 1814).
74. Madrid, 6 Jan. 1779, AHN, FCH, leg. 6732.
75. San Lorenzo, 10 Nov. 1783, AGS, DGT, Inv. 25, leg. 15.
76. The problem was posed in Antonio José Rodríguez Hernández, *Los tambores de Marte: el reclutamiento en Castilla durante la segunda mitad del siglo XVII (1648–1700)* (Valladolid: Universidad de Valladolid-Castilla Ediciones, 2011). See also Carmen Sanz Ayán, 'Negociadores y capitales holandeses en los sistemas de abastecimientos de pertrechos navales de la monarquía hispánica durante el siglo XVII', *Hispania* 182 (1992), 915–45. Alicia Esteban Estríngana, 'Administración militar y negocio de guerra en los Países Bajos católicos. Siglo XVII', in Ana Crespo and Manuel Herrero, eds, *España y las 17 Provincias de los Países Bajos. Una revisión historiográfica (XVI–XVIII)* (Córdoba: Universidad de Córdoba, 2002), 65–100. Antonio Jiménez Estrella and Francisco Andújar Castillo, eds, *Los nervios de la guerra: Estudios sociales sobre el Ejército de la Monarquía Hispánica (siglos XVI–XVIII): nuevas perspectivas* (Granada: Comares, 2007).
77. Anne Dubet, *Un estadista francés en la España de los Borbones: Juan Orry y las primeras reformas de Felipe V (1701–1706)* (Madrid: Biblioteca Nueva, 2008), 54.
78. José Calvo Poyato, 'La industria militar española durante la Guerra de Sucesión', *Revista de historia militar* 33 (1989), 51–71.
79. Jean-Pierre Dedieu, 'Les Intermédiaires privés dans les finances royales espagnoles sous Philippe V et Ferdinand VI', in Vicent Meyzie, ed., *Crédit public, crédit privé et institutions intermédiaires: Monarchie française, monarchie hispanique, XVIe–XVIIIe siècles* (Limoges: Presses Universitaires de Limoges et du Limousin, 2012), 223–39 and see n. 9. To the French group of Orry Jean-Pierre Dedieu also adds Sartine, 'Les Groupes financiers et industriels au service du roi. Espagne, fin XVIIe–début XVIIIe siècle', in Anne Dubet and Jean-Philippe Luis, eds, *Les Financiers et la construction de l'État—France, Espagne (XVIIe–XIXe siècle)* (Rennes: P. U. Rennes, 2011), 87–104 at 103.
80. Guillermo Pérez Sarrión, *La península comercial: Mercado, redes sociales y Estado en España en el siglo XVIII* (Madrid: Marcial Pons, 2012).
81. Michael Zylberberg, 'Des affaires à l'administration: un échec de François Cabarrus', in Bernard Vincent and Jean Pierre Dedieu, eds, *L'Espagne, l'État, les Lumières: mélanges en l'honneur de Didier Ozanam* (Madrid: Casa de Velázquez, 2004), 109–19.

82. Rafael Torres Sánchez, 'In the Shade of Power. Monopolist Entrepreneurs, the State and Spanish Military Victualling in the Eighteenth Century', in Jeff Fynn-Paul, ed., *War, Entrepreneurs, and the State* (Leiden: Brill, 2013), 37.
83. Rafael Torres Sánchez, 'Los navarros en la provisión de víveres a la armada española durante el siglo XVIII', in *Volver a la 'hora navarra': La contribución Navarra a la construcción de la monarquía española en el siglo XVIII* (Pamplona: EUNSA, 2009), 213–64.
84. Manuel Díaz Ordóñez, 'El riesgo de contratar con el enemigo. Suministros ingleses para la Armada Real española en el siglo XVIII', *Revista de historia naval* 21 (2003), 65–74.
85. According to Gabriel Arrieta (*Alphabeto y cartilla militar* (Cadiz: Imprenta Real de Marina de D. Manuel Espinosa de los Monteros, 1757), 447) the total number of soldiers in infantry regiments was 59,712, of which 12,672 belonged to foreign regiments.
86. In mid-century there were 9 foreign infantry regiments; by 1781 this had risen to 12, with a theoretical total of 24,768 men. José Luis Terrón Ponce, *Ejército y política en la España de Carlos III* (Madrid: Ministerio de Defensa, 1997), 86.
87. Morriss, *The Foundations of British Maritime Ascendancy*, 171.
88. Stephen Conway, *Britain, Ireland, & Continental Europe in the Eighteenth Century: Similarities, Connections, Identities* (Oxford: Oxford University Press, 2011). Along the same lines, but for the specific case of the navy, see Andrew Martin Rodger, 'From the "Military Revolution" to the "Fiscal-Naval State"', *Journal for Maritime Research* 13 (2011), 119–28.
89. Rafael Guerrero Elecalde, *Las elites vascas y navarras en el gobierno de la Monarquía Borbónica: Redes sociales, carreras y hegemonía en el siglo XVIII (1700–1746)* (Bilbao: Universidad del País Vasco, 2012), 157.
90. See the reflections on this matter in Agustín González Enciso, 'La promoción industrial en la España Moderna: intervención pública e iniciativa privada', in Luis Antonio Ribot and Luigi de Rosa, eds, *Industria y Época Moderna* (Madrid: Actas, 2000), 15–46; Agustín González Enciso, 'El "Estado económico" en la España del siglo XVIII', *Memoria y civilización: anuario de historia de la Universidad de Navarra* 6 (2003), 97–139.
91. San Lorenzo, 28 Oct. 1783, AGS, DGT, Inv. 25, leg. 15.
92. Inocencio García, administrador general de la casa de negocio del marqués de Valdeolmos, 18 Feb. 1741, AGS, SSH, leg. 640.
93. Gerbaut, Cadiz 18 Feb. 1760. Solicitud de Antonio Soria, vecino de Castril. AGS, Marina, leg. 609.
94. Francisco Andújar Castillo, 'Guerra, venalidad y asientos de soldados en el siglo XVIII', *Studia historica. Historia moderna* 35 (2013), 235–68.
95. This is repeated in several military contracts. Several of them appear in AGS, DGT, Inv. 25, leg. 14.
96. Dubet, *Un estadista francés*, 191.
97. Marqués de Esquilache to Sebastián Gómez de la Torre, Aug. 1767, AGS, SSH, leg. 644.
98. Raúl Cabello Vázquez, 'Ciencia y guerra en los albores de la química como disciplina: programa francés para la producción de pólvora', in Jesús Astigarraga et al., eds,

Ilustración, ilustraciones (San Sebastián: Real Sociedad Bascongada de Amigos del País y Sociedad Estatal de Conmemoraciones Culturales, 2009), 715–34.

99. The annual consignment paid by the Real Hacienda was increased by 35% between 1775 and 1808 to 1,125,000 *rsv*. The Tesorería General's total artillery cost was 5.8 million, representing slightly less than 20%: Aguilar Escobar, *Cañones de bronce*, 269.
100. 'Neither was the new method completely satisfactory since the pieces, in some cases, turned out to be frailer than those cast with the old techniques', Aguilar Escobar, *Cañones de bronce*, 199.
101. Lord Grantham, Madrid, 16 June 1774, PRO, SP-94, fo. 195.
102. Torres Sánchez, 'Velas sin Cañones', 1727.
103. Aguilar Escobar: *Cañones de bronce*, 117; García-Torralba Pérez, *La Artillería Naval Española en el Siglo XVIII*, 67.
104. Valdez-Bubnov, *Poder naval*, 298.
105. 1780, AHN, FCH, leg. 6732.
106. Morriss, *The Foundations of British Maritime Ascendancy*, 130.
107. Miriam Núñez Torrado, 'Estudios de costes en la renta de la pólvora', 69.
108. Luis María de Salazar, *Juicio crítico*, 127 (Letter xxiv, May 1814).
109. Rafael Torres Sánchez, 'Contractor State and Mercantilism. The Spanish-Navy Hemp, Rigging and Sailcloth Supply Policy in the Second Half of the Eighteenth Century', in Richard Harding and Sergio Solbes, eds, *The Contractor State and its Implications, 1659–1815* (Las Palmas: Universidad de Las Palmas, 2013), 317–44.
110. A good example of the consequences of enforcement of the *Ordenanza de Montes* is given in María Baudot Monroy, 'Barcos para el Rey. Julián de Arriaga, la madera y la construcción naval (1752–1759)', in Manuel Reyes García Hurtado, ed., *La Armada española en el siglo XVIII: Ciencia, hombres y barcos* (Madrid: Sílex, 2012), 297–328. See also Álvaro Aragón Ruano, 'La historiografía forestal sobre época moderna en el panorama internacional, español y vasco: una revisión bibliográfica', *Vasconia: Cuadernos de historia* 37 (2011), 117–40.
111. Salazar, *Juicio crítico*, 33 (Letter xxvi, July 1814. De los montes pertenecientes a la marina).

CHAPTER 3

1. Quoted by John A. Lynn, *Giant of the Grand Siècle: The French Army, 1610–1715* (Cambridge: Cambridge University Press, 1997), 108.
2. Judith A. Miller, *Mastering the Market: The State and the Grain Trade in Northern France, 1700–1850* (Cambridge: Cambridge University Press, 1998), 15–17.
3. Martin Van Creveld, *Supplying War: Logistics from Wallenstein to Patton*, 2nd edn (Cambridge: Cambridge University Press, 2004), 5–17.
4. David Parrott, *The Business of War: Military Enterprise and Military Revolution in Early Modern Europe* (Cambridge: Cambridge University Press, 2012).
5. John A. Lynn, *Giant of the Grand Siècle: The French Army, 1610–1715* (Cambridge: Cambridge University Press, 1997), 117.
6. A good example of the chaos that might ensue is the weakening of state administration in Spain during the War of Independence in the early nineteenth century: Jesús Cantera Montenegro, 'La otra guerra: la lucha por la subsistencia. Acuartelamiento, vestuario y alimentación durante la Guerra de la Independencia', *Cuadernos de Historia Moderna* 9 (2010), 147–65.

7. Janet Macdonald, *Feeding Nelson's Navy: The True Story of Food at Sea in the Georgian Era* (London: Chatham, 2006), 7.
8. Roger Knight and Martin Wilcox, *Sustaining the Fleet, 1793–1815: War, the British Navy and the Contractor State* (Woodbridge: The Boydell Press, 2010), 19–45.
9. Roger Morriss, *The Foundations of British Maritime Ascendancy: Resources, Logistics and the State, 1755–1815* (Cambridge: Cambridge University Press, 2011), 271–320.
10. Richard Harding, *The Emergence of Britain's Global Naval Supremacy: The War of 1739–1748* (Woodbridge: The Boydell Press, 2010).
11. There was also a third option, i.e. a direct agreement between military personnel and private agents and with the government's blessing, as occurred in the English case with the 'regimental agents', see Alan James Guy, *Oeconomy and Discipline: Officership and Administration in the British Army, 1714–1763* (Manchester: Manchester University Press, 1985), 59.
12. The Russian army used the number and distribution of soldiers' bread rations as a way of reducing the high desertion rate, John Keep, 'Feeding the Troops: Russian Army Supply Policies during the Seven Years War', *Canadian Slavonic Papers* 29 (1987), 24.
13. An update of the role played by *situados* in the Spanish monarchy's military expenditure set-up can be found in Carlos Marichal and Johanna Graffenstein, eds, *El secreto del Imperio español: los situados coloniales en el siglo XVIII* (Mexico: El Colegio de México, Instituto Mora, 2012). An essential reference for understanding the local dimension of military supplies in the Americas is still Juan Marchena Fernández, 'Capital, créditos e intereses comerciales a fines del periodo colonial: los costos del sistema defensivo americano. Cartagena de Indias y el Sur del Caribe', *Tiempos de América* 9 (2002), 3–38.
14. This issue has been thoroughly studied for the Americas: Stanley J. and Barbara H. Stein, *Apogee of Empire: Spain and New Spain in the Age of Charles III, 1759–1789* (Baltimore: Johns Hopkins University Press, 2003), but much the same occurred in the case of the Philippines, Luis Alonso Álvarez, *El costo del imperio asiático: La formación colonial de las islas Filipinas bajo dominio español, 1565–1800* (Mexico: Universidade da Coruña, Instituto Mora, 2009), 305–28.
15. Juan Marchena Fernández, *Ejército y milicias en el mundo colonial americano* (Madrid: MAPFRE, 1992), 227. Due to the ongoing dearth of wheat flour, cassava apparently had to be used for making the sailors' hardtack, called 'cazave' in Spanish, in the Americas and on the expedition of Rodrigo Torres in 1740: María Baudot Monroy, *La defensa del Imperio: Julián de Arriaga en la Armada (1700–1754)* (Madrid: Ministerio de Defensa, 2013), 185.
16. See also Johanna Graffenstein, 'El abasto de la escuadra y las plazas militares del gran Caribe, con harinas y víveres novohispanos, 1755–1779', in Yuste López and Matilde Souto, eds, *El comercio exterior de México 1713–1850: Entre la quiebra del sistema imperial y el surgimiento de una nación* (Mexico: UNAM, 2000), 42–83.
17. The towns' victualling contribution was constant during the whole century: Severo Aguirre, *Prontuario Alfabético y Cronológico por Orden de Materias de las Instrucciones, Ordenanzas, Reglamentos, Pragmáticas y demás Reales Resoluciones No Recopiladas que han de observarse para la Administración de Justicia y Gobierno en los Pueblos del Reino* (Madrid: Benito Cano, 1799), 211–43. An example is found in Emilio Fernández Maldonado, *El sargento español en el Siglo de las Luces 1685–1760* (Madrid: Ministerio de Defensa, 1999), 85.

18. Representación a SM sobre el estado de cada uno de los regimientos de infantería, Madrid, 18 Aug. 1770, Archivo Campomanes, legs 18, 28. Quoted by José Luis Terrón Ponce, *Ejército y política en la España de Carlos III* (Madrid: Ministerio de Defensa, 1997), 99.
19. David Goodman, *El poderío naval español: Historia de la armada española del siglo XVII* (Barcelona: Peninsular, 2001), 217–18.
20. The make-up of the ration was fixed in 1717 in the navy ordinances decreed by Patiño. Quoted by Carlos Pérez Fernández-Turégano, *Patiño y las reformas de la administración en el reinado de Felipe V* (Madrid: Ministerio de Defensa, 2006), 107. This was repeated in the ordinances of 1725. Isidoro Guzman Raja, 'Normativa contable en la Armada española durante el periodo 1700–1850: especial referencia a la administración de provisiones', *De Computis: Revista española de historia de la contabilidad* 5 (2006), 65–142.
21. Witness the example of the extraordinary victualling of the amphibious fleet that set sail for the Americas in 1781, which called for 5,400,000 victual rations to be brought together in Cadiz. Miguel Múzquiz to Luis Manuel Quiñones, Madrid, 24 Sept. 1781, AGS, SSH, leg. 51. Several examples in María Baudot, ed., *El Estado en guerra: expediciones navales españolas en el siglo XVIII* (Madrid: Polifemo, 2014).
22. Figures from AGS, DGT, Inv. 25, leg. 14 and 15.
23. Ernesto López Losa, 'The Legacy of Earl J. Hamilton: New Data for the Study of Prices in Spain, 1650–1800', *Investigaciones de Historia Económica* 9 (2013), 75–87. Enrique Llopis Agelán and Héctor García Montero, 'Precios y salarios en Madrid, 1680–1800', *Investigaciones de historia económica: revista de la Asociación Española de Historia Económica* 7 (2011), 295–309.
24. See e.g. the accounts presented by Antonio Rubio, war commissioner and factor for the victualling of the court and royal residences, for the supplies 'coming from Seville', while the royal household and court were in the Andalusian city. Seville, 4 Aug. 1733, AGS, DGT, Inv. 24, leg. 14.
25. Contract with Bernabé Soto for victualling the Court and Royal Estates, San Ildefonso, 20 Sept. 1743, AGS, DGT, Inv. 25, leg. 14.
26. Francisco Andújar has shown that these 'elite' armed forces were a valuable source of privilege and social and military promotion: Francisco Andújar Castillo, 'Élites de poder militar: Las Guardias Reales en el siglo XVIII', in Juan Luís Castellano, Jean Pierre Dedieu, and María Victoria López, eds, *La pluma, la mitra y la espada: Estudios de historia institucional en la Edad Moderna* (Madrid: Marcial Pons, 2000), 65–94; Francisco Andújar Castillo, 'La Corte y los militares en el siglo XVIII', *Estudis* 27 (2001), 91–120.
27. Rafael Torres Sánchez, 'Cuando las reglas del juego cambian. Mercados y privilegio en el abastecimiento del ejército español en el siglo XVIII', *Revista de historia moderna* 20 (2002), 487–511.
28. Urban Ruiz Velarde to José Campillo, Madrid, 8 Nov. 1726, AGS, SSH, leg. 640.
29. This general accounting office was set up on 1 Dec. 1730 under Fermín Folch. AGS, DGT, Inv. 25, leg. 14.
30. Several accounting statements of this provision during the 1730s in AGS, SSH, leg. 640.
31. In fact this did not include the whole army. This list excluded the seven battalions of Swiss 'who receive no bread', the six battalions in Orán, and seven in Ceuta. In all, in 1738 a total number of 109 battalions were taken into account. The list, on the contrary, includes part of the supply of victuals to the navy, precisely 3,300 daily rations

to the navy troops (3,000 in Cadiz and 300 in Ferrol: *Contabilidad de la Provisión de víveres de 1738*, AGS, SSH, leg. 640.

32. In sum, this victualling arrangement ate up over 3 million *reales* a year. This figure was considerably swollen with incorporation of the cost of straw supplied to this troop, which in this year was 1,177,976 *rsv*. This was the cost of the 471,187 *arrobas* delivered to the troops of the court and royal estates. We have no figures for the cost of straw for the rest of the army this year. The figures for 1738 are in AGS, SSH, leg. 640.
33. Victualling *asiento* signed by Banco Nacional de San Carlos for garrison victualling, Madrid, 19 June 1786, AGS, DGT, Inv. 25, leg. 14.
34. Victualling contract of 'four garrisons of Africa', Pedro de Astrearena, Marqués de Murillo, 1745–55, AGS, SSH, leg. 113.
35. Figures from the Tesorería General, in AGS, DGT, Inv. 16, Guión 24, leg. 49.
36. Antonio Miguel Bernal, ed., *Dinero, Moneda y Credito en la Monarquia Hispánica* (Madrid: Marcial Pons, 2000).
37. Irving Anthony A. Thompson, *Guerra y decadencia, gobierno y administración en la España de los Austrias, 1560–1620* (Barcelona: Crítica, 1981).
38. Carlos Álvarez Nogal, *El crédito de la monarquía hispánica en el reinado de Felipe IV* (Burgos: Junta de Castilla y León, Consejería de Educación y Cultura, 1997). Mauricio Drelichman and Hans-Joachim Voth, *Lending to the Borrower from Hell: Debt, Taxes, and Default in the Age of Philip II* (Princeton: Princeton University Press, 2014). Hans-Joachim Voth and Mauricio Drelichman, 'The Sustainable Debts of Philip II: A Reconstruction of Castile's Fiscal Position, 1566–96', *Journal of Economic History* 70 (2010), 813–42.
39. Carmen Sanz Ayán, 'Negociadores y capitales holandeses en los sistemas de abastecimientos de pertrechos navales de la monarquía hispánica durante el siglo XVII, *Hispania* 182 (1992), 915–45.
40. Luis Perdices de Blas and John Reeder, *El mercantilismo: política económica y Estado nacional* (Madrid: Editorial Síntesis, 1998).
41. Gerónimo de Uztariz, *Theórica, y práctica de comercio, y de marina* (Madrid: Imprenta de Antonio Sanz, 1742).
42. José Calvo Poyato, 'La industria militar española durante la Guerra de Sucesión', *Revista de historia militar* 33 (1989), 51–71.
43. Henry Kamen, *La Guerra de Sucesión en España, 1700–1715* (Barcelona: Grijalbo, 1974); Joaquim Albareda Salvadó, *La Guerra de Sucesión de España (1700–1714)* (Madrid: Crítica, 2010), 77.
44. Anne Dubet, *Un estadista francés en la España de los Borbones: Juan Orry y las primeras reformas de Felipe V (1701–1706)* (Madrid: Biblioteca Nueva, 2008), 153.
45. Dubet, *Un estadista francés*, 191.
46. Santiago Aquerreta, 'La participación de los financieros navarros en la Guerra de Sucesión: el abastecimiento de víveres al ejército', in Rafael Torres Sánchez, ed., *Capitalismo mercantil en la España del siglo XVIII* (Pamplona: EUNSA, 2000), 273–14.
47. Pedro Rodríguez de Campomanes, *Discurso sobre la educación popular de los artesanos y su fomento* (Madrid: Imprenta de Antonio Sancha, 1775), 420.
48. Ildefonso Pulido Bueno, *José Patiño: El inicio del gobierno político-económico ilustrado en España* (Huelva: Artes Gráficas Andaluzas, 1998).
49. For information on the business activities of Aguerri see Carmen Sanz Ayan, 'La problemática del abastecimiento de los Ejércitos de Extremadura y Cataluña durante 1652', *Temas de Historia Militar, 2º Congreso de Historia Militar* (Zaragoza: 1988), 221–36,

and, by the same author, *Los banqueros de Carlos II* (Valladolid: Universidad de Valladolid, 1989), 378–82. The characteristics of the company set up by Valdeolmos and Goyeneche have been analysed in Santiago Aquerreta, 'La participación de los financieros nacionales en la Guerra de Sucesión: el abastecimiento de víveres al ejército', in Rafael Torres, ed., *El capitalismo mercantil en España siglo XVIII* (Pamplona: EUNSA, 2000), 83–123.

50. A biography of this house in the reign of Charles in Julio Caro Baroja, *La hora navarra del siglo XVIII* (Pamplona: Diputación Foral, 1969), 49–60. According to this author, although they came from Lower Navarre and with residence in Zaragoza, they ended up moving to Madrid at the end of the century, joining the busy group of Navarre merchants in the court, forming part of its Congregation of San Fermín, and doing business with some of its members, like the Goyeneche. On the economic activity of this group see Santiago Aguerreta, *Negocios y finanzas en el siglo XVIII: la familia Goyeneche* (Pamplona: EUNSA, 2001).
51. There are many reference works on the tie-ins between *asientos* and taxation revenue rights during the Habsburg era. One of the most recent and interesting in Carlos Álvarez Nogal, *El crédito de la monarquía hispánica en el reinado de Felipe IV* (León: Publicaciones Junta Castilla y León, 1997). In the one-year grain victualling contract for the army of Aragón, in Valencia and Catalonia alone the Casa del Marqués de Valdeolmos earned a credit with the Real Hacienda of 46 million *reales*, according to Henry Kamen, *La guerra de Sucesión en España* (Barcelona: Grijalbo, 1974), 82.
52. During these decades we find the Casa de Valdeolmos tendering in several military victualling *asientos*, always under the name of Pedro López de Ortega, 'administrator of the house and business of the Marqués de Valdeolmos', AGS, DGT, Inv. 25, leg. 4.
53. Troop victualling in 1740–1. The bid put in by Casa de Valdeolmos was made through its administrator Inocencio García, AGS, SSH, leg. 640.
54. Urban Ruíz Velarde to José Campillo, 'Un pliego para la Provisión Gral de Viveres, por un año (1727). Todas las tropas menos las guardias de Corps e infantería de la Corte y veinte leguas de ella', 8 Nov. 1726, AGS, SSH. leg. 640.
55. Jean-Pierre Dedieu 'Les Groupes financiers et industriels au service du roi. Espagne, fin XVIIe-début XVIIIe siècle', in Anne Dubet and Jean-Philippe Luis, eds, *Les Financiers et la construction de l'Ètat—France, Espagne (XVIIe–XIXe siècle)* (Rennes: Presses Universitaires de Rennes, 2011), 87–104.
56. José Miguel Delgado Barrado, *Aquiles y Teseos: Bosquejos del reformismo borbónico (1701–1759)* (Granada: Universidad de Granada, 2007). The aim in view was to limit the conception of public administration and finances as a private business. It was a similar case to that of the French *fermiers*, whose 'private enterprise in public finance' was the fruit of a progressive campaign by the state against the build-up of debt and in the hope that bringing them into the administration would improve their managerial efficiency. See J. F. Bosher, *French Finances 1770–1795: From Business to Bureaucracy* (Cambridge: Cambridge University Press, 1970), 92. A compendium of the main criticisms made of this system in Spain's political-economic works of the first half of the eighteenth century is in Pablo Fernández Albaladejo, 'El decreto de suspensión de pagos de 1739: análisis y explicación', *Moneda y Crédito* 142 (1977), 51–81. The author argues that the crown's suspension of payments in 1739 was the result of the control over public finances wielded by private business. The climate of intellectual hostility was matched by open social rejection, much

the same as in France itself: Daniel Dessert, *Argent, pouvoir et societé au grand siécle* (Paris: Fayard, 1984), 242

57. RO of José Patiño to Tomás de Iriberri, Treasurer General, Madrid, 11 Dec. 1730, AGS, DGT, Inv. 16, Guión 24, leg. 4.
58. 'Order for setting up a Contaduría General for settling the cost and expense for the Real Hacienda of supplying bread and barley for the accounting year beginning I-XII-1730'; the proceedings aimed to ascertain and keep a track of 'the price at which each bread ration and *fanega* of barley went out to the troops'. The administrative history of the Contaduría from 1730 to 1739 can be reconstructed in AGS, DGT, Inv. 25, leg. 14. Although all the references we have found on changing the provisioning method are related to the army, at the beginning of the 1730s the rumour was rife that it was to be applied also in the navy, for a navy *asiento* bid made in 1730 by Miguel Arizcun asked for a series of safeguards for not getting left high and dry with the purchased goods 'in the event that Your Majesty should choose to bring said provision under your Real Hacienda', 1 Oct. 1730, AGS, DGT, Inv. 25, leg. 15.
59. Daniel A. Baugh, *British Naval Administration in the Age of Walpole* (Princeton, NJ: Princeton University Press, 1965), 448–52.
60. Fermín Foich, 18 Nov. 1739, AGS, SSH, leg. 640.
61. See Michael J. Braddick, *The Nerves of State: Taxation and the Financing of the English State, 1558–1714* (Manchester: Manchester University Press, 1996), and John Brewer, *The Sinews of Power: War, Money and the English State, 1688–1783* (New York: Alfred A. Knopf, 1989).
62. Duncan Crewe, *Yellow Jack and the Worm: British Naval Administration in the West Indies, 1739–1748* (Liverpool: Liverpool University Press, 1993), 298.
63. The English victualling system strengthened as the solvency of its public finances increased. This was the key to its success because it underpinned the merchants' confidence in state business and tapped into the improvement in economic conditions. The system proved its mettle during the Seven Years War, when products flooded to the army and there was no need to seek them or grant anyone privileges to find them. Witness how London merchants rushed to meet the English army and navy's supply needs, and the Victualling Board's only concern was to control the quality of the products. David Hancock, *Citizens of the World: London Merchants and the Integration of the British Atlantic Community, 1735–1785* (Cambridge: Cambridge University Press, 1995), 222–3; Roger Morriss, *The Foundations of British Maritime Ascendancy: Resources, Logistics and the State, 1755–1815* (Cambridge: Cambridge University Press, 2011), 271–20.
64. AGS, SSH, leg. 640.

CHAPTER 4

1. For a development of this thesis in the specific case of industrial policy, see Guillaume Garner, 'Caméralisme et territoire. Ètat, espace et économie dans le discours économique allemand au XVIIIe siècle', *Revue du Nord* 85 (Oct.–Dec. 2003), 729–45.
2. Rafael Torres Sánchez, *Volver a la 'hora navarra': La contribución Navarra a la construcción de la monarquía española en el siglo XVIII* (Pamplona: EUNSA, 2010).
3. Santiago Aquerreta, 'La casa de Arizcun 1725–1742: las estrategias financieras de un hombre de negocios en el Madrid de la Ilustración', in José A. Ferrer Benimeli, ed., *El Conde de Aranda y su tiempo* (Zaragoza: Institución Fernando el Católico, 2000), 659–78. María Concepción Hernández Escayola, *Negocio y*

servicio: finanzas públicas y hombres de negocios en Navarra en la primera mitad del siglo XVIII (Pamplona: EUNSA, 2004).

4. Rafael Torres Sánchez, 'Los navarros en la provisión de víveres a la armada española durante el siglo XVIII', in Rafael Torres Sánchez, ed., *Volver a la 'hora navarra': La contribución Navarra a la construcción de la monarquía española en el siglo XVIII* (Pamplona: EUNSA, 2009), 213–64.
5. María Concepción Hernández Escayola, *Negocio y servicio: finanzas públicas y hombres de negocios en Navarra en la primera mitad del siglo XVIII* (Pamplona, EUNSA, 2004).
6. Santiago Aquerreta, *Negocios y familias en el siglo XVIII: la familia Goyeneche* (Pamplona: EUNSA, 2001).
7. AGS, SSH, leg. 640.
8. Rafael Escobedo Romero, *El tabaco del rey: la organización de un monopolio fiscal durante el Antiguo Régimen* (Pamplona: EUNSA, 2007).
9. AGS, SSH, leg. 293.
10. The trend is shown in José Miguel Palop Ramos, 'El ejército en Valencia durante el siglo XVIII: Alojamientos y cuarteles', Ricardo Franch Benavent and Rafael Benítez Sánchez-Blanco, eds, *Estudios de historia moderna: en homenaje a la profesora Emilia Salvador Esteban* (Valencia: Universitat de València, 2008), 403–30.
11. AGS, SSH, leg. 640.
12. Eduardo Escartín Sánchez, *La intendencia de Cataluña en el siglo XVIII* (Barcelona: Santandreu, 1995), 266.
13. Rafael Torres Sánchez, *La llave de todos los tesoros: La Tesorería General de Carlos III* (Madrid: Silex, 2012), 151–73.
14. Fermín Folch, 22 Sept. 1740, AGS, SSH, leg. 640.
15. AGS, DGT, Inv. 25, leg. 14.
16. AGS, SSH, leg. 641.
17. AGS, DGT, Inv. 25, leg. 14.
18. Decreto, 23 Nov. 1755, AGS, SSH, leg. 642.
19. Campillo to Folch, Madrid, 21 Feb. 1742. AGS, SSH, leg. 640.
20. Vicente Llombart, 'La política económica de Carlos III ¿Fiscalismo, cosmética o estímulo al crecimiento?', *Revista de historia económica* 11 (1994), 11–39.
21. Michel Zylberberg, 'Un centre financier "péripherique": Madrid dans la seconde moitié du XVIIIe siècle', *Revue Historique* 546 (1983), 265–309. Michel Zylberberg, *Une si douce domination: Les milieux d'affaires français et l'Espagne vers 1780–1808* (Paris: Ministère des Finances, 1993).
22. The difficult transition until finding the Cinco Gremios Mayores is described in AGS, SSH, leg. 645.
23. Madrid, 16 Nov. 1749, Santos to Ensenada, AGS, SSH, leg. 640.
24. The negotiation is described in AGS, SSH, leg. 640.
25. Francisco Mendinueta, 'Provisión por Comisión', 1753 and 1754, AGS, DGT, Inv. 25, leg. 14.
26. Madrid, 9 Aug. 1754, AGS, SSH, leg. 641.
27. Madrid, 18 Jan. 1759, AGS, SSH, leg. 641.
28. Rafael Torres Sánchez, 'La Hora navarra y el triunfo de los navarros. El banquero navarro Juan Bautista Dutari y sus relaciones con Navarra durante el siglo XVIII', in Agustín González Enciso, ed., *Navarros en la Monarquía española en el siglo XVIII* (Pamplona: EUNSA, 2007), 283–308.
29. For more information on the munitions *asiento* see Agustín González Enciso in Stephen Conway and Rafael Torres Sánchez, eds, *The Spending of the States:*

Military Expenditure during the Long Eighteenth Century: Patterns, Organisation and Consequences, 1650–1815 (Saarbrücken: VDM, 2011), 285–312.

30. Francisco Mendinueta to Miguel Muzquiz, 4 June 1757, AGS, SSH, leg. 641.
31. Rafael Torres Sánchez, 'Campomanes y el comerciante y financiero Simón Aragorri', in Dolores Mateos Dorado, ed., *Campomanes doscientos años después* (Oviedo: Publicaciones de la Universidad de Oviedo, 2003), 709–18. Jesús Astigarraga, 'Un nuevo sistema económico para la monarquía española. Las "Reflexiones sobre el estado actual del comercio de España" (1761), de Simón de Aragorri', *Revista de historia industrial* 52 (2013), 13–42.
32. Madrid, 20 Dec. 1754, AGS, SSH, leg. 640.
33. Stanley J. Stein, 'Un raudal de oro y plata que corría sin cesar de España a Francia: Política mercantil española y el comercio con Francia en la época de Carlos III', *Actas del Congreso Internacional sobre Carlos III y la Ilustración* (Madrid: Ministerio de Cultura, 1989), ii. 219–87.
34. AGS, SSH, leg. 641.
35. María Victoria López-Cordón, María Ángeles Pérez, and María Teresa Martínez de Sas, *La casa de Borbón* (Madrid: Alianza Editorial, 2000), 227.
36. Marqués de Esquilache, AGS, SSH, leg. 641.
37. For more information on these bids see AGS, SSH, legs 641 and 642.
38. Francisco Mendinueta to Marqués de Esquilache, Madrid, 12 Apr. 1763, AGS, SSH, leg. 642.
39. Zylberberg, *Une si douce domination*, 167.
40. AHN, Consejos, 21 Aug. 1789, leg. 34.498.
41. For more information on this army see Agustín González Enciso, 'Spain's Mobilisation of Resources for the War with Portugal in 1762', in Huw V. Bowen and Agustín González Enciso, eds, *Mobilising Resources for War: Britain and Spain at Work During the Early Modern Period* (Pamplona: EUNSA, 2006), 159–90.
42. AGS, SSH, 24 Mar. 1763, leg. 642.
43. The demonstration before the Marqués de Esquilache was carried out in Madrid, in the Convento de Agustinos, Recoletos del Prado, probably at the end of 1762. AHN, Consejos, leg. 34.498.
44. AHN, Consejos, 21 Aug. 1789, leg. 34.498.
45. The deed of empowerment of Francisco Dughes, expressly referring to his intervention in the victualling *asiento*, is kept in the AHPM, Ramón Antonio Aguado, 18.968, fo. 425, Madrid, 21 Apr. 1763.
46. Salvador Querejazu to Esquilache, 23 Apr. 1763, AGS, SSH, leg. 642.
47. AHPM, 18.965, 15 Apr. 1754, fo. 343.
48. AHPM, 18.965, 10 Sept. 1753, fo. 229; AHPM, 18.965, 1 Jan. 1754, fos. 324, 465.
49. AHPM, 18.965, fo. 624; AHPM, 18.966, fo. 90.
50. AHPM, 18.966, 27 Oct. 1756, fo. 163; AHPM, 18.967, 4 Oct. 1760, fo. 536; AHPM, 18.968, 15 Feb. 1763, fo. 307.
51. Juan Carlos Sola Corbacho, 'El mercado de crédito en Madrid (1750–1808)', in Rafael Torres Sánchez, ed., *Capitalismo mercantil en la España del siglo XVlII* (Pamplona: EUNSA, 2000), 211–46.
52. AHPM, 18.965, 10 May 1754, fo. 510; AHPM, 18.966, 7 Aug. 1756, fo. 134; AHPM, 18.968, 29 Mar. 1756, fo. 405.
53. This Madrid credit network worked in a very similar way to the Paris market analysed in Philip T. Hoffman, Gilles Postel-Vinay, and Jean-Laurent Rosenthal, *Priceless*

Markets: The Political Economy of Credit in Paris, 1660–1870 (Chicago: University of Chicago Press, 2000).

54. AHPM, 18.965; (1743) 19 Dec. 1754, fo. 630; AHPM, 18.966, 24 Mar. 1756, fo. 73; AHPM, 18.968, 9 Sept. 1763, fo. 527.
55. AHPM, 18.965, 21 Oct. 1754, fo. 602; AHPM, 18.967, 10 Jan. 1759, fo. 11; AHPM, 18.967, 12 Jan. 1759, fo. 17.
56. AHPM, 18.966, 16 Nov. 1758, fo. 646; AHPM, 18.968, 5 Aug. 1763, fo. 500; AHPM, 18.968, 13 July 1763, fo. 483.
57. AHPM, 18.966, 24 May 1756, fo. 108.
58. The *asiento* approved in 21 June 1756 and the accounts thereof in Archivo General de Simancas, Dirección General del Tesoro, Inv. 25, leg. 14. For this *asiento* Florenza and Partearroyo received from the government 1,714,520 *rsv*.
59. AHPM, 18.968, 9 March 1760, fo. 353, 7 May 1763, fo. 434.
60. AGS, DGT, Inv. 25, leg. 14.
61. AHN, Consejos, leg. 34.498. Álvaro Aragón Ruano and Alberto Angulo Morales, 'The Spanish Basque Country in Global Trade Networks in the Eighteenth Century', *International Journal of Maritime History* 25 (2013), 149–72 at 154.
62. The *asiento* was approved on 21 May 1763, AGS, DGT, Inv. 25, leg. 14.27; AHN, Consejos, leg. 34.498.
63. AGS, SSH, 22 Aug. 1763, leg. 642.
64. Juan Guillot Matutares to Marqués de Esquilache, AGS, SSH, La Coruña, 3 Dec. 1763, leg. 642.
65. AHN, Consejos, leg. 34.498.
66. AHN, Consejos, leg. 34.498.
67. Querejazu to Esquilache, Madrid, Sept. 1763, AGS, SSH, leg. 642.
68. Francisco Azcaya to Francisco Antonio Ibarrola, 4 Nov. 1763, AGS, SSH, leg. 642.
69. AHN, Consejos, leg. 34.498.
70. This ruling was handed down on 9 Nov. 1763; on 11 Nov. 1763 Someruelos informed Esquilache that the trial had reached its final ruling, AGS, SSH, leg. 642.
71. AHN, Consejos, leg. 34.498.
72. Marqués de Ossun, Ambassador of France, to Esquilache, 13 Dec. 1763, AGS, SSH, leg. 642.

CHAPTER 5

1. Miguel Capella and Antonio Matilla, *Los Cinco Gremios Mayores de Madrid* (Madrid: Cámara de Comercio de Madrid, 1957). On its track record as a great business group see Rafael Torres Sánchez, 'In the Shade of Power: Monopolist Entrepreneurs, the State and Spanish Military Victualling in the Eighteenth Century', in Jeff Fynn-Paul, ed., *War, Entrepreneurs, and the State* (Leiden: Brill, 2013), 260–83.
2. AGS, DGT, Inv. 25, leg. 22.
3. Virginia Tovar Martín, *Los Cinco Gremios Mayores de Madrid: Artífices de la entrada pública en la capital de España de los Reyes Don Fernando VI y Doña Bárbara de Braganza, octubre de 1746* (Madrid: Cámara de Comercio de Madrid, 1980).
4. 13 June 1779, AHN, Hacienda, lib. 10.820.
5. AGS, SSH, leg. 640.
6. José Patiño to Marqués de Valdebueno, San Ildefonso, 4 Aug. 1733, AGS, DGT, Inv. 25, leg. 14.
7. José Luis Gómez Urdáñez, *El proyecto reformista de Ensenada* (Lleida: Milenio, 1995).

8. Bernabé de Soto to Marqués de la Ensenada, Aranjuez, 3 June 1744. AGS, DGT, Inv. 25, leg. 14.
9. The rivalry of these businesspeople for making with this *asiento* can be pieced together from the contracts, auctions, and bids carried out. AGS, SSH, legs 640 and 641.
10. AGS, SSH, leg. 641.
11. Francisco Soria Zaldibar and Francisco Martínez de Vallejo to Conde de Valparaiso, Madrid, 5 Sept. 1758. AGS, DGT, Inv. 25, leg. 14.
12. Contract in AGS, SSH, leg. 642.
13. Jorge Pinto Rodríguez, 'Los Cinco Gremios Mayores de Madrid y el comercio colonial en el siglo XVIII', *Revista de Indias* 51 (1991), 293–326.
14. Rafael Torres Sánchez, 'Los navarros en la provisión de víveres a la Armada española durante el siglo XVIII', in Rafael Torres Sánchez, *Volver a la 'hora navarra': La contribución Navarra a la construcción de la monarquía española en el siglo XVIII* (Pamplona: EUNSA, 2009), 213–64.
15. Rafael Torres Sánchez, 'El gran negocio de la época, la provisión de víveres al ejército por Francisco Mendinueta (1744–1763)', in Santiago Aquerreta, ed., *Francisco Mendinueta: Finanzas y mecenazgo en la España del siglo XVIII* (Pamplona: EUNSA, 2002), 101–34.
16. María Antonia O'Brien (Cristóbal Partearroyo's wife) to Miguel Múzquiz, Madrid, 17 Feb. 1768, AGS, SSH, leg. 644.
17. On the life-annuity business, AGS, SSH, leg. 485. Rafael Torres Sánchez, 'Seguro de hombres y auxilio de reyes. El Fondo Vitalicio y la Royal Exchequer española de Carlos III', *Obradoiro de historia moderna* 15 (2006), 139–72.
18. Rafal Torres Sánchez, 'Lana y banca. Los servicios financieros al negocio lanero en el siglo XVIII', in Agustín González Enciso, ed., *El negocio de la lana en España (1650–1830)* (Pamplona: EUNSA, 2001), 235–68.
19. Juan Sola Corbacho, 'El mercado de crédito en Madrid (1750–1808)', in Rafael Torres Sánchez, ed., *Capitalismo mercantil en la España del siglo XVIII* (Pamplona: EUNSA, 2000), 211–46.
20. The British Library, Manuscript Collection, MS 10255, Francisco Vicente de Gorvea, Madrid, 18 Jan. 1769.
21. Ventura de Argumosa to Miguel Múzquiz, Guadalajara, 25 Aug. 1768, AGS, SSH, leg. 644.
22. Partearroyo and Larralde to Miguel Múzquiz, Madrid, 23 Jan. 1768, AGS, SSH, leg. 644.
23. Pinto Rodríguez, 'Los Cinco Gremios Mayores de Madrid', 293–326.
24. Marqués de Esquilache, Madrid, 26 Dec. 1771, AGS, SSH, leg. 113.
25. Ángel Iturrioz Magaña, *Estudio del subsidio y excusado (1561–1808): contribuciones económicas de la diócesis de Calahorra y La Calzada a la Royal Exchequer* (Logroño: Instituto de Estudios Riojanos, 1987).
26. Juan Bautista Laurnaga and Antonio Martínez de Santidrian to Marqués de Esquilache, 11 July 1764, AGS, SSH, leg. 644.
27. Accounts in AGS, SSH, leg. 643. Contract of 1762 in AGS, DGT, Inv. 25, leg. 14.
28. José Melchor de Urquijo and Francisco Vicente de Gorbea to Miguel Múzquiz, 30 May 1768, Madrid, AGS, DGT, Inv. 25, leg. 14.
29. The *asiento* bid was put in on 30 May 1768 and the award came on 10 June 1768. José Melchor de Urquijo and Francisco Vicente de Gorbea to Miguel Múzquiz, Madrid, AGS, DGT, Inv. 25, leg. 14.
30. Madrid, AGS, DGT, Inv. 25, leg. 14.

31. See Rafael Torres Sánchez, *La llave de todos los tesoros: La Tesorería General de Carlos III* (Madrid: Silex, 2012).
32. Cosme Gómez Carrasco, 'Parientes, amigos y patronos. Red, movilidad y reproducción social en la burguesía y la élite de poder a finales del Antiguo Régimen (Albacete, 1750–1808)', *Studia Histórica* 29 (2007), 427–63.
33. Francisco Andújar Castillo, 'El fuero militar en el siglo XVIII. Un estatuto de privilegio', *Chronica Nova* 23 (1996), 11–31, and Rafel Torres Sánchez, 'Cuando las reglas del juego cambian. Mercados y privilegio en el abastecimiento del ejército español en el siglo XVIII', *Revista de historia moderna* 20 (2002), 487–511.
34. RO, 27 Apr. 1769, AGS, DGT, Inv. 25, leg. 14.
35. RO, 15 Nov. 1770, AGS, DGT, Inv. 25, leg. 14.
36. AGS, SSH, leg. 268.
37. Response to the governor of Cadiz, 21 Nov. 1770, AGS, SSH, leg. 645.
38. Pedro Rodríguez Campomanes to Miguel Múzquiz, 10 Jan. 1770, AGS, SSH, leg. 643.
39. Michel Zylberberg, *Une si douce domination: les milieux d'affaires français et l'Espagne vers 1780–1808* (Paris: Ministère des Finances, 1993).
40. See José Miguel Medrano and Carlos Malamud, 'Las actividades de los Cinco Gremios Mayores en el Perú. Apuntes preliminares', *Revista de Indias* 48 (1988), 421–33.
41. Rafael Torres Sánchez, 'Campomanes y el comerciante y financiero Simón Aragorri', in Dolores Mateos Dorado, ed., *Campomanes doscientos años después* (Oviedo: Universidad de Oviedo, 2003), 709–18. For information on the life and thinking of this merchant, see Jesús Astigarraga, 'Las "Reflexiones sobre el estado actual del comercio de España" (1761), de Simón de Aragorri: contenido, estudio de fuentes y primera interpretación', *Documentos de trabajo de la Asociación Española de Historia Económica* 9 (2011).
42. Secret report on the proposal of Simón Aragorri, 3 Oct. 1771, AGS, SSH, leg. 645.
43. Proposal of Francisco Cabarrús for the extraction of silver coin by *asiento* to Miguel Múzquiz, Madrid, 30 July 1778, AHN, Diversos, leg. 31. This early and hitherto unknown proposal by Cabarrús was not taken into account by Pedro Tedde, 'Cabarrús y el monopolio de extracción de la plata', *Economía y Sociedad en la España moderna y contemporánea* (Madrid: Editorial Síntesis, 1996), 115–35. This author, however, believes it to be essential for a proper understanding of the financier's career.
44. Rafael Torres Sánchez, 'Financiers et politiques. Francisco Montes et François Cabarrus (1770–1790)', in Anne Dubet, ed., *Administrer les finances royales dans la monarchie espagnole (XVIe–XIXe siècles)* (Rennes: Presses Universitaires de Rennes, 2008), 103–20.
45. Resolution of Pedro Lerena, 3 Sept. 1789, AGS, SSH, leg. 647.
46. Terms and conditions of the *asiento* by administration of the Cinco Gremios Mayores, 30 Oct. 1790, AGS, SSH, leg. 647.
47. José Canga Argüelles, *Diccionario de Hacienda con aplicación a España* (Madrid: Imprenta de Don Marcelino Calero y Portocarrero, 1834), 524.
48. Gordon E Bannerman, *Merchants and the Military in Eighteenth-Century: British Army Contracts and Domestic Supply, 1739-1763* (London: Pickering & Chatto Publishers, 2008). Gordon Bannerman, 'The Impact of War on the British Economy, 1739–1770: Contracting as a Facet of Economic Vibrancy'. My thanks to the author for allowing me to read this interesting work.>

CHAPTER 6

1. Patrick K. O'Brien, 'The Nature and Historical Evolution of an Exceptional Fiscal State and its Possible Significance for the Precocious Commercialization and Industrialization of the British Economy from Cromwell to Nelson', *Economic History Review* 64 (2011), 408–46.
2. N. A. M. Rodger, 'From the "Military Revolution" to the "Fiscal-Naval State"', *Journal for Maritime Research* 13 (2011), 119–28.
3. Richard Harding, 'Parliament and the British Fiscal-Military State: Ideology, Consent and State Expenditure in Britain, 1739–1748', in Stephen Conway and Rafael Torres, eds, *The Spending of States: Military Expenditure during the Long Eighteenth Century: Patterns, Organisation, and Consequences, 1650–1815* (Saarbrücken: VDM, 2011), 31–50.
4. Roger Morriss, *The Foundations of British Maritime Ascendancy: Resources, Logistics and the State, 1755–1815* (Cambridge: Cambridge University Press, 2011).
5. Along the same line see Clive Wilkinson, *The British Navy and the State in the Eighteenth Century* (Woodbridge: The Boydell Press, 2004).
6. Rafael Torres Sánchez, *La llave de todos los tesoros: La Tesorería General de Carlos III* (Madrid: Silex, 2012), 129–266.
7. There has still been very little research as yet into eighteenth-century Spanish navy finances. The best work to hand is that of José Patricio Merino Navarro, *La Armada española en el siglo XVIII* (Madrid: Fundación Universitaria Española, 1981), 112–78, which could be fleshed out with Jacques A. Barbier, 'Indies Revenues and Naval Spending: The Cost of Colonialism for the Spanish Bourbons, 1763-1805', *Jahrbuch für Geschichte von Staat, Wirtschaft und Gesellschaft Lateinamerikas* 21 (1984), 169–88. Also useful is José Manuel Serrano Álvarez, 'El gasto naval en España e Indias (1715–1759). El caso de Tierra Firme', *Revista de historia naval* 20 (2002), 25–34, and financial information is also given in Iván Valdez-Bubnov, *Poder naval y modernización del Estado: política de construcción naval española (siglos XVI–XVIII)* (Mexico: Unam, 2011). For the reign of Charles III see Torres Sánchez, *La llave de todos los tesoros*, 199–266. The best work on economic legislation of the Armada is still Antonio Raquejo Alonso, *Historia de la administración y fiscalización económica de las fuerzas armadas* (Madrid: Ministerio de Defensa, 1992). A good example of the possibility of studying ordinances for the study of finances in Isidoro Guzmán Raja, 'Normativa contable en la Armada española durante el periodo 1700–1850: especial referencia a la administración de provisiones', *De Computis: revista española de historia de la contabilidad* 5 (2006), 65–142.
8. Sergio Solbes Ferri, 'Campillo y Ensenada: el suministro de vestuarios para el ejército durante las campañas de Italia (1741–1748)', *Studia historica. Historia moderna* 35 (2013), 201–34.
9. Olivier Chaline, Philippe Bonnichon, and Charles-Philippe de Vergennes, eds, *Les Marines de la Guerre d'Indépendance Américaine (1763–1783)* (Paris: Les Presses de l'université Paris-Sorbonne, 2013), 12.
10. 'Estado militar. Armada Española en 1796', Cadiz, December 1796. Reproduced in Adolfo de Castro, *Historia de Cádiz y su provincia* (Madrid: Imp. de la Revista médica, 1858), 517.
11. Marina Alfonso Mola, 'Corso y flota de Indias: Los convoys ingleses apresados en 1780 y 1795', in Bibiano Torres Ramírez, ed., *Andalucía América y el mar* (Seville: Diputación de Huelva, 1991), 196–224. See also Mario Luis Ocaña Torres,

El corso marítimo español en el estrecho de Gibraltar (1700–1802) (Algeciras: Instituto de Estudios Campogibraltareños, 1993).

12. e.g. the sale of 'surplus flax tow produced by shipyard hemp combs', Ferrol, 1768, AGS (Archivo General de Simancas), Marina, leg. 606.
13. The obligation for Havana also to draw up a yearly budget was expressly included in 1776 on the grounds 'that a squadron should be considered to be based there permanently': Ordenanza 1776, in Jesús María Alía Plana, *Ordenanzas fundacionales de la Armada* (Madrid: Port Royal, 1997), 391.
14. It was this treasury of the Real Giro of Paris that was in charge of sustaining the Spanish squadrons for the invasion of Great Britain sent to the English Channel in 1779 to 1781. Although most of the crew were taken from their bases in Spain, there did remain in Brest a squadron led by Miguel Gastón, which had to be sustained by means of direct purchases from French suppliers or by purchases made by the Spanish consul of Bordeaux, Manuel de las Heras, or the Spanish ambassador in Paris: AHN, Hacienda, lib. 6734.
15. Castejón to Miguel Gastón, San Ildefonso, 27 Sept. 1779, AGS, Marina, leg. 591. The squadron treasurer was Hermenegildo Llanderal. The Finance Ministry urgently sent 3 million *reales* through the Real Giro of Paris, its treasurer Francisco Ventura de Llovera.
16. Marqués de Castejón to Miguel Múzquiz, 12 June 1780, AGS, SSH, leg. 50.
17. In an attempt to clear up this problem, an order was sent out in 1777 establishing the obligation of navy departments to pay all duties belonging to the Royal Exchequer for goods purchased, whereafter the Tesorería General would reimburse each department for the sum paid: RO, 7 Nov. 1777, AGS, SSH, leg. 51.
18. The main direction of these flows was from Cadiz to Cartagena and Ferrol: Marqués de Zambrano to Múzquiz, Madrid, 24 Apr. 1779, AGS, Marina, leg. 591.
19. Chaline, Bonnichon, and de Vergennes, eds, *Les Marines de la Guerre*, 12.
20. When referring to its shipyard, José Patricio Merino admitted that 'The biggest lacuna, without any doubt, is Havana, a singular circumstance that always remains apart': José Patricio Merino Navarro, *La Armada española en el siglo XVIII* (Madrid: Fundación Universitaria Española, 1981), 130.
21. The works that helped to gauge the scale of the problem were those of G. Douglas Inglis, 'The Spanish Naval Shipyard at Havana in the Eighteenth Century', in *New Aspects of Naval History: Selected Papers From the Fifth Naval History Symposium* (Baltimore: Nautical Aviation and Publishing Co. of America, 1985), 47–58; María Mestre Prat de Padua and David Matamoros Aparicio, 'La organización del astillero de La Habana durante el siglo XVIII', *Jahrbuch für Geschichte Lateinamerikas* 34 (1997), 89–103. The best studies, however, are those made by Carlos Martínez Shaw and Marina Alfonso Mola, 'Los astilleros de la América colonial', *Historia general de América Latina* 3 (1999), 279–304, and, above all, José Manuel Serrano Álvarez, *El astillero de La Habana y la construcción naval militar (1700–1750)* (Madrid: Ministerio de Defensa, 2008). For the second half of the century the above can be complemented by other works: Allan J. Kuethe and José Manuel Serrano Álvarez, 'El astillero de la Habana y Trafalgar', *Revista de Indias* 67 (2007), 763–76. José Manuel Serrano Álvarez, 'La revitalización del Astillero de La Habana en época de Lorenzo Montalvo, 1765–1772', *Revista de historia naval* 27 (2009), 71–100.
22. Bibiano Torres Ramírez, *La Armada de Barlovento* (Seville: Escuela de Estudios Hispanoamericanos, 1981), 216.

23. An ambitious plan was drawn up for building two 80-gun ships of the line. This was later increased to four ships of the line. José Manuel Serrano Álvarez, 'La revitalización del Astillero de La Habana en época de Lorenzo Montalvo, 1765–1772', *Revista de historia naval* 27 (2009), 91.
24. Allan J. Kuethe and José Manuel Serrano Álvarez, 'El astillero de la Habana y Trafalgar', *Revista de Indias* 67 (2007), 770.
25. Real Instrucción, 14 Nov. 1766. Conde de Macuriege to Julián Arriaga, Havana, 25 Mar. 1774, AGS, Marina, leg. 596. For each ship the *junta* submitted an individualized budget, breaking down payments made to officers, infantry, artillery, and crew.
26. Nine boats were used for the sea transport of cut wood alone. These tasks involved the payment of free workers and the maintenance of slaves. An important factor was the purchase and maintenance of many draught oxen. Juan Bautista Bonet, Havana, 31 Dec. 1778, AGS, Marina, leg. 591.
27. Shipments of naval supplies from Europe is a subject that has been little studied as yet, even though it is crucial for understanding the construction of an Atlantic trading space. There are, however, a few studies showing the scale and fluidity of these shipments to Havana. See José Quintero González, 'La Carraca y La Habana: aproximación al intercambio de pertrechos entre arsenales', *Revista de historia naval* 24 (2006), 57–66.
28. Johanna Von Grafenstein Gareis, 'El abasto de la escuadra y las plazas militares de gran Caribe, con harinas y víveres novohispanos, 1755–1779', in Carmen Yuste López and Matilde Souto Mantecón, eds, *El comercio exterior de México, 1713–1850: Entre la quiebra del sistema imperial y el surgimiento de una nación* (México: Instituto de Investigaciones Históricas-UNAM, 2000), 42–83.
29. Agustín González Enciso, *España y USA en el siglo XVIII: crecimiento industrial comparado y relaciones comerciales* (Valladolid: Universidad de Valladolid, 1979), and Linda Salvucci, 'Atlantic Intersections: Early American Commerce and the Rise of the Spanish West Indies (Cuba)', *Business History Review* 79 (2005), 781–800.
30. Juan Bautista Bonet, Havana, 31 Dec. 1778, AGS, Marina, leg. 591.
31. Richard Harding claims that crew illness was one of the main problems posed by British expeditions against the Americas. Richard Harding, *The Emergence of Britain's Global Naval Supremacy: The War of 1739–1748* (Woodbridge: The Boydell Press, 2010). Havana's Junta de Marina considered that the number of daily hospital stays in that port could be established 'at about 3 percent, on the basis of past experience, at a cost of about 3 *reales* each one', AGS, Marina, leg. 591.
32. By way of example, Fernando de Leyba, captain of Luisiana's infantry battalion, had asked for his mother living in Barcelona to be succoured by the treasury of that city at 8 pesos per month, duly allocated from his salary. Julián de Arriaga to Miguel de Múzquiz, 18 May 1775, AGS, SSH, leg. 61.
33. Héctor R. Feliciano Ramos, *El contrabando inglés en el Caribe y el Golfo de México (1748–1778)* (Seville: Diputación Provincial, 1990), 307.
34. José Manuel Serrano Álvarez, *Fortificaciones y Tropas: El gasto militar en Tierra Firme, 1700–1788* (Seville: Universidad de Sevilla, 2002), 377.
35. e.g. the purchases made were then defrayed by the Navy Secretariat of France to the treasury of the Spanish Royal Exchequer in Madrid: De Castries to Ventura Llovera, Paris 2 June 1781 (on this occasion 21,175 *pesos fuertes*), AHN, Hacienda, lib. 6458.
36. Carlos Marichal, *Bankruptcy of Empire: Mexican Silver and the Wars between Spain, Britain and France, 1760–1810* (Cambridge: Cambridge University Press, 2007), 40–1.

37. As well as Havana, the Mexican *situado* was sent to Luisiana, Santo Domingo, Puerto Rico, Cumaná, the French navy, and to pay the Casa Cabarrús. For the sums involved see Johanna Gareis, *Nueva España en el Circuncaribe, 1779–1808: Revolución, competencia imperial y vínculos intercoloniales* (Mexico: Universidad Nacional Autónoma de México, 1997), 139.
38. James A. Lewis, 'Nueva España y los esfuerzos para abastecer La Habana, 1779–1783', *Anuario de Estudios Americanos* 33 (1976), 101–26. See also Juan Ortíz Escamilla, *El teatro de la guerra: Veracruz, 1750–1825* (Castellón de la Plana: Universitat Jaume I, 2008).
39. The donations from the Condes de Regla and the Conde de Valenciana and others for building the ships Regla and Mexicano, both 114 gunners, built in Havana with the contributions from these rich owners of Mexican mines: Marichal, *Bankruptcy of Empire*, 37.
40. On this matter see the reflections of Marie-Therese Boyer-Xambeau, 'À la recherche d'un âge d'or des marchés financiers: intégration et efficence au XVIII siècle', *Cahiers d'Économie Politique* 21 (1992), 33–65.
41. Juan Marchena Fernández, 'Capital, créditos e intereses comerciales a fines del periodo colonial: los costos del sistema defensivo americano. Cartagena de Indias y el Sur del Caribe', *Tiempos de América* 9 (2002), 3–38.
42. Regina Grafe and Alexandra Irigoin have flagged up the extension of this relation in the Americas in the second half of the eighteenth century and the positive role it played in Spain's survival in the Americas: Regina Grafe and Alexandra Irigoin, 'A Stakeholder Empire: The Political Economy of Spanish Imperial Rule in America', *Economic History Review* 65 (2011), 1–43.
43. Alonso María de Cárdenas, Havana, 1 Mar. 1779, AGS, Marina, leg. 591.
44. Witness the charging of 9,300 *reales* of current silver 'which produced a premium of 38,750 *pesos fuertes* changed for that currency from several individuals at a rate of 3%', Ignacio Peñalver y Cardenas, Havana, 1 Apr. 1779, AGS, Marina, leg. 591.
45. In 1778 the Havana navy took in 82,978 *pesos fuertes* from this activity, representing 7% of the year's total income, whereas in war years the revenue from this activity added up to only 70,214 pesos, i.e. hardly 1% of the funds received by the navy treasury. Even so, the attractiveness of this business still soared in war years since the currency exchange premium as from January 1780 stood at 13%.
46. Ignacio Peñalver y Cardenas, Havana, 1 Oct. 1779, AGS, Marina, leg. 591.
47. Judging from the number of bread rations supplied to Spanish armies in the mid eighteenth century, about one in every four soldiers in Spain was quartered in Catalonia: AGS, SSH, leg. 640. As the second half of the eighteenth century unfurled, Catalonia was gradually ousted by Andalusia as the most militarized region, while still holding onto second place: by about 1766 29.7% of the Spanish army's bread rations were consumed in Andalusia, but Catalonia remained in second place with 25.7%: AGS, SSH, leg. 644. To put these figures in their proper perspective, Catalonia accounted for between 6 and 8% of Spain's population during the eighteenth century.
48. Jacques A. Barbier, 'Towards a New Chronology for Bourbon Colonialism: The *'Depositaría de Indias'* of Cadiz, 1722–1789', *Ibero-Amerikanisches Archiv* 6 (1980), 335–53; see also Torres Sánchez, *La llave de todos los tesoros*, 117.
49. Juan Torrejón Chaves, 'Estructura y organización de la producción en los arsenales de la Marina española del siglo XVIII', *Revista de historia naval* 19 (2001), 55–82.

50. Manuel Claro Delgado, 'Cádiz y las expediciones militares a Indias en el siglo XVIII', in *Milicia y sociedad en la baja Andalucía (siglos XVIII y XIX): actas VIII Jornadas Nacionales de Historia Militar* (Seville: Cátedra General Castaños, 1999), 3–20.
51. Quintero González, 'La Carraca y La Habana', 58. When the coastguard squadron of Cartagena submitted its 1770 budget, it worked on the premise that most of the supplies would come from Cadiz, 'but on the grounds that the shipments of rigging, canvass, nails, iron and flour that must come from Spain be checked as requested by this ministry with such punctuality as hitherto has been performed by the navy *intendente* of Cadiz, otherwise the budget would be inflated hugely if this essential wherewithal should fail and should then have to be bought in the Americas', Domingo Hernani to Pedro Mesía de la Cerda, Cartagena de Indias, 31 Aug. 1769, AGS, Marina, leg. 596. The correspondence of the Secretaría de Indias gives a good idea of the host of shipments sent. Several examples in Rafael Torres Sánchez, 'Tejiendo una Hacienda Imperial. "Unir los manejos de la Royal Exchequer de España y América" en el reinado de Carlos III', in Michel Bertrand and Zacarías Moutoukías, eds, *Changement institutionnel et fiscalité dans le monde hispanique (1750–1850)* (Toulouse: Université de Toulouse, 2014).
52. Juan Jaime López González, 'Una firma comercial sueca en Cádiz y su relación con los arsenales españoles a finales del siglo XVIII', *Actas I Congreso de Historia de Andalucía: Andalucía moderna (siglo XVIII)* (Córdoba: 1978), 287–99.
53. Roger Morriss, *The Foundations of British Maritime Ascendancy: Resources, Logistics and the State, 1755–1815* (Cambridge: Cambridge University Press, 2011). See also Roger Knight and Martin Wilcox, *Sustaining the Fleet, 1793–1815: War, the British Navy and the Contractor State* (Woodbridge: The Boydell Press, 2010).
54. David Syrett, *The Royal Navy in European Waters during the American Revolutionary War* (Columbia: University of South California Press, 1998).
55. It was knocked down to José Ortega, a resident of Cadiz: Cadiz, 6 Oct. 1784, AGS, Marina, leg. 606.
56. As recognized by the *junta* of Cadiz, the dearth of some products could have been surmounted only with the participation of private merchants, 'who are leading and have received in the shipyard itself a growing amount of iron and nails provided by private merchants of Cadiz, representing a huge expenditure in the budgets', Juan de Ulloa to Castejón, Isla de León, 23 Mar. 1781, AGS, Marina, leg. 593.
57. Francisco Bances, Isla de León, 19 Mar. 1782, AGS, Marina, leg. 594.
58. The option, in fact, was an ultimatum: 'they would rather receive payment in Cadiz than forfeit it completely, and I do not deem them so imprudent as to turn this down in default of any sooner payment', Montes to Múzquiz, 5 Nov. 1780, AGS, SSH, leg. 51.
59. The navy *intendente* estimated this exchange premium to be 1.5 or 2% but deemed it to be very convenient in so far as it forestalled the danger of payment defaults. Francisco Bances to Castejón, Isla de León, 12 July 1782, AGS, Marina, leg. 594. When extraordinary costs piled up, however, and therewith payment defaults, discounts could soar to 6%.
60. List of existing funds. Out of a total of 653,482 *rsv.* Tomás Cerviño, Ferrol, 1 Jan. 1784, AGS, Marina, leg. 595.
61. Maria Teresa Pérez Crespo Muñoz, *El arsenal de Cartagena en el siglo XVIII* (Madrid: Editorial Naval, 1992); see also Rafael Torres Sánchez, 'La palanca de la riqueza. Las repercusiones del arsenal en el crecimiento de Cartagena durante el

siglo XVIII', in Manuel-Reyes García Hurtado, ed., *Ferrol año cero: Una ciudad de la Ilustración* (Ferrol: Ediciones Embora, 2007), 157–89.

62. Alfredo Martín García, *Una sociedad en cambio: Ferrol a finales del Antiguo Régimen* (Ferrol: Embora, 2003), and 'La política de reconstrucción naval borbónica y el reino de Galicia: el real astillero de Esteiro (s. XVIII)', in Agustín Guimerá Ravina and Víctor Peralta Ruiz, eds, *Actas de la VIII Reunión Científica de la Fundación Española de Historia Moderna: El equilibrio de los imperios: de Ultrecht y Trafalgar* (Madrid, 2005), 747–60.
63. Witness the comments of the naval authorities of Cartagena on credit possibilities and the repercussions of payment defaults: 'there are few well-off subjects, locally, to turn to in case of need, such as the present one, since all funds are tied up in shops and foodstuff traders, who supply the shipyard staff and other employees in return for payment and any payment delays render these shopkeepers incapable of supplying the shipyard over and beyond a month and a half at the most', José de Roxas to Castejón, Cartagena, 30 June 1781, AGS, SSH, leg. 51.
64. Múzquiz to Castejón, Madrid, 13 Nov. 1781, AGS, Marina, leg. 593.

CHAPTER 7

1. Porfirio Sanz Camañes, ed., *Tiempo de cambios: Guerra, diplomacia y política internacional de la Monarquía Hispánica (1648–1700)* (Madrid: Actas, 2012).
2. Christopher Storrs, *The Resilience of the Spanish Monarchy, 1665–1700* (New York: Oxford University Press, 2006), 75.
3. David Goodman, *El poderío naval español: Historia de la armada española del siglo XVII* (Barcelona: Peninsular, 2001), 383.
4. Juan M. Castanedo Galán, *Guarnizo, un astillero de la Corona* (Madrid: Editorial Naval, 1993), 57.
5. Lourdes Odriozola Oyarbide, 'La construcción naval en el País Vasco. Siglos XVI–XVIII', *Itsas Memoria: revista de estudios marítimos del País Vasco* 2 (1998), 93–146.
6. Rafael Palacio Ramos, 'Los últimos galleones: el fin de la construcción naval para la Corona en el *Astillero* de Colindres', *Revista de historia naval* 27 (2009), 7–30.
7. Iván Valdez-Bubnov, *Poder naval y modernización del Estado: política de construcción naval española (siglos XVI–XVIII)* (Mexico: Unam, 2011), 91–5.
8. Marina Alfonso Mola and Carlos Martínez Shaw, 'Los *Astilleros* de la América colonial', *Historia General de América Latina: Consolidación del orden Colonial* 3 (2000), 279–303.
9. Fernando Serrano Mangas, *Los galeones de la carrera de Indias, 1650–1700* (Madrid: CSIC, 1986).
10. Bibiano Torres Ramírez, *La Armada de Barlovento* (Seville: Escuela de Estudios Hispano-Americanos, 1981).
11. Hermes Tovar Pinzón, 'Remesas, situados y *Real Hacienda* en el siglo XVII', in Antonio Bernal, ed., *Dinero, Moneda y Credito en la Monarquia Hispánica* (Madrid: Marcial Pons, 2000), 241–68.
12. Pablo Emilio Pérez-Mallaina Bueno and Bibiano Torres Ramírez, *La Armada del mar del sur* (Seville: Escuela de Estudios Hispano-Americanos, 1987), 113–15 and 103.
13. Didier Ozanam, 'La política exterior de España en tiempos de Felipe V y de Fernando VI', in Ramón Menéndez Pidal, *Historia de España* (Madrid: Cervera Pery, 1985).

14. The list of eighteenth-century navy ships built, bought, removed from service, or lost has been drawn up from various sources: MS Almirante Vigodet: 'Relación de los navíos que formaron parte de la Armada Española, desde principios del siglo XVIII', Gervasio de Artiñaño, *La Arquitectura naval española (en madera): Bosquejo de sus condiciones y rasgos de su evolución* (Madrid: Ateneo, 1914), 346–66. MS 471, AMN; Buques de la Armada, MS 8770, BN; and MS 2215, 12–7, AMN.
15. Valdez-Bubnov, *Poder naval*, 151, 153.
16. Pablo Emilio Pérez-Mallaina, *Política Naval Española en el Atlántico 1700–1715* (Seville: Escuela de Estudios Hispano-Americanos, 1982), 41, 390.
17. *Rande, 1702. Arde o mar. Catálogo de la exposición conmemorativa del tercer centenario de la batalla de Rande* (Vigo: Consorcio Zona Franca de Vigo, 2002).
18. Aingeru Zabala, 'La Guerra de Sucesión en el mar Cantábrico', *Itsas Memoria: revista de estudios marítimos del País Vasco* 5 (2006), 325–56.
19. Juan Marchena Fernández, 'De las "reliquias" de Felipe V a la gran Armada Oceánica de 1750: guerra y marina durante la primera mitad del siglo XVIII', in Juan José Sánchez Baena, Celia Chain Navarro, and Lorena Martínez Solis, eds, *Estudios de Historia Naval: Actitudes y medios en la Real Armada del siglo XVIII* (Murcia: Ministerio de Defensa, 2011), 49–90 at 71.
20. Marchena Fernández, 'De las "reliquias" de Felipe V', 49–90 at 72.
21. Valdez-Bubnov, *Poder naval*, 133.
22. Pablo Emilio Pérez-Mallaina, *Política Naval Española en el Atlántico 1700–1715* (Seville: Escuela de Estudios Hispano-Americanos, 1982), 400.
23. Concepción De Castro, *A La Sombra De Felipe V: Jose Grimaldo Ministro Responsable (1703–1726)* (Madrid: Marcial Pons, 2004). Anne Dubet, *Un estadista francés en la España de los Borbones: Juan Orry y las primeras reformas de Felipe V (1701–1706)* (Madrid: Biblioteca Nueva, 2008).
24. Allan J. Kuethe and Kenneth J. Andrien, *The Spanish Atlantic World in the Eighteenth Century: War and the Bourbon Reforms, 1713–1796* (Cambridge: Cambridge University Press, 2014).
25. José Calvo Poyato, 'La industria militar española durante la Guerra de Sucesión', *Revista de historia militar* 33 (1989), 51–71.
26. Pablo Emilio Pérez-Mallaina, *Política Naval Española en el Atlántico 1700–1715* (Seville: Escuela de Estudios Hispano-Americanos, 1982), 421.
27. José Patricio Merino Navarro, *La Armada española en el siglo XVIII* (Madrid: Fundación Universitaria Española, 1981). Hugo O'Donnell, 'Las reformas de la Armada', *Temas de Historia Militar, II Congreso de Historia Militar* I (1988), 341–74.
28. Pablo Emilio Pérez-Mallaina Bueno, *Política Naval Española en el Atlántico 1700–1715* (Seville: Escuela de Estudios Hispano-Americanos, 1982), 379.
29. Dionisio Perona Tomás, *Los orígenes del Ministerio de Marina: la Secretaría de Estado y del Despacho de Marina, 1714–1808* (Madrid: Instituto de Historia y Cultura Naval, 1999).
30. Roger Morriss, *The Foundations of British Maritime Ascendancy: Resources, Logistics and the State, 1755–1815* (Cambridge: Cambridge University Press, 2011), 113.
31. Pablo Emilio Pérez-Mallaina Bueno and Bibiano Torres Ramírez, *La Armada del mar del sur* (Seville: Escuela de Estudios Hispano-Americanos, 1987), 109.
32. Ana Crespo Solana, *La Casa de la Contratación y la Intendencia General de la Marina en Cádiz, 1717–1730* (Cadiz: Universidad de Cádiz, 1996).

33. Carlos Álvarez-Nogal, and Christopher Chamley, 'Debt Policy under Constraints: Philip II, the Cortes, and Genoese Bankers', *Economic History Review* 67 (2014), 192–213.
34. Valdez-Bubnov, *Poder naval*, 100.
35. Kuethe and Andrien, *The Spanish Atlantic World in the Eighteenth Century*.
36. Dionisio Perona Tomás, *Los origenes del Ministerio de Marina: la Secretaría de Estado y del Despacho de Marina, 1714–1808* (Madrid: Instituto de Historia y Cultura Naval, 1999).
37. José Quintero González, *La Carraca: El primer arsenal ilustrado español (1717–1776)* (Madrid: Ministerio de Defensa, 2004), 68.
38. Merino Navarro, *La Armada española*, 27.
39. Quintero González, *La Carraca*, 224, 234.
40. Maria Teresa Pérez Crespo Muñoz, *El arsenal de Cartagena en el siglo XVIII* (Madrid: Editorial Naval, 1992), 36. Rafael Torres Sánchez, 'La palanca de la riqueza. Las repercusiones del arsenal en el crecimiento de Cartagena durante el siglo XVII', in Manuel-Reyes García Hurtado, ed., *Ferrol año cero: Una ciudad de la Ilustración* (Ferrol: Ediciones Embora, 2007), 157–89.
41. Pérez Crespo Muñoz, *El arsenal de Cartagena*, 183.
42. Juan A. Granados Loureda, 'El arsenal y astillero de Ferrol en el siglo XVII: de A Graña a Trafalgar', *Congress Minutes of Technology of the Ships of Trafalgar, a Homage to their Designers and Constructors* (Madrid-Cadiz, 2005). Alfredo Martín García, 'La política de reconstrucción naval borbónica y el reino de Galicia: el real astillero de Esteiro (s. XVIII)', in Agustín Guimerá Ravina and Víctor Peralta Ruiz, eds, *Actas de la VIII Reunión Científica de la Fundación Española de Historia Moderna: El equilibrio de los imperios: de Ultrecht y Trafalgar* (2005), 747–60.
43. Cited by Valdez-Bubnov, *Poder naval*, 200.
44. Valdez-Bubnov, *Poder naval y modernización del Estado*, 164.
45. Castanedo Galán, *Guarnizo, un astillero de la Corona*, 137.
46. Valdez-Bubnov, *Poder naval*, 179.
47. Juan M. Castanedo Galán, 'Un asiento singular de Juan Fernández de Isla. La fábrica de ocho navíos y la reforma de un astillero', in Carlos Martínez Shaw, ed, *El derecho y el mar en la España moderna* (Granada: Universidad de Granada, 1995), 457–76 at 461.
48. Mestre Prat de Pàdua, 'La construcción naval de guerra en la España del siglo XVIII. El marco legal de los procesos de financiación', in Carlos Martínez Shaw, ed., *El derecho y el mar en la España moderna* (Granada: Universidad de Granada, 1995), 299–322.
49. José Alcalá-Zamora, *Historia de una empresa siderúrgica española: los altos hornos de Liérganes y La Cavada, 1622–1834* (Santander: Consejería de turismo, 1974).
50. Castanedo Galán, *Guarnizo, un astillero de la Corona*, 63.
51. María Lourdes Odriozola Oyarbide, 'La construcción naval en Gipuzkoa: siglos XVI–XVIII', *Itsas memoria: revista de estudios marítimos del País Vasco* 2 (1998), 93–146.
52. Jesús Maiso González, *La difícil modernización de Cantabria en el siglo XVIII: D. Juan F. de Isla y Alvear* (Santander: Librería Estudio, 1990), 350.
53. Valdez-Bubnov, *Poder naval*, 301.
54. Cited by Castanedo Galán, *Guarnizo, un astillero de la Corona*, 69.
55. Marcelino Manuel Sobrón Iruretagoyena, 'Algunos aspectos del estudio de costes y otras consideraciones en los *asientos* de Guarnizo', in Carlos Martínez Shaw, ed., *El*

derecho y el mar en la España moderna (Granada: Universidad de Granada, 1995), 477–88 at 488.

56. Carlos Martínez Shaw and Marina Alfonso Mola, 'Los astilleros de la América colonial', *Historia general de América Latina* 3 (1999), 279–304; Jorge Ortiz Sotelo, *La Real Armada en el Pacífico Sur: El Apostadero Naval del Callao 1746–1824* (México: Iberoamericana, 2015).
57. Martínez Shaw and Alfonso Mola, 'Los astilleros de la América colonial', 292–7.
58. Germán Luis Andrade Muñoz, *Un mar de intereses: La producción de pertrechos navales en Nueva España, siglo XVIII* (México: Instituto Mora, 2006), 62.
59. Cited by Martínez Shaw and Alfonso Mola, 'Los astilleros de la América colonial', 297.
60. José Manuel Serrano Alvarez, *El astillero de La Habana y la construcción naval militar (1700–1750)* (Madrid: Ministerio de Defensa, 2008), 37.
61. Allan J. Kuethe and José Manuel Serrano Álvarez, 'El *astillero* de la Habana y Trafalgar', *Revista de Indias* 67 (2007), 763–76.
62. José Quintero González, 'La Carraca y La Habana: aproximación al intercambio de pertrechos entre arsenales', *Revista de historia naval* 24 (2006), 57–66.
63. Ovidio Ortega Pereyra, *El Real Arsenal de La Habana* (Havana: Editorial Letras Cubanas, 1998).
64. Serrano Alvarez, *El astillero de La Habana*, 48.
65. Valdez-Bubnov, *Poder naval*, 231
66. Valdez-Bubnov, *Poder naval*, 232.
67. José Manuel Serrano Álvarez, 'El poder y la gloria: élites y asientos militares en el astillero de La Habana durante el siglo XVIII', *Studia historica. Historia moderna* 35 (2013), 99–125.
68. Serrano Alvarez, *El astillero de La Habana*, 74.
69. Germán Luis Andrade Muñoz, *Un mar de intereses: La producción de pertrechos navales en Nueva España, siglo XVIII* (México: Instituto Mora, 2006), 81.
70. Montserrat Gárate Ojanguren, *Comercio ultramarino e Ilustración: la Real Compañía de La Habana* (San Sebastián: Real Sociedad Bascongada de los Amigos del País, 1993).
71. Santiago Luxán, Montserrat Gárate, and José Manuel Ródriguez, *Cuba-Canarias-Sevilla: El estanco español del tabaco y Las Antillas (1717–1817)* (Las Palmas: Ediciones del Cabildo de Gran Canaria, 2012), 246.
72. Gárate Ojanguren, *La Real Compañía Guipuzcoana de Caracas* (Donostia: Sociedad Guipuzcoana de Ediciones y Publicaciones, 1990).
73. Kuethe and Andrien, *The Spanish Atlantic World in the Eighteenth Century*, 146.
74. Serrano Alvarez, *El astillero de La Habana*, 100.
75. Kuethe and Serrano Alvarez, 'El *astillero* de la Habana y Trafalgar', 763–76.
76. Serrano Alvarez, *El astillero de La Habana*, 118–19.
77. José Rodríguez Labandeira, 'La política económica de los Borbones', in Miguel Artola, ed., *La economía española al final del Antiguo Régimen* (Madrid: Alianza, 1982), 107–84. Alcalá-Zamora, *Historia de una empresa siderúrgica española*; Juan Helguera Quijada, 'Las reales fábricas', in Francisco Comín, ed., *Historia de la empresa pública* (Madrid: Espasa Calpe, 1991), 51–87; and Juan Helguera Quijada, 'Empresas y empresarios manufactureros en la España del siglo XVIII', in Francisco Comín and Pablo Martín, eds, *La empresa en la Historia de España* (Madrid: Civitas, 1996), 115–40.
78. R. J. B. Knight, 'Construction et entretien de la flotte anglaise durant les guerres anglo-françaises (1688–1815)', in Martine Acerra, José Merino, Jean Meyer, and

Michel Vergé-Franceschi, ed., *Les Marines de guerre européennes, XVIIe–XVIIIe siècles* (Paris: Presses de l'Université de Paris-Sorbonne, 1985), 47–62 at 59.

79. Roger Morriss, *The Foundations of British Maritime Ascendancy: Resources, Logistics and the State, 1755–1815* (Cambridge: Cambridge University Press, 2011), 135.
80. Pierrick Pourchasse, 'Buying Supplies from Your Enemy or How the French Navy Stocked up with Products from the North in the Eighteenth Century', in Richard Harding and Sergio Solbes, eds, *The Contractor State and its Implications, 1659–1815* (Las Palmas: Universidad de Las Palmas de Gran Canaria, 2012), 253–72.
81. Castejón to Múzquiz, 3 Sept. 1781, AGS, SSH, leg. 51.
82. Gerónimo Ceballos, Santander, 5 Dec. 1766, AGS, Marina, leg. 607.
83. María Baudot Monroy, 'Barcos para el Rey. Julián de Arriaga, la madera y la construcción naval (1752–1759)', in Manuel Reyes García Hurtado, ed., *La Armada española en el siglo XVIII: Ciencia, hombres y barcos* (Madrid: Silex, 2012), 297–328 at 327.
84. Valdez-Bubnov, *Poder naval*, 45.
85. Valdez-Bubnov, *Poder naval*, 317.
86. María Baudot Monroy, 'Barcos para el Rey. Julián de Arriaga, la madera y la construcción naval (1752–1759)', in Manuel Reyes García Hurtado, ed., *La Armada española en el siglo XVIII: Ciencia, hombres y barcos* (Madrid: Silex, 2012),, 297–328.
87. José María Juan-García Aguado, *José Romero Fernández de Landa: un ingeniero de marina en el siglo XVIII* (Santiago: Universidade da Coruña, 1998). Valdez-Bubnov, *Poder naval y modernización del Estado*', 346.

CHAPTER 8

1. Manuel Díaz Ordóñez, *Amarrados al negocio: Reformismo borbónico y suministro de jarcia para la Armada Real (1675–1751)* (Madrid: Ministerio de Defensa, 2009).
2. Cited by José Patricio Merino Navarro, *La Armada española en el siglo XVIII* (Madrid: Fundación Universitaria Española, 1981), 107.
3. María Teresa Pérez Crespo Muños, *El arsenal de Cartagena en el siglo XVIII* (Madrid: Editorial Naval, 1992), 153.
4. Merino Navarro, *La Armada española*, 269 and 328–9.
5. Merino Navarro, *La Armada española*, 81.
6. Cadiz, 17 Apr. 1757, Juan Gerbaut, AGS, Marina, leg. 606. More examples in legs 611 and 612.
7. AGS, Marina, leg. 604.
8. Many examples in AGS, Marina, legs 604, 605, and 606.
9. Examples in AGS, Marina, leg. 606.
10. Merino Navarro, *La Armada española*, 354–6.
11. AGS, Cadiz, 1784, Marina, leg. 606.
12. On the military jurisdiction: José Cepeda Gómez, 'El fuero militar en el siglo XVIII', in Enrique Martínez Ruíz and Magdalena de Pazzis, eds, *Instituciones de la España Moderna, Las Jurisdicciones* (Madrid: Actas, 1996), 393–404.
13. Merino Navarro, *La Armada española*, 344. Lourdes Odriozola, 'La industria naval guipuzcoana y la producción de navíos para el Rey (1650–1799)', *Boletín de la Real Sociedad Bascongada de los Amigos del País* 1 (1994), 3–41.
14. The *asientos* with Italian businesspeople in AGS, Marina, leg. 605.
15. Criticism of Castelini's *asiento* in AGS, Cartagena, 5 Feb. 1767, Marina, leg. 605.
16. AGS, Havana, 10 July 1766, Marina, leg. 606.
17. AGS, Cadiz, 1784, Marina, leg. 606.

18. Ferrol, 29 Nov. 1776, AGS, Marina, leg. 607.
19. Marqués de Someruelos to Julián Arriaga, AGS, 1761, Marina, leg. 605.
20. Asiento de madera para la Carraca, Andrés Morales, vecino de Huelva, Cadiz, 17 July 1767, AGS, Marina, leg. 598.
21. AFB, Judicial, *Corregidor*, Civil, 694–523.
22. AGS, DGT, 1760, Inv. 25, leg. 15.
23. Rafael Torres Sánchez, 'Comercio y *asientos* militares. Hacia la integración comercial del Cantábrico en el siglo XVIII', *Cuadernos de Investigación Histórica* 17 (1999), 81–108.
24. AGS, Marina, leg. 606. In the end the *asiento* was knocked down to Matías Abadiano on 14 July 1774.
25. Ravago, *Ministro de Marina* in Santander, to Arriaga, 29 Oct. 1761, AGS, Marina, leg. 605.
26. Ignacio María Carrión Arregui, 'Tecnología tradicional y desarrollo de una industria pesada: la fabricación de anclas en Guipuzkoa (siglos XVI–XVIII)', *Revista de historia industrial* 7 (1995), 199–214.
27. Tellechea records the traditional story of the early 1730s journey made by the master anchor-maker Juan Fermín de Guilisasti to Holland at the behest of the Real Compañía de Caracas, gleaning technical superiority that then boosted industrial production. J. Ignacio Tellechea, 'Juan Fermín de Guilisasti y sus anclas', *Real Sociedad Bascongada de los Amigos del País* 31 (1975), 285–90.
28. Carrión Arregui, 'Tecnología tradicional y desarrollo', 208.
29. María Lourdes Odriozola Oyarbide, 'La Real Fábrica de anclas de Renteriola: un intento fallido', *Real Sociedad Bascongada de los Amigos del País* 46 (1990), 41–77.
30. Odriozola Oyarbide, 'La Real Fábrica de anclas de Renteriola', 46–7.
31. José Ignacio Tellechea Idígoras, *Anclas en Hernani: El registro de cartas de D. Francisco Antonio de Oquendo, Inspector de la Fábrica de Anclas (1750–1755)* (San Sebastián: Caja Ahorros, 1977), 11–12.
32. Tellechea Idígoras, *Anclas en Hernani*, 12.
33. Rafael Guerrero Elecalde, *Las elites vascas y navarras en el gobierno de la Monarquía Borbónica: Redes sociales, carreras y hegemonía en el siglo XVIII (1700–1746)* (Vitoria: Universidad del País Vasco, 2012).
34. Emiliano Fernández de Pinedo, 'From the Bloomery to the Blast-Furnace: Technical Change in Spanish Iron-making (1650–1850)', *Journal of European Economic History* 17 (1988), 7–32.
35. Álvaro Aragón Ruano, 'Atraso e innovación tecnológicos en la siderurgia guipuzcoana durante el Antiguo Régimen', *Studia historica. Historia moderna* 33 (2011), 235–59.
36. José Manuel Barrenechea, ed., *Moral y economía en el siglo XVIII: Antología de textos sobre la usura: Zubiaur, Calatayud, los Cinco Gremios Mayores y Uría Nafarrondo* (Vitoria: Gobierno Vasco, 1995).
37. Asiento de fábrica de anclas para los tres arsenales, 1776–1779, José Roger, AGS, Marina, leg. 606.
38. AFB, Judial *Corregidor*, Civil, 185, 2.
39. Informes de Jorge Juan sobre la calidad y defectos de las anclas, AGS, Marina, leg. 606.
40. Asiento de cal para el arsenal de Ferrol, Rodrigo González Villar, 1758–63, AGS, Marina, leg. 606.
41. Daniel Peribáñez Caveda, *Comunicaciones y comercio marítimo en la Asturias preindustrial, 1750–1850* (Gijón: Junta del Puerto, 1992), 473.

42. Asiento de cal para el arsenal de Ferrol, Rodrigo González Villar, 1758–63, AGS, Marina, leg. 606.
43. Xán Carmona Badía, 'Sargadelos en la historia de la siderurgia española', *Revista de historia industrial* 3 (1993), 11–40.
44. Ofelia Rey has made a detailed analysis of the conflicts sparked off in Galicia by privileged access to timber resources by some *asentistas*: Ofelia Rey, *Montes y Política Forestal en la Galicia del Antiguo Régimen* (Santiago: Universidad de Santiago, 1995), 236.
45. *Asiento* de Fábrica de Anclas, Banco de San Carlos, 1785, AGS, Marina, leg. 606.
46. Ignacio Carrión, *La siderurgia guipuzcoana en el siglo XVIII* (Bilbao: Universidad del País Vasco, 1991).
47. Agustín González Enciso, 'Military Expenditure and Entrepreneurial Promotion in Modern Spain: An Unsuccessful Expedient. The Example of the Eugui Munitions Factory', in Stephen Conway and Rafael Torres Sánchez, eds, *The Spending of the States: Military Expenditure during the Long Eighteenth Century: Patterns, Organisation and Consequences, 1650–1815* (Saarbrücken: VDM, 2011), 285–312.
48. AGS, Marina, leg. 606.

CHAPTER 9

1. Philip J. Stern and Carl Wennerlind observed, 'the word "mercantilism" itself appeared nowhere in Smith's writings, nor for that matter in the works of his predecessors or interlocutors', Philip J. Stern and Carl Wennerlind, eds, *Mercantilism Reimagined. Political Economy in Early Modern Britain and Its Empire* (New York: Oxford University Press, 2014), 3.
2. Steven Pincus, 'Rethinking Mercantilism: Political Economy, the British Empire, and the Atlantic World in the Seventeenth and Eighteenth Centuries', *William and Mary Quarterly* 69 (2012), 3–34.
3. Patrick K. O'Brien, 'The Nature and Historical Evolution of an Exceptional Fiscal State and its Possible Significance for the Precocious Commercialization and Industrialization of the British Economy from Cromwell to Nelson', *The Economic History Review* 64 (2011), 408–46.
4. Rafael Torres Sánchez, ed., *War, State and Development: Fiscal-Military States in the Eighteenth Century* (Pamplona: EUNSA, 2007), 28.
5. Parts of this chapter were first published in Richard Harding and Sergio Solbes, eds, *The Contractor State and its Implications, 1659–1815* (Las Palmas: Universidad de Las Palmas, 2013), 317–44.
6. Gerónimo Uztáriz, *Theórica, y práctica de comercio, y de marina* (Madrid: Aguilar, 1742, 1968), 163. The work of this author is analysed in Reyes Fernández Durán, (*Gerónimo de Uztáriz (1670–1732): Una política económica para Felipe V* (Madrid, Minerva, 1999).
7. Uztáriz, *Theórica, y práctica de comercio, y de marina*, 164.
8. A summary of the literature on the creation of rigging and canvas in Galicia is given in Manuel Díaz Ordóñez, *Amarrados al negocio: Reformismo borbónico y suministro de jarcia para la Armada Real (1675–1751)* (Madrid: Ministerio de Defensa, 2009), 197–209. This should be rounded out with the account of the dependence on Dutch supplies for this project, given in Carmen Sanz Ayán, 'Negociadores y capitales holandeses en los sistemas de abastecimientos de pertrechos navales de la monarquía hispánica durante el siglo XVII', *Hispania* 182 (1992), 915–45.

9. For more information on the Colbertist influence on the renewal of mercantilist thought in the second half of the seventeenth century, see Agustín González Enciso, 'La política industrial en el siglo XVIII', in Luis Ribot, ed., *Pensamiento y política económica en la Época Moderna* (Madrid: Actas, 2000), 141–50.
10. In general, Uztáriz's thinking had a tremendous influence on Spanish eighteenth-century thinkers and his ideas were brought to a very wide audience within Spain and also abroad by way of translations: Jonathan Carlyon, 'Gerónimo de Uztáriz and the Economic Shades of Enlightment in Spain', *Cuaderno internacional de estudios humanísticos* 12 (2009), 7–24. The English translation came out in 1751 and the French in 1753; see N. Guasti, 'Forbonnais e Uztáriz: le ragioni di una traduzione', *Cuadernos aragoneses de economía* 8:1 (1998), 125–41.
11. Díaz Ordóñez, *Amarrados al negocio*, 186–7.
12. Ramón Serrera Contreras, *Lino y cáñamo en Nueva España (1777–1800)* (Seville: EEHA, 1974), 61.
13. Díaz Ordóñez, *Amarrados al negocio*, 186.
14. Gerónimo Uztáriz, *Theórica, y práctica de comercio, y de marina*, 216.
15. Antonio de Ulloa, *La Marina: fuerzas navales de la Europa y costas de Berbería* (Cadiz: Universidad, 1773, 1995), 208.
16. Ulloa, *La Marina: fuerzas navales de la Europa*, 208.
17. 30 Oct. 1748, quoted by Díaz Ordóñez, *Amarrados al negocio*, 99.
18. Serrera Contreras, *Lino y cáñamo en Nueva España*, 96.
19. Castejón to Múzquiz, 2 Oct. 1781, AGS, SSH, leg. 51.
20. 1784, quoted by Díaz Ordóñez, *Amarrados al negocio*, 110.
21. Serrera Contreras, *Lino y cáñamo en Nueva España*, 35.
22. Gerbaut to Arriaga, Cadiz, 30 Oct. 1767. Marqués de Monteverde to Arriaga, 22 Apr. 1767, AGS, Marina, leg. 613.
23. Gerbaut to Arriaga, Cadiz, 30 Oct. 1767. Marqués de Monteverde to Arriaga, 22 Apr. 1767, AGS, Marina, leg. 613.
24. Manuel Travieso, Cartagena, 8 Aug. 1778. AGS, Marina, leg. 591.
25. Manuel Travieso, Cartagena, 8 Aug. 1778. AGS, Marina, leg. 591.
26. Junta de Ferrol, 15 Sept. 1778, AGS, Marina, leg. 591.
27. Díaz Ordóñez, *Amarrados al negocio*, 197.
28. José Quintero González, *La Carraca: El primer arsenal ilustrado español (1717–1776)* (Madrid: Ministerio de Defensa, 2004). Díaz Ordóñez, *Amarrados al negocio*, 270.
29. Montserrat Gárate Ojanguren, *La Real Compañía Guipuzcoana de Caracas* (Donostia: Sociedad Guipuzcoana de Ediciones y Publicaciones, 1990); *Comercio ultramarino e Ilustración: la Real Compañía de La Habana* (San Sebastián: Real Sociedad Bascongada de los Amigos del País, 1993).
30. Díaz Ordóñez, *Amarrados al negocio*, 395.
31. Santiago Aquerreta, *Negocios y finanzas en el siglo XVIII: la familia Goyeneche* (Pamplona: EUNSA, 2001).
32. Quintero González, *La Carraca*, 467; Serrera Contreras, *Lino y cáñamo en Nueva España*, 95.
33. Merino Navarro, *La Armada Española en el siglo XVIII*, 267.
34. José Patricio Merino Navarro, *La Armada Española en el siglo XVIII* (Madrid: Fundación universitaria española, 1981), 107.
35. RO, 6 Nov. 1781, Serrera Contreras, *Lino y cáñamo en Nueva España*, 198.
36. Serrera Contreras, *Lino y cáñamo en Nueva España*, 231.
37. Isla de León, 24 Aug. 1779, AGS, Marina, leg. 592.

38. Zambrano to Múzquiz, 21 Jan. 1778, AGS, SSH, leg. 268.
39. Ulloa, *La Marina: fuerzas navales de la Europa*, 217.
40. Rafael Torres Sánchez, *Constructing a Fiscal-Military State in Eighteenth-Century Spain* (Aldershot: Palgrave Macmillan, 2015).
41. Patrick Karl O'Brien, 'Taxation for British Mercantilism from the Treaty of Utrecht (1713) to the Peace of Paris (1783)', in Rafael Torres Sánchez, ed., *War, State and Development: Fiscal-Military States in the Eighteenth Century* (Pamplona: EUNSA, 2007), 295–356.
42. José Patricio Merino Navarro, 'Cultivos industriales: el cáñamo en España, 1750–1800', *Hispania* 130 (1975), 567–84 at 572.
43. Quintero González, *La Carraca*, 463.
44. AGS, Marina, leg. 613.
45. Agustín Navarrete to Alfonso Alburquerque, Barcelona, 28 Aug. 1781, AGS, SSH, leg. 51.
46. Esteban Gaztambide to Castejón, Granada, 19 Oct. 1781, AGS, SSH, leg. 51.
47. Secretaría de Marina to the Comandante General de Marina de Cartagena, Madrid, 23 Feb. 1781, AGS, Marina, leg. 593.
48. Francisco Cantos to Francisco Montes, AGS, SSH, leg. 51.
49. Secretaría de Marina to Gastambide, Madrid, 10 Dec. 1782, AGS, Marina, leg. 594.
50. Castejón to Múzquiz, 1 Dec. 1781, AGS, SSH, leg. 51.
51. Castejón to Múzquiz, 1 Dec. 1781, AGS, SSH, leg. 51.
52. Castejón to Múzquiz, 2 Oct. 1781, AGS, SSH, leg. 51.
53. Esteban Gaztambide to Castejón, Granada, 19 Oct. 1781, AGS, SSH, leg. 51.
54. *Secretaría de Marina* to the Comandante General de Marina de Cartagena, Madrid, 23 Feb. 1781, AGS, Marina, leg. 593.
55. Junta de Marina de Cádiz, Isla de León, 6 Apr. 1781, AGS, Marina, leg. 593.
56. José Canga Argüelles, *Diccionario de Hacienda con aplicación a España* (Madrid: Imprenta de Don Marcelino Calero y Portocarrero, 1834).
57. Pierrick Pourchasse, 'Buying Supplies from your Enemy or How the French Navy Stocked up with Products from the North in the Eighteenth Century', in Richard Harding and Sergio Solbes, eds, *The Contractor State and its Implications, 1659–1815* (Las Palmas: Universidad de Las Palmas, 2013), 253–72.
58. AGS, Marina, leg. 787.
59. Bilbao, 6 Nov. 1754, AGS, Marina, leg. 613.
60. Arriaga to Valdeparaiso, on the problem of authorizing Juan Antonio de Yunibardia to take out 1,792,000 *reales* from Bayonne after selling 10,000 *quintales* of Riga hemp in Ferrol. Madrid, 16 Mar. 1757, AGS, Marina, leg. 48.
61. Rafael Torres Sánchez, 'Comercio y asientos militares. Hacia la integración comercial del Cantábrico en el siglo XVIII', *Cuadernos de Investigación Histórica* 17 (1999), 81–108.
62. Response to Gerónimo de Retortillo, protégé of Simón de Aragorri, San Ildefonso, 28 Aug. 1761, AGS, Marina, leg. 613.
63. Bilbao, 9 May 1767. AFB, Judicial, Consulado/Mercantil, 2255/50.
64. Gerbaut to Arriaga, Cadiz, 30 Oct. 1767, AGS, Marina, leg. 613.
65. Ferrol, 19 Apr. 1773, AGS, DGT, Inv. 25, leg. 15.
66. Múzquiz to Zambrano, El Pardo, 11 Feb. 1775. AGS, DGT, Inv. 25, leg. 15.
67. My thanks go to Pierrick Pourchasse (Université de Bretagne Occidentale, France) for allowing me to read his work, 'Buying Supplies from your Enemy or How the French Navy Stocked Up with Products from the North in the XVIIIth Century'.

68. José Guerrero García to Conde de Clonard, Madrid, 17 Sept. 1774. AGS, SSH, leg. 50.
69. AGS, SSH, leg. 8.
70. Conde de Clonard to Miguel Múzquiz, Cadiz, 21 Sept. 1774, AGS, SSH, leg. 50.
71. Miguel Múzquiz to Julián de Arriaga, San Ildefonso, 23 Sept. 1774, AGS, SSH, leg. 50.
72. Castejón to Múzquiz, 1 Sept. 1778, AGS, SSH, leg. 50.
73. Felipe Chone and Conde de Clonard also worked with the house of Felipe Kcarney and Francisco Hayden. Executed in Madrid, 21 Jan. 1772, AGS, Dirección General del Tesoro (DGT), Inv. 15, leg. 15.
74. AGS, Marina, leg. 609. Madrid, 19 Aug. 1773, AGS, DGT, Inv. 25, leg. 15. San Ildefonso, 28 Aug. 1773.
75. Northern hemp provision contract, San Lorenzo 17 Oct. 1778, Museo Naval, Biblioteca IMP-C6/38.
76. Castejón to Múzquiz, 16 Feb. 1780, AGS, SSH, leg. 51.
77. Zambrano to Múzquiz, 21 Jan. 1778. AGS, SSH, leg. 268.
78. Zambrano to Múzquiz, 29 Apr. 1776, AGS, SSH, leg. 269.
79. AGS, SSH, leg. 293.
80. Liquidation of the effects belonging to the company Chone y Soto in St Petersburg. Floridablanca to Múzquiz, 20 Sept. 1781, AGS, SSH, leg. 10. The reason for this bankruptcy is given by the firm itself in AHN, Estado, leg. 3210.
81. Castejón to Múzquiz, 7 July 1781. AGS, SSH, leg. 51.
82. Floridablanca to Múzquiz, El Pardo, 5 Feb. 1782, AGS, Marina, leg. 592.
83. Castejón to Múzquiz, Madrid, 16 June 1781, AGS, SSH, leg. 51. The accounts subsequently presented by Normande refer to the period 1781–4. Flor to Lerena, Madrid, 2 June 1785, AGS, SSH, leg. 10.
84. Enrique Martínez Ruiz and Magdalena Pi Corrales, *Commerce and Navigation between Spain and Sweden throughout History* (Madrid: Fundacion Berndt Wistedt, 2000), 171, and Jörg Ulbert and Gérard Le Bouëdec, *La Fonction consulaire à l'époque modern: l'affirmation d'une institution économique et politique, 1500–1800* (Rennes: Presses universitaires de Rennes, 2006), 349.
85. St Petersburg, 5 Aug. 1781, AHN, Hacienda, leg. 6734. Esteban Drouilhet to Floridablanca, 26 June 1781, AGS, SSH, leg. 51.
86. He drew the bills against the Treasury of the Real Giro de Amsterdam. Pedro Normande drew on the treasurer of Amsterdam 'up to the sum of 4000 roubles' for expenses incurred on the royal service, 6 Feb. 1780, AHN, Hacienda, leg. 6731.
87. e.g. the taking out of insurance in Amsterdam on the Russian ship 'Ana Martina', which had brought 'navy effects of the king', to the value of 670 *ducados de plata* 'against Floridablanca' which had been presented by Agustín Queneu, 16 Dec. 1781, AHN, Hacienda, leg. 6734.

CHAPTER 10

1. Roger Knight, 'Changing the Agenda: The "New" Naval History of the British Sailing Navy', *The Mariner's Mirror* 97:1 (2011), 225–42.
2. Richard Harding, *Seapower and Naval Warfare, 1650–1830* (Annapolis: Naval Institute Press, 1999), 212; 'Amphibious Operations', in J. Hattendorf, ed., *The Oxford Encyclopaedia of Maritime History* (New York: Oxford University Press, 2007).

3. Richard Harding, 'Operaciones anfibias británicas, 1700–1815', in Agustín Guimerá Ravina y José María Núñez, eds, *Guerra Naval en el Revolución y el Imperio: Bloqueos y operaciones anfibias, 1793–1815* (Madrid: Pons Historia, 2008), 39–58 at 41.
4. Part of this chapter was first published in Rafael Torres Sánchez, 'Monopoly or the Free Market. Two Ways of Tackling the Expenditure. The Minorca Expedition (1781–1782)', in Stephen Conway and Rafael Torres Sánchez, eds, *The Spending of the States: Military Expenditure during the Long Eighteenth Century: Patterns, Organisation and Consequences, 1650–1815* (Saarbrücken: VDM, 2011), 285–312.
5. Conde del Asalto to Miguel Múzquiz, Barcelona, 4 Aug. 1781, AGS, Guerra, leg. 1465.
6. Estado de Fuerzas (forces list) sent by Crillon in Minorca, signed by Juan Roca, Mahón, 1 Jan. 1782. The figures for the French regiments date from 1 Feb. 1782: AHN, Estado, leg. 4230. For more details of the incorporation of the Spanish and French forces to the expeditionary force and a good summary of the taking of Minorca, see the works of José Terrón Ponce, *La reconquista de Menorca por el duque de Crillon (1781–82), aspectos militares y políticos* (Mahón: Editorial Menorca, 1981), and *La toma de Menorca (1781–82) en los escritos autobiográficos y epistolario del Duque de Crillon* (Mahón: Institut Menorquí d'Estudis, 1999).
7. José Juan Vidal, 'Crisis de subsistències i aprovisionament blader de Mallorca durant el segle XVIII', *Randa* 26 (1990), 103–32.
8. Joan Hernández Andreu, 'Trets de l'economia menorquina des de l'època britànica fins a mitjan segle XIX', *Randa* 45 (2000), 7–29.
9. David Whamond Donaldson, *Britain and Menorca in the Eighteenth Century* (Milton Keynes: Open University, 1994), iii. 428.
10. Amador Mari Puig, 'El comerç del blat al port de Maó. 1792–1802', *Estudis d'Història Econòmica* 2 (1989), 133–57.
11. Tom Henderson McGuffie, *The Siege of Gibraltar* (London: Batsford, 1965), 105; Desmond Gregory, *Minorca, the Illusory Prize: A History of the British Occupations of Minorca between 1708 and 1802* (London: Fairleigh Dickinson University Press, 1990), 183.
12. Donaldson, *Britain and Menorca*, 349, 268. According to Richard Harding, the British purchases in Italy and Barbary for Mahón were really nothing new, since the latter formed part of the regular supply zones set up by the English. Richard Harding, 'Gibraltar: A Tale of Two Sieges, 1726–1727 and 1779–1783', in *Gibraltar as a Naval Base and Dockyard* (Portsmouth: Ray Riley Naval Dockyards Society, 2006), ii.
13. As Crillon himself later acknowledged to Miguel Múzquiz, Mahón, 1 Dec. 1781, AGS, SSH, leg. 748. See also Gregory, *Minorca, the Illusory Prize*, 145.
14. Miguel Bañuelos to Floridablanca, Palma, 1 Feb. 1781, with undated letters from Sollerich et al. AHN, Estado, leg. 4205-1. The relations between Great Britain and Russia in Minorca had been stepped up since the 1768–74 war between Russian and Turkey, when the English government allowed the Russian fleet to use Mahón as a base, as a way of offsetting their deteriorating trading relations with Turkey. Gregory, *Minorca, the Illusory Prize*, 141.
15. John Drinkwater, *A History of the Late Siege of Gibraltar (Facsimil de la edición 1786)* (Valencia: Paris-Valencia, 1989). Many more references are made to these relief supplies throughout the book. The success of these shipments can be gauged from the fact that Murray's requests to London were mainly for soldiers rather than supplies.

Even the expeditions of Rodney and the next one of 1781 centred on Gibraltar shipped in munitions rather than supplies.

16. Solleric to Floridablanca, Palma, 16 June 1780, AHN, Estado, leg. 4205-1.
17. Francesc Hernández Sanz, 'Un corsario menorquín (1779–1781)', *Cultura i societat a Menorca* 1 (1987), 54–110 at 56.
18. Amador Marí Puig, 'Cors i comerç a Menorca. La comercialització de les preses (1778–1781)', *Jornades d'estudis històric locals. El comerç alterniu* 8 (1989), 201–16 at 214.
19. Marí Puig, 'Cors i comerç a Menorca, 203.
20. Miguel Bañuelos to Floridablanca, Palma, 29 Jan. 1781, AHN, Estado, leg. 4205.
21. Miguel Cuadrado y Sanes to Marqués de Sollerich (in Palma) Ciutadella, 30 May 1781, AHN, Estado, leg. 4205.
22. Sollerich to Múzquiz, Palma, 28 May 1781, AHN, Estado, leg. 4205.
23. AGS, SSH, leg. 646.
24. Communiqué by Floridablanca to the Junta de Estado, Madrid, 20 Apr. 1781, AHN, Estado, leg. 4230.
25. Crillon to Ventura on board the San Pascual, 6 Aug. 1781, AHN, Estado, leg. 4230.
26. Communiqué by Floridablanca to the Junta de Estado, Madrid, 20 Apr. 1781, AHN, Estado, leg. 4230.
27. Anonymous communiqué to Floridablanca, Mahón, 22 Aug. 1781, AHN, Estado, leg. 4230.
28. The inventories of the value of the prizes, stores, and San Felipe Fort in AGS, Guerra, leg. 478. According to Micaela Mata, 53 English stores were taken, with victuals and arms: Micaela Mata, *Conquistas y reconquistas de Menorca* (Barcelona: Imp. Juvenil, 1984), 205.
29. Crillon to Floridablanca, Mahón, 23 Oct. 1781, AHN, Estado, leg. 4230.
30. Múzquiz to Floridablanca, Madrid, 16 Dec. 1781, AGS, SSH, leg. 748.
31. Instructions to Múzquiz, Aranjuez, 6 June 1781, AHN, Estado, leg. 4230.
32. Pedro Montenegro to Múzquiz, Mahón, 15 Sept. 1781, AGS, SSH, leg. 747. Crillon to Conde del Asalto, 8 Oct. 1781, AHN, Estado, leg. 4230.
33. San Ildefonso, 17 Aug. 1776, AGS, DGT, Inv. 25, leg. 15; Madrid, 12 Sept. 1777 (term from 1 Jan. 1778 to 30 Dec. 1782), AGS, SSH, leg. 647.
34. Ángel Sanz Tapia, *El final del Tratado de Tordesillas: la expedición del virrey Cevallos al Río de la Plata* (Valladolid: Junta de Castilla y León, 1994), 265.
35. Luis Manuel de Quiñones to Múzquiz, Madrid, 9 Sept. 1781, AGS, SSH, leg. 51.
36. In 1780 he was treasurer of the army of Extremadura, AGS, DGT, Inv. 6, leg. 11. The appointment was made on 8 June 1780, AGS, Guerra, leg. 1489.
37. Pedro Montenegro to Múzquiz, Cadiz, 29 June 1781, AGS, SSH, leg. 747.
38. Montenegro to Múzquiz, Cadiz, July 1781, AGS, SSH, leg. 747.
39. Múzquiz to Montenegro, 1 July 1781, AGS, Guerra, leg. 3763.
40. Múzquiz to Montenegro, 1 July 1781, AGS, Guerra, leg. 3763.
41. Pedro Montenegro, AGS, DGT, Inv. 25, leg. 25.
42. Order of 10 Aug. 1781, AGS, DGT, Inv. 25, leg. 25.
43. AHN, Estado, 4230, Floridablanca to Múzquiz, 19 June 1781, Instruction to Duc de Crillon.
44. Instruction by Crillon to the field army. On board the ship San Pascual, 29 July 1781, AHN, Estado, leg. 4230.
45. The list of ships is given in AGS, Guerra, leg. 3760. On the navigation of the convoy, see José Gella Iturriaga, 'El convoy y el desembarco de 1781 en Menorca', *Revista de historia naval* 1 (1983), 9–30.

46. Mahón. Crillón to Floridablanca, 4 Feb. 1782, AGS, SG, leg. 3760.
47. AGS, SSH, leg. 271.
48. Pedro Montenegro to Múzquiz, Mahón, 6 Sept. 1781, AGS, SSH, leg. 748.
49. A good idea of the importance of this business can be gained from this year's revenue figure of 22,000 pounds, while the general *Talla* (Aragon-wide tax) of Majorca amounted to 32,000 pounds.
50. Carlos Pablo Manera Erbina, 'Resistir I créixer. Canvi econòmic i classes socials a la Mallorca del segle XVIII', *Randa* 26 (1990), 7–83.
51. Manera Erbina, 'Resistir i créixer', 46–7, 79, and 82.
52. Gerónimo Rivera, Palma, 6 Sept. 1781, AGS, SSH, leg. 748.
53. Mahón, 28 Aug. 1781, AGS, SSH, leg. 748.
54. Pedro Montenegro to Múzquiz, Mahón, 6 Sept. 1781, AGS, Guerra, leg. 478.
55. Montenegro to Múzquiz, 3 Oct. 1781, AGS, SSH, leg. 748.
56. Crillon to Múzquiz, Mahón, 1 Dec. 1781, AGS, Guerra, leg. 748.
57. Crillon to Múzquiz, Mahón, 1 Dec. 1781, AGS, Guerra, leg. 748.
58. Romualdo de Tobar to Múzquiz, Palma, 21 Sept. 1781, AGS, SSH, leg. 747.
59. Montenegro to Múzquiz, Cadiz, 17 July 1781, AGS, SSH, leg. 747.
60. Conde del Asalto to Múzquiz, Barcelona, 23 Dec. 1781, AGS, SSH, leg. 747.
61. The detail of this provision and its accounts in Floridablanca to Diputados Cinco Gremios Mayores, Madrid, 8 May 1785, AGS, SSH, leg. 646.
62. Montenegro to Múzquiz, Mahón, 28 Aug. 1781, AGS, Guerra, leg. 478.
63. Montenegro to Múzquiz, Mahón, 28 Aug. 1781, AGS, SSH, leg. 748.
64. Montenegro to Múzquiz, Mahón, 28 Aug. 1781, AGS, SSH, leg. 748.
65. Múzquiz to Montenegro, Madrid, 25 Sept. 1781, AGS, Guerra, leg. 3760.
66. Múzquiz to Montenegro, Madrid, 25 Sept. 1781, AGS, Guerra, leg. 3760.
67. Montenegro to Múzquiz, Mahón, 6 Sept. 1781, AGS, Guerra, leg. 3763.
68. Manuel Cabriada to Diputados Cinco Gremios Mayores, Mahón, 2 Oct. 1781, AGS, SSH, leg. 748.
69. Mahón, 2 Oct. 1781, AGS, SSH, leg. 748.
70. Manuel Cabriada to Diputados Cinco Gremios Mayores, Mahón, 8 Oct. 1781, AGS, SSH, leg. 748.
71. Baños and Castillo to Múzquiz, Madrid, 19 Oct. 1781, AGS, SSH, leg. 748.
72. Múzquiz to Montenegro, Madrid, 22 Oct. 1781, AGS, Guerra, leg. 3763.
73. Floridablanca to Múzquiz, Madrid, 16 Dec. 1781, AGS, Guerra, leg. 3760.
74. Montenegro to Múzquiz, 1 Sept. 1781, AGS, SSH, leg. 748.
75. Settlement account, Rosa to Luis Zanoni, 19 Oct. 1785.
76. Múzquiz to Marqués de las Hormazas, Madrid, 17 Dec. 1781, AGS, Guerra, leg. 3762.
77. Montenegro to Múzquiz, Mahón, 8 Dec. 1781, AGS, SSH, leg. 748.
78. On the relations of these politicians with the financier, see Rafael Torres Sánchez, 'Financiers et politiques. Francisco Montes et François Cabarrus (1770–1790)', in Anne Dubet, ed., *Administrer les finances royales dans la monarchie espagnole (XVIe–XIXe siècles)* (Rennes: Presses Universitaires de Rennes, 2008), 103–20.
79. Pedro López de Lerena, *Memoria sobre las rentas públicas y balanza comercial de España (1789–1790)* (Madrid: Instituto de Estudios Fiscales, 1990).
80. Conde del Asalto to Múzquiz, Barcelona, 23 Dec. 1781, AGS, SSH, leg. 748.
81. Crillon to Múzquiz, Mahón, 1 Dec. 1781, AGS, SSH, leg. 748.
82. Montenegro to Múzquiz, Mahón, 3 Oct. 1781, AGS, Guerra, leg. 3762.
83. Lerena to Múzquiz, 11 Jan. 1782, AGS, Guerra, leg. 3763.

84. Lerena to Múzquiz, Mahón, 15 Jan. 1782, AGS, Guerra, leg. 479.
85. Lerena to Múzquiz, Mahón, 4 Aug. 1782, AGS, SSH, leg. 748.
86. Lerena to Múzquiz, Mahón, 1 Feb. 1782, AGS, Guerra, leg. 479.
87. Múzquiz to Portes, Madrid, 23 Oct. 1781, AGS, Guerra, leg. 3762.
88. Múzquiz to Portes, Madrid, 18 Jan. 1782, AGS, Guerra, leg. 3762.
89. Galabert to Múzquiz, Valencia, 11 May 1782, AGS, SSH, leg. 748.
90. Lerena to Múzquiz, Mahón, 8 Apr. 1782, AGS, SSH, leg. 748.

Bibliography

Aguilar Escobar, Antonio, *Cañones de bronce para el Ejército: Historia de la Real Fundición de Sevilla en el siglo XVIII* (Madrid: Adalid, Ministerio de Defensa, 2010).

Aguirre, Severo, *Prontuario Alfabético y Cronológico por Orden de Materias de las Instrucciones, Ordenanzas, Reglamentos, Pragmáticas y demás Reales Resoluciones No Recopiladas que han de observarse para la Administración de Justicia y Gobierno en los Pueblos del Reino* (Madrid: Benito Cano, 1799).

Albareda Salvadó, Joaquim, *La Guerra de Sucesión de España (1700–1714)* (Madrid: Crítica, 2010).

Alcalá-Zamora, José, *Historia de una empresa siderúrgica española: los altos hornos de Liérganes y La Cavada, 1622–1834* (Santander: Consejería de turismo, 1974).

Alfonso Mola, Marina, 'Corso y flota de Indias: Los convoys ingleses apresados en 1780 y 1795', in Bibiano Torres Ramírez, ed., *Andalucía América y el mar* (Seville: Diputación de Huelva, 1991), 196–224.

Alía Plana, Jesús Maria, *Ordenanzas fundacionales de la Armada* (Madrid: Port Royal, 1997).

Allen, Douglas W., 'The British Navy Rules: Monitoring and Incompatible Incentives in the Age of Fighting Sail', *Explorations in Economic History* 39 (2002), 204–31.

Álvarez Luis Alonso, *El costo del imperio asiático: La formación colonial de las islas Filipinas bajo dominio español, 1565–1800* (México: Universidade da Coruña, Instituto Mora, 2009), 305–28.

Álvarez-Nogal, Carlos, *El crédito de la monarquía hispánica en el reinado de Felipe IV* (Burgos: Junta de Castilla y León, Consejería de Educación y Cultura, 1997).

Álvarez-Nogal, Carlos, 'Centralized Funding of the Army in Spain: The Garrison Factoría in the Seventeenth Century', in Jeff Fynn-Paul, ed., *War, Entrepreneurs, and the State in Europe and the Mediterranean, 1300–1800* (Leiden: Brill, 2014), 235–59.

Álvarez-Nogal, Carlos, and Chamley, Christopher, 'Debt Policy under Constraints: Philip II, the Cortes, and Genoese Bankers', *Economic History Review* 67 (2014), 192–213.

Andrade Muñoz, Germán Luis, *Un mar de intereses: La producción de pertrechos navales en Nueva España, siglo XVIII* (México: Instituto Mora, 2006).

Andújar Castillo, Francisco, 'El fuero militar en el siglo XVIII. Un estatuto de privilegio', *Chronica Nova* 23 (1996), 11–31.

Andújar Castillo, Francisco, 'Élites de poder militar: Las Guardias Reales en el siglo XVIII', in Juan Luis Castellano, Jean-Pierre Dedieu, and María Victoria López, eds, *La pluma, la mitra y la espada: Estudios de historia institucional en la Edad Moderna* (Madrid: Marcial Pons, 2000), 65–94.

Andújar Castillo, Francisco, 'La Corte y los militares en el siglo XVIII', *Estudis* 27 (2001), 91–120.

Andújar Castillo, Francisco, *El sonido del dinero: Monarquía, ejército y venalidad en la España del siglo XVIII* (Madrid: Marcial Pons, 2004).

Andújar Castillo, Francisco, 'Guerra, venalidad y asientos de soldados en el siglo XVIII', *Studia historica. Historia moderna* 35 (2013), 235–68.

Aquerreta, Santiago, 'La casa de Arizcun 1725–1742: las estrategias financieras de un hombre de negocios en el Madrid de la Ilustración', in José A. Ferrer Benimeli, ed.,

El Conde de Aranda y su tiempo (Zaragoza: Institución Fernando el Católico, 2000), 659–78.

Aquerreta, Santiago, 'La participación de los financieros navarros en la Guerra de Sucesión: el abastecimiento de víveres al ejército', in Rafael Torres Sánchez, ed., *Capitalismo mercantil en la España del siglo XVIII* (Pamplona: EUNSA, 2000), 273–314.

Aquerreta, Santiago, *Negocios y finanzas en el siglo XVIII: la familia Goyeneche* (Pamplona: EUNSA, 2001).

Aragón Ruano, Álvaro, 'Atraso e innovación tecnológicos en la siderurgia guipuzcoana durante el Antiguo Régimen', *Studia historica. Historia moderna* 33 (2011), 235–59.

Aragón Ruano, Álvaro, 'La historiografía forestal sobre época moderna en el panorama internacional, español y vasco: una revisión bibliográfica', *Vasconia: Cuadernos de historia* 37 (2011), 117–40.

Aragón Ruano, Álvaro, and Angulo Morales, Alberto, 'The Spanish Basque Country in Global Trade Networks in the Eighteenth Century', *International Journal of Maritime History* 25 (2013), 149–72.

Arrieta, Gabriel de, *Alphabeto y cartilla militar* (Cadiz: Imprenta Real de Marina de D. Manuel Espinosa de los Monteros, 1757).

Artiñaño, Gervasio de, *La Arquitectura naval española (en madera): Bosquejo de sus condiciones y rasgos de su evolución* (Madrid: Ateneo, 1914).

Astigarraga, Jesús, 'Las "Reflexiones sobre el estado actual del comercio de España" (1761), de Simón de Aragorri: contenido, estudio de fuentes y primera interpretación', *Documentos de trabajo de la Asociación Española de Historia Económica* 9 (2011).

Astigarraga, Jesús, 'Un nuevo sistema económico para la monarquía española. Las "Reflexiones sobre el estado actual del comercio de España" (1761), de Simón de Aragorri', *Revista de historia industrial* 52 (2013), 13–42.

Baker, Norman, *Government and Contractors: The British Treasury and War Supplies, 1775–1783* (London: The Athlone Press, 1971).

Bannerman, Gordon, *Merchants and the Military in Eighteenth-Century Britain: British Army Contracts and Domestic Supply, 1739–1763* (London: Pickering & Chatto, 2007).

Barbier, Jacques A., 'Towards a New Chronology for Bourbon Colonialism: The "*Depositaria de Indias*" of Cadiz, 1722–1789', *Ibero-Amerikanisches Archiv* 6 (1980), 335–53.

Barbier, Jacques A., 'Indies Revenues and Naval Spending: The Cost of Colonialism for the Spanish Bourbons, 1763-1805', *Jahrbuch für Geschichte von Staat, Wirtschaft und Gesellschaft Lateinamerikas* 21 (1984), 169–88.

Barrenechea, José Manuel, ed., *Moral y economía en el siglo XVIII: Antología de textos sobre la usura: Zubiaur, Calatayud, los Cinco Gremios Mayores y Uría Nafarrondo* (Vitoria: Gobierno Vasco, 1995).

Baudot Monroy, María, 'Barcos para el Rey. Julián de Arriaga, la madera y la construcción naval (1752–1759)', in García Hurtado and Manuel Reyes, eds, *La Armada española en el siglo XVIII: Ciencia, hombres y barcos* (Madrid: Silex, 2012), 297–328.

Baudot Monroy, María, *La defensa del Imperio: Julián de Arriaga en la Armada (1700–1754)* (Madrid: Ministerio de Defensa, 2013).

Baugh, Daniel A., *British Naval Administration in the Age of Walpole* (Princeton: Princeton University Press, 1965).

Bonney, Richard, ed., *The Rise of the Fiscal State in Europe* (Oxford: Oxford University Press, 1999).

Bosher, J. F., *French Finances 1770–1795: From Business to Bureaucracy* (Cambridge: Cambridge University Press, 1970).

Bowen, Huw, 'Trading with the Enemy. British Private Trade and the Supply of Arms to India, c. 1750–1820', in Richard Harding and Sergio Solbes, eds, *The Contractor State and its Implications, 1659–1815* (Las Palmas: Universidad de Las Palmas, 2013), 35–56.

Bowen, Huw and González Enciso, Agustín, eds, *Mobilising Resources for War: Britain and Spain at Work During the Early Modern Period* (Pamplona: EUNSA, 2006).

Boyer-Xambeau, Marie-Thérèse, 'A la recherche d'un âge d'or des marchés financiers: intégration et efficence au XVIII siècle', *Cahiers d'Économie Politique* 21 (1992), 33–65.

Braddick, Michael J., *The Nerves of State: Taxation and the Financing of the English State, 1558–1714* (Manchester: Manchester University Press, 1996).

Brandon, Pepijn, 'Global Power, Local Connections: the Dutch Admiralties and their Supply Networks', in Richard Harding and Sergio Solbes, eds, *The Contractor State and its Implications, 1659–1815* (Las Palmas: Universidad de Las Palmas, 2013), 57–80.

Brandon, Pepijn, 'Accounting for Power: Bookkeeping and the Rationalization of Dutch Naval Administration', in Jeff Fynn-Paul, ed., *War, Entrepreneurs, and the State in Europe and the Mediterranean, 1300–1800* (Leiden: Brill, 2014), 151–69.

Brewer, John, *The Sinews of Power: War, Money and the English State, 1688–1783* (New York: Cambridge University Press, 1989).

Buchet, Christian, *Marine, économie et société: un exemple d'interaction: l'avitaillement de la Royal Navy durant la guerre de sept ans* (Paris: Champion, 1999).

Cabello Vázquez, Raúl, 'Ciencia y guerra en los albores de la química como disciplina: programa francés para la producción de pólvora', in Jesús Astigarraga et al., *Ilustración, ilustraciones* (San Sebastián: Real Sociedad Bascongada de Amigos del País y Sociedad Estatal de Conmemoraciones Culturales, 2009), 715–34.

Calvo Poyato, José, 'La industria militar española durante la Guerra de Sucesión', *Revista de historia militar* 33 (1989), 51–71.

Canga Argüelles, José, *Diccionario de Hacienda con aplicación a España* (Madrid: Imprenta de Don Marcelino Calero y Portocarrero, 1834).

Cantera Montenegro, Jesús, 'La otra guerra: la lucha por la subsistencia. Acuartelamiento, vestuario y alimentación durante la Guerra de la Independencia', *Cuadernos de Historia Moderna* 9 (2010), 147–65.

Capella, Miguel, and Matilla, Antonio, *Los Cinco Gremios Mayores de Madrid* (Madrid: Cámara de Comercio de Madrid, 1957).

Carmona Badía, Xán, 'Sargadelos en la historia de la siderurgia española', *Revista de historia industrial* 3 (1993), 11–40.

Carmona Badía, Xán, 'Antonio Raimundo Ibáñez, un empresario en el filo de dos épocas', in Joaquín Ocampo, ed., *Empresa y empresarios en el norte de España (Siglo XVIII)* (Oviedo: Trea, 2012), 69–90.

Caro Baroja, Julio, *La hora navarra del siglo XVIII* (Pamplona: Diputación Foral, 1969).

Carrión Arregui, Ignacio María, *La siderurgia guipuzcoana en el siglo XVIII* (Bilbao: Universidad del País Vasco, 1991).

Carrión Arregui, Ignacio María, 'Tecnología tradicional y desarrollo de una industria pesada: la fabricación de anclas en Guipuzkoa (siglos XVI–XVIII)', *Revista de historia industrial* 7 (1995), 199–214.

Castanedo Galán, Juan Manuel, *Guarnizo, un astillero de la Corona* (Madrid, Editorial Naval, 1993).

Castanedo Galán, Juan Miguel, 'Un asiento singular de Juan Fernández de Isla. La fábrica de ocho navíos y la reforma de un astillero', in Carlos Martínez Shaw, ed., *El derecho y el mar en la España moderna* (Granada: Universidad de Granada, 1995), 457–76.

Castro, Adolfo de, *Historia de Cádiz y su provincia* (Madrid: Imp. de la Revista médica, 1858).
Castro, Concepción de, *A La Sombra De Felipe V: Jose Grimaldo Ministro Responsable (1703–1726)* (Madrid: Marcial Pons, 2004).
Cepeda Gómez, José, 'El fuero militar en el siglo XVIII', in Enrique Martínez Ruíz and Magdalena Pazzis, eds, *Instituciones de la España Moderna, Las Jurisdicciones* (Madrid: Actas, 1996), 393–404.
Chaline, Olivier, Bonnichon, Philippe, and Vergennes, Charles-Phillippe, eds, *Les Marines de la Guerre d'indépendance américaine: 1763–1783* (Paris: Presses de l'université Paris-Sorbonne, 2013).
Charters, Erica, 'The Caring Fiscal-Military State during the Seven Years War, 1756–1763)', *Historical Journal* 52 (2009), 921–41.
Claro Delgado, Manuel, 'Cádiz y las expediciones militares a Indias en el siglo XVIII', *Milicia y sociedad en la baja Andalucía (siglos XVIII y XIX): actas VIII Jornadas Nacionales de Historia Militar* (Seville: Cátedra General Castaños, 1999), 3–20.
Contamine, Philippe, ed., *War and Competition between States* (Oxford: Clarendon, 2000).
Conway, Stephen, 'Public and Private Contributions to the Mobilization of Manpower and Resources for War in Mid-Eighteenth-Century Britain and Ireland', in Huw V. Bowen, and Agustín González Enciso, eds, *Mobilising Resources for War: Britain and Spain at Work During the Early Modern Period* (Pamplona: Eunsa, 2006), 37–58.
Conway, Stephen, *Britain, Ireland, and Continental Europe in the Eighteenth Century: Similarities, Connections, Identities* (Oxford: Oxford University Press, 2011).
Conway, Stephen, 'Provisioning the Combined Army in Germany, 1758–1762: Who Benefited?', in Richard Harding and Sergio Solbes, eds, *The Contractor State and its Implications, 1659–1815* (Las Palmas: Universidad de Las Palmas, 2013), 81–102.
Conway, Stephen, 'Entrepreneurs and the Recruitment of the British Army in the War of American Independence, 1775–1783', in Jeff Fynn-Paul, ed., *War, Entrepreneurs, and the State in Europe and the Mediterranean, 1300–1800* (Leiden: Brill, 2014), 111–30.
Conway, Stephen, and Torres Sánchez, Rafael, eds, *The Spending of the States: Military Expenditure during the Long Eighteenth Century: Patterns, Organisation and Consequences, 1650–1815* (Saarbrücken: VDM, 2011).
Crespo Solana, Ana, *La Casa de la Contratación y la Intendencia General de la Marina en Cádiz, 1717–1730* (Cadiz: Universidad de Cádiz, 1996).
Crewe, Duncan, *Yellow Jack and the Worm: British Naval Administration in the West Indies, 1739–1748* (Liverpool: Liverpool University Press, 1993).
Daunton, Martin, 'The Fiscal-Military State and the Napoleonic Wars: Britain and France Compared', in David Cannadine, ed., *Trafalgar in History: A Battle and Its Afterlife* (London: Palgrave Macmillan, 2006), 18–43.
Daunton, Martin, *State and Market in Victorian Britain: War, Welfare, and Capitalism* (Woodbridge: The Boydell Press, 2008).
Dedieu, Jean-Pierre, 'Les Groupes financiers et industriels au service du roi. Espagne, fin XVIIe-début XVIIIe siècle', in Anne Dubet and Jean-Philippe Luis, eds, *Les Financiers et la construction de l'État—France, Espagne (XVIIe–XIXe siècle)* (Rennes: Presses Universitaires de Rennes, 2011), 87–104.
Dedieu, Jean-Pierre, 'Les Intermédiaires privés dans les finances royales espagnoles sous Philippe V et Ferdinand VI', in Vicent Meyzie, ed., *Crédit public, crédit privé et institutions intermédiaires : Monarchie française, monarchie hispanique, XVIe–XVIIIe siècles* (Limoges: Presses Universitaires de Limoges et du Limousin, 2012), 223–39.
Delgado Barrado, José Miguel, *Aquiles y Teseos: Bosquejos del reformismo borbónico (1701–1759)* (Granada: Universidad de Granada, 2007).

Dessert, Daniel, *Argent, pouvoir et societé au grand siécle* (Paris: Fayard, 1984).
Díaz Ordóñez, Manuel, 'El riesgo de contratar con el enemigo. Suministros ingleses para la Armada Real española en el siglo XVIII', *Revista de historia naval* 21 (2003), 65–74.
Díaz Ordóñez, Manuel, *Amarrados al negocio: Reformismo borbónico y suministro de jarcia para la Armada Real (1675–1751)* (Madrid: Ministerio de Defensa, 2009).
Dincecco, Mark, 'Fiscal Centralization, Limited Government and Public Revenues in Europe, 1650–1913', *Journal of Economic History* 69 (2009), 48–103.
Drelichman, Mauricio and Hans-Joachim Voth, *Lending to the Borrower from Hell: Debt, Taxes, and Default in the Age of Philip II* (Princeton: Princeton University Press, 2014).
Donaldson, David Whamond, *Britain and Menorca in the Eighteenth Century* (Milton Keynes: Open University, 1994).
Drinkwater, John, *A History of the Late Siege of Gibraltar (Facsimil de la edición 1786)* (Valencia: Paris-Valencia, 1989).
Dubet, Anne, ed., *Administrer les finances royales dans la monarchie espagnole (XVIe–XIXe siècles)* (Rennes: Presses Universitaires de Rennes, 2008).
Dubet, Anne, *Un estadista francés en la España de los Borbones: Juan Orry y las primeras reformas de Felipe V (1701–1706)* (Madrid: Biblioteca Nueva, 2008).
Dunning, Chester, and Smith, Norman S., 'Moving beyond Absolutism: Was Early Modern Russia a "Fiscal-Military" State?', *Russian History* 33 (2006), 19–43.
Earle, Peter, 'The Sinews of Power: War, Money and the English State, 1688–1783', *Economic History Review* 43 (1990), 142.
Edling, Max, *A Revolution in Favor of Government: Origins of the U.S. Constitution* (Oxford: Oxford University Press, 2003).
Escartín Sánchez, Eduardo, *La intendencia de Cataluña en el siglo XVIII* (Barcelona: Santandreu, 1995).
Escobedo Romero, Rafael, *El tabaco del rey: la organización de un monopolio fiscal durante el Antiguo Régimen* (Pamplona: EUNSA, 2007).
Espino López, Antonio, 'La historiografía hispana sobre la guerra en la época de los Austrias. Un balance, 1991–2000', *Manuscrits* 21 (2003), 161–91.
Esteban Estríngana, Alicia, 'Administración militar y negocio de guerra en los Países Bajos católicos. Siglo XVII', in Ana Crespo and Manuel Herrero, eds, *España y las 17 Provincias de los Países Bajos: Una revisión historiográfica (XVI–XVIII)* (Córdoba: Universidad de Córdoba, 2002), 65–100.
Esteban Estríngana, Alicia, 'El suministro de pólvora en el ejército de Flandes. Sobre la gestión directa y delegada del aprovisionamiento militar (siglo XVII)', in Enrique García Hernán and Davide Maffi, eds, *Guerra y Sociedad en la Monarquía Hispánica. Política, Estrategia y Cultura en la Europa Moderna (1500–1700)* (Madrid: Fundación MAPFRE, Ediciones del Laberinto, CSIC, 2006), ii. 473–522.
Feliciano Ramos, Héctor R., *El contrabando inglés en el Caribe y el Golfo de México (1748–1778)* (Seville: Diputación Provincial, 1990).
Félix, Jöel, 'Victualling Louis XV's armies: The Munitionnaire des Vivres de Flandres et d'Allemagne and the Military Supply System', in Richard Harding and Sergio Solbes, eds, *The Contractor State and its Implications, 1659–1815* (Las Palmas: Universidad de Las Palmas, 2013), 103–30.
Fernández Albaladejo, Pablo, 'El decreto de suspensión de pagos de 1739: análisis y explicación', *Moneda y Crédito* 142 (1977), 51–81.
Fernández de Pinedo, Emiliano, 'From the Bloomery to the Blast-Furnace: Technical Change in Spanish Iron-making (1650–1850)', *Journal of European Economic History* 17 (1988), 7–32.

Fernández Durán, Reyes, *Gerónimo de Uztariz (1670–1732): Una política económica para Felipe V* (Madrid: Minerva, 1999).

Fernández Maldonado, Emilio, *El sargento español en el Siglo de las Luces 1685–1760* (Madrid: Ministerio de Defensa, 1999).

Fynn-Paul, Jeff, ed., *War, Entrepreneurs, and the State in Europe and the Mediterranean, 1300–1800*, (Leiden: Brill, 2014).

Gárate Ojanguren, Montserrat, *La Real Compañía Guipuzcoana de Caracas* (Donostia: Sociedad Guipuzcoana de Ediciones y Publicaciones, 1990).

Gárate Ojanguren, Montserrat, *Comercio ultramarino e Ilustración: la Real Compañía de La Habana* (San Sebastián: Real Sociedad Bascongada de los Amigos del País, 1993).

García-Torralba Pérez, Enrique, *La Artillería Naval Española en el Siglo XVIII: Su evolución técnica y su recíproca influencia con la arquitectura del buque* (Madrid: Ministerio de Defensa, 2010).

Gareis, Johanna, *Nueva España en el Circuncaribe, 1779–1808: Revolución, competencia imperial y vínculos intercoloniales* (Mexico: Universidad Nacional Autónoma de México, 1997).

Garner, Guillaume, 'Caméralisme et territoire. État, espace et économie dans le discours économique allemand au XVIIIe siècle', *Revue du Nord* 85 (2003), 729–45.

Gella Iturriaga, José, 'El convoy y el desembarco de 1781 en Menorca', *Revista de historia naval* 1 (1983), 9–30.

Glesener, Thomas, 'La estatalización del reclutamiento de soldados extranjeros en el siglo XVIII', in Manuel Reyes García Hurtado, ed., *Soldados de la Ilustración: El ejército español en el siglo XVIII* (A Coruña: Universidade da Coruña, 2012), 237–61.

Glete, Jan, *War and the State in Early Modern Europe: Spain, the Dutch Republic and Sweden as Fiscal-Military States, 1500–1660* (London: Routledge, 2002).

Gómez Carrasco, Cosmo, 'Parientes, amigos y patronos. Red, movilidad y reproducción social en la burguesía y la élite de poder a finales del Antiguo Régimen (Albacete, 1750–1808)', *Studia Histórica* 29 (2007), 427–63.

Gómez Urdáñez, José Luis, *El proyecto reformista de Ensenada* (Lleida: Milenio, 1995).

González Enciso, Agustín, *España y USA en el siglo XVIII: crecimiento industrial comparado y relaciones comerciales* (Valladolid: Universidad de Valladolid, 1979).

González Enciso, Agustín, 'La promoción industrial en la España Moderna: intervención pública e iniciativa privada', in Luis Antonio Ribot and Luigi de Rosa, eds, *Industria y Época Moderna* (Madrid: Actas, 2000), 15–46.

González Enciso, Agustín, 'El "Estado económico" en la España del siglo XVIII', *Memoria y civilización: anuario de historia de la Universidad de Navarra* 6 (2003), 97–139.

González Enciso, Agustín, 'Spain's Mobilisation of Resources for the War with Portugal in 1762', in Huw V. Bowen and Agustín González Enciso, eds, *Mobilising Resources for War: Britain and Spain at Work During the Early Modern Period* (Pamplona: EUNSA, 2006), 159–90.

González Enciso, Agustín, 'Military Expenditure and Entrepreneurial Promotion in Modern Spain: An Unsuccessful Expedient. The Example of the Eugui Munitions Factory', in Stephen Conway and Rafael Torres Sánchez, eds, *The Spending of the States: Military Expenditure during the Long Eighteenth Century: Patterns, Organisation and Consequences, 1650–1815* (Saarbrücken: VDM, 2011), 285–312.

González Enciso, Agustín, 'Estado militar y empresarios de industrias militares', in Agustín González Enciso, ed., *Un Estado Militar: España, 1650–1820* (Madrid: Actas, 2012), 423–47.

González Enciso, Agustín, 'La renovación del asiento de transporte de municiones y armas en 1793 y el protagonismo de una familia navarra', *Memoria y Civilización* 15 (2012), 51–69.

González Enciso, Agustín, 'Buying Cannons Outside: When, Why, How Many? The Supplying of Foreign Iron Cannons for the Spanish Navy in the Eighteenth Century', in Richard Harding and Sergio Solbes, eds, *The Contractor State and its Implications, 1659–1815* (Las Palmas: Universidad de Las Palmas, 2013), 135–58.

González Enciso, Agustín, 'Del *contractor state* al Estado fabricante. El cambio de propiedad en la fábrica de municiones de Eugui en 1766', *Revista de historia de la economía y de la empresa,* BBVA 7 (2014), 455–84.

Goodman, David, *El poderío naval español: Historia de la armada española del siglo XVII* (Barcelona: Peninsular, 2001).

Goosens, Thomas, 'The Grip of the State? Government Control over Provision of the Army in the Austrian Netherlands, 1725–1744', in Jeff Fynn-Paul, ed., *War, Entrepreneurs, and the State in Europe and the Mediterranean, 1300–1800* (Leiden: Brill, 2014), 193–14.

Grafe, Regina, and Irigoin, Alexandra, 'A Stakeholder Empire: The Political Economy of Spanish Imperial Rule in America', *Economic History Review* 65 (2011), 1–43.

Grafenstein Gareis, Johanna von, 'El abasto de la escuadra y las plazas militares de gran Caribe, con harinas y víveres novohispanos, 1755–1779', in Carmen Yuste López and Matilde Souto Mantecón, eds, *El comercio exterior de México, 1713–1850: Entre la quiebra del sistema imperial y el surgimiento de una nación* (México: Instituto de Investigaciones Históricas-UNAM, 2000), 42–83.

Graham, Aaron, 'Auditing Leviathan: Corruption and State Formation in Early Eighteenth-Century Britain', *English Historical Review* 128 (2013), 806–38.

Graham, Aaron, 'Public Service and Private Profit: British Fiscal-Military Entrepreneurship Overseas, 1707–12', in Jeff Fynn-Paul, ed., *War, Entrepreneurs, and the State in Europe and the Mediterranean, 1300–1800* (Leiden: Brill, 2014), 87–110.

Granados Loureda, Juan A., 'El arsenal y astillero de Ferrol en el siglo XVII: de A Graña a Trafalgar', *Congress Minutes of Technology of the Ships of Trafalgar, a Homage to their Designers and Constructors* (Madrid-Cadiz, 2005).

Gregory, Desmond, *Minorca, the Illusory Prize: A History of the British Occupations of Minorca between 1708 and 1802* (London: Fairleigh Dickinson University Press, 1990).

Guerrero Elecalde, Rafael, *Las elites vascas y navarras en el gobierno de la Monarquía Borbónica: Redes sociales, carreras y hegemonía en el siglo XVIII (1700–1746)* (Vitoria: Universidad del País Vasco, 2012).

Guy, Alan James, *Oeconomy and Discipline: Officership and Administration in the British Army, 1714–1763* (Manchester: Manchester University Press, 1985).

Guzmán Raja, Isidoro, 'Normativa contable en la Armada española durante el periodo 1700–1850: especial referencia a la administración de provisiones', *De Computis. Revista española de historia de la contabilidad* 5 (2006), 65–142.

Hancock, David, *Citizens of the World: London Merchants and the Integration of the British Atlantic Community, 1735–1785*, (Cambridge: Cambridge University Press, 1995).

Harding, Richard, *Seapower and Naval Warfare, 1650–1830* (Annapolis: Naval Institute Press, 1999).

Harding, Richard, 'Gibraltar: A Tale of Two Sieges, 1726–1727 and 1779–1783', *Gibraltar as a Naval Base and Dockyard* (Portsmouth: Ray Riley Naval Dockyards Society, 2006), ii.

Harding, Richard, 'Amphibious Operations', in John B. Hattendorf, ed., *The Oxford Encyclopaedia of Maritime History* (New York: Oxford University Press, 2007).

Harding, Richard, 'Operaciones anfibias británicas, 1700–1815', in Agustín Guimerá Ravina and José María Núñez, eds, *Guerra Naval en el Revolución y el Imperio: Bloqueos y operaciones anfibias, 1793–1815* (Madrid: Marcial Pons, 2008), 39–58.

Harding, Richard, *The Emergence of Britain's Global Naval Supremacy: The War of 1739–1748* (Woodbridge: The Boydell Press, 2010).

Harding, Richard, 'Parliament and the British Fiscal-Military State: Ideology, Consent and State Expenditure in Britain, 1739–1748', in Stephen Conway and Rafael Torres Sánchez, eds, *The Spending of the States: Military Expenditure during the Long Eighteenth Century: Patterns, Organisation and Consequences, 1650–1815* (Saarbrücken: VDM, 2011), 31–50.

Harding, Richard, 'Contractors, Warship of the Royal Navy and Sea Power, 1739–1748', in Richard Harding and Sergio Solbes, eds, *The Contractor State and its Implications, 1659–1815* (Las Palmas: Universidad de Las Palmas, 2012), 159–176.

Harding, Richard, and Solbes, Sergio, eds, *The Contractor State and its Implications, 1659–1815* (Las Palmas: Universidad de Las Palmas, 2012).

Harling, Philip, and Mandler, Peter, 'From "Fiscal-Military" State to Laissez-Faire State, 1760–1850', *Journal of British Studies* 32 (1993), 44–70.

Helguera Quijada, Juan, 'Las reales fábricas', in Francisco Comín and Pablo Martín, eds, *Historia de la empresa pública en España* (Madrid: Espasa Calpe, 1991), 51–87.

Helguera Quijada, Juan, 'Empresas y empresarios manufactureros en la España del siglo XVIII', in Francisco Comín and Pablo Martín, eds, *La empresa en la Historia de España* (Madrid: Civitas, 1996), 115–40.

Hernández Andreu, Joan, 'Trets de l'economia menorquina des de l'època britànica fins a mitjan segle XIX', *Randa* 45 (2000), 7–29.

Hernández Escayola, María Concepción, *Negocio y servicio: finanzas públicas y hombres de negocios en Navarra en la primera mitad del siglo XVIII* (Pamplona: EUNSA, 2004).

Hernández Sanz, Francesc, 'Un corsario menorquín (1779–1781)', *Cultura i societat a Menorca* 1 (1987), 54–110.

Hoffman, Philip T., Postel-Vinay, Guilles, and Rosenthal, Jean-Laurent, *Priceless Markets: The Political Economy of Credit in Paris, 1660–1870* (Chicago: University of Chicago Press, 2000).

Ibáñez Molina, Manuel, 'Rentas Provinciales, administración real y recaudadores en el reino de Felipe V (1700–1739)' (Granada: Doctoral thesis, microfiches, 1985).

Inglis, G. Douglas, 'The Spanish Naval Shipyard at Havana in the Eighteenth Century', in *New Aspects of Naval History: Selected Papers From the Fifth Naval History Symposium* (Baltimore: Nautical Aviation and Publishing Co. of America, 1985), 47–58.

Innes, Joanna, 'The Domestic Face of the Military-Fiscal State: Government and Society in Eighteenth-Century Britain', in Lawrence Stone, ed., *An Imperial State at War: Britain from 1689 to 1815* (London: Routledge, 1994), 96–127.

Iturrioz Magaña, Ángel, *Estudio del subsidio y excusado (1561–1808): contribuciones económicas de la diócesis de Calahorra y La Calzada a la Real Hacienda* (Logroño: Instituto de Estudios Riojanos, 1987).

Jiménez Estrella, Antonio, 'Asentistas militares y fraude en torno al abastecimiento de pólvora en el reino de Granada (siglo XVI)', *Investigaciones históricas: Época moderna y contemporánea* 30 (2010), 11–30.

Jiménez Estrella, Antonio, and Andújar Castillo, Francisco, eds, *Los nervios de la guerra: Estudios sociales sobre el Ejército de la Monarquía Hispánica (siglos XVI–XVIII): nuevas perspectivas* (Granada: Comares, 2007).

Juan Vidal, José, 'Crisis de subsistències i aprovisionament blader de Mallorca durant el segle XVIII', *Randa* 26 (1990), 103–32.

Juan-García Aguado, José María, *José Romero Fernández de Landa: un ingeniero de marina en el siglo XVIII* (Santiago: Universidade da Coruña, 1998).

Kamen, Herny, *La Guerra de Sucesión en España, 1700–1715* (Barcelona: Grijalbo, 1974).

Kaps, Klemens, 'Entre el servicio estatal y los negocios transnacionales: el caso de Paolo Greppi, cónsul imperial en Cádiz (1774–1791)', in Marcela Aglieti et al., eds, *Los cónsules de extranjeros en la Edad Moderna y principios de la Edad Contemporánea* (Madrid: Ediciones Doce Calles, 2013), 225–36.

Keep, John, 'Feeding the Troops: Russian Army Supply Policies during the Seven Years War', *Canadian Slavonic Papers* 29 (1987), 24–44.

Knight, Roger, 'Construction et entretien de la flotte anglaise durant les guerres anglo-françaises (1688–1815)', in Martine Acerra, José Merino, and Jean Meyer, eds, *Les Marines de guerre européennes, XVIIe–XVIIIe siècles* (Paris: Presses de l'Université de Paris-Sorbonne, 1985), 47–62.

Knight, Roger, 'Changing the Agenda: The "New" Naval History of the British Sailing Navy', *Mariner's Mirror* 97 (2011), 225–42.

Knight, Roger, *Britain against Napoleon: The Organization of Victory, 1793–1815* (London: Penguin, 2014).

Knight, Roger, and Wilcox, Martin, *Sustaining the Fleet, 1793–1815: War, the British Navy and the Contractor State* (Woodbrige: The Boydell Press, 2010).

Knight, Roger, and Wilcox, Martin, 'War, Government and the Market: The Direction of the Debate on the British Contractor State, *c.*1740–1815', in Richard Harding and Sergio Solbes, eds, *The Contractor State and its Implications, 1659–1815* (Las Palmas: Universidad de Las Palmas, 2012), 175–98.

Kuethe, Allan J., and Andrien, Kenneth J., *The Spanish Atlantic World in the Eighteenth Century: War and the Bourbon Reforms, 1713–1796* (Cambridge: Cambridge University Press, 2014).

Kuethe, Allan J., and Serrano Álvarez, José Manuel, 'El astillero de la Habana y Trafalgar', *Revista de Indias* 67 (2007), 763–76.

Lewis, James A., 'Nueva España y los esfuerzos para abastecer La Habana, 1779–1783', *Anuario de Estudios Americanos* 33 (1976), 101–26.

Lind, Gunner, 'Beyond the Fiscal-Military Road to State Formation: Civil Society, Collective Identities and the State in the Old Danish Monarchy, 1500–1850', *Balto-Scandia* 18 (2012), 1–11.

Llombart, Vicente, 'La política económica de Carlos III ¿Fiscalismo, cosmética o estímulo al crecimiento?', *Revista de historia económica* 11 (1994), 11–39.

Llopis Agelán, Enrique, and García Montero, Héctor, 'Precios y salarios en Madrid, 1680–1800', *Investigaciones de historia económica: revista de la Asociación Española de Historia Económica* 7 (2011), 295–309.

López Cordón, María Victoria, Pérez, María Ángeles, and Martínez de Sas, María Teresa, *La Casa de Borbón* (Madrid: Alianza Editorial, 2000).

Lopez de Lerena, Pedro, *Memoria sobre las rentas públicas y balanza comercial de España (1789–1790)* (Madrid: Instituto de Estudios Fiscales, 1990).

López González, Juan Jaime, 'Una firma comercial sueca en Cádiz y su relación con los arsenales españoles a finales del siglo XVIII', *Actas I Congreso de Historia de Andalucía: Andalucía moderna (siglo XVIII)* (Córdoba, 1978), 287–99.

López Losa, Ernesto, 'The Legacy of Earl J. Hamilton. New Data for the Study of Prices in Spain, 1650–1800', *Investigaciones de Historia Económica* 9 (2013), 75–87.

Luxán, Santiago, Gárate, Montserrat, and Rodríguez, José Manuel, *Cuba-Canarias-Sevilla: El estanco español del tabaco y Las Antillas (1717–1817)* (Las Palmas: Ediciones del Cabildo de Gran Canaria, 2012).

Lynn, John A., *Giant of the Grand Siècle: The French Army, 1610–1715* (Cambridge: Cambridge University Press, 1997).

Macdonald, Janet, *Feeding Nelson's Navy: The True Story of Food at Sea in the Georgian Era* (London: Chatham, 2006).

McGuffie, Tom Henderson, *The Siege of Gibraltar* (London: Batsford, 1965).

Maiso González, Jesús, *La difícil modernización de Cantabria en el siglo XVIII: D. Juan F. de Isla y Alvear* (Santander: Librería Estudio, 1990).

Manera Erbina, Carlos Pablo, 'Resistir i créixer. Canvi econòmic i classes socials a la Mallorca del segle XVIII', *Randa* 26 (1990), 7–83.

Manera Erbina, Carlos Pablo, 'Mallorca en el planeta mediterrani. Les principals línies d'inversió del capital comercial (1700–1900)', *Randa* 42 (1999), 81–148.

Mann, Michael, 'Putting the Weberian State in its Social, Geopolitical and Militaristic Context: A Response to Patrick O'Brien', *Journal of Historical Sociology* 19 (2006), 364–73.

Marchena Fernández, Juan, *Ejército y milicias en el mundo colonial americano* (Madrid: MAPFRE, 1992).

Marchena Fernández, Juan, 'Capital, créditos e intereses comerciales a fines del periodo colonial: los costos del sistema defensivo americano. Cartagena de Indias y el Sur del Caribe', *Tiempos de América* 9 (2002), 3–38.

Marchena Fernández, Juan, 'De las "reliquias" de Felipe V a la gran Armada Oceánica de 1750: guerra y marina durante la primera mitad del siglo XVIII', in Juan José Sánchez Baena, Celia Chain Navarro, and Lorena Martínez Solis, eds, *Estudios de Historia Naval: Actitudes y medios en la Real Armada del siglo XVIII* (Murcia: Ministerio de Defensa, 2011), 49–90.

Marí Puig, Amador, 'Cors i comerc a Menorca. La comercialització de les preses (1778–1781)', *Jornades d'estudis historic locals El comerc alterniu* 8 (1989), 201–16.

Marí Puig, Amador, 'El comerç del blat al port de Maó', *Estudis d'Història Econòmica* 2 (1989), 133–57.

Marichal, Carlos, *Bankruptcy of Empire: Mexican Silver and the Wars between Spain, Britain and France, 1760–1810* (Cambridge: Cambridge University Press, 2007).

Marichal, Carlos, and Graffenstein, Johanna, eds, *El secreto del Imperio español: los situados coloniales en el siglo XVIII* (México: El Colegio de México-Instituto Mora, 2012).

Martí, Ricard, *Cataluña armería de los Borbones: Las armas y los armeros de Ripoll, Barcelona, Manresa, Igualada . . . de 1714 a 1794* (Barcelona: Salvatella, 2004).

Martín García, Alfredo, *Una sociedad en cambio: Ferrol a finales del Antiguo Régimen* (Ferrol: Embora, 2003).

Martín García, Alfredo, 'La política de reconstrucción naval borbónica y el reino de Galicia: el real astillero de Esteiro (s. XVIII)', in Agustín Guimerá Ravina and Víctor Peralta Ruiz, eds, *Actas de la VIII Reunión Científica de la Fundación Española de Historia Moderna: El equilibrio de los imperios: de Ultrecht y Trafalgar* (2005), 747–60.

Martínez Ruiz, Enrique, and Pi Corrales, Magdalena, *Commerce and Navigation between Spain and Sweden throughout History* (Madrid: Fundación Berndt Wistedt, 2000).

Martínez Shaw, Carlos, and Alfonso Mola, Marina, 'Los astilleros de la América colonial', *Historia general de América Latina* 3 (1999), 279–304.

Mata, Micaela, *Conquistas y reconquistas de Menorca* (Barcelona: Imp. Juvenil, 1984).

Medrano, José Miguel, and Malamud, Carlos, 'Las actividades de los *Cinco Gremios Mayores* en el Perú. Apuntes preliminares', *Revista de Indias* 48 (1988), 421–33.

Merino Navarro, José Patricio, 'Cultivos industriales: el cáñamo en España, 1750–1800', *Hispania* 130 (1975), 567–84.

Merino Navarro, José Patricio, *La Armada española en el siglo XVIII* (Madrid: Fundación Universitaria Española, 1981).

Mestre Prat de Padua, María, 'La construcción naval de guerra en la España del siglo XVIII. El marco legal de los procesos de financiación', in Carlos Martínez Shaw, ed., *El derecho y el mar en la España moderna* (Granada: Universidad de Granada, 1995), 299–322.

Mestre Prat de Padua, María, and Matamoros Aparicio, David, 'La organización del astillero de La Habana durante el siglo XVIII', *Jahrbuch für Geschichte Lateinamerikas* 34 (1997), 89–103.

Miguel Bernal, Antonio, ed., *Dinero, Moneda y Credito en la Monarquia Hispánica* (Madrid: Marcial Pons, 2000).

Miller, Judith A., *Mastering the Market: The State and the Grain Trade in Northern France, 1700–1850* (Cambridge, Cambridge University Press, 1998).

Morgan, Kenneth, 'Mercantilism and the British Empire, 1688–1815', in Donald Winch and Patrick Karl O'Brien, eds, *The Political Economy of British Historical Experience, 1688–1914* (Oxford: Oxford University Press, 2002), 165–91.

Morris, Roger, *The Foundations of British Maritime Ascendancy: Resources, Logistics and the State, 1755–1815* (Cambridge: Cambridge University Press, 2011).

North, Douglass C., Wallis, John J., and Weingast, Barry R., *Violence and Social Orders: A Conceptual Framework for Interpreting Recorded Human History* (New York: Cambridge University Press, 2012).

Núñez Torrado, Miriam, 'Estudios de costes en la renta de la pólvora de nueva España ante la implantación de un nuevo sistema de gestión (1766–1785)', *Revista española de financiación y contabilidad* 111 (2002), 47–74.

O'Brien, Patrick Karl, 'The Formation of a Mercantilist State and the Economic Growth of the United Kingdom 1453–1815', United Nations University, Research Paper 2006/75.

O'Brien, Patrick Karl, 'Taxation for British Mercantilism from the Treaty of Utrecht (1713) to the Peace of Paris (1783)', in Rafael Torres Sánchez, ed., *War, State and Development: Fiscal-Military States in the Eighteenth Century* (Pamplona: EUNSA, 2007), 295–356.

O'Brien, Patrick K., 'The Nature and Historical Evolution of an Exceptional Fiscal State and its Possible Significance for the Precocious Commercialization and Industrialization of the British Economy from Cromwell to Nelson', *Economic History Review* 64 (2011), 408–46.

O'Brien, Patrick Karl, 'A Global Perspective for the Comprehension of Fiscal State Formation across Eurasia from the Rise of Venice to the Opium War', in Richard Harding and Sergio Solbes, eds, *The Contractor State and its Implications, 1659–1815* (Las Palmas: Universidad de Las Palmas, 2012), 223–42.

Ocaña Torres, Mario Luis, *El corso marítimo español en el estrecho de Gibraltar (1700–1802)* (Algeciras: Instituto de Estudios Campogibraltareños, 1993).

O'Donnell, Hugo, 'Las reformas de la Armada', *Temas de Historia Militar, II Congreso de Historia Militar* I (1988), 341–74.

O'Donnell, Hugo, 'Luis María de Salazar, capitán de navío, ministro de Marina', *Cuadernos monográficos del Instituto de Historia y Cultura Naval* 54 (2007), 115–28.

Odriozola Oyarbide, María Lourdes, 'La Real Fábrica de anclas de Renteriola: un intento fallido', *Real Sociedad Bascongada de los Amigos del País* 46 (1990), 41–77.

Odriozola Oyarbide, María Lourdes, 'La industria naval guipuzcoana y la producción de navíos para el Rey (1650–1799)', *Boletín de la Real Sociedad Bascongada de los Amigos del País* 1 (1994), 3–41.

Odriozola Oyarbide, María Lourdes, 'La construcción naval en Gipuzkoa: siglos XVI–XVIII', *Itsas memoria: revista de estudios marítimos del País Vasco* 2 (1998), 93–146.

Ortega Pereyra, Ovidio, *El Real Arsenal de La Habana* (Havana: Editorial Letras Cubanas, 1998).

Ortiz Escamilla, Juan, *El teatro de la guerra: Veracruz, 1750–1825* (Castellón de la Plana: Universitat Jaume I, 2008).

Ortiz Sotelo, Jorge, *La Real Armada en el Pacífico Sur: El Apostadero Naval del Callao 1746–1824* (México: Iberoamericana, 2015).

Ozanam, Didier, 'La política exterior de España en tiempos de Felipe V y de Fernando VI', in Ramón Menéndez Pidal, ed., *Historia de España* (Madrid: Cervera Pery, 1985).

Palacio Ramos, Rafael, 'Los últimos galleons: el fin de la construcción naval para la Corona en el *Astillero* de Colindres', *Revista de historia naval* 27 (2009), 7–30.

Palop Ramos, José Miguel, 'El ejército en Valencia durante el siglo XVIII: Alojamientos y cuarteles', in Ricardo Franch Benavent and Rafael Benítez Sánchez-Blanco, eds, *Estudios de historia moderna: en homenaje a la profesora Emilia Salvador Esteban* (Valencia: Universitat de València, 2008), 403–30.

Parrott, David, *The Business of War: Military Enterprise and Military Revolution in Early Modern Europe* (Cambridge: Cambridge University Press, 2012).

Patricio Merino Navarro, José, *La Armada española en el siglo XVIII* (Madrid: Fundación Universitaria Española, 1981).

Paul, Helen Julia, 'The Royal African Company's Contractors', in Richard Harding and Sergio Solbes, eds, *The Contractor State and its Implications, 1659–1815* (Las Palmas: Universidad de Las Palmas, 2012), 243–52.

Paul, Helen Julia, 'Suppliers to the Royal Company and the Royal Navy in the Early Eighteenth Century', in Jeff Fynn-Paul, ed., *War, Entrepreneurs, and the State in Europe and the Mediterranean, 1300–1800* (Leiden: Brill, 2014), 131–50.

Perdices de Blas, Luis, and Reeder, John, *El mercantilismo: política económica y Estado nacional* (Madrid: Editorial Síntesis, 1998).

Pérez Crespo Muñoz, María Teresa, *El arsenal de Cartagena en el siglo XVIII* (Madrid: Editorial Naval, 1992).

Pérez Fernández-Turégano, Carlos, *Patiño y las reformas de la administración en el reinado de Felipe V* (Madrid: Ministerio de Defensa, 2006).

Pérez Sarrión, Guillermo, *La península comercial: Mercado, redes sociales y Estado en España en el siglo XVIII* (Madrid: Marcial Pons, 2012).

Pérez-Mallaina Bueno, Pablo Emilio, *Política Naval Española en el Atlántico 1700–1715* (Seville: Escuela de Estudios Hispano-Americanos, 1982).

Pérez-Mallaina Bueno, Pablo Emilio, and Torres Ramírez, Bibiano, *La Armada del mar del sur* (Seville: Escuela de Estudios Hispano-Americanos, 1987).

Peribáñez Caveda, Daniel, *Comunicaciones y comercio marítimo en la Asturias preindustrial, 1750–1850* (Gijón: Junta del Puerto, 1992).

Perona Tomás, Dionisio, *Los orígenes del Ministerio de Marina: la Secretaría de Estado y del Despacho de Marina, 1714–1808* (Madrid: Instituto de Historia y Cultura Naval, 1999).
Phillips, Carla Rahn, *Seis galeones para el rey de España: la defensa imperial a principios del s. XVII* (Madrid: Alianza Editorial, 1991).
Pincus, Steven, 'Rethinking Mercantilism: Political Economy, the British Empire, and the Atlantic World in the Seventeenth and Eighteenth Centuries', *William and Mary Quarterly* 69 (2012), 3–34.
Pinto Rodríguez, Jorge, 'Los *Cinco Gremios Mayores* de Madrid y el comercio colonial en el siglo XVIII', *Revista de Indias* 51 (1991), 293–326.
Pool, Bernard, *Navy Board Contracts 1660–1832: Contract Administration under the Navy Board* (London: Longmans, Green, 1966).
Pourchasse, Pierrick, 'Buying Supplies from Your Enemy or How the French Navy Stocked Up with Products from the North in the Eighteenth Century', in Richard Harding and Sergio Solbes, eds, *The Contractor State and its Implications, 1659–1815* (Las Palmas: Universidad de Las Palmas de Gran Canaria, 2012), 253–72.
Prat de Pàdua, Mestre, 'La construcción naval de guerra en la España del siglo XVIII. El marco legal de los procesos de financiación', in Cerlos Martínez Shaw, ed., *El derecho y el mar en la España moderna* (Granada: Universidad de Granada, 1995), 299–322.
Pulido Bueno, Ildefonso, *José Patiño: El inicio del gobierno político-económico ilustrado en España* (Huelva: Artes Gráficas Andaluzas, 1998).
Quintero González, José, *La Carraca: El primer arsenal ilustrado español (1717–1776)* (Madrid: Ministerio de Defensa, 2004).
Quintero González, José, 'La Carraca y La Habana: aproximación al intercambio de pertrechos entre arsenales', *Revista de historia naval* 24 (2006), 57–66.
Rande, 1702: Arde o mar. Catálogo de la exposición conmemorativa del tercer centenario de la batalla de Rande (Vigo: Consorcio Zona Franca de Vigo, 2002).
Raquejo Alonso, Antonio, *Historia de la administración y fiscalización económica de las fuerzas armadas* (Madrid: Ministerio de Defensa, 1992).
Redlich, Fritz, *The German Military Enterpriser and His Work Force: A Study in European Economic and Social History* (Wiesbaden: F. Steiner, 1964).
Rey, Ofelia, *Montes y Política Forestal en la Galicia del Antiguo Régimen* (Santiago: Universidad de Santiago, 1995).
Rodger, Andrew Martin, 'From the "Military Revolution" to the "Fiscal-Naval State"', *Journal for Maritime Research* 13 (2011), 119–28.
Rodríguez de Campomanes, Pedro, *Discurso sobre la educación popular de los artesanos y su fomento* (Madrid: Imprenta de Antonio Sancha, 1775).
Rodríguez Hernández, Antonio José, *Los tambores de Marte: el reclutamiento en Castilla durante la segunda mitad del siglo XVII (1648–1700)* (Valladolid: Universidad de Valladolid-Castilla Ediciones, 2011).
Rodríguez Labandeira, José, 'La política económica de los Borbones', in Miguel Artola, ed., *La economía española al final del Antiguo Régimen* (Madrid: Alianza, 1982), 107–84.
Rowlands, Guy, *The Financial Decline of a Great Power: War, Influence, and Money in Louis XIV's France* (Oxford: Oxford University Press, 2012).
Rowlands, Guy, 'Agency Government in Louis XIV's France: The Military Treasurers of the Elite Forces', in Jeff Fynn-Paul, ed., *War, Entrepreneurs, and the State in Europe and the Mediterranean, 1300–1800* (Leiden: Brill, 2014), 215–34.
Sakul, Kahraman, 'The Evolution of Ottoman Military Logistical Systems in the Later Eighteenth Century: The Rise of A New Class of Military Entrepreneur', in Jeff

Fynn-Paul, ed., *War, Entrepreneurs, and the State in Europe and the Mediterranean, 1300–1800* (Leiden: Brill, 2014), 307–28.

Salazar, Luis María, *Juicio crítico de la marina militar de España dispuesto en cartas de un amigo a otro* (Madrid: D. Miguel de Burgos, 1814).

Salvucci, Linda, 'Atlantic Intersections: Early American Commerce and the Rise of the Spanish West Indies (Cuba)', *Business History Review* 79 (2005), 781–800.

Sanz Ayán, Carmen, 'La problemática del abastecimiento de los Ejércitos de Extremadura y Cataluña durante 1652', *Temas de Historia Militar, 2º Congreso de Historia Militar* (Zaragoza: 1988), 221–36.

Sanz Ayán, Carmen, *Los banqueros de Carlos II* (Valladolid: Universidad de Valladolid, 1989).

Sanz Ayán, Carmen, 'Negociadores y capitales holandeses en los sistemas de abastecimientos de pertrechos navales de la monarquía hispánica durante el siglo XVII', *Hispania* 182 (1992), 915–45.

Sanz Camañes, Porfirio, ed., *Tiempo de cambios: Guerra, diplomacia y política internacional de la Monarquía Hispánica (1648–1700)* (Madrid: Actas, 2012).

Sanz Tapia, Ángel, *El final del Tratado de Tordesillas: la expedición del virrey Cevallos al Río de la Plata* (Valladolid: Junta de Castilla y León, 1994).

Serrano Álvarez, José Manuel, 'El gasto naval en España e Indias (1715–1759). El caso de Tierra Firme', *Revista de historia naval* 20 (2002), 25–34.

Serrano Álvarez, José Manuel, *Fortificaciones y Tropas: El gasto militar en Tierra Firme, 1700–1788* (Seville: Universidad de Sevilla, 2002).

Serrano Alvarez, José Manuel, *El astillero de La Habana y la construcción naval militar (1700–1750)* (Madrid: Ministerio de Defensa, 2008).

Serrano Álvarez, José Manuel, 'La revitalización del Astillero de La Habana en época de Lorenzo Montalvo, 1765–1772', *Revista de historia naval* 27 (2009), 71–100.

Serrano Álvarez, José Manuel, 'El poder y la gloria: élites y asientos militares en el astillero de La Habana durante el siglo XVIII', *Studia historica. Historia moderna* 35 (2013), 99–125.

Serrano Mangas, Fernando, *Los galeones de la carrera de Indias, 1650–1700* (Madrid: CSIC, 1986).

Serrera Contreras, Ramón, *Lino y cáñamo en Nueva España (1777–1800)* (Seville: EEHA, 1974).

Sobrón Iruretagoyena, Marcelino Manuel, 'Algunos aspectos del estudio de costes y otras consideraciones en los *asientos* de Guarnizo', in Cerlos Martínez Shaw, ed., *El derecho y el mar en la España moderna* (Granada: Universidad de Granada, 1995), 477–88.

Sola Corbacho, Juan Carlos, 'El mercado de crédito en Madrid (1750–1808)' in Rafael Torres Sánchez, ed., *Capitalismo mercantil en la España del siglo XVlII* (Pamplona: EUNSA, 2000), 211–46.

Solbes Ferri, Sergio, 'Contracting and Accounting: Spanish Army Expenditure in Wardrobe and the General Treasury Accounts in the Eighteenth Century', in Richard Harding and Sergio Solbes, eds, *The Contractor State and its Implications, 1659–1815* (Las Palmas: Servicio de publicaciones y difusión científica de la ULPGC, 2012), 273–93.

Solbes Ferri, Sergio, 'Campillo y Ensenada: el suministro de vestuarios para el ejército durante las campañas de Italia (1741–1748)', *Studia historica. Historia moderna* 35 (2013), 201–34.

Stein, Stanley J., 'Un raudal de oro y plata que corría sin cesar de España a Francia: Política mercantil española y el comercio con Francia en la época de Carlos III', *Actas del Congreso Internacional sobre Carlos III y la Ilustración* (Madrid, 1989), ii. 219–87.

Stein, Stanley, J. and Stein, Barbara H., *Apogee of Empire: Spain and New Spain in the Age of Charles III, 1759–1789* (Baltimore: Johns Hopkins University Press, 2003).
Stern, Philip J., and Wennerlind, Carl, eds, *Mercantilism Reimagined: Political Economy in Early Modern Britain and Its Empire* (New York: Oxford University Press, 2014).
Storrs, Christopher, *The Resilience of the Spanish Monarchy, 1665–1700* (New York: Oxford University Press, 2006).
Storrs, Christopher, ed., *The Fiscal Military State in Eighteenth-Century Europe* (Burlington: Ashgate, 2008).
Storrs, Christopher, *The Fiscal-Military State in Eighteenth-Century Europe: Essays in Honour of P.G.M. Dickson* (Farnham: Ashgate, 2009).
Syrett, David, *Shipping and the American War* (London: Athlone, 1970).
Syrett, David, *The Royal Navy in European Waters during the American Revolutionary War* (Columbia: University of South California Press, 1998).
Tallet, Frank, and Trim, D. J. B., *European Warfare 1350–1750* (Cambridge: Cambridge University Press, 2010).
Tedde, Pedro, 'Cabarrús y el monopolio de extracción de la plata', *Economía y Sociedad en la España moderna y contemporánea* (Madrid Editorial Síntesis:, 1996), 115–35.
Teijeiro de la Rosa, Juan Miguel, *La Real Hacienda militar de Fernando VII: el cuerpo administrativo militar* (Madrid: Ministerio de Defensa, Secretaría General Técnica, 1995).
Tellechea Idígoras, José Ignacio, 'Juan Fermín de Guilisasti y sus anclas', *Real Sociedad Bascongada de los Amigos del País* 31 (1975), 285–90.
Tellechea Idígoras, José Ignacio, *Anclas en Hernani: El registro de cartas de D. Francisco Antonio de Oquendo, Inspector de la Fábrica de Anclas (1750–1755)* (San Sebastián: Caja Ahorros, 1977).
Terrón Ponce, José Luis, *La reconquista de Menorca por el duque de Crillon (1781–82), aspectos militares y politicos* (Mahón: Editorial Menorca, 1981).
Terrón Ponce, José Luis, *Ejército y política en la España de Carlos III* (Madrid: Ministerio de Defensa, 1997).
Terrón Ponce, José Luis, *La toma de Menorca (1781–82) en los escritos autobiográficos y epistolario del Duque de Crillon* (Mahón: Institut Menorquí d'Estudis, 1999).
Thiele, Andrea, 'The Prince as Military Entrepreneur? Why Smaller Saxon Territories Sent Holländische Regimenter (Dutch Regiments) to the Dutch Republic', in Jeff Fynn-Paul, ed., *War, Entrepreneurs, and the State in Europe and the Mediterranean, 1300–1800* (Leiden: Brill, 2014), 170–92.
Thompson, Irving A., *Guerra y decadencia, gobierno y administración en la España de los Austrias, 1560–1620* (Barcelona: Crítica, 1981).
Tilly, Charles, *Coerción, capital y los Estados europeos, 990–1990* (Madrid: Alianza Editorial, 1992).
Torrejón Chaves, Juan, 'Estructura y organización de la producción en los arsenales de la Marina española del siglo XVIII', *Revista de historia naval* 19 (2001), 55–82.
Torres Ramírez, Bibiano, *La Armada de Barlovento* (Seville: Escuela de Estudios Hispano-Americanos, 1981).
Torres Sánchez, Rafael, 'Comercio y asientos militares. Hacia la integración comercial del Cantábrico en el siglo XVIII', *Cuadernos de Investigación Histórica* 17 (1999), 81–108.
Torres Sánchez, Rafael, 'Producir o comprar, la demanda de la corona española de productos industriales en el siglo XVIII', in Luis Antonio Ribot and Luigi de Rosa, eds, *Industria y Época Moderna* (Madrid: Actas, 2000), 95–131.

Torres Sánchez, Rafael, 'Lana y banca. Los servicios financieros al negocio lanero en el siglo XVIII', in Agustín González Enciso, ed., *El negocio de la lana en España (1650-1830)* (Pamplona: EUNSA, 2001), 235–68.

Torres Sánchez, Rafael, 'Cuando las reglas del juego cambian. Mercados y privilegio en el abastecimiento del ejército español en el siglo XVIII', *Revista de historia moderna* 20 (2002), 487–511.

Torres Sánchez, Rafael, 'El gran negocio de la época, la provisión de víveres al ejército por Francisco Mendinueta (1744–1763)', in Santiago Aquerreta, ed., *Francisco Mendinueta: Finanzas y mecenazgo en la España del siglo XVIII* (Pamplona: EUNSA, 2002), 101–34.

Torres Sánchez, Rafael, 'Campomanes y el comerciante y financiero Simón Aragorri', in Dolores Mateos Dorado, ed., *Campomanes doscientos años después* (Oviedo: Universidad de Oviedo, 2003), 709–18.

Torres Sánchez, Rafael, 'Las dificultades de ser financiero extranjero en la España de Carlos III', *I Coloquio Internacional 'Los extranjeros en la España Moderna'* (Málaga: Universidad de Málaga, 2003), 771–80.

Torres Sánchez, Rafael, 'Seguro de hombres y auxilio de reyes. El Fondo Vitalicio y la *Real Hacienda* española de Carlos III', *Obradoiro de historia moderna* 15 (2006), 139–72.

Torres Sánchez, Rafael, 'La Hora navarra y el triunfo de los navarros. El banquero navarro Juan Bautista Dutari y sus relaciones con Navarra durante el siglo XVIII', in Agustín González Enciso, ed., *Navarros en la Monarquía española en el siglo XVIII* (Pamplona: EUNSA, 2007), 283–308.

Torres Sánchez, Rafael, 'La palanca de la riqueza. Las repercusiones del arsenal en el crecimiento de Cartagena durante el siglo XVIII', in Manuel-Reyes García Hurtado, ed., *Ferrol año cero: Una ciudad de la Ilustración* (Ferrol: Ediciones Embora, 2007), 157–89.

Torres Sánchez, Rafael, 'The Triumph of the Fiscal-Military State in the Eighteenth Century. War and Mercantilism', in Rafael Torres Sánchez, ed., *War, State and Development: Fiscal-Military States in the Eighteenth Century* (Pamplona: EUNSA, 2007), 13–44.

Torres Sánchez, Rafael, ed., *War, State and Development: Fiscal-Military States in the Eighteenth Century* (Pamplona: EUNSA, 2007).

Torres Sánchez, Rafael, 'Financiers et politiques. Francisco Montes et François Cabarrus (1770-1790)', in Anne Dubet, ed., *Administrer les finances royales dans la monarchie espagnole (XVIe–XIXe siècles)* (Rennes: Presses Universitaires de Rennes, 2008), 103–20.

Torres Sánchez, Rafael, 'Velas sin Cañones. La eficacia de las reformas artilleras tras la Guerra de los Siete Años', in Francisco Morales Padrón, ed., *Piratería, Corso y Guerra Marítima: XVII Coloquio de Historia Canario-Americana* (Las Palmas de Gran Canaria: Cabildo de Gran Canaria, 2008), 1717–28.

Torres Sánchez, Rafael, 'Los navarros en la provisión de víveres a la Armada española durante el siglo XVIII', in Rafael Torres Sánchez, *Volver a la 'hora navarra': La contribución Navarra a la construcción de la monarquía española en el siglo XVIII* (Pamplona: EUNSA, 2010), 213–64.

Torres Sánchez, Rafael, 'Monopoly or the Free Market. Two Ways of Tackling the Expenditure. The Minorca Expedition (1781–1782)', in Stephen Conway and Rafael Torres Sánchez, eds, *The Spending of the States: Military Expenditure during the Long Eighteenth Century: Patterns, Organisation and Consequences, 1650–1815* (Saarbrücken: VDM, 2011), 285–312.

Torres Sánchez, Rafael, 'Los Cinco Gremios Mayores y la provisión de víveres al ejército español en el siglo XVIII', *Studia Histórica. Edad Moderna* 34 (2012), 407–32.

Torres Sánchez, Rafael, 'Contractor State and Mercantilism. The Spanish-Navy Hemp, Rigging and Sailcloth Supply Policy in the Second Half of the Eighteenth Century', in Richard Harding and Sergio Solbes, eds, *The Contractor State and its Implications, 1659–1815* (Las Palmas: Universidad de Las Palmas, 2012), 317–44.

Torres Sánchez, Rafael, *La llave de todos los tesoros. La Tesorería General de Carlos III* (Madrid: Sílex, 2012).

Torres Sánchez, Rafael, 'La política de abastecimiento de cáñamo a la Armada en la segunda mitad del siglo XVIII', *Revista de historia naval* 116 (2012), 47–71.

Torres Sánchez, Rafael, 'Eighteenth-Century Spain as a Contractor State', *International Journal of Maritime History* 23 (2013), 253–7.

Torres Sánchez, Rafael, 'In the Shade of Power. Monopolist Entrepreneurs, the State and Spanish Military Victualling in the Eighteenth Century', in Jeff Fynn-Paul, ed., *War, Entrepreneurs, and the State* (Leiden: Brill, 2013), 260–84.

Torres Sánchez, Rafael, 'Tejiendo una Hacienda Imperial. "Unir los manejos de la *Real Hacienda* de España y América" en el reinado de Carlos III', in Michel Bertrand and Zacarías Moutoukías, eds, *Changement institutionnel et fiscalité dans le monde hispanique (1750–1850)* (Toulouse: Université de Toulouse, 2014).

Torres Sánchez, Rafael, *Constructing a Fiscal-Military State in Eighteenth-Century Spain* (Basingstoke: Palgrave Macmillan, 2015).

Tovar Martín, Virginia, *Los Cinco Gremios Mayores de Madrid: Artífices de la 'entrada pública en la capital de España de los Reyes Don Fernando VI y Doña Bárbara de Braganza, octubre de 1746'* (Madrid: Cámara de Comercio de Madrid, 1980).

Tovar Pinzón, Hermes, 'Remesas, situados y *Real Hacienda* en el siglo XVII', in Antonio Bernal, ed., *Dinero, Moneda y Credito en la Monarquia Hispánica* (Madrid: Marcial Pons, 2000), 241–68.

Ulbert, Jörg, and Le Bouëdec, Gérard, *La Fonction consulaire à l'époque modern: l'affirmation d'une institution économique et politique, 1500–1800* (Rennes: Presses universitaires de Rennes, 2006).

Ulloa, Antonio de, *La Marina: fuerzas navales de la Europa y costas de Berbería* (Cádiz: Universidad de Cadiz, 1773, 1995).

Uztariz, Gerónimo de, *Theórica, y práctica de comercio, y de marina* (Madrid: Imprenta de Antonio Sanz, 1742).

Valdez-Bubnov, Iván, *Poder naval y modernización del Estado: política de construcción naval española (siglos XVI–XVIII)* (Mexico: Unam, 2011).

Van Creveld, Martin, *Supplying War: Logistics from Wallenstein to Patton*, 2nd edn (Cambridge: Cambridge University Press, 2004).

Vidal, Jose Juan, 'Crisis de subsistències i aprovisionament blader de Mallorca durant el segle XVIII', *Randa* 26 (1990), 103–32.

Villar Ortiz, Covadonga, *La renta de la pólvora en Nueva España (1569–1767)* (Seville: CSIC, 1988).

Voth, Hans-Joachim, 'Debt, Default and Empire: State Capacity and Economic Development in England and Spain in the Early Modern Period', *Economic History Review* (in press, 2015).

Vries, Peer, 'Governing Growth: A Comparative Analysis of the Role of the State in the Rise of the West', *Journal of World History* 13 (2002), 67–138.

Wilkinson, Clive, *The British Navy and the State in the Eighteenth Century* (Woodbridge: The Boydell Press, 2004).

Yun-Casalilla, Bartolomé K., O'Brien, Patrick, and Comín, Francisco, eds, *The Rise of Fiscal States: A Global History, 1500–1914* (Cambridge: Cambridge University Press, 2012).

Zabala, Aingeru, 'La Guerra de Sucesión en el mar Cantábrico', *Itsas memoria: revista de estudios marítimos del País Vasco* 5 (2006), 325–56.
Zylberberg, Michel, 'Un centre financier "péripherique": Madrid dans la seconde moitié du XVIIIe siècle', *Revue Historique* 546, (1983), 265–309.
Zylberberg, Michael, *Une si douce domination: Les milieux d'affaires français et l'Espagne vers 1780–1808* (Paris: Ministère des Finances, 1993).
Zylberberg, Michael, 'Des affaires à l'administration: un échec de François Cabarrus', in Bernard Vincent and Jean-Pierre Dedieu, eds, *L'Espagne, l'État, les Lumières: mélanges en l'honneur de Didier Ozanam* (Madrid: Casa de Velázquez, 2004), 109–19.

Index

The manufacturer's authorised representative in the EU for product
safety is Oxford University Press España S.A. of El Parque Empresarial
San Fernando de Henares, Avenida de Castilla, 2 - 28830 Madrid
(www.oup.es/en or product.safety@oup.com). OUP España S.A. also acts
as importer into Spain of products made by the manufacturer.
Printed and bound by CPI Group (UK) Ltd, Croydon, CR0 4YY
14/09/2026
02216306-0007